CAN'T TOUCH MY SOUL

CAN'T TOUCH MY SOUL

A GUIDE FOR LESBIAN SURVIVORS OF CHILD SEXUAL ABUSE

DONNA RAFANELLO

Manufactured in the United States of America.

This trade paperback original is published by Alyson Publications,
P.O. Box 4371, Los Angeles, California 90078-4371.
Distribution in the United Kingdom by Turnaround Publisher Services Ltd.,
Unit 3, Olympia Trading Estate, Coburg Road, Wood Green,
London N22 6TZ England.

First edition: June 2004

04 05 06 07 08 a 10 9 8 7 6 5 4 3 2 1

ISBN 1-55583-776-X

Credits
Cover photography by Veronique Rolland/Getty Images.
Cover design by Louis Mandrapilias.

“The spirit remains untouched by the experience of sexual trauma. The spirit is the center, the essence of who we are.… We are much more than our physical body, our emotional experiences, and our mental abilities… No matter what your experience has been, your spirit remains beautifully free of it all. And ultimately it is your own powerful spirit that will heal you.”

—Wayne Kritsberg and Ceci Miller-Kritsberg, *The Invisible Wound: The New Approach to Healing Childhood Sexual Abuse*

I dedicate this book to all the brave women who shared their stories with me. They took the next step in their own healing in the hopes of helping other women who suffer in silence.

And to Lisa and Sadie, my reasons for living—your love makes everything possible.

CONTENTS

ACKNOWLEDGMENTS

In writing this book I needed an emotional support system that could see me through the dark hours spent listening to the painful accounts of child sexual abuse shared with me by survivors as well as those spent revisiting my own abuse memories. Rather than any need for technical support or writing assistance, my greatest need was for people who believed in me and my experiences as a survivor, understood the need for the book, and kept me going when the emotional and physical demands of this project took its toll. For everyone who offered me encouragement during this process, I give my sincere thanks. My; deepest gratitude goes out to my dear friends Joan, Jennie, Ingrid, and Paula, and my sister, Katey. Your love and support mean everything to me. It saw me through.

Thanks to my editor, Angela Brown, at Alyson and Dan Cullinane for believing in this book from the start and for helping to make my dream of writing this book a reality.

And to Mom and Dad: My love for you surpasses any obstacles that life could put in our path. Your undying faith in me and my ability to fulfill my dreams of being a writer have been a source of strength for me always. I hope that in reading this book you are able to understand finally what I have been unable to say in words and why telling my story, and providing a forum for other survivors to tell theirs, is so very important to me.

INTRODUCTION

"WE DO NOT WRITE IN ORDER TO BE UNDERSTOOD;
WE WRITE IN ORDER TO UNDERSTAND."
—C. DAY LEWIS

Each survivor's journey is personal and unique. In providing a forum for survivors to tell their stories and attempting to find common threads in their experiences, I do not mean to diminish each woman's experience—both their challenges and triumphs. While recognizing the variability in survivors' experiences, we also understand that there are predictable phases in the sexual abuse recovery process. Part of what I set out to do in this book is normalize the recovery process for lesbian survivors. I find like Hall (1999) did that while there are some lesbian-specific issues, overall the experiences of female survivors—both lesbian and heterosexual—are remarkably similar. So many of us spend enormous amounts of time—years of our lives—suffering under the false assumption that no one could possibly understand our experience, that no one has endured what we have. While this is, of course, true on some level, the aloneness we feel as survivors is not altogether accurate. As the stories told here attest, we are not alone in our suffering. Many have suffered as we have. And the beauty of recognizing this tragic truth is in appreciating how much we stand to learn from each other.

The parallel issues that confront lesbians who are survivors of childhood sexual abuse are well articulated by Struve (n.d.). In his work as a clinical social worker, Struve identifies nine issues that affect survivors and gay men and lesbians; these contribute to the dynamics of "double layering" for gay men and lesbians who are also survivors. These issues serve as the conceptual framework for the following discussion of lesbian survivors and will be echoed throughout this book's pages.

1. isolation and the feeling of being separate and unsupported
2. secrecy, lies, and deception

3. disclosure and its repercussions: chaos, conflict, anxiety, and blame
4. hypervigilance: always watching for and anticipating signs of danger
5. shame and the resulting negative self-image and self-hatred
6. vulnerability to assault
7. sexuality: difficulty accepting healthy attitudes toward sex and sexuality
8. intimacy: hindered by mistrust, controlling dynamics, and lack of support
9. dissociation as a survival strategy and learning to live "split lives"

"Writing gives one the strength to give birth to the inner conscience and the courage to look it in the eye."
—Vanessa Scrivens, *A Truth of Being*

As an avid reader all my life, I've always tried to find the answers in books. So when I needed help in making sense of my own sexual abuse, I turned to books. I found many excellent ones on the topic of child sexual abuse but none that addressed the unique experiences of lesbian survivors. As a writer, I decided I could be the one to create such a book, a resource for other lesbian survivors like myself. How thrilled I was the day that Angela Brown from Alyson Books called to tell me she was interested in talking with me about my book! Little did I realize the personal and professional journey I was about to begin. In writing this book I've had to face my old demons again and recommit to my healing. In talking with survivors—courageous women all—I've had my faith in the human spirit restored. How generous and open you all were in sharing your stories, how willing to help others! I am inspired and awed by your spirit. This book is for all of us. And I have come to appreciate, in talking with all of you, how important contributing to this book has been to your own healing and your desire to help other survivors. Here's some of what you told me:

"It was good for me to process this stuff. I saw things I hadn't seen before." —Sue

"Talking to you is nudging me to look at things differently." —Mary Lou

"Thank you for this opportunity. I just can't explain how, in my heart, I know that there will be much healing from telling my story about the real me and allowing myself to unmask." —Tammy

"I'm hopeful that my story will help. Maybe somebody will read it and recognize something and get some help and maybe understand why they act the way they do." —Nedhera

"It was a nice touchstone—determining where I am with all of these issues." —Tammie

"Telling your story is so healing, especially in this form. In talking today I've taken another step." —Mary Lou

"I look forward to being part of something that might help another survivor get through all the muck. It's such a hard journey. I guess, selfishly, it's always nice to connect with people who understand too." —Mary

"I'm very interested in getting my story out there. I want to be part of something that gives back." —Wendy

Over and over again the women I interviewed told me how important the subject of lesbian survivors is and how surprising it is that so little is written about it.

"It is an ignored angle on an important subject." —Deborah

"There's a need for this type of information out there. Because when I started questioning myself, I started going to libraries, but I didn't find any information on being abused and being gay. I think this book will help me answer some questions. Not so much 'You're gay because of this,' but that I wasn't alone with my sexuality and also the fact that I was abused. Because I separated the two things—I dealt with them in separate ways even though they were both part of me, so they were

working together. I think it would have helped me to have both of these integrated." —Diana

"What you are doing with the book addresses the challenges of aloneness and isolation—common to both lesbians and survivors—in a very meaningful way. This has been a unique opportunity to revisit my situation as a lesbian and as a survivor—something I've been doing in intensive bits and pieces both by myself and in therapy for the past 11 years. The opportunity to pass along some of my ideas seemed too good to pass up." —Levie

Estimates are that 1 in 3 women will be victims of sexual abuse by the age of 18. Most sexual abuse is incest. The definition of abuse I use here (from the Sexual Assault Center at Harborview Medical Center in Seattle Washington) is an inclusive one: "Child sexual abuse is the sexual exploitation of a child who is not developmentally capable of understanding or resisting the contact, and/or who is psychologically or socially dependent on the offender. It may involve fondling, exhibitionism, masturbation, and genital penetration" (cited in Fortune, 1983). Abuse includes gestures, comments, and observation as well as actual body contact (Courtois, 1988). There are two criteria for child sexual abuse as defined here. The first is the lack of consent on the part of the victim. According to David Finkelhor (1979), "Children, by definition, cannot give or withhold consent when approached sexually by an adult because they are immature, uninformed, and usually dependent on the adult. Consequently, they lack the real power to resist" (cited in Fortune, 1983). Therefore, any sexual contact between an adult and a child is abusive. Courtois (1988) clarifies, "Children involved sexually with adults may be said to submit rather than to consent to the activity." According to Fortune (1983), the second criterion for understanding child sexual abuse has to do with "whose self-interest is being served by the sexual contact and who is injured." When the child is being used for sexual stimulation of an adult or another person, this "sexual use of a child disregards the child's welfare. The child becomes an object exclusively to meet the needs of the offender. The act is exploitative and, consequently, damaging to the child." I agree with Ellen Bass and Laura Davis's belief that "violation is determined by your experience as a child—your body, your feelings, your spirit." Some abuse is not even physical, but it still leaves real psychological scars.

Despite the compelling arguments made by writers and activists (e.g., Garnets, 2002a; Nestle, Wilchins, and Howell, 2002) about a wide range of gender possibilities, I've focused here on lesbians who identify as lesbian and who exclusively seek relationships with women. As Ann Ferguson (1981) argues, it isn't meaningful to talk about a woman as a lesbian if she doesn't acknowledge herself to be one. She offers the following definition:

> A lesbian is a woman who has sexual and erotic-emotional ties primarily with women or who sees herself as centrally involved with a community of self-identified lesbians whose sexual and erotic-emotional ties are primarily with women and who is herself a self-identified lesbian (cited in the Boston Lesbian Psychologies Collective, 1987).

While I appreciate that there is a great deal of power in the exploration of gender construction and gender choices, such a discussion is beyond the scope of this book. Therefore, women I interviewed who identify as bisexual, gender-queer, or other than lesbian are not included in this book.

"The universe is made of stories, not atoms."
—Muriel Rukeyser

More than 130 women contacted me to share their stories. Of these, I communicated with 60 women in depth. I could not tell each story in its entirety, but I have included portions of each woman's experience. The survivors represent a diverse group of women. You will hear from women who vary in age, economic background, and race. Some are in committed lesbian relationships; others are single. There are mothers and nonmothers. These women were abused under a wide range of circumstances and by a variety of perpetrators. You will read about women who are at different stages of the healing process and women whose approaches to healing have varied. Lesbian survivors who share their stories here range in age from 18–66 years and live in urban, suburban, and rural communities in 28 states, New Zealand, and Canada. They are Hispanic, African-American, Latina, White, Asian, Native-American, and Polynesian. Some subsist on Social Security benefits, permanently disabled with depression and post–traumatic stress disorder; others are supported financially by their partners. Others are students and at-home mothers. Paid positions include psychologists, college professors, ranchers, writers, scientists, youth counselors, nurses, advocates, healers, artists, Web site developers, social workers, bookstore managers, secretaries, tutors, customer service representatives, marketing researchers, landscape architects, carpenters, ministers, and lab technicians. Some struggle to make ends meet while others live comfortably. They represent the diversity of the lesbian experience and their stories, as you will read, are powerful testaments to the capacity of women to reclaim their lives and to do what they can to improve the lives of other women. I am inspired by their example.

Responding to advertisements in national lesbian magazines and flyers posted in gay and lesbian bookstores and community centers across the country and at the Michigan Womyn's Music Festival, lesbian survivors sought me out to tell their stories. While I was initially surprised and thrilled to receive so many responses to my call for stories, my enthusiasm was tempered by my realization of the tremendous pain and suffering that all of these women had suffered. How I wish that there were no need for this book, no sexual abuse of children to report or to heal from. But in our efforts to create a world where children are valued and protected from such abuse, sharing our stories is vitally important. I write this book in that endeavor.

This will not be an easy book to read. Some of the information may be triggering. Please take care of yourself while you move through the chapters. Reach out for support when you need it. If you find yourself feeling overwhelmed by your feelings or are considering hurting yourself or others please seek immediate assistance from a trusted friend or family member or go to your local hospital emergency room. Respect the cues that your body is giving you to pace yourself and your healing process. This is not a race to be won by sprinting through the stages of recovery; in fact, the real work of healing happens in slow, methodical steps and cannot be rushed. There are no quick fixes. Devote yourself to the long haul. While at times discouraging in its slowness, healing will happen if we respect ourselves in the process. Honoring ourselves by listening to what our bodies and emotions are telling us is an important step to reclaiming our power and learning to love—and trust—ourselves again.

Many of us continue to feel the ravages of the abuse in our bodies and in the memories we hold in our minds long after the abuse has ended. Psychotherapist Nicki Roth (1993), who has spent years working with incest survivors, describes their inner strength. "My clients use words like *soul* or *spirit* or *inner self* or *inner voice.* They all talk about a part of themselves that is untouchable, powerful, intelligent, and private that has guided them through the most difficult of times." The abuse hurts us in unimaginable ways, but it can't touch our soul.

the fact that your body is going to be gone as well and your loved [illegible]

[illegible]

CHAPTER 1

Remembering

"I was later to discover that memory could save, that it had power, that it was often the only recourse of the powerless, the oppressed, or the brutalized."
—Alice Sebold, *Lucky*

There has never been a time when I didn't remember the abuse. I don't know whether this is a blessing or a curse. I hear the lament of survivors who are piecing together memory fragments and know this isn't the case with me. I also know that the vivid memories of the abuse, the smell and taste of my abuser, and the feel of my abuser on me are like poison to my body. And try as I might to forget the details or to diminish their capacity to sicken me, I still relive the abuse in my mind time and time again. The intensity of the memories, however, does diminish a little over time, and my ability to handle these flashbacks improves. And I have come to respect this healing journey that I am on. I have grown to accept that facing memories head-on and feeling the feelings associated with them is the only way I can begin to put the experience behind me. It's true what they say: What you resist persists. When I focus my energy on forgetting the abuse, consciously and unconsciously my mind stalls there. But when I focus intently on the abuse for short times, I am better able to move on to other things. This is not without great pain—looking at the abuse anew—but then I always knew healing would involve some discomfort. I've come to appreciate that the pain I feel now in remembering is not and will never be as great as the pain I endured while the abuse was happening. *I survived the worst part,* I remind myself. I can handle the pain of remembering. I am a survivor.

Feeling the Feelings

"You can't heal if you can't feel."
—Debbie Ford, *The Dark Side of the Light Chasers*

Many of us lack affect when telling the stories of our abuse. We reveal none of our feelings as we recount the atrocities we suffered as children. As Mary Lou said, "I was totally shut down. When I look at childhood photos of myself and share them with my friends, they say, 'You're gone.'" We learned as children that the more pain, anger, or fear we expressed, the greater our suffering. We may even have been teased about our outcries. The only way to survive was to stop having feelings. Don't let our abuser see that he or she has affected us. We have separated the *fact* of our abuse from our *feelings* about the abuse as a way to survive the pain. It is only when we learn to trust others that we can begin to connect our feelings to the facts of our experience.

Telling the story of our abuse is very difficult. While we have battled—and in some cases overcome or at least slightly diminished—our feelings of guilt and shame, we are still reluctant to describe the abuse we suffered. In telling of our experiences we relive the details and this often stirs things up for us again, painful memories and issues we would just as soon leave buried. Still, the power of telling our stories cannot be overestimated. When we find our voice and speak out about the abuse we reclaim control over our lives and we reach out to other survivors who have suffered in silence. Our stories are in the details, and so I include the personal accounts of the abuse we have suffered here, not to sensationalize or titillate but to reveal the truth about the hurts we have known and the pain we still hold inside. When we can speak directly of the abuse we suffered in detail, we begin to let go of its hold on us.

Our abusers included male and female relatives, friends of the family, and other trusted adults. Decades of research on sexual abuse reveals that the majority of victims are female, the majority of perpetrators male, and much of the sexual abuse is perpetrated by either a family member or by someone known to the child. New research suggests same-sex incest and incest perpetrated by females have been underreported, leading us to believe these are rarities (Courtois, 1988). These occurrences may be underreported because they break numerous taboos—incest, homosexuality, and the nurturing role of women. Survivors can feel additional shame and stigma when their abuse experience is out of the ordinary. If our abuser was a family member or if force was used, our psychological distress is likely to be greater (Hyman, 2000). Specifically, incest between close relations often causes more serious aftereffects (Courtois, 1988). I share the survivors' stories here by type of abuser, understanding they represent the diverse experiences of child sexual abuse survivors, including social factors (ethnicity, socioeconomic class, religion), age at onset of abuse, duration and frequency of abuse, and types of sexual behavior.

Fathers and Other Male Relatives

"My father started the sexual abuse when he took over my bath time. He always made sure to wash all the nooks and crannies—my vagina and rectum. From there it progressed to other 'special' things that were just for me and him to know about, to help me learn about my body. They would help me when I was married so I could please my husband. He taught me how to masturbate myself and him. I learned how to kiss and love his penis. I learned how to give really good blow jobs and how to be really quiet and nonexpressive. No one was supposed to hear us, or they would know. That was all part of the secret." —Mo

"When I was 9 and my bust required a bra and my periods started, that's when the abuse began. My father would come in my bedroom at night, two or three times a week. I had the top bunk, my sister was on the bottom one. He would run his hands all over me, but especially my breasts, which he would squeeze and knead. He would kiss me and talk to me. I tried to pretend I was asleep most of the time. If I resisted him, I learned quickly that there were consequences. A day or two later I would receive a punishment from him, far out of proportion to the misbehavior. My mother would look puzzled but would never question him about it." —Jacque

"Dad would put pictures of his penis around the house—in the medicine cabinet and in drawers—where we would find them. There was a window beside the toilet in the house where I grew up. An arm would grope through the screen. Fear-building things. My father would scare you so you'd be submissive. The abuse ran the gamut; the sexual and emotional abuse started when I was 4 and included penetration." —Sarah

"I remember my uncle calling me into his room to play a game called 'Find the Keys.' I knew this game and didn't like it. He had cut holes in the bottom of his pockets. I can't honestly say how many times this happened, but enough that I knew what he wanted me to do. I was between 3 and 5 years old." —Missy

"My dad had a thing where every night he would take me into my bedroom. He would shut the door, and he always started with spanking." —Kris

"When I was 8 or 9 years old my father molested me. He fondled me and kissed me in inappropriate ways. This happened when he had been drinking and my mother was away or they had had a fight. I can remember this happening until I was 15 and refused his advances." —Maggie

"My dad began abusing me when I was about 4 years old, beginning with requests that I touch his penis. Fairly soon after that it escalated to include requests that I perform oral stimulation of his penis. At other times he performed cunnilingus. During the early stages he would leave me after being stimulated—I assume to masturbate. Over the years the abuse came to include sodomy, physical abuse along with the sexual violations, and eventually full-fledged intercourse." —Levie

"My mother remarried when I was 5. I hated the guy. He put his hand down my pajamas while I watched television. He forced me into his walk-in closet to suck his dick. He came into my room at night repeatedly and did other things to my body I can't remember." —Robin

"When I was 5, my mom had to see the doctor and my stepdad had us

in the car waiting for her. This kid, a boy, riding a bike flipped me off for looking at him. And I said, 'Daddy, what does that mean?' He said, 'I'll show you later.' I had no idea that it would lead to sexual abuse. He showed me a film first, then the sexual abuse started." —Laura

"Once my grandfather went in his trailer and masturbated. When he ejaculated he did it on a paper towel and came outside to show me 'how babies are made.' He would make me masturbate by lying on my stomach with my hands in fists between my legs. I was uncomfortable doing it in front of him." —Juli

"My first memory is around 6 years old. My uncle would start with patting on me, slowly moving up my legs, telling me he loved me the whole time. He would touch me, my clitoris, put his fingers inside me. It was never brutal or sadistic, more of a slow coercing. My mother completely trusted him. He manipulated situations to have a lot of access to me as a child. The abuse went on for years. My grandmother witnessed him molesting me when I was 9. She turned her head, walked away, and never did anything about it. I don't think she wanted to believe it was true. Not her own baby boy!" —Kristie

"My father had multiple sclerosis. I was sent to my uncle so I wouldn't get my father sick or kill him. I protested for a while, but my parents insisted. At age 3 or 4 my aunt was warming up the tub and I was in a robe and my uncle fondled me. And he would insert himself in me. There was blood and everything. I wished that my aunt would wake up and save the day. He would always say, 'Who do you love the best?' I felt that the uncle who abused me loved me the most. He pressed against my genitals and breasts even at Dad's funeral." —Debbie

"It was unwanted attention and unwanted touching by my older brother. He would say 'One more time. It'll stop after this.' But he had said that before." —Christy

"My abuser was my brother, four years my senior. The sexual abuse started when I was 3 or 4 years old. The abuse lasted until I was in my

mid teens and could defend myself. Although actual penetration never took place, everything short of it did." —Serena

"From the ages of 3 to 6 my oldest brother abused me. I loved frogs. They were my best friends. He abused me with them; rubbed me with them, penetrated me with them. It was ritualistic abuse." —Wendy

Mothers and Other Female Relatives

"My mother was pretty much out of control, I expect, even before I was born. She was actually undiagnosed mentally ill for a long, long time. My sisters and I had a tortured childhood. Have you seen the movie Sybil*? It was like that."* —Jill

"The experience I had with my aunt was that she was sexually, physically, and emotionally abusive to me. My mother wasn't around a lot. As a single parent she was out working, and she was also alcoholic. My aunt was the one there at night, so she could pretty much do what she wanted to do." —Nedhera

"When I was 10, my 17-year-old stepsister walked in on me while I was masturbating. I was nude and my fingers were inside my vagina. She proceeded to tell me that if I would let her do anything she wanted to me she wouldn't tell. I was frightened to death. She forced me to say yes. Then she finger-raped me, giving me a horrifying orgasm. From then on she dominated me sexually and otherwise until I left for the university when I was 18. She gave me to other females and actually whored me to some. She forced me to bring girls my age to her. The most awful times were when she made me suck on a dog." —Amy

Friends of the Family

"My parents' good friend had a son who would come over and we would play together. I was 7 and he was 15. I really liked him. He was nice to me. He would bring me presents and let me hang out with his friends

and stuff. He made me feel special. One afternoon he talked me into playing a new game. Things progressed and before long I was giving him oral sex and he would perform it on me too. Eventually he had sex with me. It was awful because I hated him, but I really liked him too. The abuse continued for three years until my fifth grade teacher suspected something and called Child Protective Services." —Elizabeth

"During a game with my friend's older brother, he captured me, blindfolded me, and put me down in a deep hole in the yard that I couldn't climb out of. He did everything you can imagine to me." —Kyrce

"My best friend's father abused me between the ages of 7 and 11. I went over to her house nearly every weekend, so he had an amazing amount of access." —Mollie

"When I was 3, I was molested by a 60-year-old farmhand who was working for my parents. The abuse continued for two years. I was raped at age 4. I had bladder and kidney infections that required prescriptions and surgery. I was frequently in the hospital. One medication I took was not for kids under 5, and it messed up my ears. I am severely hearing impaired and this gets worse with age." —Lynn

Neighbors

"I remember my mother leaving my brother and I, ages 2 and 4, with a 15-year-old neighbor boy for a few afternoons. He made me kiss him and eventually perform oral sex on him. Actually, I kind of remember him cramming his dick down my throat and making me gag and puke this awful-tasting stuff. I remember him fingering me and licking me, then sitting me on his lap and hurting me, inserting his dick in my vagina and anus. I remember he had me under a big shaggy cedar tree behind our house. My mother walked past us and he covered my mouth and continued to pump until he came, with my eyes wide open in horror. My mother did not see us." —Tammy

Teachers, Clergy, and Other Trusted Adults

"The abuse started at the end of 11th grade. My abuser was a coach and teacher of mine and a friend of my parents. He was a real fun, outgoing person, and for some reason he and I just started to get together. He was, at the time, the coolest adult. He'd let me have a drink when I was at his house baby-sitting. He was just a good person to talk to. He built up my trust for a year before the abuse started. The abuse continued through my senior year." —Delphene

"When I was in boarding school at age 9, Father Terry used to call me to the Presbytery. I had to go down to the back room, which always had the blinds drawn and was dark and smelly. He would make me sit on his knee and tell me what I was supposed to have done (e.g., peering through a hole in the boys' toilet and things like that). Then I would have to tell it all back to him in detail. At the time I didn't know exactly what he was doing, but I now realize he would masturbate to erection while I was giving him the graphic details he had just given me! Then in the confessional he would demand that I go through it all again. He said I was a sinner and could go to hell for my actions. I started to believe that maybe I had done all the things he said I was doing. In my second year at that school he tried once again, but I wouldn't cooperate. He then punished me by telling all the kids on the playground that I was a bad girl and they weren't to play with me. So I was pretty isolated. He was also the priest that came around to all the schools and tested us on religious knowledge. He always asked me questions I had no hope of answering and then brought me out front and humiliated me." —Misha

"A youth leader, a female youth leader, sexually abused me." —Max

Multiple Abusers

We know that the younger the age of onset, the more likely that the child will be multiply molested either within or outside the family (Walsh, 1986).

"My mother is disturbed. She married my father, who is an alcoholic and from a really abusive family. He's a violent, rapist kind of guy. He got me pregnant when I was 12, and I ended up having an abortion. My mother also had her own little relationship with me. She wanted a girlfriend and sexually abused me." —Liz

"I was raped repeatedly as a young child. Even though it was clear to my parents that I had spent a good deal of time alone with two men who were discovered to be pedophiles, they chose to ignore what had happened. Image in our small Mormon farming community was everything." —Cristi

"My mom didn't like to have sex, only on Sundays before Dad started his work week. So the rest of the week was up to me. I was sexually and physically abused and neglected from very young. I had vaginal infections and liver, kidney, and urinary tract infections. I couldn't tell what hurt and what didn't on my body. The sexual abuse went on into my adulthood. For a while I wondered if my daughter was my father's child. My mother was sexual with me too. She would show me '69' in magazines and masturbate in front of me." —Tabitha

"I was first abused at age 4 by an uncle. Then I was abused over many years by my older sister, then my older brother. There were other isolated incidents that involved a cousin, neighborhood boys, and male friends of my sister." —Brooke

"My earliest memories of my father sexually abusing me were when I was an infant. This abuse continued until the age of 19. My father was also involved with another man who had three children. As a group, both men hurt me and the other children. My father also had acquaintances sexually assault me." —Katie

"I had three major abusers in my life. The abuse from my uncle lasted a couple of years. They moved away when I was 9 or 10. The abuse from my brother occurred when he was home on leave or visiting us with his family. The last time he cornered me I was in my late

teens. The abuse from my father continued until I was 10 or 11 years old." —Mo

"My parents gave me away at the age of 12 to breed me. My parents could see that I was gay before I could see it myself and sexually gave me away the moment they recognized it, hoping to force a change in me." —Jan

"My sexual abusers are many. I once counted 11, including uncles, cousins, sisters, and friends of the family. My abuse ranged from finger penetration at the age of 4 or 5, penile penetration when I was in kindergarten, oral copulation, fondling, and being forced to provide sexual favors to women, teens at the time." —Noemi

"My grandmother was very busy with the farm, so two uncles and at least one outsider abused me. I was blamed for it." —Naomi

"My family is insane. I was not only sexually abused; I was physically abused, lots of bloodshed. I was given psychoactive drugs. I was neglected. I witnessed the torture and killing of animals." —Barbara

"My parents were sexually inappropriate. They would have sex while I was sitting on the bed or standing in my crib. They were selfish, or they just didn't care. I thought I would have to help by having sex with Dad because of Mom's MS. It was a bizarre place to grow up. Part of me knew that other parents didn't do this. It was a clothing-optional household after 6 o'clock. There was no door on the full bath because my mother's wheelchair didn't fit. Of course, they could have found another solution for privacy. My father's brother was a child molester. He lived with us. He molested me when I was 2." —Reg

"I had three perpetrators. The first was a male relative. At age 3 he masturbated me and asked me, 'Can I kiss your pussy?' The second perpetrator was the father of a friend. He had seven daughters. He raped all of them and the neighborhood girls, like me, who slept over. This happened between the ages of 7 and 10. He was oral with me, digital

penetration, and masturbated me in the middle of the night with three other girls next to me. At some point I stopped going there overnight. Then on the day after the last day of school of sixth grade I was taking flowers to the student teacher by bus by myself. I asked a man for directions. He strangled me, digitally masturbated me, and raped me with his penis. I thought, I can live through this because I've been through this. *But he splintered me. He tore me open. I stopped a car and the driver gave me the words for what had happened to me. He took me to the police station. My parents were devastated. I cried and my Mom rocked me."* —Kathy

"When my mother died of cancer when I was 2, I was placed in an orphanage. The children there were overseen by various house mothers who would bring their adolescent sons as 'helpers.' These boys would display themselves to us and encourage us to fondle them. They would carry on under their mother's noses. They enjoyed having an audience. When they became more brazen they would perform oral and anal sex on the children, infants to 5-year-olds. It was a progression, an evolution of abuse. The mothers would occasionally participate by holding us down for their sons. I would put up monumental resistance. I was abused from age 3 to 5. There was so much violence to my physical flesh." —Marian

"When I was in boarding school, a 12- to 13-year-old girl would come to my bed and do digital penetration after lights-out and when I was asleep. When I was 11, I worked for the local butcher, a family acquaintance, before and after school. He trapped me in the back room and began fondling my breasts and kissing them. He smelled of alcohol even though it was about 8 A.M. *I got out when he was interrupted by a customer coming into the shop. I never went back."* —Misha

"In addition to abuse by my brother, I also remember sitting on my grandfather's lap. He was rubbing me and I was in diapers. I was also abused by an uncle, my brother's friend, and also my brother's female friend." —Wendy

The devastating emotional impact of child sexual abuse is enormous. In *The Right to Innocence*, Beverly Engel (1989) writes:

> Childhood sexual abuse is such an overwhelming, damaging, and humiliating assault on a child's mind, soul, and body that she cannot escape emotional damage. The abuse invades every facet of one's existence: It affects self-esteem, relationships with others, sexuality, one's ability to be successful, one's ability to trust others, and physical health. It causes victims to be self-destructive, over-controlling, and abusive of others, as well as addiction to alcohol, drugs, and food and attraction to love partners who abuse them physically, verbally, and emotionally. Its victims come to feel ashamed, guilty, powerless, depressed, afraid, and angry.

My own abuse story begins when I was 12. My older brother, two years my senior, began abusing me at night while I was sleeping in my bed. I would awaken to the feel of his penis or testicles in my hand, the feel of him pulling at my clothes, or the feel of his breath on my cheek, pleading with me to let him touch me. The initial touching, and his forcing me to touch him, progressed to oral sex and intercourse. The abuse continued for six years. I can clearly remember the constant dread that I would be awakened in the night by his advances. The shadow of a figure in a doorway can still make me jump. The feel of his weight on top of me, the smell of his breath in my face, the feel of insistent pawing at my skin, and the sticky feel of semen and blood are all memories I carry with me from my childhood. But more than the physical sensations, I remember feeling scared, alone, and exhausted, for years.

Ellen Bass and Laura Davis, authors of the acclaimed *Courage to Heal* (1988)—for many survivors the bible for healing the effects of childhood sexual abuse—describe how "all abuse is damaging, and the trauma does not end when the abuse stops. If you were abused as a child, you are probably experiencing long-term effects that interfere with your day-to-day functioning." Delphene spoke for many survivors when she described the overwhelming effects the abuse had had on her life: "*The abuse confused me, made me unsure of everything.*" The power to reclaim our feelings, particularly given the rules we learned about not speaking out within our dysfunctional childhood households, is eloquently captured by Mollie who said, "*I grew up with people doubting my feelings left and right.*" Bass and Davis describe how survivors learned to block the physical pain during the abuse. "But since you can't block feelings selectively, you simply stopped feeling." Often we turn our feelings inside out, trying to make them more socially acceptable. We hide our feelings to be pleasing, to avoid making waves. This is called *reaction formation* (Van der Kolk, 1987). We pretend to like our abuser, we pretend we're not hurting inside, we become perfectionists and straight-A students, while deep inside we know we are fooling only ourselves.

The untreated effects of abuse are chronic and lead to secondary effects as well. The most common of these include depression, eating disorders, substance abuse, anxiety, dissociative disorders, somatization disorders, and explosive disorders (Courtois, 1988). Survivors might also experience domestic violence or other sexual violence as adults. "The aftermath of childhood abuse can manifest itself at any age in a variety of ways. Internally, it can appear as depression, anxiety, suicidal thoughts, or post–traumatic stress; it can also be expressed outwardly as aggression, impulsiveness, delinquency, hyperactivity, or substance abuse" (Teicher, 2002). Recent brain research has revealed physiological changes in the brain's structure as a result of abuse. Reductions in the size of the hippocampus and amygdala in survivors of child abuse have been documented. These changes are related to dissociative symptoms and depression, irritability, and hostility, respectively. In addition, significant brain wave abnormalities have been found in patients with a history of early trauma, including incest. Abnormal EEG activity in the temporal lobe is often seen in people with a greatly increased risk for suicide and self-destructive behaviors. The use of threat or force and duration of abuse, rather than the overall severity of the abuse, are related to more psychological distress in the long term (Bennett, 2000). Abuse by a father figure and severe abuse are also more damaging psychologically (Ketring and Feinauer, 1999).

In *Trauma and Addiction*, psychotherapist Tian Dayton (2000) describes *relationship trauma* as the "internal earthquake or loss of psychological and emotional ground that happens when people you love and need in order to feel secure in the world are lost in their own addictions, psychological illnesses or addictive behaviors, when the relationships you depend upon for survival are ruptured." Krystal (1968) calls the profound changes to a person's personality as a result of trauma *disaster syndrome* which includes: loss of capacity to use support, chronic recurrent depression with feelings of despair, psychosomatic symptoms, emotional "anesthesia" or blocked ability to react affectively, and alexithymia or inability to recognize and make use of emotional reactions. In addition, there are numerous personality changes common to individuals who have experienced trauma: learned helplessness, anxiety, depression, emotional constriction, disorganized inner world, traumatic bonding, cycles of reenactment, loss of ability to modulate emotions (black-and-white thinking), emotional triggering, distorted reasoning, loss of trust and faith, hypervigilance, loss of ability to take in support, fused feelings, emotional numbness (alexithymia), loss of spontaneity, high-risk behaviors, survival guilt, development of rigid psychological defenses, and desire to self-medicate (Dayton, 2000).

Child sexual abuse has been identified as a significant predictor of a woman's educational attainment and annual earnings (Hyman, 2000). The experience of child sexual abuse appears to adversely affect the economic status of adult lesbian women by interfering with their ability to acquire the skills necessary to be successful in the workplace and by shaping women's functioning in other areas, such as physical and mental health. It has been found that women who are employed are healthier than nonemployed women; women who are not employed often report poor health as their reason for not working. According to Hyman, child sexual abuse often adversely affects a developing girl's self-esteem and shapes her school experiences, thereby affecting her educational attainment and future earnings. Hyman (2000), in describing the economic consequences of child sexual abuse to lesbians, described how the abuse experience "may affect each of the three factors known to affect a woman's salary: her information about occupations, her risk-taking behaviors, and her self-confidence."

Hyman's research corroborates that of Putnam and Trickett (cited in Strong, 1998) who found that many aftereffects of abuse interfered with learning: dissociation, depression, lower self-esteem, distraction, memory problems, and aggressive or withdrawn behavior.

The key issue affecting survivors is, of course, self-esteem. The feeling of being unloved, unwanted, worthless, and without value can threaten to overwhelm us and shapes all of our behavior. Unwanted sexual attention experienced by children is associated with poorer self-esteem, body image, and body anxiety in young women (Whealin and Jackson, 2002). Davis (1992) describes this feeling of low self-esteem when she writes, "If you ever really knew me, you wouldn't want to know me or love me." How many of us have said that to ourselves, and believed we were unworthy, undeserving of love in some sort of fundamental way that could not be altered?

"When the abuse started I was 8. I started to have problems with my self-image and self-esteem. I began to withdraw from friends and life in general. I used to self-mutilate. I stopped trusting men and felt uncomfortable when anyone was close to me." —Kim

"Saying no to anything is frightening, and I am always afraid that the person to whom I say no will withdraw their love, affection, or respect." —Mollie

"I can't get angry at my abusers; I get angry at myself. It's my fault in a million ways. I feel there's something intrinsically wrong with me. I have a deep sense of shame and worthlessness." —Lynn

"I believe the abuse has affected mostly everything about how I have chosen to live my life. By some standards I am considered a success. However, by my standards, I am only barely above mediocrity. Yes, I have a degree from an Ivy League institution, and yes, I am soon to receive my doctorate, and yes, I have a fairly impressive job. But generally I feel I am 'just getting by.' It is very hard for me to be compassionate or understanding about my own struggles. Intellectually I understand it all. Emotionally, I look at myself as a failure." —Lisa

"As a youth I was withdrawn, shy, quiet, and scared. I would not put myself in any situation that I might have to be looked at individually." —Serena

"I felt useless, awful, ugly, and worthless. There was a black cloud following me around everywhere. I constantly craved everyone's love and attention while at the same time feeling completely unworthy of it and absolutely positive I'd never get it." —Cory

"I put myself down all the time, which makes my girlfriend mad." —Melissa

"I had a chronic 'I'm not good enough' feeling." —Kathy

"I have always struggled with trust, self-hate, and self-doubt. I also struggle with the feeling that I don't really fit in anywhere and the feeling that I can't make the world safe enough." —Levie

"I feel that I'm no good or not worthy of love. I have never had a meaningful relationship." —Naomi

To appreciate the pervasive impact of childhood sexual abuse we must recognize how it affects self-perceptions, feelings, relationships with others, achievement, and values. As a result of low self-esteem, survivors tend to be self-destructive. These destructive habits can be categorized in five areas: physical pain or danger, addictions, sexual acting out, negative self-talk, and suicidal ideation or actions (Roth, 1993). The women I interviewed described the pervasive effects the abuse had had on their lives in this way:

"The abuse really messed up my life." —Debbie

"I have lived my whole life as a survivor. I exhibited most of the classic signs of molestation. I wet the bed until a teen, had blackouts when I didn't know what was happening, had low self-esteem. I read The Courage to Heal *and could check off most of the 72 indicators of sexual abuse."* —Deborah

"I sought out people who would hurt me. I was raised Catholic and was taught that the more you hurt, the better you are as a person. I was seeking out chaos." —Sarah

"I have had a host of psychotic and post–traumatic stress symptoms since my early childhood. My experiences went unrecognized as such until my freshman year of college when I was diagnosed and hospitalized four times for a psychotic disorder." —Mollie

"The abuse affected me in the classic ways: poor self-esteem, self-loathing, a hatred for the feminine, hatred for my body, fear of sexual contact, particularly with a male. I was not at peace. The split in my psyche from the dissociating had left a gaping hole. In my teens I felt mentally unstable, that my life was not my own, that my own needs and desires did not matter." —Cristi

"It has left me with severe and lasting emotional and psychological problems. I am unable to work, unable to have a normal adult relationship (sexual problems, inability to fall in love, unable to feel connected to another human being, trust issues, anger and hostility issues, low self-esteem). It is overwhelming for me to do normal life stuff like housekeeping or driving." —Barbara

"Sometimes it feels like a big snowball getting bigger and bigger. I resent the way the abuse has made me manage my life. The money I spend on therapy. The abuse affects everything: Who I date, what I can do in bed, what I eat, who I eat with. I don't eat in front of people I don't trust." —Reg

"It affected all areas of my life—sexually, emotionally, physically. There is no part that it didn't touch." —Kathy

"I have difficulty with self-control if I want something. I try to ask myself if I 'need' what I want so I'm not spending money on things I don't need. I used to spend too much time at work. I've disciplined myself to leave when it's time to go now. I think my peers would say that I am friendly, but they don't know much about my personal life." —Maggie

"My life has been changed in every way by the abuse. I think that all of my choices, all my nonchoices, were shaped by the abuse. Everything that the abuse did is who I am today, though I've evolved. Who knows what my journey would have been if I hadn't been abused?" —Jill

Many survivors describe feeling emotionally disconnected from the experience, as if they were watching the abuse happen to someone else. We develop defense mechanisms, in this case *dissociation,* to live with the pain of the abuse. When you recall the abuse, your emotions "go numb." Another form of dissociation is referred to as "splitting off," the feeling of leaving your body while you were being sexually abused. Dissociation allowed you to function while the abuse was happening.

"When I'm talking about it it's almost like I'm talking about someone else." —Kris

"Dissociation is like when you're out of your body. I think I got pretty good at that. I learned to do it when my father was molesting me. The way it's affected me since then is in not being in tune with my body. When I hurt myself it's like it doesn't register with me." —Jacque

"When the neighbor boy molested me I remember feeling numb, not participating. I had an urge to flee. I tried to leave the situation, in my head. During sex I always felt that I was out of my body." —Amanda

"I visualized that I was laying up close to the ceiling kind of looking down on what was happening. Like that was another part of me. Sometimes the idea of another place entered in too. I've always used nature and gardens and being outside as an escape or a coping. I'd always rather be outside. I felt safe there. Part of it was that if you're out in the open, he can't do anything." —Jacque

"I have the typical signs of abuse, like spacing out and dissociating." —Cory

"I went to therapy because I wanted to experience a normal range of

emotion. I had gotten to a point where I didn't feel anything. Sad and bad feels all the same to me. It's hard for me to distinguish my emotions and to determine cause and effect. 'What made me feel this way?'" —Reg

"My parents were violent when I tried to tell them I didn't agree with them. I soon learned to swallow what I felt to avoid punishment. I became so out of touch with my feelings that at the end of high school I denied feeling any 'bad' emotions." —Cristi

According to Bratton (1999), dissociation allows us "to separate core self from the abuse." In this way, it's comforting for survivors to realize that "dissociation means the spirit, the soul, was never touched by the abuse." The alternative, of fully experiencing the physical and emotional pain of the abuse—would have been devastating.

Many of us attempt to self-medicate the emotional pain resulting from trauma. We seek out substances and experiences to solve our problems—to kill the pain or numb the hurt—but this solution becomes a primary problem, addiction. In experiencing trauma we lose our ability to put our feelings into words. "When we are traumatized," Dayton (2000) writes, "we lose contact with our real and authentic emotions. They become covered by psychological defenses and emotional armoring." We choose to self-medicate with chemicals (drugs or alcohol), as well as behavioral addictions that affect our brain chemistry (bingeing, purging, or withholding food), or engaging in high-risk or high-intensity activities such as excessive work behaviors, risky sex, or gambling. These behaviors affect the pleasure centers of the brain, enhancing "feel-good" chemicals, thus minimizing the pain. So in addition to distancing themselves emotionally from the abuse, as described above, survivors describe the ways they have tried to dull or numb the pain by abusing substances or food. The mood-altering qualities of these substances help take away the pain (Bratton, 1999).

The desire to self-medicate or self-soothe—with drugs, alcohol, food, sex, spending, gambling, and a variety of other things—is a psychological defense. Our attempts to self-medicate give us temporary relief from our pain. But as Dr. Kathryn Zerbe, author of *The Body Betrayed*, describes, "When we persistently try to hide our true feelings we soon lose touch with how we really feel." At the root of most of our coping skills is the attempt to numb or control the effects of the abuse. According to Starzecpyzel (1987), "Issues around control are also central to the incest survivor's psychology. Perfectionism, various forms of food control (obesity, anorexia, bulimia), money issues, and excessive striving for success or achievement are defenses against not having had control." Noted child development expert Stanley Greenspan (1999, cited in Dayton, 2000) speaks of growth-producing and growth-inhibiting environments for children. In growth-producing environments, the parent is attuned to the child and there is no gap between words and actions. Consistency and authenticity are the norm. Children have parental behavior and routines they can count on. This means that children's energy is freed up to meet the challenges and opportunities of their own lives. In growth-inhibiting environments, the child's energy is devoted to developing strategies to ward off painful, confusing, and inconsistent behavior. In such cases, children become internally preoccupied with bringing sense and order to external and internal chaos so they can feel safe.

A dual diagnosis of post–traumatic stress disorder and addiction is common for adult children who have grown up in homes where emotional, psychological, and physical abuse were prevalent (Dayton, 2000). When our childhood is out of control we often resort to coping mechanisms to convince ourselves that we are in control at all times.

"*I'm always a perfectionist.*" —Meg

"*I strove for perfection and quiet recognition in my schoolwork and job. I am an extremely Type A personality now—controlling, assertive, winner takes all. All extremes, I guess you could say.*" —Serena

"*I became an achiever and went underground.*" —Mary Lou

"*I became a compulsive cleaner. I thought if my house was perfect, then no one would have a reason to look closer at me. I was a perfect student and won praise and love. I tried to be the perfect person for everyone. Whatever they needed, I could do it, be it. All my things were perfect.*

Everything in my room and life was just right. I folded clothes in a specific way. Everything had its place, and I knew where everything was. I was safe and no one could get me. If something was unfolded or rearranged it would make me uneasy. I felt violated. If I left my house by a certain door I had to reenter it the same way. Light switches were turned off in a sequence. The list keeps going. These behaviors grew in number and severity depending on the level of abuse or emotional upheaval I was experiencing." —Mo

"I'm obsessive-compulsive and have been that way since I was a child. It's something that made me spend a lot of time alone. It got worse as I got older. I didn't want people to catch me doing my washing and arranging and stuff, so I isolated myself pretty well. It's something that every day reminds me and makes me angry for feeling different. Like toothbrushing. I can brush my teeth for an hour at a time and totally lose track of time. It's like in my mind I'm washing that dick out of my mouth." —Kris

Personally I have done many things to avoid feeling the effects of the abuse. As a teenager and young adult I was a binge drinker; I think the term I liked to use was social drinker. I drank to forget, to loosen up, to have an excuse for the sexually promiscuous behavior I engaged in that I would never have done had I been sober. I've battled a weight problem since the abuse started at age 12. I recognize now that I hide behind the weight, somehow tricking myself into thinking I'm safe if I'm overweight—no one will approach me sexually if I'm not thin. I have struggled with anorexia, bulimia, and compulsive overeating. Food has been my rescuer. Instead of feeling the feelings, I push them down with food. My drug of choice is sugar—cookies, cake, doughnuts. The sugar high pulls me out of the blues, at least temporarily. I'm ashamed to say I've been a compulsive shopper; I've bought things I didn't need and couldn't afford. Sometimes I buy gifts for people so they'll think well of me and so I could uphold an image of myself as a person of wealth. I experienced a tremendous high when I was buying things and then deep remorse and regret when I arrived home with my purchases. I'd hide my purchases from my partner and lie about where things came from. I'd say I received things as gifts or exchanged things for them. I have battled with debt for many years. I'm beginning to see the way my overeating and spending habits are connected to my feeling trapped and worthless. Recognizing these as problems for me has spurred me to get the help I need to continue my healing.

It takes courage to recognize we have a problem and then do something about it. Here's what some courageous women say about their struggles and triumphs.

"I don't drink, since 1995. I think I would have been an alcoholic. I noticed some of the danger signs and thought, This is unhealthy." —Reg

"I started drinking at 13. By 16 I was addicted to cigarettes, alcohol, and various drugs. I was in a car accident at 17 that scared me. I realized I was turning out just like my parents, so I stopped. I swore to get clean. By 18 I was off everything and have been ever since." —Rowan

"Getting sober let me deal with the abuse, let the feelings come up." —Marty

Food addictions, as many of us know firsthand, help us avoid life's difficulties because of the preoccupation—or obsession—with food. It's a way to numb out, to dull the pain. As Lynn said, *"I have had issues with food and alcohol; anything not to have to feel."* And Deborah said, *"I eat to feel something or not to feel something."* Food may be used to fill up the individual or as a replacement for people or friendships (Zerbe, 1993). As Lisa said, *"I find most of my solace in food. I find very little emotional reward from interacting with others."* Disordered eating and a variety of issues around food were common in the survivors I spoke with, as well as in the literature on eating disorders. Here are the ways in which survivors described their struggles with food:

"Food is a big deal. As a kid, food was a way my parents neglected me. My parents never looked at me. I was nonexistent to them. Food is some sort of a friend, a comfort to me. I was bulimic as an adult. I always was a fat kid, and now I'm a fat adult." —Reg

"All my life I've been anorexic. When I was 70 pounds at 5 foot 6 I was in the ICU for severe anorexia." —Tabitha

"I've had issues with food my whole life. I'm heavier now than I've ever been. I'm eating a lot and not exercising at all. I'm punishing myself for my last relationship ending." —Chris

"I started using food to deal with my pain as a young child. I binged often." —Katie

"I have an eating disorder and suffer from obesity. I believe this is a direct result of not being able to handle my feelings." —Cory

"My compulsive overeating began at age 3. I was bulimic in high school, and this continued into my 30s." —Mary Lou

"I'm a comfort eater and a boredom eater. When I feel stressed out or when I feel upset, usually I'll turn to food." —Lyndsey

"Over the past few years I have struggled with an on-again, off-again pattern of disordered eating. When I tell myself I can't use cutting to deal with whatever is upsetting me, I find myself restricting instead. It is much easier for me to turn my feelings into physical pain or discomfort—and thereby punish myself—than it is for me to deal with them constructively." —Mollie

"I drank a lot to numb the pain. I didn't know where to turn." —Jan

"I have a history of relapsing with alcohol over post–traumatic stress disorder." —Kyrce

"I have an addiction to drugs that can be somewhat attributed to my abuse and how I was raised. Me and my family have a tendency to completely phase out whatever we're dealing with." —Kristie

"I was abusing prescription tranquilizers." —Naomi

"I was a drug user and drank a lot of alcohol. I was trying to run away." —Whitney

"What I liked about coke and methamphetamine is that I felt out of control for a reason. I was controlling my out-of-controlness. I was whacked out half the time and started to do all these crazy things. I'd sit down and do $150 worth of cocaine myself. I think I just got too much into myself." —Delphene

"At times I would go in the fridge and take a beer to relax myself. I didn't understand why I would do that. Now I see that it's very common. People think that drinking is a way of getting relaxed. In reality it's a depressant." —Diana

"At 14 I was into pot and then alcohol. This continued for 10 years. I was self-medicating and wanted to be more outgoing. A lot was going on in the house. I ended up in an inpatient substance abuse treatment program. When someone suggested that I was an alcoholic and an incest survivor, I said, 'You're crazy.'" —Chris

"I was a heavy drug user, in and out of jail. Now my addictions are pain meds and pot." —Laura

Several survivors describe how their attempts to self-medicate helped them to deny the impact of the abuse as well as keep them from recognizing their lesbianism.

"My addiction was full-blown in college. If I wasn't abusing, I would not have had sex with men or married. The substances and food covered up the abuse and my sexual identity. Until I stopped my compulsive overeating and bulimia, I didn't know I was lesbian." —Mary Lou

"I did every drug I could get my hands on, not coincidentally when I decided I was gay." —Missy

"The abuse has affected me greatly—inability to love or be loved. Hate

for myself and my body; growing up confused about my gender and sexuality. I continue to struggle with my body image, intimacy, food, and a constant struggle for the desire to live and survive." —Noemi

"First I got sober, then I got in touch with my anger, and then I got my body back. That was significant. Then I came out to myself. It's amazing what can happen when you stop drowning your feelings." —Marty

Child sexual abuse is associated with lifetime alcohol abuse in both lesbian and heterosexual women (Hughes, Johnson, and Wisnack, 2001; Lehmann, Lehmann, and Kelly, 1998). Victims of unresolved childhood trauma are considerably more likely to develop post–traumatic stress disorder symptoms in adulthood, which can and often do lead to addiction (Dayton, 2000). Reliance on bars for socializing is also a distinct problem in the lesbian community. A recent review of the literature revealed three major findings about lesbians' alcohol use: (1) Lesbians tend to drink more than other women; (2) Rates of drinking do not decline with age; and (3) Lesbians report greater difficulties related to alcohol consumption (Abbott, 1998). Claire Renzetti argues that "Alcohol and drugs have historically been palliatives for the stress [of the gay and lesbian experience]. Excessive drinking is associated with avoidant coping" (cited in Hefferman, 1998). Avoidant coping is the preferred style of many lesbians and survivors who struggle to accept their sexuality. As Sue said, *"I know I'm a lesbian, but every time I start drinking again I find myself hopping in bed with a guy. Why? I don't know. I wind up feeling like shit after, and still haven't figured out why I do it. I certainly don't enjoy it. I think the booze convinces me I will."* How much more burdensome life can seem to the lesbian survivor who struggles with conflicted feelings about her own healthy sexual attraction toward other women and the painful experience of sexual abuse.

Alcohol is also associated with lesbians committing abusive acts against their partners as well as being the victim of abusive acts (Schilit, Lie, and Montaigne, 1990).

"I attended a group for lesbian perpetrators of domestic violence. I

learned that the behavior stops you from feeling. Once I wasn't acting out or throwing things, I could deal with my feelings better." —Cory

Substance abuse recovery is complicated by a history of childhood sexual abuse (Hall, 1996). Research has found that adolescents who suffer physical and sexual abuse have higher rates of depression and alcohol use disorders (Clark et al, 2002). Research on substance abuse treatment for survivors found that survivors who receive treatment have significantly more problems related to drug use and psychological adjustment at follow-up than do women who have not experienced child abuse (Kang et al, 1999). Lesbian survivors in alcohol recovery reported a wide range of issues including multiple addictions, self-harm, isolation, sexual problems, depression, self-loathing, physical illness, and inability to work. Unfortunately, most treatment centers are reluctant to address sexuality and related problems (Neisen and Sandall, 1990). Therefore, lesbians in substance abuse treatment programs fail to receive the sensitive treatment they need to heal. Abbott's findings (1998) support the need for treatment programs tailored to survivors' needs. Finally, researchers warn that heavy alcohol use has implications for lesbians' health and is a risk factor for disease (Aaron et al, 2001).

"Anyone can become angry, that is easy...but to be angry with the right person, to the right degree, at the right time, for the right purpose, and in the right way... this is not easy."
—Aristotle

One of the key emotions that survivors self-medicate is anger. They're afraid of feeling and expressing their anger for fear that it will overwhelm them. "Rage is the long-suppressed response to the abuse," explains Roth (1993). Survivors are resistant to expressing their rage, knowing all too well the destructive nature of anger. They are terrified of turning into their abusers and attempt to hold all their anger inside. Often when you find yourself automatically reacting over the simplest thing in an angry or defensive manner, or find yourself trying to escape life by indulging in your vices more than you normally do, it's most likely due to an event linked to a past situation. Therapy can be effective in teaching us how to recognize these triggers and how to bring ourselves under control before expressing our rage. When our feelings get too painful for us to deal with, we get rid of the feelings by seeing the problem as being not inside but outside, not about us but about someone else. This is the defense mechanism *projection.*

"I've had anger all my life. It didn't occur to me until a year ago that maybe this is why. I'm working on it. I control my anger now instead of the other way around. I look at it, learn from it, and keep it under control. I am in charge of my emotions and memories. I refuse to let them control my life." —Missy

As many of us are all too aware, survivors usually turn their anger at their perpetrators inward first, on themselves. We experience tremendous guilt and shame over what has happened. We become depressed, even suicidal, feeling we are to blame for our circumstances. We believe there must be something wrong with us that caused this to happen. Many of us express our rage during adolescence through rebellion and in self-destructive behaviors: suicidal gestures and behavior, self-mutilation, substance abuse, poor choice of friends and partners, sexual promiscuity and prostitution, and runaway attempts (Courtois, 1988).

With help and support, we can begin to turn this around and put the blame where it belongs—on our abusers. This can be a very lengthy and painful process. After all, for most of us, our abusers were friends or family members, the people who were supposed to love and protect us. It can feel emotionally overwhelming and unsafe to direct our anger at our father, brother, mother, or uncle. Zerbe (1993) describes the paradox in this way: "The abused person may fear for her very survival, yet often depends on those who hurt her, which leads her to disavow her anger at all costs." The distortion of our anger comes out in a variety of ways, many that we don't even recognize as anger. Anger is often disguised as passive-aggressive behavior, depression, manipulativeness, anxiety, and somatic complaints (Courtois, 1988).

As Kristie describes, when we experience trauma we have trouble tolerating intense emotions without feeling overwhelmed. This can lead us to continue relying on dissociation (Dayton, 2000). *"I was extremely angry for years with no idea of how to express it."* This is characteristic of trauma survivors who are described as alexithymic (emotionally numbed) and who are given to sudden outbursts of anger or rage (Dayton, 2000). This is closely tied to survivors' inability to modulate their emotions. Survivors are emotionally and psychologically wired for intensity. We are easily triggered into anger, withdrawal, or shutdown.

"I'm mad at the world at times." —Naomi

"I think if I deal with this abuse and my family's disowning me, I could control my issues with anger." —Tammy

"My anger comes out at people on the street and is trapped in my body—my weight, my back, and my legs. In the last six months in therapy, I've felt like I'd really like to strangle, kill, my parents. I would break things. I have a rage, a well-founded rage. My feelings of worthlessness, depression, and self-blame have turned into anger now." —Cory

I have a big anger issue. Things set me off and I become a raving lunatic. It's usually over a competency issue—people who can't do their jobs. Mom was really smart, and people would say, 'Why can't you be more like your mother?' I was berated for not being good enough. Dad said I'd never amount to anything. The only emotion allowed in the household when I was growing up was rage." —Reg

Novotni and Petersen's research (2001) indicates that "anger isn't precise. It's a fire that burns anything in its path. Anger often lashes out at inappropriate targets. This is called *displacement.* This lack of precision sometimes makes it hard to figure out the real cause of our anger. It's no wonder many of us are afraid of this unharnessed emotion." Relaxation exercises and other techniques we can perform for ourselves to control the intensity of our anger can be very helpful as Marie came to appreciate saying, *"I still struggle with anger issues and knowing how to express them, but I am learning how to maintain self-control."*

On a lighter note, Sue was able to find humor in a difficult situation where her anger literally knocked her out:

"There was this intense rage just beneath the surface. I was staying with a friend and I was saying some pretty horrible things and just couldn't stop yelling at her. I called my therapist who told me to go out in the woods, find a stick, take a few swings at the tree, and say out loud what was making me so angry. Well, I thought she was nuts until I tried it. After the fourth of fifth stick broke I began to realize what I was yelling about. Not just about the abuse as a child, but all the other individuals who abused me. I threw the stick at the tree. Not a good idea. It bounced off the tree and came back to hit me, right between the eyes, knocking me out. I woke up lying flat on my back, staring up at the trees and blue sky, and laughing like hell. That day I stopped being angry about the abuse. I highly recommend the tree therapy. Just don't throw the damn stick!"

While humorous, Sue's example does illustrate the point that physical outlets can be healthy ways to manage anger. Strenuous exercise like tennis, squash, racquetball, or jogging can help discharge tension. Activities like breaking pencils or shredding magazines, hitting pillows, screaming, or drawing can also help.

"The problems of alcoholism and drug addiction have strong links to depression. The search for highs may often begin as a flight from lows."
—Nathan S. Kline, MD

Many survivors criticize themselves for the way they coped. But according to Bass and Davis (1988), "Coping is nothing to be ashamed of. You survived, and it's important to honor your resourcefulness." While some of the ways you've coped have developed into strengths, others have become self-defeating patterns. As Bass and Davis explain, "Healing requires that you differentiate between the two. Then you can celebrate your strengths while you start changing the patterns that no longer serve you." Symptoms and defenses must be understood in context and not pathologized (Courtois, 1988). What you are feeling are normal reactions to abnormal events (Bratton, 1999). Therapists treating dysfunctional families, including alcoholic and incestuous families, have found these families often have multiple problems associated with regulation and control and that overlap exists between different types of family problems (Courtois, 1988). A variety of addictions and different types of compulsive behaviors are mechanisms used by these families to defend against their shame issues (Fossum and Mason, 1986). These include:

- compulsively abusing themselves: abusing drugs and alcohol, physically inflicting pain and injury, overworking, overexercising, or starving themselves
- compulsively abusing others: physical, sexual, and emotional abuse of children or spouses
- compulsions related to money and material goods: compulsive shopping, overspending, hoarding, saving, and shoplifting
- compulsions related to sexuality: compulsive voyeurism, exhibitionism, masturbation, affairs and casual encounters, use of pornography, obscene calls, incest and rape
- compulsions related to food: anorexia nervosa, bulimia, obsessive dieting, and overeating

Within the context of shame-based family systems, survivors' coping strategies can be understood as both attempts to deal with shame and learned behaviors. Dayton (2000) describes self-soothing as one of the primary developmental tasks for children. For those of us who have lived with trauma, learning healthy ways of self-soothing is a critical developmental task that will help us to seek comfort in healthy—not addictive or self-destructive—ways.

Many survivors discount the impact of the abuse on their lives, which is another common defense mechanism—*minimization*—a way to cope with the emotional pain associated with trauma. When we tell ourselves *It wasn't that bad,* we are trying to lessen the pain that the abuse caused us. Unfortunately, our minds, and certainly our bodies, rarely believe what we are trying to convince ourselves of. Courtois (1988) believes these attempts to downplay or deny the consequences of the abuse do not indicate that the experience was nonabusive, but rather we "have not yet been able to acknowledge its full impact." Sometimes we discount our experiences, saying someone has it worse than we do. We think these "downward comparisons" will somehow help us feel better. As long as we're not the worst off we can handle it. Unfortunately, these comparisons don't help us. They only serve to distance us from our feelings and continue our detachment.

"The type of abuse, the incest, was not horrific. So it was fondling, penetration—but with a finger—and it wasn't done in a way that was particularly terrifying." —Margie

"The extent of the abuse was not as severe as some others." —Christy

Still other survivors, like Jacque, maintain—as I do—that all abuse is harmful:

"Since my father never raped me or tried to have intercourse with me, I get the idea that people think, Oh, well, then you didn't have that big of a problem. *They are quick to say, 'Oh, he just molested you.' And it's like, what are you talking about? Psychologically it was still just as harmful. I wondered if my story would be taken as seriously because of that."* —Jacque

An interesting phenomenon occurred in my interviews with survivors. In volunteering to share their stories, some women suggested that even as survivors they might not measure up. Despite my assurances that each survivor's story is important, some survivors maintained that their own stories might not be "good enough" for the purposes of the book.

"I may not be what you need. I hope that if I am not that I haven't wasted your time." —Dana

"I feel like a failure at being a victim because I don't remember what happened." —Deborah

Some survivors, after years of turning their anger on themselves, finally acknowledge the trauma they have suffered and react loudly in righteous indignation. They rail at the injustice that their abusers have resumed their lives while they continue to suffer.

"The last I heard he had gotten married. It angered me that he could just go on with his life. That he could have a relationship while what he did to me has affected me and every relationship I have had. He should be punished for what he did to me. There should be consequences for his actions." —Kirsten

"I would get livid when I would see my former boss in town. I was training to be an advocate for victims of sexual assault but was told I carried too much anger to be effective in my role." —C.J.

"I struggle with the fact that nothing was ever done to any of my abusers. Everyone seems to think that this kind of thing just happens. The justice system makes me sick. A man can rape a young person and go to jail for three years, whereas a person in possession of marijuana can go for 40 years." —Missy

Marian also feels tremendous anger toward her abusers and their accomplices—the adolescent boys and their mothers in the orphanage where she lived from ages 3 to 5—and recognizes the way she has generalized her anger at her abusers toward all mothers of sons and continues to struggle to live her life on her terms.

"It's still very difficult to see mothers of sons. I want to throttle them. I refuse to spend time on them. Further, if I attribute my present life to events of the past, I'm giving my abusers power over me. I could stay in bed for the rest of my life, but I'm not going to let the abuse ruin me."

Similarly, Cory describes her suffering and her will to survive: "*I feel the ramifications of the abuse every day. It's overwhelming, but I'm making it back.*"

Elizabeth's cry echoes what so many of us have felt as the sting of betrayal, the lost innocence of our youth when she says of her parents, "*They were supposed to protect me.*" Incest involves four levels of betrayal: (1) the abuse itself and the betrayal of the family member perpetrator; (2) nonresponse by the nonoffending parent or other relatives or friends, (3) nonresponse by professionals such as teachers, social workers, nurses, or doctors; and (4) betrayal of the self, when the child denies her own reality and experience in order to cope (Courtois, 1988). In this way, the layers of abuse reach beyond the dyad of abuser and victim and affect the survivor's relationships with others in her world, like ripples on the water.

Children who are sexually abused are forced to grow up too fast through a process called *parentification.* Such children are described as "little adults" or "mature beyond their years." Marian said she was one such child: "*My adoptive parents remarked that I acted like an adult even at 5.*" Knowing too much too soon can have lasting effects on a child's development. Being robbed of innocence and forced to leave behind the carefree attitude of youth is one of the saddest consequences of abuse. Feeling angry about this loss is appropriate and necessary for healing.

Dealing With Gaps in Memory

"Small children cannot survive the truth; for purely biological reasons they have no choice but to repress what they know."
—Alice Miller

It's estimated that about half of all survivors suffer some form of memory loss. This is an important way of coping with the abuse, by protecting us from overwhelming or continuous psychological strain (Maltz, 1991). Memory loss has both physiological (see Hyman, above) and psychological bases. Psychologically, memory loss is related to the concept of repression, which has three elements: (1) It is the selective forgetting of materials that cause the individual pain; (2) It is not under voluntary control; and (3) Repressed material is not lost but instead is stored in the unconscious and can be returned to consciousness if the anxiety that is associated with the memory is removed (Holmes, 1998). Sometimes we repress memories of the abuse for many years, emotionally unable to handle the pain that remembering would bring. Deborah's therapist had this to say about trying to recover repressed memories of the abuse: "*'It's a waste of time. The memories will return when you're ready for them.' I'm not good at keeping myself safe. Because I don't feel safe, I don't remember what happened.*" As Finney (1992) describes, "Our minds rationally protect us from information that is too painful in order to give us time to make the mental adjustments that enable us to cope."

"I've remembered a lot after suppressing it for 30 years." —Tammie

"Eleven years ago, at age 53, I began recovering memories of having been abused by my father from ages 4 through 11, and by the older of my two brothers when I was 8 years old. I remember my father telling me that if I told my mother about the sexual abuse, he would kill us both. I repressed the memories of my abuse for more than 40 years." —Levie

"I didn't know what exactly happened to me until a few months ago, and even now I'm still not entirely sure of the details. I do know that something happened, and I know that it went on for a few years between ages 7 and 10. Everything fits—from the raging yeast infections I had in second and third grade to the severe and medically unexplainable stomachaches that woke me in the middle of the night during those years to special articles of clothing I wear in my dreams." —Mollie

"I never forgot my stepfather's abusing me. But it wasn't until after the birth of my first child—when I starting having flashbacks—that I really started thinking about what happened to me. Then I remembered my grandfather showing me his penis when I was 4. I told my mother that he had two penises—one flaccid one and one erect one." —Robin

"The earliest memory I have is of being abused at 2 or 3. I don't know who it was, but I know it was a man. Part of me wants to know. I can't say it wasn't my dad." —C.J.

"I always felt I had some reason to be angry with my mother, but I never understood the intensity of my anger until I recovered the memories of sexual abuse by my dad and brother. Then it seemed logical, albeit somewhat unfair, that I blamed her for not protecting me from the sexual abuse." —Levie

"I realized the abuse after I was married and had two children. Things would come back in flashes. The memories weren't connected to any other memory, so it was confusing. When I realized what had happened I was devastated. The memories were very unsettling. It's difficult to verbalize." —Margaret

"My ex encouraged me to go through my childhood photo album. Seeing my vulnerability triggered the memories. When I started to recover the abuse memories, everything really caved in." —Wendy

"I started having nightmares in high school. Flashbacks. Things were coming to my mind and I wasn't clear on what they were. I thought about what my dreams were, all the memories. I don't remember much about my childhood. You know how you block these things? It's a way of protecting yourself." —Diana

"I think I always knew something was wrong, but I never quite knew what it was. It wasn't until I was 24 that I started putting things together from my past and started having body memories and feeling memories of some sort of sexual abuse. To this day I'm not certain who perpetrated it on me. My body has not allowed me to get the full picture of the event. I think it happened when my parents would wake us up in the middle of the night to use the bathroom. We were all bed-wetters. There is a lot I do remember, but not the details of the sexual abuse. I believe that both of my parents were inappropriate sexually, but I'm not exactly sure how." —Mary

Memory repression is "forgetting" about the abuse. This defense mechanism or coping strategy keeps us from living in constant painful awareness of the abuse. As such, amnesia is a form of numbing (Courtois, 1988). It can be understood in the context of brain development. Trauma memories are stored in parts of the brain that were formed early in humans' evolution as fight, flight, or freeze responses to preserve survival. The cortex, or the part of the brain where we think about and reflect upon what we do, was developed later in human evolution. Because of this we tend to have difficulty reflecting upon, remembering or placing into context memories related to trauma (Dayton, 2000). Additionally, it is known that the younger you were when you were sexually abused, the more likely it is that you experienced memory loss around the abuse incident(s). During depression the center of memory, the hippocampus, loses nerve-to-nerve links. Brain imaging research shows that it is altered in size and shape in victims of trauma such as sexual abuse (Dayton, 2000). Most survivors carry no outward signs that they have been sexually abused, other than the "blank spots" in their memory to cover the painful event. (Kritsberg and Miller-Kritsberg, 1993). Bass and Davis (1988) encourage survivors to trust their feelings, saying, 'If you are unable to remember any specific instances [of abuse] but still have a feeling that something abusive happened to you, it probably did."

Remembering occurs in numerous ways and often in a fragmented or disconnected fashion. Understanding this can be reassuring to survivors who recover memories in snapshots and glimpses. First, memory can return physiologically, through body memories and perceptions. You might retrieve colors, specific visions or images, hear sounds, experience smells, odors, and taste sensations. Your body might react in pain reminiscent of the abuse. Other physiological reactions include the stress reactions of fight, flight, or freeze, states of hyperactivity and arousal (including sexual), anxiety, temperature change, and age regression (Courtois, 1998).

Many of the women who spoke with me shared their experiences with repressed memories and their pain of "not knowing for sure."

"I don't have clear memories of the abuse, just flashes and glimpses." —Reg

"I repressed the memories of my abuse for more than 40 years." —Levie

"I only have bits and pieces of memories around the abuse. I can't remember where we lived as kids, what some of my teachers or schoolmates' names were. I just go along with the stories my brothers tell." —Whitney

"I hardly remember, just flashbacks mainly." —Tammy

"I don't remember much about my childhood. I would say from when I was 6 until I was 13 or 14 I blocked everything. My younger sister will tell me things like the fun things we did together, and I'm like, 'I don't remember this.' In high school I started having nightmares, many flashbacks. Things were coming to my mind and I wasn't clear on what they were. I didn't remember a single thing about what had happened until I started having nightmares." —Diana

"I struggle with dissociating all the time. It's like living in eight different worlds at one time. I forget things." —Liz

"It started early, like 18–24 months. I know this because we are DID, multiple personality. There are, like, 20 of us, and the youngest is 18–24 months." —Dana

"My understanding of truth can change from day to day. And my commitment must be to truth rather than to consistency."
—Ram Dass

Dissociation can be as subtle as "spacing out" for a brief time or as extreme as blocking the memory of the abuse entirely. This is called *traumatic amnesia.* You may have no recollection of the abuse whatsoever or only a vague sense that something happened. Or, you may know you are terrified of a certain person or place—but have no idea why (Haines, 1999).

"When I think about my life I think it's been incredibly lucky. I was always able to split myself into little parts, into different buckets in my head. This was my saving grace." —Liz

"I didn't realize I had been sexually abused until I was probably 15 or 16 because I basically only have one memory of it. It's a still image, not a moving image, but I can see it in my mind as clear as day. In the image I can see myself and the perpetrator as if I were at a corner of a room up at the top in the ceiling looking down. It didn't occur to me that this was an actual happening until I heard somebody else share their story and it was similar to mine." —Lyndsey

"I'm still piecing things together about the abuse. Even though my dreams were frequent reminders of the trauma, I was clueless as to their origins. I had had inklings that I may have been abused. There were whole sections of my childhood that were blank. Memories are starting to come back now about the abuse. Most of them involve the church leader. He used a lot of psychological crap about the church to have his way with me, telling me that he was preparing me to be a good wife, that I was special because he was showing me secrets of the temple, but we had to keep them quiet." —Cristi

Survivors describe their difficulty situating events in time or on a timeline.

"I have vivid memories of certain situations that I can recall, but a timeline of events is beyond my recollection." —Marie

"Time is lumpy for me." —Liz

"I have a huge problem with timelines. I don't remember going to school my last year. I don't remember doing any homework. But then there are stretches where it's clear as day. It's just funny. There's a lot of gaps." —Delphene

"My memories are so sketchy it's hard to put it into any chronological order." —Missy

Sometimes we consciously try to block memories of the abuse in hopes of controlling its effects on our life.

"Once I decided that I was not going to allow my inner demons to affect me anymore, it was like I decided, 'You're not going to think about it. You're not going to talk about it or acknowledge anything about the abuse to anybody.' You know, cordon myself off. Set those parameters." —Noemi

There are many gaps in my memories of my childhood. My family likes to joke that I can't remember any of the family vacations we took. My father has even expressed disappointment in me for not remembering the special vacations he paid for. I wish I could remember. But I know I must be blocking out the memories for a reason. The vacations I do remember are filled with incidents of the abuse. I don't remember the restaurants we ate in or the sites we saw. I remember the bedrooms and the sheets and the ceilings in the rooms where my brother abused me. I remember having toileting accidents on vacations when I was a preteen. I am growing to accept the gaps in my memories because I know the block is protecting me from additional pain.

"I was being abused by my father and uncle between the ages of 6 and 7. I can't remember first grade at all." —Lynn

"I didn't remember the abuse when I entered therapy. My therapist asked me if I had been abused because of what she was seeing and hearing. Now I remember some things and then my memory goes bizarre." —Kyrce

"I had a dream where I asked Dad to show me about sex. I expected him to say, 'Get out of here, you harlot.' Instead he took my hand, smiled, and led me into the bedroom where we had sex in my parents' bed. In the dream it was very pleasurable. I also had another dream involving my dad where I had escaped into the barn attic. Finally, I

asked my father if he sexually abused me, and he said he never touched me. Then both he and Mom tried to discredit me, saying that I was mentally unstable. I do not know if my father sexually abused me. Intuitively I feel that it is yes." —Cristi

"Just a couple of years ago I asked my mom why I had to see a psychiatrist when I was in fourth grade. She looked startled that I didn't know, and told me that a teacher had called and said that I was masturbating behind my desk in the back of the room. I had no recollection of that or anything like that. But I do remember having a strong interest in sex always." —Deborah

"I had blank spots in my memory until one day when I was masturbating and I had a flashback of bloody summer shorts, like I got my period. That happened the day my brother abused me." —Dorian

Several women described the way getting clean and sober had freed them up to recover memories of the abuse and reclaim their sexuality.

"I had blocked it out of my memory completely until I spent 28 days in alcohol rehab." —Sue

"Since I dealt with my lesbianism, alcohol is no longer my crutch." —Tammy

Several survivors described their initial frustration—and then growing acceptance—that they could not control the recovery of memories.

"New memories are coming up. The details are coming up. I get discouraged with that." —Rowan

"I am probably not your ideal survivor anyway. I am 44 years old and still don't know for sure; nor do I know who the perpetrator would have been. Since I'm not sure of the perpetrator I may not be of any use to you. Because I don't feel safe, I don't remember what happened. It would be easier to know what happened, to know what to respond to. It's like being a little bit fucked

up. I had a dream a few years ago. I was in a store buying a puzzle. The puzzle pieces were clouds. A woman said to me, 'You need this box to be able to see the whole picture.' I think that was prophetic. I feel like a failure at being a victim because I don't remember what happened." —Deborah

"There are some memories that I simply don't have. There's a whole five-year period where everything is extremely fuzzy. And I've done a lot of digging, believe me." —Jill

"It's more OK now than it used to be to not have memories. I can't force them." —Cory

"I went through a lot of stress and anxiety because I could not force myself to remember. It continues to be in my life in a way that I can't control. I wanted desperately to remember because I thought otherwise no one would believe me. But on the other hand there were definite things in my life and behaviors and feelings that I dealt with that I knew had to have some correlation. My therapist taught me that thank God I don't remember. Obviously I couldn't deal with it then, and I probably can't deal with it now. I've come to the point where I'm grateful for the repressed memories because other survivors that I've spoken to have to live with vivid memories, and luckily I don't have to. If at some point in my life I do remember, I'll take it day by day. But I don't see it as something that I need to validate the experience." —Lyndsey

Understanding what we do about repression, Courtois (1998) cautions survivors about working too hard or too compulsively to recall abuse memories. She reminds us of the "internal wisdom of our psychological defenses" and that memories return in their own good time. Fears of abandonment, being disbelieved, blamed, further shamed, or rejected that keep our memories at bay require discussion and reassurance. Courtois suggests that survivors who are struggling to remember ask themselves, *What do you have to give up to remember? What do you lose?* Giving up fantasies about their childhoods and relationships with family members involves painful loss. Keeping memories locked away inside of us is one way we can preserve the fantasies about our childhoods and our families. Deborah hopes that if she is patient and gives herself the space to heal, the memories will come back.

"I hope that maybe as the fog starts to lift and as I gradually bring order to things I've struggled with forever, perhaps I'll have the psychic space to start coming to terms with it."

Believing It Happened

"An unacknowledged trauma is like a wound that never heals over and may start to bleed again at any time."
—Alice Miller

Lynn Finney, author of *Reach for the Rainbow*, says, "We doubt our own memories because we do not want to believe such terrible things could have happened." Denial, as a coping strategy, allows us to repress our memories of the abuse for many years. It allows us to distance ourselves from the painful reality of our childhood and leaves us confused about what really happened. Often we convince ourselves that the abuse was "not that bad" or that "dwelling on it" will not serve any useful purpose. As all too many of us, however, have learned firsthand, denying the effects of the abuse can lead to long-lasting physical and emotional problems. When we isolate ourselves, try to forget the abuse, or use alcohol or drugs to suppress the memories, we usually develop additional problems, including depression, anxiety, or dependence on alcohol or drugs. We must face the memories directly, as difficult and painful as that is, in order to let them go once and for all. The only way to resolve the hurt of abuse is to acknowledge and feel the pain of the experience (Courtois, 1988).

"You can never find yourself until you face the truth."
—Pearl Bailey

Closely related to the issue of repressed memories is the self-doubt that plagues us as survivors. While we *know* something happened to us, the sexual abuse taboo keeps us questioning ourselves and our perceptions. Believing concrete details of the abuse will prove it happened, we begrudge the way our mind tries to protect us by repressing memories.

"I had read so much about abuse that I just had this doubt if it really had happened. Am I crazy? Did this really happen?" —Diana

"I was questioning myself. Did it happen? I worry if the memories are accurate." —Amanda

"Having no confirmation of the abuse is the hardest part. All my abusers are dead. It's confusing even though I know it really happened." —Lynn

"I thought for a long time it was a dream. Was it reality or not?" —Christy

"As an adult, I returned to the orphanage where I had been abused. My sister and I visited there and took pictures of the buildings. The staff didn't believe I had lived there. They said it had always been a boarding school for boys. But I knew it had happened there just as I remembered." —Marian

In *The Right to Innocence*, Beverly Engel (1989) writes, "If you have ever had reason to suspect you may have been sexually abused, even if you have no explicit memory of it, the chances are very high you were. It is not something you would *choose* to suspect or 'make up.'" In 15 years of clinical practice she says she has never worked with a client who initially suspected she was sexually abused but later discovered she had not been. Bass and Davis maintain the same belief, that trusting our feelings is essential. This can be very difficult, of course, because, as Haines (1993) says, incest is "the ultimate training in not trusting one's self."

Sometimes it's possible for us to receive confirmation of the abuse and validation of our experience through conversations with others.

"I had these snippets, but I didn't really know until I was visiting a cousin after college and found out my uncle had abused his own sister, a neighbor, cousins, and me." —Reg

"It wasn't until I had a chance to be with my great-aunt that I got support from a family member. She told me she was almost raped by her father, my grandfather, but somebody walked in and stopped it. Then I came to understand that he had done this to someone besides me." —Margie

At other times, the confirmation comes to us in dreams, as it did for Cristi:

"I had recurring dreams where I was being chased by a very angry bull that wanted to destroy me. I escaped by climbing the ladder into the barn—something I now attribute to leaving my body during the abuse. In another recurring dream I was kneeling half-naked in the backyard. I felt something penetrate me vaginally from behind, which felt good. When I turned to see what it was, I saw the family dog penetrating me with his penis. Another recurring dream took place at my grandma's house, where a dragon monster popped out of the toaster in my uncle's bedroom and was again trying to destroy me. I'm not sure that this uncle didn't do something to me also, as I spent a lot of time at Grandma's house alone while he was around. I had not had sexual intercourse with a male as a teen or as an adult, thinking that I was still a virgin. The discovery that I had no hymen and had vaginal scarring left me upset yet relieved that perhaps there was physical evidence of the abuse."

Psychologically speaking, Kritsberg and Miller-Kritsberg (1993) write, "To live with the pain of ongoing abuse, you have to develop defenses." These defenses include denial—which tells you what happened to you really did not happen to you at all (so you won't have to experience the pain). Accepting that you were abused means acknowledging that it happened, that you couldn't prevent it, and that you survived. Believing the abuse happened and trusting our memories is particularly difficult because family and friends don't want to face it and will often deny it happened or tell us to "get over it." We know facing the truth about our experiences is the first step in healing; receiving acknowledgment that the abuse happened, if possible, and trusting our own perceptions is critical.

"While my brother denies abusing me and I have no proof, the older of his two daughters recovered memories of having been sexually abused by him at virtually the same time that I did and with absolutely no contact with me or knowledge of my memories. I continue to believe that he abused me. I continue to struggle to believe that even the basic substance of my recovered memories is accurate. The timing of the False Memory Syndrome Foundation was disastrous for me. It began forming when I began recovering memories. I struggle mightily with the fact that I can't conclusively prove that I was sexually abused, yet neither can I dismiss my recovered memories of abuse. I have compiled a list of fewer than 10 quite weak reasons why I should not believe my memories to be valid. This is in contrast to nearly 30 remarkably solid reasons why I should." —Levie

"When I learned just a few years ago from my mom that I had masturbated secretively under my desk in school, I was stunned and embarrassed beyond belief. When I was finally able to think about it, it just further confirmed my suspicion that I'd been molested." —Deborah

"My dad acts like nothing really happened. My mom denies it, and my stepfather laughs and says I liked it. In our family we keep secrets to save face. I guess I learned that no one cared or was going to protect me, so I stopped telling and just tried to live with it." —Rowan

"My aunt says, 'Just put it behind you.'" —Dana

Believing the abuse happened includes grieving for the loss of our childhood (Zerbe, 1993). Lyndsey likens the experience of accepting her abuse history to the experience of coming out as a lesbian. Trusting our perceptions and feelings is essential to our living lives of integrity—being true to ourselves.

CHAPTER 2

COPING

Why do some survivors struggle to live full and satisfying lives while others thrive? Why can some manage productive careers and home lives while others struggle with addiction and mental illness? What makes the difference? Child development researchers say the difference is *resilience.* Resilience researcher Emmy Werner (1989, cited in Dayton, 2000) identified four elements that buffer children. First, resilient children tend to have likable personalities at birth that attracted people to want to care for them. Second, they are of at least average intelligence. Third, they did not have another child born into their family before they had reached the age of two. And fourth, they had at least one person with whom they had developed a strong bond of attachment as children in their family of origin or extended family. Courtois (1988) asserts that most accounts of survivors lack an appreciation of the creative ways these women devised as children and adults to cope with their experience and its aftermath.

FORGIVING YOURSELF

"It is hard to fight an enemy who has outposts in your head."
—Sally Kempton

A child who has been abused believes it is her fault. Instead of getting angry at her abuser, she gets angry at herself. As Dorian said, "*We need to discuss this so that the victim isn't the one who feels guilty for letting it happen to them.*" This makes sense when you understand child development and attachment theory. From a child's perspective, the world revolves around her. This is called *egocentrism* (Roth, 1993). Children believe they can cause things just by thinking about them (*magical thinking*). One of the deepest scars we have as survivors is guilt. In a child's mind, she can make things happen just by wishing and wanting it to be so. This magical thinking is the basis of many amusing anecdotes we have all heard about children. It is no wonder that a child who is abused will feel responsible for this behavior, particularly if she wanted the attention of her abuser in some form, as Levie and Kyrce explain.

"The abuse by my dad didn't always feel abusive. Much of the time is was sexually gratifying and made me feel special and important." —Levie

"I thought it was normal. I never felt my father's attention was inappropriate." —Kyrce

In addition, it is important to understand that children form strong attachments to those responsible for their care and nurturance. Therefore a relative, a family friend, or a trusted coach or pastor becomes someone the child can trust. When the trust is betrayed, the child does not see this as evidence of the abuser's sickness or ill will, but as her own worthlessness or evil in corrupting the relationship. Speaking to her abuser in a letter, Barbara says:

"Not so long ago I realized that in my own way I'm just as stupid, useless, and ugly as you are. Within myself, I've always known that I'm not any better than you. But still, somehow, I never though that I could be as bad."

Blaming ourselves may also be an attempt to gain some sense of control over what happened. Believing we caused the abuse counters our feelings of helplessness and powerlessness (Maltz, 1991). If we feel we caused the abuse, we feel better in some way that the abuse was under our control; we made it happen, it was not made to happen to us. She was not asking for the abuse, but in her childish understanding, she believes she was. "If she is the cause," Roth explains, "she can be the cure." She refuses to relinquish her last ounce of dignity by letting her abuser know the depth of her pain; she refuses to shed a tear, register any pain, or display any affect. As children we blame ourselves for having caused the abuse since no other explanation is available and blaming the perpetrator—usually a family member—is too threatening (Courtois,

1998). Many survivors try to be good, both to deal with their guilt and to earn acceptance and love. They say to themselves, "If only I can be good enough, then the abuse will stop. Since it is not stopping, I must be bad and have to keep trying to be good." Serena explains, *"As a young adult I continued to be who everyone thought I should be: college grad, married, good job, house by age 22, children planned by age 25."*

Sexual abuse survivors focus more on self-blame than on holding offenders responsible (Owens, 2001). Roth (2001) explains, however, that "we are not responsible for what happened to us as children, but we are responsible for what we do with our pain as adults." Taking this a step further, feminist therapists Groves and Schondel (1996) argue:

> Incest is a major component of the training ground of the patriarchy.... Women and children receive messages that they are responsible for the actions of men and to be silent.... The female victim of abuse, through her experience of being silent, typically learns that women are victims. She may continue this silence when victimized as an adult or remain silenced when her child reports victimization.

"Many women feel they were responsible for the abuse that was perpetrated again them. Partly this is developmental. When we are children we believe we are omnipotent, all powerful."
—JoAnn Loulan

The painful truth is that children believe they are responsible for events that happen in their lives. These feelings of guilt and responsibility continue into adulthood.

"I thought it was my fault. I blamed myself for everything." —Pat

The feelings of guilt are particularly strong if we feel we cooperated, at times initiated, or derived pleasure from the abuse. Failing to resist or stop the abuse is strong enough to contribute to our feelings of guilt. But as Fortune (1983) explains, it is the sexual dimension of the abuse that contributes to the confusion for the child. "The child may experience positive physical feelings, affection, and a sense of self-worth simultaneously with terror and powerlessness. This combination, confusing to the child, encourages self-blame and discourages her or him from seeking help to stop the abuse."

"With my dad it wasn't just sex, there was a lot of physical violence. And to me it was easier to just give in to the sex instead of going to school beat up." —Kris

"I did what I was told. Masturbating felt good, and I listened to my grandfather." —Juli

"Between the ages of 8 and 11 years old, my oldest brother convinced me to perform oral sex on him. He would try bribing me with money. Sometimes I just did it to shut him up." —Whitney

"Sometimes when my stepfather would come into my room I would let him because then he would leave me alone for a little while. Other times I let him do it so that he would be nicer to me. I stopped pretending that I was asleep mostly because I was tired of fighting him off." —Melissa

"I still struggle with my part in it all." —Mary Lou

"I blamed myself because the abuse went on for a period of time. Why didn't I do something more to stop him? You know, looking back on him now, my coach wasn't that big of a man. I could've tried harder or something. Why didn't I fight until my death? I'm still going through that process of questioning why it isn't my fault." —Delphene

"I wonder why I wasn't stronger about resisting my father." —Jacque

If we enjoyed the attention we received from our abusers or had any pleasurable physical reactions to his or her touch, our self-loathing is only intensified. None of this is to suggest that we enjoyed or wanted the abuse. We didn't want it nor deserve it. However, enjoying the friendship or loving attention of a parent or relative and the pleasure of sexual touch—to which our bodies involuntarily respond—is fairly typical of the experiences of survivors, and one of the most devastating aspects of the abuse. Our recollections of our "special" relationships with our abusers and the sometimes-pleasurable touch we experienced can leave us questioning our role in the abuse. But we needn't be confused about one fundamental truth: We didn't ask for the abuse. We didn't want it. And if we could have stopped it, we would have.

"When I was sleeping on the floor, watching TV, my brothers would undress me and take turns getting on top of me. I didn't know what was happening, but I did know that part of me enjoyed it. Later I would entice them by falling asleep on the floor more often. This is the part of the situation which was the hardest to live with, knowing that I enjoyed what they were doing. I felt a strong sense of anger associated with it." —Marie

"My father abused us until we didn't enjoy it. But our bodies will enjoy it automatically." —Dana

According to Courtois (1988), "Many juveniles abuse younger children as a traumatic reenactment of their own abuse or because they have had inappropriate sexual stimulation or modeling in their own families." Diana describes her desire to abuse others as she had been abused:

"I grew up thinking it was my fault. I felt dirty for letting it happen. I lost my innocence. I don't think I was a child for much. When I was 6 I remember wanting to do to a cousin what my cousin has done to me. Like, 'Let's go to the room and let's play doctor.' I'm so glad nothing happened."

We assume responsibility for what happened instead of placing the responsibility squarely on our perpetrators where it belongs.

"The abuse kept me silent for 30 years. I was always raised to tell my parents the truth. This was the one and only thing they didn't know about me. On some level I would feel like I was lying to them every day of my life." —Whitney

"A lot of times I feel that I am damaged goods, or that I have too much emotional baggage to be in a relationship of any sort, or that I am not fit for existence on my own. I think, though, that the process of remembering has changed me more than the abuse changed me. Both destroyed my innocence, but remembering now what happened more than half a lifetime ago makes me wonder if I'm really the same person that I thought I was." —Mollie

"My mother savagely abused me physically and emotionally. More than likely, this was related to her suspicion that something was happening between me and my father. In some ways, I was treated like 'the other woman.'" —Lisa

"People have told me it's not my fault. It didn't sink in until once a week my therapist was saying it to me too." —Amanda

"I had to forgive myself and let go of the hate. The hate I had was a trap for me. I understand that it's not my fault, but you don't get over it." —Rowan

When we are revictimized in the course of our lives, this only serves to reinforce our belief that we caused the abuse, and indeed brought it on ourselves.

"It was so hard because for a while I felt like it was my fault. After my father I was raped by three different men, at 15, 23, and 29. I feel negative about myself sometimes when I think about how many times it's happened and why I couldn't stop it." —Kim

"Besides my uncle I was also abused by friends of the family. I would let them do things to me." —Debbie

Years ago a therapist suggested a technique for getting in touch with my inner child. Having long struggled with feelings of guilt and shame about the abuse, I wanted to understand how the abuse could have continued to happen for years when I didn't want it to. Was I responsible? Could I have done something to stop it? Why didn't I? My therapist suggested spending time with children of the age I was when the abuse started to see how they act, to understand their development. I remember visiting a neighborhood playground where a group of 12-year-old girls were playing on the jungle gym. They looked so young to me. Their prepubescent bodies were just starting to develop breasts and they were alternately self-conscious and pleased with their budding womanhood. They talked quietly to each other about their dreams for the future and ridiculed themselves for believing they could be successful. Hearing their conversations and seeing their developing bodies made me realize the devastation of the abuse all over again. I had been sexually abused at a critical point in my development. All the tensions around the physical changes in my body and my emotional reactions to these had been overwhelmed by the abuse. I realized I couldn't have done anything to stop the abuse. I was abused as a child, not as the adult reflecting back on the events. The vulnerability of a 12-year-old girl is painful for me to look at. There's so much expectation and excitement about the future and relationships and sex that were tainted for me. The exercise was useful in helping me to see what I hadn't before. I felt responsible for the abuse because I was viewing it through the eyes of an adult rather than the child that I was when it happened. Now I need to forgive the 12-year-old I was for not stopping the abuse. It wasn't her fault. She didn't want it to happen. She felt powerless to stop it and in reality, given my family dynamics, she was. Now I carry my fifth grade school picture in my wallet to remind me of who I was before the abuse—the little girl lost. I like to think that in carrying her with me at all times I am beginning to heal her and she is forgiving me.

Diana shares a similar realization:

"I remember my partner saying to me, 'It's not your fault. You were just a victim. You were a kid, for crying out loud.' It was the first time it hit me that it was little kids this guy came to. I was a little kid at the time, 4 years old. I never saw it that way. I always thought of me, the adult who I was."

Delphene came to this realization with the help of a dream:

"I've had this one dream where I'm a little girl standing on a long country road by a tree and I just feel bad for her. And it's me. In the past year or two I've started realizing that it wasn't my fault. And I get angry that such a little, innocent girl… That it really wasn't my fault. It helped to change my outlook on it all. Now I don't have to blame myself."

As we come to understand that the family system made the abuse possible, we can begin to let go of the self-blame that has tormented us for years. The traits and characteristics of incestuous families are well documented (Courtois, 1988). Many survivors I spoke with described their families using these characteristics without making the connection between these traits and the occurrence of incest:

- collective denial and shared secrets
- duplicity and deceit between family members
- social isolation
- role confusion and boundary diffusion
- child triangulated into the parents' marriage
- poor tolerance for differences
- overly moralistic
- no touch except bad touch
- inadequate parenting
- low humor and high sarcasm
- children may be unwanted and treated that way
- unpredictability and intermittent reinforcement
- violence and the threat of violence
- no one to turn to

Seen in this context, incest is a manifestation of family dysfunction. And healing occurs when we appreciate the role we play(ed) in our families of origin and assert our rights to craft new roles for ourselves and create new relationships with family members on our own terms.

The Mind-Body Connection

"The truth about childhood is stored up in our body and lives in the depth of our soul. Our intellect can be deceived, our feelings can be numbed and manipulated, our perception shamed and confused, our bodies tricked with medication. But our soul never forgets. And because we are one, one whole soul in one body, someday our body will present its bill."
—Alice Miller

Research by scientists, including Robert Sapolsky of Stanford University, shows that a young brain does its best to cope with a threatening environment (Blum, 2002): "It restructures. It notches up the stress response. It keeps the body poised for flight. It floods the nervous system with angst." Unfortunately, when the child grows up, her brain has already been shaped to panic. The state of hyperalertness triggers stress-related hormones that cause real wear and tear on the system and are linked to the destruction of brain cells and memory loss. Repression, the common defense mechanism, has been shown to depress healthy immune system function. It appears that the psychic strength needed to keep the memories pushed down drains the survivor of much needed vitality physically, mentally, and emotionally (Dayton, 2000). Pennebaker's research (1990, cited in Dayton, 2000), reveals that expressing and processing emotions has a positive influence on immune functions and our resistance to disease.

Memories can occur somatically through pain or illness (often without medical diagnosis), nausea, and what are called *conversion symptoms*, such as paralysis and numbing (Courtois, 1998). Levie describes her experience this way:

"I developed facial paralysis at the specific ages when the abuse was going on. When I began recovering memories of the abuse, my face would often feel numb after I talked about a memory. That scared me. I thought the paralysis might be returning. It never did, but the numbness would occur quite predictably after I talked or wrote about a memory. I tend to believe that the childhood facial paralysis was a strong mind-body con-

nection—that as I was repressing the memories of the abuse, the facial paralysis accompanied the mind paralysis concerning the abuse. At least three therapists have commented that they think there is a possible, or even likely, connection between the bouts of paralysis and the repression of my abuse memories." —Levie

In their study, Putnam and Trickett (cited in Strong, 1998) found that abused girls had dramatically higher rates of somatization (the conversion of emotional stress into physical symptoms), mainly headaches, stomachaches, nausea, vomiting, and other pain symptoms, than did their nonabused peers. It is believed that physical symptoms can be signals from the nerve endings that are holding on to feelings (Bratton, 1999). Headaches, stomach problems and difficulty swallowing, and shortness of breath may be indications that nerves are blocked by layers of emotion.

"The study of self-injury makes clear that the mind and body are inextricably linked, each feeding from the other's nourishment or starving from the other's neglect. The body is, indeed, the temple of the soul. Cutters are living proof that when the body is ravaged, the soul cries out. And when the soul is trampled upon, the body bleeds."
—Marilee Strong, *A Bright Red Scream*

Self-injury is one way that survivors make their emotional pain visible. Self-injury is defined as "the physical alteration of one's own body tissue, via cutting, scratching, burning, or purposefully breaking bones" (Goldman, 2001). Cutters, as they are sometimes called, typically irritate the wounds to prevent healing and wear long-sleeved shirts and pants to hide the marks. Cutting can be a powerful coping mechanism for dealing with overwhelming emotional pain and gaining control over an out-of-control mind and body (Strong, 1998). Repetitive self-mutilators may become depressed and suicidal because they cannot control their self-mutilation and because they feel that no one truly understands what they are feeling.

According to Goldman (2001). "Self-injurers feel so depressed, so numb, that hurting themselves is, paradoxically, the only way they feel alive." This is similar to the motivation for other destructive habits that survivors engage in to feel better. In fact, Karen Conterio, founder of the nation's first inpatient center for self-injurers, says, "The internal conflict is so overwhelming they can't articulate it emotionally." At SAFE (Self-Abuse Finally Ends) in Naperville, Illinois, Conterio has identified the strongest risk factor for self-injury as a "poor—or nonexistent—family communication network." About 50% of all self-injurers have a history of being physically—and often emotionally or sexually—abused. In one way, self-injurers want to punish the body as if the body was "bad for betraying them. When they start to heal, the pain is immense." Research conducted by Dr. Barbara Stanley at the New York State Psychiatric Institute and Columbia University found a possible link between self-injury and the release of pain-regulating opiates. This may explain why sufferers are able to cut or burn themselves, undeterred by pain that would otherwise prove unbearable. Another explanation, offered by Strong (1998), is that cutting may serve as a way to reclaim control over one's body or allow the cutter to play out the roles of victim, perpetrator, and loving caretaker, soothing self-inflicted wounds and watching them heal. For others, the sight of blood is literally proof that they are alive, drawing them out of their dissociative states.

In the largest study ever conducted on cutting, Armando Favazza and Karen Conterio (cited in Strong, 1998) found that:

> Cutters describe themselves as feeling empty inside, unable to express emotions in words, afraid of getting close to anyone, and wanting desperately to stop their emotional pain.... They grew up in families full of anger and double messages in which they were told to be strong and prevented from expressing their feelings. More than half were troubled by sexual feelings and a large number hated parts of their anatomy.

In this way, says psychiatrist and professor James Chu of Harvard Medical School, in the face of severe stress people experience a chronic disconnectedness in which they detach from their own surroundings, even from their own bodies. This detachment is characteristic of survivors who use substances (drugs, alcohol, food) and experiences (gambling, shopping)—as described earlier—to not feel the feelings associated with the abuse. In fact, childhood sexual abuse is the single most common causal factor for cutting (Strong, 1998) and a leading cause of post–traumatic stress disorder and dissociative disorders—the primary diagnoses of self-mutilators—and, not coincidentally, survivors of child sexual abuse.

Cutting has been revealed as a response to physical or sexual abuse (Crowe, 1996). It is "a means of establishing a sense of self while perpetuating a sense of the body as a site for abuse." It appears that when language fails to capture survivors' pain, they use the body as a place to write their message. Survivors, then, "signify distress" while perpetuating "the body's role as an object of abuse." Jeffreys (2000), in examining cutting from a feminist perspective, criticizes arguments for modification and "body art," calling cutting one of several "harmful cultural practices of self-mutilation" that is carried out by groups who lack social status and who have suffered abuse.

There is no single therapeutic approach that works with all self-injurers, since the roots of the disorder are so varied. Acute symptoms need to be brought under control with medication and behavior modification in order for the patient to be able to tolerate exploring deeper issues. If the underlying trauma is not resolved, the patient will likely relapse into cutting or replace it with some other destructive coping behavior (Strong, 1998). Other self-destructive behaviors that go hand in hand with cutting must also be treated, such as alcohol and drug abuse, eating disorders, and sex and relationship addictions. As with all survivors who seek therapy, self-injurers have to want to get better.

Child abuse changes children's brains. Recent scientific evidence shows that because childhood abuse occurs during the critical formative time when the brain is being physically sculpted by experience, the impact of severe stress can leave an indelible imprint on its structure and function. Such abuse, it seems, induces a "cascade of molecular and neurobiological effects that irreversibly alter neural development" (Teicher, 2002). Therefore, methods like psychodrama—expressive methods that use the whole person, mind and body—are more effective than traditional talk therapy in helping survivors to recall memories more completely (Dayton, 2000). When we openly confront painful feelings we begin to resolve the trauma and lower the overall stress on the body.

"When you're depressed, the whole body is depressed, and it translates to the cellular level."
—O. Carl Simonton, MD

There is also the very real link between psychological suffering and physical complaints. Survivors have been found to have more premenstrual symptoms, both physical and emotional, than women who have not suffered abuse (Al-Mateen et al, 1999). Baker (1998) and Maltz (1991) describe a wide range of physical and somatic complaints among abused children. In addition, Hyman's review of the literature (2000) revealed that several health concerns of lesbians may be associated with the experience of child sexual abuse: pelvic pain, gynecological problems, migraine headaches, asthma, epileptic seizures, digestive system problems, and increased lifetime risk of surgery. In addition, survivors were more likely to engage in behaviors that would put them at risk. Hyman found that child sexual abuse was a significant predictor of the number of health problems a woman reported.

According to Dr. Kathryn Zerbe (1993), the severe split between mind and body cuts the survivor off from experiencing her physical self and her emotions. Having no way to express her feelings or to reduce inner tensions verbally, she channels her feelings through her body.

"I live out of my body. I live in my head." —Deborah

"Then there's the physical stuff. I feel sometimes like my skin is crawling or burning." —Liz

Zerbe focuses on eating disorders, but the same could be said about the chronic pain, disease, and illness that many survivors suffer. As such, eating disorders, according to Zerbe, represent "a last bastion of self-regulation and autonomy." Often eating disorders are associated with a history of family discord, physical or sexual abuse in the family, and a personal or family history of depression and other psychiatric disorders. An eating disorder, Zerbe says, "is most dangerous, because it pits soul against body." Survivors who struggle with eating disorders—anorexia, bulimia, and compulsive overeating—as we have heard—often struggle to express their feelings in words. Treatment involves helping the survivor to recognize and name her feelings instead of "displacing emotional struggles onto her body."

"I tend not to realize how heavy I am. Sometimes I've been kind of startled when I went to sit in a chair and I didn't fit. Or catching a glimpse of myself in a store window and saying, 'Is that really me?' It's like somehow the mind and body aren't totally connected." —Jacque

"Self-care is a big issue for me. I'll have bruises and I don't know how I got them. I really used to be disconnected from my body and would discount any physical sensations. 'Cold is all in your head,' I would say. It's hard for me to figure out when to go to the doctor and what to tell them. Everything was a big secret in my family. Nothing was ever bad enough to go to the doctor." —Reg

Emotional pain often finds expression more easily in physical symptoms (Zerbe, 1993). As Chris described, "*I developed laryngitis recently. My dad is visiting now.*" Viewed in this way, addictions and sexual promiscuity may be seen as "attempts to define and reestablish the body boundary" as invaded during the abuse. This issue is explored more fully later in *Respecting Our Bodies.*

"Clearly, it's no mystery to me that today I remain obese to eliminate any chance of being viewed in sexual terms." —Lisa

"After the abuse, my relationship with my body changed. I didn't want a relationship with my body anymore." —Lynn

Binges can also be seen as a "surrender of control—a merging with food and a quest for nurturance" (Zerbe, 1993). Bingeing has been explained within the family context. When parents place enormous emphasis on looking good at the expense of recognizing true, but unpleasant, feelings, daughters' relationships with their bodies suffer. In the treatment process, women must learn that they are using the eating disorder to make significant statements about their need to suffer. We can view the eating disorder as a way for the body to speak about issues of concern that were raised early on, when words were not available.

When asked about the mind-body connection—or the way in which their bodies held the pain of the abuse—survivors shared many different experiences on a common theme. These body memories and physical complaints manifested during the time of the abuse and continued into the present. Cory and Katie described their body memories this way:

"I trust my body. It'll react before my head does. I have to trust that. My mother creeps me out. I became aware of the abuse and my body just reacted to her. She actually made me nauseous. I think it was my body's way of saying how toxic she is for me, because my head couldn't put it together." —Cory

"My body has physical memories of the abuse." —Katie

In some instances, it is the stress of living with abuse and the abuse memories that causes a breakdown in our body leading to disease as described earlier.

"I developed petit mal epilepsy after the rape and have had grand mal epilepsy with seizures from age 12 to now." —Kathy

"I have suffered from migraine headaches and backaches. I had two back surgeries for ruptured disks." —Maggie

"The abuse changed me in every way. I believe it is why I can't walk." —Jan

"I suffered from headaches, stomachaches, nightmares, anxiety, and cried myself to sleep all the time." —Tammy

"I carry a lot of excess weight and struggle with migraine headaches." —Cristi

"I have myofascial pain syndrome, which prevents my muscles from flexing. It affects my hips and back. I see a massage therapist to get deep tissue release and acupuncture. I have problems socializing with large crowds of people and suffer anxiety in new situations, and I have irritable bowel syndrome." —Nedhera

"Sometimes I have physical problems, and I'm not sure if they're caused by emotions or if the physical causes the emotional. The teacher did some serious damage to my anus. The doctors back then also suspected damage to my right ovary. I've had menstrual problems forever. I have a hard time making a bowel movement." —Delphene

"The stress of the abuse broke my body down to the point that I was diagnosed with breast cancer. I'm currently in remission, but all the treatment from that has messed my bones up. I've had two breaks. And now I've been diagnosed with this chronic afibrillation in my heart." —Jill

Mary Lou describes her experience with somatic psychotherapy as being successful in addressing the mind-body connection:

"I lived in chronic pain from keeping secrets. I know that trauma is held in our bodies. Somatic psychotherapy was awesome. The touch techniques release the emotions. It is possible to change the effects of trauma on the body and change personality."

As for me, there are many ways in which my body *remembers* the abuse. For years I have suffered with tension headaches, temporomandibular (jaw) disorder, chronic laryngitis, irritable bowel syndrome, debilitating menstrual pain, and chronic pain and inflammation in my joints. When I first committed to writing this book, I developed back pain that immobilized me. I consider this immobility to be a metaphor for my inability to escape the abuse. I marvel at my body's ability to communicate the message to me in such concrete terms. Since then I have developed coping skills to deal with the pain and to offer my body the care and respect it deserves.

Related to the mind-body connection is the way in which we choose to interact with the health care system. Here Kirsten describes the way that surviving abuse has affected the way she makes decisions about her health that empower her rather than victimize her. Medical examinations and procedures may be seen as negative by survivors because they involve touching and are otherwise invasive (Courtois, 1988). Confinement and being in the control of an authority figure is also anxiety-producing. Such experiences may even produce body memories of the abuse or flashbacks.

"Dealing with men has been difficult. I'd rather deal with women and do when I have control over the situation. It has been difficult to find women in the health system, thus making it more stressful to find adequate care. The abuse has put me on the defensive, more aware of having to protect myself, of not putting up with any further abuse. It is not so much that there is a fear of a male physician assaulting me—although the possibility is certainly there—but I do not trust men. I have a very severe response to them touching me. One time when I became very ill and had to be taken to the emergency room. It seemed like I had a very bad bladder infection. They weren't satisfied with the urine sample and wanted to do a pelvic exam. I was so ill that I wasn't thinking right. I allowed a male doctor to do the procedure. For days after I was unable to sleep. I felt violated. I blamed myself for not asking for a female doctor or just refusing. To this day I still get very upset when I think about it." —Kirsten

Depression

It is estimated that 65% of sexual abuse survivors suffer from depression (Wood, 1993). And a history of child sexual abuse—victimization—is strongly associated with adult depression (Matthews et al, 2002; Otis and Skinner, 1996; Whiffen, Thompson, and Aube, 2000). Yale University neurobiologist Ronald Dorman, Ph.D., says, "Stress-related events may kick off 50% of all depression, and early life stress can prime people for later depression" (Marano, 1999). Self-esteem has also been identified as the strongest predictor of depression in both lesbians and gay men (Otis and Skinner, 1996).

During depression, the amygdala, which is the center of negative emotions in the brain and informs the brain of threat, runs unchecked—in other words, everything feels threatening—while the center of memory, the hippocampus, loses nerve-to-nerve links. Brain imaging research shows that both of these centers of the brain are altered in size and shape in victims of trauma such as sexual abuse. Currently, research shows that stress or trauma early in life permanently sensitizes neurons and receptors throughout the central nervous system so that they perpetually over-respond to stress. (Dayton, 2000).

Michael Faenza, president and CEO of the National Mental Health Association, says, "Clinical depression is a major health crisis from which children and teens are not immune" (NMHA, 1999). And psychiatrist Dr. Frank Putnam of the National Institute of Mental Health calls child sexual abuse the single biggest risk factor for mental illness (Strong, 1998). Recent studies, however, show that parents are often unaware of the warning signs of depression. Children and adolescents don't necessarily act sad and withdrawn the way adults who are depressed do. They may act out and behave aggressively. "As a result," Faenza says, "less than one third of children and teens with depression ever receive treatment." As Mary told me, "*Looking back now, I realize I was depressed. But at the time, who knew?*" Suniya Luther, professor of psychology and education at Columbia's Teachers College, found that girls who are close to their mothers are at a far lower risk of depression (Marano, 2002).

Recent research has found higher levels of depression and a greater history of psychological distress among gay men and lesbians (Lehmann, Lehmann, and Kelly, 1998; O'Neill, 1998; White and Martinez, 1997). These problems have been attributed to the chronic stress of living as a gay man or lesbian in our society. Many gay men and lesbians report periods of depression as adolescents (Mackay, 1999). Moreover, the National Lesbian Health Care Survey (Bradford, Ryan, and Rothblum, 1994) found that the majority of lesbians surveyed had thought about suicide at some time, and 18% had attempted suicide. Nineteen percent of the sample had been victims of incest, and 75% had received counseling at some time. Some researchers have suggested that sexual orientation may represent an important but poorly understood risk factor for depression as well as suicidal ideation and behavior (Matthews et al, 2002). With all of this said, it is evident that the lesbian survivor is at increased risk for experiencing depression in her lifetime. Support from friends and family have been identified as having a positive effect (Oetien and Rothblum, 2000; Otis and Skinner, 1996), however some researchers theorize that survivors may be at particular risk for depression because they experience interpersonal problems that inhibit their capacity to derive support from others.

"Depression is a treatable biological disease characterized by changes in brain chemistry, but it is unusual for this to occur in the absence of an environmental trigger" (Rosenthal, 2000). Repressed anger is a particularly common trigger in women. Most cases of depression are caused by life's circumstances, which is why mental health professionals often use the term *situational depression.* A trigger for situational depression can be an "absence of resolution" regarding traumas and abuses you suffered as a child, including sexual abuse, incest, violence, and physical abuse (Rosenthal, 2000). Loss is a core theme for lesbian survivors (Guyer, 2000; Hall, 1999). Growing up in abusive homes, many of us were not protected from violence, nor nurtured, guided, or loved. "In losing their safety," Hall concluded, "they lost their very childhoods" (1999).

As you reflect on what you have heard thus far about survivors' experiences—and perhaps your own—you begin to understand the devastating effects of depression, most of it undiagnosed. Depression can affect memory and concentration and strain relationships. People who are depressed show little or no responsiveness to others, often lacking patience and understanding. If untreated, depression can produce physical symptoms. For example, eating and sleeping can be disrupted. Depression can cause headaches, backaches, and stomachaches. Symptoms that persist may be signs of depression.

Let's get more specific. There are two main types of depression. First is the depression that has an apparent cause—like child sexual abuse—even though the reaction to it may be excessive or abnormally prolonged. Depression, however, can also develop for no apparent reason and without a trigger. According to Dr. Isadore Rosenfeld (1999), that's the worst kind. "We just feel like there's no point to anything, the future is bleak—yet we don't know why." Isaacs (1998, cited in Dayton, 2000) describes depression as "a combination of feelings that are more or less in a traffic jam. The individual cars need to move so traffic can move freely. Perhaps the depression is part anger, part sadness, and part fear. Working with each feeling gives us a place to start. What are you sad about? What are you angry about? Who are you angry at, you or someone else?"

Warning signs of depression include mood changes, loss of interest, lack of enjoyment, changes in sleep patterns, changes in appetite, work or school difficulties, and self-criticism (Hales and Hales, 2002). The National Depression Screening Day's series of 10 questions is designed to quickly screen for depression (2002). Ask yourself if the following statements apply to you:

- I'm unable to do the things I used to do.
- I feel hopeless about the future.
- I can't make decisions.
- I feel sluggish or restless.
- I'm gaining or losing weight.
- I get tired for no reason.
- I'm sleeping too much, or too little.
- I feel unhappy.
- I become irritable or anxious.
- I think about dying or killing myself.

If you answered yes to five or more of these questions, and you have felt this way every day for several weeks, there is a good chance you are suffering from depression and should seek the help of a psychiatrist or other health care professional. The American Psychiatric Association describes symptoms of a major depression in this way:

- You experience changes in appetite—either no appetite, often resulting in weight loss, or eating ravenously so that you've gained weight.
- You experience sleep problems—insomnia or wanting to sleep all the time.
- You have no energy and are often fatigued.
- You're restless and irritable.
- You have feelings of worthlessness, hopelessness or inappropriate guilt.
- You have difficulty thinking, making decisions, or concentrating.
- You have thoughts of death or suicide or attempts at suicide.

The National Institute of Mental Health adds these symptoms:

- chronic aches and pains that don't respond to treatment
- excessive crying

Other tip-offs that may not be "major" but which you should address include:

- You feel pessimistic about your life.
- You have a "What difference does it make?" attitude.
- You avoid old friends.
- Crowds bother you.
- You don't get along with people.
- You have poor memory. You've had to start writing things down.
- You're not doing nearly as well as you used to at work or school.
- You have unexplained headaches, backaches, and stomachaches.
- You've made a will and have been thinking about your funeral.

Many women find that they suffer from repeated episodes of low blood sugar, known as *hypoglycemia.* This is usually caused by consuming too many carbohydrates, which produces an initial rush of energy, followed by a tremendous crash, which is sometimes known as *postprandial depression* (or postmeal depression). In fact, during episodes of depression, it's not unusual to crave simple carbohydrates such as sugars and sweets (Rosenthal, 2000). While consuming too much sugar can contribute to depression, exercise can prevent, or help you cope with, depression. Many of us have heard the health benefits of aerobic cardiovascular exercise, including the feel-good endorphins that aerobic exercise produces. Now research has shown that endorphins actually decrease the incidence of depression, while inactivity and sedentary living breed depression.

According to Rosenfeld (1999), many people who are depressed mask the way they feel, sometimes even from themselves. They may appear to be functioning normally. However, "even mild depression stifles spontaneity and creativity; it affects relationships with family, friends, and on the job. If it persists long enough it almost inevitably produces physical symptoms such as weight loss or weight gain, poor appetite, fatigue, irritability, stomach problems, lack of sex drive, insomnia—you name it, depression will do it." Survivors I spoke with described their struggles with depression.

"Lately I feel like the world has already ended and I'm already dead. Some great things have happened recently, but I can't feel them. I can't feel anything but horror and darkness and misery. There's no joy in a good thing anymore, just overwhelming fear and confusion. I am tired and I want permanent sleep. I just want the pain to stop. Dear God! I just want the pain to stop." —Barbara

"There is irreparable damage from the abuse. When you commit a sin against the core spirit of a person, it cannot be healed. If people are too hurt, maybe they can't recover." —Tabitha

"I suffer from depression. Sometimes things are too hard. It's all just an indescribable mountain to climb." —Liz

The good news is that depression can now almost always be treated successfully (Rosenfeld, 1999). Of course, in order to benefit from therapy, you must first realize that you are depressed, and you must seek the help that's there for you. Bencosme (2002) clarifies, "Depression cannot be cured, only managed. Depression enters into our lives as a messenger to bring us valuable information about issues we need to tend to within our psychological life...If we can stop trying to eradicate depression, we can begin to honor its existence in our lives; we can then become aware of our needs, wants, motivations, and goals." People who have been traumatized tend to alternate in their emotional responses between intense fear or rage and numbness, dissociation, or shutdown. They do not have the ability to modulate the intensity of their emotions or talk about what matters most (Dayton, 2000). Developing emotional literacy—the ability to convert feelings into words—gives us the ability to "talk out" rather than "act out" our feelings. These are important skills for all survivors, whether they suffer from depression or not. Learning to identify and express our emotions is a critical life skill. Dayton (2000) proposes four stages of emotional literacy: (1) Feel the fullness of the emotion, (2) Label it, (3) Explore the meaning and function of the feeling within oneself, and (4) Choose whether or not to communicate our inner state to another person. In this way dealing with our emotions becomes a conscious, thoughtful process. Despite media attention to the use of medication for the treatment of depression, Hales and Hales (2002) indicate that "Studies have shown that cognitive-behavioral therapy—which focuses on teaching new ways to deal with stress and sadness, such as changing unrealistic or highly negative ways of thinking—can be as effective as medication."

The bad news is that depression, if left untreated, can be fatal. Post–traumatic stress disorder in combination with child abuse increases a woman's risk for making a suicide attempt (Thompson et al, 2000). A significant relationship has been found between a history of sexual abuse and suicidal behavior in childhood and adulthood (Courtois, 1988). Sexually abused therapy clients were twice as likely as nonabused clients to have made at least one suicide attempt in the past and more frequently reported suicidal ideation at intake. Among the sexual abuse clients, greater suicidality is associated with multiple perpetrators, concurrent physical abuse, and abuse involving intercourse.

"I have some mental problems, and I have borderline personality disorder, major depressive disorder, and post–traumatic stress disorder. I

tried to kill myself with drugs and liquor. I'm in a much better place now but still have problems. I can't seem to keep a job." —Laura

"In college I attempted to kill myself by overdosing on muscle relaxants. Later a decision was made to hospitalize me for suicidal ideation. Between being depressed about my weight—I am morbidly obese and it impacts my appearance and my mobility—and being depressed about my abuse, I always feel like I am in a never-ending cycle of distress and soothing effects." —Lisa

"If it hadn't been for the abuse, I wouldn't feel so emotionally and mentally conflicted, so tortured inside, so unsure of myself. I wouldn't hate myself and the human race. I wouldn't want to hurt myself or to die sometimes. I'm pinned down under so many old bruises, trapped beneath thick layers of scars where it's impossible to reach anyone or to be reached." —Barbara

"I'm disabled, not able to work because of mental problems due to the abuse. I get nervous leaving the house. I've been on Social Security disability since 1990 because of major depression, post–traumatic stress disorder, anxiety disorder, and schizo-affective disorder. At one time I was sleeping a lot, not getting out of bed or taking a shower. I thought the best thing to do was to leave this world. I refilled my meds and overdosed. I stopped breathing. I had a flashback when they were trying to hold me down. I felt the rescuers wanted to hurt me. They thought I would die and called the relatives. I survived and my partner took me in." —Debbie

"I wasn't diagnosed as bipolar until after high school. Bipolar disorder usually manifests in young teenagers as depression and not mania, so everybody just assumed I was a teenager with hormones." —Lyndsey

The American Association of Suicidology in Washington, D.C. (2002), has identified the following feelings as characteristic of people considering suicide:

- can't stop the pain
- can't think clearly
- can't make decisions

- can't see any way out
- can't sleep, eat or work
- can't get out of depression
- can't make the sadness go away
- can't see a future without pain
- can't see themselves as worthwhile
- can't get someone's attention
- can't seem to get control

Here are some common warning signs:

- talks about committing suicide
- has trouble eating or sleeping
- experiences drastic changes in behavior
- withdraws from friends and/or social activities
- loses interest in hobbies, work, school, etc.
- prepares for death by making out a will and final arrangements
- gives away prized possessions
- has attempted suicide before
- takes unnecessary risks
- has had recent severe losses
- is preoccupied with death and dying
- loses interest in their personal appearance
- increases their use of alcohol or drugs

If you see yourself here, please **stop reading** and get help. Call a friend or trusted family member or go to the emergency room at your local hospital. Help is available. Although the pain you are feeling is real and very overwhelming right now, it will subside. Remember, suicide is a permanent solution to a temporary problem. Please get help right away. I know the depth of your pain and how alone you feel, but your life matters. You deserve to be free of pain and to live a life of your own choosing.

When asked what challenges she faced as a survivor, Delphene said, *"Living. I was becoming very suicidal. I think you just get so low and you think,* It can't get worse than this."

"If I did die, I would say I couldn't survive due to a broken heart, not because I was depressed. I don't use the term depression. People are more compassionate about physical illnesses, not so for mental struggles. People should respect the right for people to let go. It's their choice to let go. I want to let go because of the abuse. It has everything to do with the trauma. Then my abusers won. They get the last laugh. I don't remember happy. I don't know if recovery—all-encompassing recovery—is possible. My image of recovery is being completely integrated, getting off tranquilizers, and meeting someone and having another family. I've lost everything I've ever known. My whole life has been a midlife crisis. What is my purpose? The physical and sexual pain is so much more bearable than the emotional pain and neglect. I need more support than most people. What could have made a difference? If my friend said, 'Come stay with me.' Or if they said, 'You get to see your daughter.'" —Tabitha

"I can suffer from overwhelming despair. More than the next person. I read about the war in Afghanistan and I wonder, Why are we still alive? What's the point?" —Marian

"I remember crying a lot. I used to cry a lot when I went to sleep, and I wouldn't know why. Thinking back now I think I was always very depressed. When I was in tenth grade a friend was shot and killed. I remember I cared about him. Maybe it hit me so hard because I was depressed. Around that time I took some pills to kill myself. I remember the whole night waiting to die. And nothing happened. But they were only cough drops, which I'm grateful for. I get angry about it now. I lost so much of my life being depressed." —Diana

"I was depressed a lot, but never really felt like telling anyone. I didn't know what to do. When I was 14 I tried to kill myself by taking a lot of aspirin, but all I did was get really sick." —Melissa

As mentioned earlier, depression is treatable. You can feel better and function better in the world with help, learning to cope with your feelings in more effective ways, as Nedhera learned: *"I still have mild depression that I have had to learn coping skills for."* Here are other survivors' reflections on their struggles with depression and triumphs over it:

"*I was saving pills for suicide. Then I decided I don't have to be like this.*" —Sarah

"*I've been depressed most of my life. Now I'm on an antidepressant and love my job and my life.*" —Chris

"*I almost didn't survive. I wrote suicide notes. I was so close to taking my own life: cutting, obsessive-compulsive disorder, panic, depression. I'm still so young, only 21. I've been at that low point. I feel lucky to be alive.*" —Amanda

"*After the '60s I was on the brink of total destruction. Before I was 20 I had spent four months in a mental hospital, and I finished off the year trying to kill myself. Now I'm disabled, completely disabled with depression. I haven't worked full-time since 1987. I first took a leave. That began my absolutely tormented trip back from the edge of darkness. I don't think you come out of everything with black and white. I think you come out with a lot of gray. A lot of good and a lot of bad. My marriage ended and I was really on the rocks. My life was completely out of control. I couldn't wait to die. I relished the idea of dying because the memories were in full swing. I flirted with death and almost succeeded in 1992. The depression that I suffered was so catastrophic. Now I'm on Zoloft. I maintain on Zoloft. I feel that it's protection from the depression that I had. And who's to say whether the depression was already genetic in my family? We've got profound mental illness throughout our family. I don't even know how to describe the place I'm in right now. The mental anguish that I experienced for a number of years was like a prison, and I couldn't imagine ever getting away. And now the intensity of the joy is equal to that anguish. I conquered it. I conquered its effects.*" —Jill

"*When I was a sophomore in high school I really began to struggle. I thought of suicide and wrote out a will. Another classmate found the will and told a teacher. I was sent to this counselor to talk about my suicidal tendencies and how they affected those who I thought were friends. I realized that this was not the right way to handle my problems.*" —Marie

"I would slip into a depression, and I would sit for days and let it eat at me. I carried the guilt and the shame of the abuse. I didn't know how to cope. Now every six weeks I have one of my 'moods.' It lasts hours, not days." —C.J.

"I decided to live, to be better than I was. I was surviving at the bottom of where human beings can be for a really long time, never really living. It was not a good place. My partner watched me in pain and this caused her pain. She encouraged me to see a therapist. I needed that outside perspective." —Amanda

Dorian describes how depression affected her ability to make good life choices for herself. *"I realized that I became depressed again because I wasn't taking time out to live. My counter-character in my book trilogy was living the life I wanted, so now I'm trying to do likewise."*

Dayton (2000) explains that when we know ourselves better, our ability to make choices that work for us improves, and in this way we "manage our own experience."

I have struggled with depression over the years. Looking back, I can see that these times usually surrounded major life changes—starting college, moving away from home, breakups. I attempted suicide twice. There have been some very dark days—or more precisely, very dark nights. While I still feel down every now and then, I have found that if I can wait until the morning, things usually look better. I am also getting better about asking for help when I need it and not allowing myself to spiral downward the way I used to.

"Before I built a wall I'd ask to know
What I was walling in or walling out."
—Robert Frost

In a fascinating look at the rewards of depression, Bratton (1999) describes how in choosing not to be depressed about the abuse, the survivor is forced to look at the issues realistically, to recognize that she cannot change or control them, and that she can look at them differently. Mo describes her struggle to overcome depression.

"Once I realized that suicide was not going to work for me I fell into deeper periods of depression. I coped with all the emotional and physical pain by hiding and building emotional barriers. I built walls so thick, so high, so deep that at times I really blocked out everything. I can best describe it as 'being there but not being there.' I did not place emotions into activities. On the outside of me I appeared to be normal in every way. I excelled and continued to be an overachiever. On the inside I suppressed everything. I stayed in my room and hid from everyone, especially myself."

A recurring theme in sexual abuse recovery work—as you have read—is dealing with our feelings—all of our feelings. We usually think that we will feel better if we don't allow ourselves to face the painful feelings inside us. The reverse is actually true. As Father John McNeill (1988) explains:

"We cannot repress and deny [our] anger without repressing and denying *all* feelings, including feelings of tenderness and love.... Feelings are like a bowl of spaghetti: You can never get only one strand—they all come together. Similarly, you can never select out just one feeling to deal with or repress. You must deal with all your feelings, including anger, or repress them all.... If we can't get in touch with our anger, or if we don't feel we have the freedom and the trust to share it, it will quickly grow into a brick wall, cutting us off from others."

"Your pain is the breaking of the shell
that encloses your understanding."
—Kahlil Gibran, *The Prophet*

Depression is a very real problem that affects many survivors. But what is important to remember is that help is available. The first step is recognizing that your suffering has a name—depression—and that medication, therapy, and other healing techniques can help you feel better and lead a more productive, fulfilling, and satisfying life.

CHAPTER 3

BREAKING THE SILENCE

"WE EACH INHERENTLY POSSESS THE COURAGE TO SPEAK OUR OWN TRUTH. GOD HAS GIVEN US THE GIFT OF COURAGE. IT LEADS THE WAY FOR ALL OTHER VIRTUES. WITHOUT COURAGE THERE WOULD BE NO COMPASSION, INTEGRITY, OR LOVE. SOMETIMES WE NEED A NUDGE—A HUG FROM ANOTHER OR MAYBE THE SIMPLE MOVEMENT OF A BRANCH IN THE WIND TO REMIND US OF OUR STRENGTH AND UNDYING SPIRIT. TO ACCEPT THE TRUTH. TO SPEAK THE TRUTH."

KAREN HOLT, AUTHOR OF *CAN YOU SEE ME?*

TELLING

"It is not difference which immobilizes us, but silence. And there are so many silences to be broken."
—Audre Lorde

"The small voices once raised here and there to tell their tales of childhood savagely destroyed have swollen to a mighty chorus, and they won't be silenced easily, no matter how determined the opposition."
—Mary Sykes Wylie

On the subject of telling, noted child sexual abuse expert Wendy Maltz (1991) writes, "Our acknowledgment of sexual abuse is not complete until we share it with others. Sharing with others often liberates us from the past." Sexual abuse occurs in silence and secrecy, leading to feelings of shame, isolation, worthlessness, and anger. Indeed, it is our inability to talk about the abuse, or even know about it consciously, that leads to pathology (Courtois, 1988). The first step toward recovery is to begin to talk about the abuse we suffered.

Psychotherapist Tian Dayton, Ph.D., describes this experience of telling as "coming out of my silences."

For many of the survivors I spoke with, telling their story to me was one of the few opportunities they had taken to share their experiences in detail, and one they welcomed.

"I am an adult survivor as well as a psychotherapist and would be more than willing to assist you in any way I can." —Hilary

"I have found that part of the healing process is sharing one's story with others so they know that they are not alone." —Bailey

"I feel I have a story that needs to be out there for others. I hated the abuse for so many years. I want so much to help others find the peace I have now." —Max

"I share my story and ask nothing in return. To know that my words could help another is enough for me." —Juli

"The more stories we tell, the more people will become aware, the less it will happen." —Delphene

"I am very happy for my story to be told." —Misha

"I know it's important to get my story out. And if it helps other people, then I'm dedicated to that cause. I feel a real need to be able to talk about it. If people ask me about it or somebody mentions that it happened to them, I always validate their experience by saying, 'It happened to me too.' And I think that that's a really empowering thing for women who have survived it. It's something that needs to be shared, if the person has the will to do it. I'm as open about it as I can be. Talking about it gives you a sense of control. I think it's part of the process of putting your life back into your own hands and making something positive out of something destructive." —Lyndsey

"What I've found helpful is being able to talk about it openly without fearing the consequences." —Nedhera

"Our experiences can only draw us closer and illustrate that we have something so powerful in common." —Missy

"The word is not just a sound or a written symbol. The word is a force; it is the power you have to express and communicate, to think, and thereby to create the events in your life."
—Don Miguel Ruiz, *The Four Agreements*

Each survivor decided for herself whether she wanted her real name to be used here or wanted to create a pseudonym and remain anonymous in the telling of her story. Many wanted to use this opportunity to come out for the first time as survivors.

"It's the power to pick up a book and see yourself in it." —Reg

"Please use my name. I need to tell my story—if not for anything else, maybe to help others out there who remain silent due to fear of the abuser." —Laura

"It's OK to use my name. It's part of coming out." —Yvonne

"My first name is OK to use. There are thousands of us old girls with that name." —Pat

"It's OK to use my real name since I incorporate the sexual abuse theme into my novels." —Dorian

Still others feared the repercussions of this decision.

"I come from a small town. I can't use my real name." —C.J.

"I would prefer that you not use my name." —Kirsten

"I was wondering if anonymity would be possible because I would be interested in telling my story, but the people I would be speaking about are still alive and I'm not interested in jeopardizing my safety in any way." —Amanda

"On the one hand, I don't want to be ashamed of myself, and telling my story is part of my process of admitting the abuse happened. Yet I want to make sure that your book is going to represent me and everyone else participating in a positive light. Because it would be something I would be exposing about myself, something very personal. It's the insecurity. I'm afraid that it's going to turn around and bite me on my ass. And yet I'd be willing to take that risk for my own purpose of dealing with it and as a Latina saying, 'Yes, abuse exists in our community.' Because of our cultural norms it tends to go unaddressed in our families. I'm at a point where I'm trying to peel all the layers off, like an onion. I've been holding this information inside me for the past 23 years." —Noemi

Several survivors have since changed their names; in telling their stories some asked that I use their birth names, signifying the child who was abused. Others wanted me to use their chosen names.

"Please feel free to identify me as Lisa. While my given name is different, Lisa is the name my family uses for me and thus it seems appropriate that I use this identity for this project."

"Call me Mary Lou, the me that was abused."

"While my name is different now, I was abused as Kathy."

"I am in the process of legally changing my name to Rowan. I'd like you to use this instead of my given name."

For others, creating a name of their own choosing was an empowering process. Some invented names, others claimed names of family members or ancestors whose spirit gave them strength. For all of these reasons, I respect survivors' choices and present their stories here as they would have them told. For many women it is the first time they are speaking out about the abuse.

Fear of Telling

"I thought in some vague way I would get in trouble if I didn't do what my uncle wanted. So I did." —Missy

When we tell the story about our abuse, the painful memories lose some of their power over us. In addition, when we sort through our memories, we are able to cope better with the distress that the abuse has caused us. Sharing our experiences is one of the suggested treatments for post–traumatic stress disorder. This is the rationale for self-help and support groups where we can share our stories with others who have had similar experiences. Of course, we cannot second guess ourselves, try as we might, to understand why we did not tell someone about the abuse when it was happening.

There are always many reasons for our silence, as well as our family and friends' inability or unwillingness to help us even when they knew of the abuse when it was happening. Jean Baker Miller (1997, cited in Dayton, 2000) identifies three dysfunctional family patterns that affect a child's development. First, secrecy binds the abused child to the perpetrator and isolates the child from the rest of the family—and the world—and leads children to blame themselves for the bad things that happen to them. In families where secrecy is perpetuated, family members routinely deny "unacceptable reality." Second, when parents are inaccessible to children, children feel abandoned but strive to keep alive their sense of the "good parent." Third, parentification occurs when a parent is unable to respond to a child's needs and casts the child in a role that better suits him or her. The parentified child puts her own needs aside and focuses on caring for others. These children are forced to develop skills before they are developmentally ready, which can lead them to feel a sense of failure and inadequacy. They end up feeling a dissonance between how others see them and how they see themselves.

These three patterns can lead to psychological problems because developmental needs are not adequately met in the family. Attempts at individuation by children who try to separate from the family are interpreted as assaults on the family system. Children from these kinds of families often reenact dynamics from their families of origin in their chosen partners. These strategies, according to Dayton (2000), help keep us disconnected in order to feel safe and prevent further violation of attachment bonds. In order to resolve these problems so we can learn to connect in healthy ways, we need to grieve what we never had.

In their longitudinal study of girls sexually abused as children, Putnam and Trickett (cited in Strong, 1998) found that how the abuse is disclosed affects a child's future mental and physical health. In cases where the abuse was accidentally discovered by a doctor, teacher, or family member, the girls were more likely to be believed and thus suffered less anxiety afterward than those who directly told of their abuse. The girls who purposely disclosed may have felt more guilt and responsibility for the events that followed their disclosure, such as the breakup of the family, the arrest of the perpetrator, and change in family circumstances, including financial hardship.

"The abuse kept me silent for 30 years. I was always raised to tell my parents the truth. This was the one and only thing that they didn't know about me. On some level I would feel like I was lying to them every day of my life." —Whitney

Many of us had parents and other adults in our lives who tacitly permitted the abuse or denied its occurrence, even when confronted with reality. (Baker, 2002, provides an excellent list of common behavioral and physical warning signs of sexually abused children.) We must remember that it is dysfunctional family systems that allow incest to occur. Incest survivors feel even more betrayed by the nonabusing yet nonprotective parent, often referred to as the "silent partner"—who either tacitly encourages the abuse or fails to recognize and stop it. Roth (1993) uses the term nonprotector to describe the parent who does not prevent or rescue the child from the abuse. *Nonprotector* implies that the nonabusing parent, usually the mother, was either unaware, unable, unavailable, or unwilling to protect the child. Alcoholic, drug-dependent, mentally ill, physically ill, chronically depressed, or absent parents are often so absorbed in their own realities they don't perceive much else around them.

Other mothers do not heed their child's protests. In other families the parent may have a sense that something is wrong but is too defensive, horrified, dependent, or frightened to confront the situation. She chooses to remain ignorant of the truth. Lesbian survivors of incest often have a strong sense of having been their mother's protector (Starzecpyzel, 1987). Wanting to protect Mom from knowledge of the abuse was one of the ways that the child could continue to relate to her.

"Let me listen to me and not to them."
—Gertrude Stein

It can be extremely painful to face the betrayal or abandonment of one's parents. What many of us experience is the painful loss of our mothers and the grieving process that follows. As painful as this deep sense of loss is, acknowledging our anger toward our mothers is usually harder. In expressing our anger toward our mothers we fear that we will eliminate all hopes that she ever loved us or ever will. As angry as we may be about our mother's role as nonprotector, we must be clear about who committed the crime. While our mothers may have been involved, in most cases she did not abuse us. (Those abused by their mothers have special challenges in this area.) Even those not abused by members of their families often feel anger toward their mothers for failing to protect them from the abuse or failing to respond in a swift and compassionate manner. A key issue for the lesbian survivor of incest, as discussed earlier, is her relationship with her mother. According to Starzecpyzel (1987):

> Particularly for the lesbian survivor of incest, therapy must involve working through the strong ambivalence about the mother. Because of the child's feelings of rejection by her mother, she must deal with a wish to reject, punish, and humiliate the mother whom she also needed and loved.... She feels extremely needy on one hand, and humiliated by what seems to be her 'weakness' with lovers (mother) on the other. At the same time, she is intensely enraged by the humiliation

of neediness in the face of inadequate response, and she subconsciously wants never to need another woman again.

"My mother said she knew about my uncle because she walked into the bathroom when he was exposing himself to me. She said she told the rest of the family. Later, when I was 4, I remember my grandmother telling me that if anyone ever told me to pull my panties down, to tell her. So I said, "Mitchell does that to me." She said she told my mother. When my father heard about this he said I was lying. My mother, my aunt, and my grandmother know about the abuse. They are sorry, and I have tried to keep a lot of it from them. My mom is paying in her heart—and I don't mean to imply I hold her responsible—she suffers in her soul with the memories too." —Missy

"I remember in college feeling like, Gosh, if I told my mom, why didn't she do anything? *I was really angry."* —Diana

Most self-injurers come from a family in which inappropriate sexual attention means love (Strong, 1998). Strong explains, "By silencing their children's voices they force them to find another language—primitive and destructive—to speak their truths." In this instance, Strong was talking about cutting, but the same could be said for eating disorders such as bulimia, anorexia, and compulsive overeating, and other forms of self-destructive behavior that act as a way of communicating our inner pain.

Survivors told me how they were forced into silence, threatened by their abusers not to tell of the abuse.

"My uncle threatened me not to tell. He said I wouldn't be believed." —Debbie

"The goat man told me not to tell my Mom because she would be mad if she found out. I told him I wouldn't tell, which I didn't." —Cristi

"The neighbor threatened me not to tell anybody, or my family wouldn't want me anymore and would send me to live with the 'bad kids.'" —Tammy

"My stepfather said he would kill my mother or my two younger sisters. I was threatened with a .44 Magnum in my mouth." —Laura

"As a child I was too scared to tell anybody for fear I would be taken away. My mom used to tell me that if I didn't act right, listen, behave, she was going to put me in a home." —Mo

Others kept silent to protect their families.

"I did not tell anyone about the abuse. I was afraid that either I would not be believed or I would be responsible for the destruction of my family." —Maggie

"At one time I wanted to go to the police and report my uncle, but I decided against it. The police would turn it against me, and I would only hurt my family all over again." —Missy

"I guess I protected Mom by not telling. I guess I felt she was weak. She was so dependent on my father that I was afraid if I did anything to stir things up, she wouldn't be able to handle it, that she'd hurt herself or have a breakdown. If I wanted her to be taken care of, with my father providing all the economic support, I couldn't tell. I don't know how much I really thought about telling anybody. At the time I don't think I would have known how to put into words what was going on. And I didn't think anyone would believe me anyway. He was such an upstanding citizen, and I was just a kid. And he was quite domineering, and we were all quite afraid of him." —Jacque

It is no wonder that most cases of child sexual abuse are not reported outside the family (Courtois, 1988). Shame-based family systems are governed by the implicit rule not to talk about painful experiences of any kind (McNeill, 1988). A sense of shame leads family members to rigidly control their emotions and to set demanding, inhuman standards for themselves. As a result, family members never expose or share deep feelings. A feminist approach to healing recognizes the role that family beliefs play in keeping the secret (Groves and Schondel, 1996). According to Groves and Schondel, "The belief that what goes on in the family is private business has been perpetuated in our society. Women and children are considered property of the male head of household. Through the perpetuation of this belief system, women and children receive messages that they are responsible for the actions of men and to be silent." This code of silence allows the abuse to begin and to be perpetuated. Many of us were given explicit or implicit messages not to talk about the abuse. Decades of research on child sexual abuse have shown that this vow of secrecy is one of the hallmarks of dysfunctional families in which abuse thrives.

"I told my mom what the baby-sitter was doing to me. Then I stopped going there, but we never talked about what happened. I was never given any help. My parents want me to forget it. 'Ignore it, and it will go away.' That method isn't working." —Amanda

"I told my mother about my uncle, and she didn't do anything to stop it." —Debbie

"I told my grandmother about the sexual abuse from my stepdad and mom. She said, 'Oh, well, these things happen.'" —Rowan

"My family knows everything that happened to me, and they basically pretend it never happened. We never discuss it, not since I was little." —Elizabeth

"My mom had to know because there were times when what Dad did made me bleed. I would clean myself up afterwards, but it would be on the bed. She did the laundry, and she never said anything to me." —Kris

"I remember in seventh grade walking into the house to tell my mother what my cousin was doing to me. The kitchen was blue and my mom was ironing. I said, 'I went to him. We were wrestling, but he was touching my private parts. He was having intercourse with me.' My mom got really angry, but all she said to me was, 'Don't talk about that. Go play

with your brothers and sisters.' I heard her talking to my dad, and he was very angry. But they never said anything to me." —Diana

"When I was a senior in high school, I started talking to my mom about it, saying, 'Sometimes Dad would…' And she was like, 'No.' She just cut me off. 'Your father would never do anything.' So there was no point. I haven't talked to her about it since." —Kris

"I always knew that my parents knew about the abuse, but they would not talk about it until 10 years ago when I confronted them with it. Their response was, 'Well, what could we do?' It is pretty scary to think you grew up with completely incompetent people as your parents." —Pat

Experts recommend that each disclosure be carefully planned. Each survivor must examine her motivations and expectations before each disclosure to decide on strategy and timing (Courtois, 1988). Courtois (1988) advises the survivor to "anticipate that family members will likely resort with familiar defenses and dysfunctional patterns as they attempt to cope with the exposure of the family secret" and remind herself, over and over again, that she was not to blame for the abuse or the pain caused by the disclosure. Often we are not believed and, in fact, are blamed for the abuse and for the turmoil that the telling creates in the family. In a shame-based family system, disclosure is viewed as disloyalty and the penalties are high. At best we may be initially supported in our telling of the abuse, but quickly reminded not to bring it up anymore.

"After I told the authorities, I told my parents. Then the town was made aware. My mom couldn't believe that I could do this to the family. My dad said to my mother, 'Well, tell your daughter that at least you love her.' And she said, 'I can't do that. She just opened up a huge can of worms.' She blamed me for so much for so long. She didn't even want me in the house, like it was all my fault. My father still calls it my 'mistake.'" —Delphene

"Initially, my mother's response was to blame me." —Margie

"I told my parents what my friend's brother had done to me the same day that it happened. When I told my parents, my mom went into hysterics. My father went into holy hell and made me tell the guy's parents what happened. But they didn't do anything about it. My father had been abusing me too. I lost my best friend over it. She said, 'Why did you have to tell? He does that to me all the time.'" —Kyrce

"About 10 years ago, when I had agreed to appear on the news regarding clergy abuse, I told my stepfather about the abuse by the priest. Dad was upset that I would publicly denounce a priest. Dad felt I was letting down the Catholic Church and defaming all priests. He was pretty angry and has never mentioned it since." —Misha

"I witnessed my aunt's sexual and physical abuse of her grandchildren. I told their mothers, who were my three cousins. And, of course, they were vehement with me that it wasn't true. They cursed me out. I felt very unsupported." —Nedhera

"After I had been in therapy for three months, I told my parents about the abuse by my brother. My father didn't believe it and wanted proof." —Christy

"I told my mother about the abuse when I was 45 and she was 65. Nine years have passed and she has not forgiven me for telling her." —Maggie

"I told my birth family about my experiences at the orphanage. They were horrified, but they didn't want to talk about it." —Marian

"When I was getting ready to go to college I wrote a letter to my family telling them about the abuse. There was no response. My mother won't talk about it. My stepfather acknowledges it, but doesn't really talk about it. My aunt believes that she was abused too, but she put it out of her head." —Julie

"One of my abusers held a prestigious calling in the church. Dad and

Mom took great pride that they were good friends with him. Mom often dropped me off to play with his daughter on Sunday afternoons. After I confronted Mom about the abuse, years after it happened, she told me that one day when he had brought me home he told her I was going to make someone a very beautiful wife someday. She thought that was a strange thing to say but ignored any implications. Later my grandfather caught my abuser fondling my uncle. He eventually moved away, and my grandmother received a legal request asking for a statement that this man had been caught fondling my uncle as he had since been caught molesting children in his new community. Grandma refused to submit the statement, saying that she did not want to tarnish her youngest son's reputation in the community." —Cristi

"My school counselor told my parents that my brothers sexually abused me. My mother took me out of the meeting room to see if it was true. The next week was hell. The department of Children and Family Services was called and my mother blamed me for 'airing out the dirty laundry.' She blamed me for not dealing with it myself. She blamed me for the potential criminal record my brothers would now possess. After a couple days I told my mother to shut up and stop blaming me." —Marie

"As a child I tried to confront my aunt about my father's abuse. I was having flashbacks, and I wanted her to validate it. She said, 'Leave it go.'" —Sarah

"As far as my parents know it's only conjecture. When I sat them down and told them that abuse had been suggested, my father said, 'You know, you tend to exaggerate a lot. Can you get post–traumatic stress disorder from nightmares? You used to have a lot of those.' I wasn't able to convince him that it's usually the nightmares that come from post–traumatic stress disorder and not the other way around. I am afraid to tell my parents all that I know about the abuse. I would like to protect them. I am afraid that they will beat themselves up over (a) letting me go to my friend's house every weekend, (b) not noticing all of the physical and emotional symptoms I had as a young girl, (c) not arguing with my pediatrician when he said that he wasn't going to investigate my yeast infections because he

knew our family too well, and d) not intervening sooner in my social life. I am also afraid that they will try to cover it all up and say, 'We told you so. She was a bad friend, and you just wouldn't listen.'" —Mollie

"When I was 14 I told one of my teachers that my father had been molesting me. This disclosure led to me telling my mother. She called one of my aunts, and I was taken to a local emergency room for a rape exam. As the last incident had occurred over two months prior there was no evidence. It was decided that others would be told that I had fabricated the story because I had been denied a new pair of shoes. Because I had reported the abuse to a teacher, I was ordered to be evaluated by a psychologist to determine if I was stable enough to stay in school. My parents chose a psychologist who was affiliated with my father's job. After three sessions with me and two with my parents, that was it. I was taken by my father to a doctor and treated with antibiotics. This was a protective measure as my father was sleeping with women other than my mother. The doctor chastised me for 'being with a man so much older.' Clearly, he was not informed that we were father and daughter. Years later I told my grandparents, who tried to be supportive, but it was difficult for them to cut ties with my father. My family knows that my father sexually abused me between the ages of 2 and 14. The overall reaction has been 'How much longer are you going to dwell on this?' and 'When are you going to move on?'" —Lisa

"When I was 20 I had a big fight with my parents, and afterward I told my mother what Dad had done to me and my sister. She didn't believe me and said she couldn't understand why I was telling such horrible lies about my father." —Jacque

"My cousins knew about the abuse, but never wanted to acknowledge it. This is where the split came. I was the cousin, and I was expendable. My mother knew about the abuse, but she was the peacemaker. She knew but did nothing about it. My aunt knew that she knew. I think my mother was afraid that we would get thrown out, that she'd have to make it on her own. It was never something that she thought she was capable of." —Nedhera

"I told my mother when I was 16. But she visited me recently and said she didn't remember me telling her. Her reaction when I was 16 was, 'Why didn't you tell me? You could've prevented it from happening to your sister.' Some other family members know as well. I feel that they all act as if it never happened." —Kristie

In telling the family secret, we are often branded as liars—scapegoated for the family problems we had the courage to speak out about. But as Bratton (1999) writes, it is not a betrayal to reveal the facts about what happened to us when we were children; "it is simply telling the truth after so many years of lies and deceit and distortion."

"In my family I'm the big liar. When I wrote my mom a letter about the abuse, she had a fit. When she asked my dad he denied it. So she said it must not have happened. What else is he going to say? 'Of course I did'? She said I was doing this to hurt her. She said it never happened. Of course, my mom denies everything." —Liz

"My mother discovered semen in my panties when I was four and took her love away. I see us in that bathroom with her angry glare asking me what that was in my panties—obviously semen—and she flipped out. My mother has consistently rejected and belittled me since. To this day we do not speak. She swept it under the proverbial carpet to keep it from my explosive father. She treats me like an outcast." —Tammy

"When she made me go to counseling, I told her what her husband had done to me. She told me right to my face, 'I don't believe you, and I think you are doing this to hurt me.' This is what I had feared all along." —Melissa

Sometimes our telling stopped the abuse.

"I told my mother at age 11 that Dad was molesting me. The next morning I was sent to school like nothing happened, but the sexual abuse stopped." —Robin

"I told my mother what the man had done to me, and he was banished from the house. I told, and they believed me and got rid of him." —Kathy

"I told my parents what the farmhand was doing to me, and he was gone the next day. My mother told me I would not have to go up there and listen to his stories again." —Lynn

Sometimes others tell for us, but the telling does not protect us.

"My sister caught my brothers with me one Sunday morning and told my parents. My parents told us not to do these things, but my brothers never stopped. This is when I first realized my parents would not help stop them. I felt as if I was in a trapped situation." —Marie

"My therapist told my mom, and she told a brother, who beat me within an inch of my life." —Barbara

"When I was in the seventh grade I reported the rape to a counselor. The counselor, who had promised not to tell, reported the incident to the police department. They, in turn, called my home to inquire about the rape. One of my sisters answered the call. That evening my mother demanded to know why the police called and whether any of it was true. She demanded that I pull down my underwear so that she could inspect my vagina. In the bedroom, as I sat at the end of the bed with her standing in front of me, I told her that none of it was true. She left me alone and never brought the issue up again." —Noemi

Children will often find ways to tell people, without words, that something is wrong. As Barbara Myers (1979) writes, "When children have pain which is hard to express, they will sometimes do destructive things to themselves and to others in order to be heard.... We must learn to do more than just see the behavior or treat the symptoms. We must learn to hear the pain and offer new survival skills" (cited in Fortune, 1983). Significant changes in children's behavior, like those listed below, signal problems that should not be ignored:

- a shift from outgoing behavior to shy, withdrawn behavior (or vice versa)
- regressive behaviors such as resuming thumb-sucking or bed-wetting
- discomfort or fear of being left alone with a particular adult or teenager
- precocious, provocative sexual behavior, such as imitation of adult sex play
- running away or drug and alcohol abuse
- nightmares or sleep disturbances

Behavioral and physical symptoms vary by the age of the child (Courtois, 1988). If parents know what to look for and are willing to see what is happening to their children, evidence of sexual abuse in children's behavior is not difficult to detect. Like Melissa, whose stealing was a cry for help:

"I actually didn't tell my mother till I got fired from my first job because of stealing. At that point I would have done anything to show my mother that I was in need of help."

"I never told anyone about the abuse. When I was flagged as a 'troubled' student in high school and sent to chemical dependency treatment for a month, I wanted treatment to save my family." —Katie

"My mom would say to me, 'When you were growing up you never wanted to take showers. You always wanted to look dirty.' That's something you know about children who are sexually abused. They don't want to draw attention to themselves. Why would you want to do that?" —Diana

"I used to set fires and do very bad things." —Tabitha

"When I told my mom that my symptoms were classic signs of abuse, she

didn't say anything, just changed the subject. I think the prevailing wisdom in my family is to get over it and move on, which I have tried to do. When I was 5 or 6, I would walk around the house just saying, 'I'm sorry.' If anything happened, for any reason, I would say, 'I'm sorry.'" —Deborah

Sometimes it is only years after the abuse has ended that we are finally able to tell of the abuse and be believed.

"My brother told me never to tell anyone, especially our parents. I just recently came to terms with withholding the truth from my parents and decided to tell them. I traveled to spend a week with them. One night I told my mother. Later that evening my father joined us, and I asked my mother to tell him the truth. They both embraced me and said it would be all right. Later, my mother told me that she would have killed him if I had told way back then. I held in all that energy for 30 years of my life! My God, what a relief it was to let it go!" —Whitney

"I told my parents that my oldest brother had abused me, and they believed me." —Wendy

"I told my Mom at 19. She believed me." —Yvonne

"My parents felt guilty, like they needed to do something. This is a lingering feeling for them, though I've told them I just need for them to understand now. It's too late for them to do anything to help me." —Brooke

"My grandfather had a special way of saying 'I love you' over the phone. That was our code that let him know I hadn't told anyone. My whole family knows. They were extremely understanding and protective and wanted to share it with any relatives who had children in my grandfather's presence." —Juli

Reg describes the importance of speaking out about our experiences and compares the experiences of coming out as a survivor and as a lesbian.

"As uncomfortable and yucky as it is, it's important to tell. Not telling sure doesn't help. Telling gets us out of our mind stuff. Being quiet about it didn't work. It didn't help me or others. Coming out as a survivor was much worse for me than coming out as a lesbian. The abuse involves other people and my responses to it, my own baggage and denial."

I never told anyone about the abuse until I was well into adulthood, and then only a few close friends and my partner. A few years ago my partner disclosed the abuse to my mother. My mother was shocked and completely unable to accept it. To this day, more than four years later, she has not said a word to me about it. To the contrary, she has done everything she can to talk in glowing terms about my brother and the wonderful person and father he is. I have told her that I do not want to talk about him, but she will not stop. I am angry at my mother for failing to protect me then and for continuing to sacrifice my life for his. This has become an obstacle for me in my relationship with her. I am guarded with her now. Although I want to talk to her about it in order to release the anger I feel eating me up inside, I have not been able to do this. One of my sisters is unable to accept that the abuse by our brother affected me; she told me that he wouldn't have done it if I had said no as she did. I told her that she didn't know what she was talking about, and I would not discuss it with her again. My youngest sister has been very supportive. While we do not discuss the details of the abuse, she has supported the choices I have made in my life to put distance between me and the family, and she has been very supportive of my writing this book.

When we are not believed nor offered comfort for the pain that we have suffered, we die a little more inside. If we allow ourselves to, we can begin to grieve for the loss of the family we wish we had, the family that let us down.

"I told my parents about the abuse in 1995. They sat quietly and listened. They asked who, and about the connection to my being a lesbian, but not a whole lot else. I don't remember that they said they were sorry it happened. I don't remember feeling happy, but I was relieved not to have that secret anymore. It's taken the charge off and made it less important. I have less of a need to live up to my parents'

expectations. They failed me. I can be independent now." —Marty

And sometimes we are fortunate enough to be surrounded by friends and family who are capable of offering us the comfort and support we so desperately need.

"My siblings know just about everything. My sisters were very supportive and protective. It sparked some memories for both of them, and now one is wondering if she was abused as well." —Mary

"At the time of my mother's death, I told my brothers and sister that I had recovered memories of having been sexually abused by my dad between the ages of 4 and 11. All three were shocked, sympathetic, and supportive. My sister deserves a paragraph of her own. She has been as believing, supportive, and sympathetic as humanly possible. In the period right after I told her about the abuse, she checked in regularly with me. Over the years she has worked very hard to become informed about incest." —Levie

"My mother has apologized for not protecting me. That was two years ago. She was never explicit about what she was apologizing for. Maybe it wasn't acknowledged the way I would have hoped, but it has been helpful to me. I was angry with my mother for a very long time. Her apology was sort of impromptu, and it was great." —Noemi

And sometimes we decide that telling of the abuse, especially when our abuser is dead, serves no useful purpose. While I do not judge survivors who decide this, I only suggest that sometimes we spend our lives protecting others from the painful truth of our abuse, while we continue to suffer in silence.

"I see no reason to tell my mom, except to maybe cry on her shoulder. She loved her father, and no good would come of it. She's just a great mother. It would only hurt her." —Margaret

Examples of reenactment were also evident in survivors' stories: their attempts to resolve the pain of family dynamics by acting it out.

My own parents' marriage dissolved during my preadolescent years as a result of my father's extramarital affair. Years later I had a series of affairs with married men, reenacting my father's infidelity and my mother's heartbreak. In this way I acted out the pain and shame that my family could not talk about.

Sarah equates the processes of coming out as a survivor and a lesbian:

"I would love to participate in anything that will bring awareness and hopefully make a difference. I know it's not possible, but I would love to see the day that child abuse of any kind is nonexistent. Until then, I will do everything in my power that I can to help. I want to tell my story because I'm tired of the abuse continuing. It's like standing up and saying I'm gay. It's so empowering when people don't feel alone."

In the days and weeks following their interviews with me, many survivors connected with me again to describe how the telling of their story had proved to be a healing experience for them.

"These questions are a novelty since I have never talked to others about these aspects of my past." —Amy

"I anticipated that this would be a heavy load for me to carry and a touch traumatic to go through. Instead I found a burden lifted, and as I told a friend, I feel remarkably well. I have been processing this with friends all week and anticipating the telling of the whole story one more time. But it seems that the healing has caught up with me, and rather than more heaviness I feel good, released, relieved, and have a new perspective on how far I've come. I thank you for this opportunity. It feels like a capstone. I am profoundly grateful." —Kathy

Confrontation

"You gain strength, courage, and confidence by every experience in which you really stop to look fear in the face.... You must do the thing you think you cannot do."
—Eleanor Roosevelt

Confrontation goes beyond disclosure and builds upon it. While disclosure involves exposing the abuse, confrontation involves challenging the abuser and other family members to face the truth about it. It can involve a variety of actions: expressing anger and other emotions; questioning reasons and motives for family circumstances, the abuse, and any lack of assistance; determining why the survivor was selected for victimization; describing the effects of the abuse on her life; demanding accountability, apology, or restitution; and preventing future abuse in the family. Confrontation, like disclosure, can be a powerful therapeutic strategy whether done indirectly (through role play or psychodrama, a letter, an audiotape, or videotape) or directly in face-to-face contact.

While survivors are often encouraged to confront their abusers as an avenue to empowerment and healing, this needs to be approached with great care (Roth, 1993). Lengthy conversations between survivors and their therapists will help to assess the wisdom of confrontation given particular family dynamics. Roth advises, "It is safer to generalize that confrontation will lead to further abuse and loss for the client than to generalize that confrontation will offer a healing experience." While confrontation may or may not be advisable, the survivor does not need to keep the abuse a secret in her family or remain engaged in dysfunctional patterns of relating. The treatment goals for the survivor are to no longer feel threatened by her abuser and to create a new identity and role for herself as a member of the family.

Adult survivors of child sexual abuse often have a strong sense of unfinished business (Fortune, 1983). Their anger, guilt, and confusion are unresolved. They may choose to act on their own behalf by confronting their abuser. Fortune explains,

> It is important to remember that a victim's desire to confront the offender always carries with it the expectation that the offender will acknowledge his offense and ask for forgiveness, preparing the way for some form of reconciliation. In fact, the offender may well continue to deny that the abuse ever took place and may be unwilling to discuss the matter at all. A victim should be prepared for this disappointment. Nonetheless,

she has done what she needed to do in confronting the abuser with his or her behavior.

When my editor at Alyson contacted me to tell me she was interested in publishing my book, I decided I needed to take the next step in my healing. I decided to confront my brother with what he had done to me. I wrote him a letter. I experienced the emotions that Kritsberg and Miller-Kritsberg (1993) describe. It was "a deeply cleansing experience. It provides a release for the intense emotions trapped inside you so that you can be free of them." I was in control of the experience and that felt great! This is what I wrote in the letter:

"I've been wanting to write you this letter for a long time. A letter was the only way I could say these words to you. I was uncomfortable with the idea of talking with you about this in person. I anticipated your response and frankly didn't want to see it. This is not about you anymore. This is about me and reclaiming my power. When I was a little girl, not much older than your oldest daughter is now, I lost my innocence. You took it from me. What you undoubtedly see as sexual experimentation between siblings was a nightmare of sexual abuse, the memory of which continues to affect me today. I learned to hate my body, men, and myself. I learned to lie—to Mom, to friends, and mostly to myself—about who I was and what I was feeling. I felt trapped in a nightmare from which there was no escape. You did this to me. I was much too young to understand the implications of sex or to handle the complex emotions that accompanied the sexual abuse. I didn't know how to make it stop. You told me that no one would believe me if I told. I guess I knew that was true. You were the favored child and no one would ever have believed you were capable of such horror. I kept the secret. I would sleep on the stairs to Mom and Dad's bedroom or at the foot of their bed hoping they would ask me what was wrong. They never did. Every day after school I would hide in my bedroom, refusing dinner and pleading excessive homework. I was always tired. I recorded the incidents of abuse in my diary, looking for a pattern that would help me anticipate your next attack. I discovered that you were more likely to attack me after a date, so I tried to stay over at a friend's house on these nights so I wouldn't be available to you. I saved all

the physical evidence of your abuse—the semen-stained pajamas, the used condoms, the empty Baby Magic lotion bottles. I tucked them in the back of my closet, hoping that someday I would have the courage to show them to someone and finally have a witness to the horror I had lived through. When I received the panicked call years ago that the house was on fire, my immediate concern was for everyone's safety. Then my thoughts quickly turned to the evidence—now destroyed. Now there was only my word as proof of the abuse that you had inflicted on me for six long years. These many years later I know that my word is enough. I am stronger now. Time, therapy, the kindness of friends, and the love of a woman have helped to heal my wounds. I know now that I am not to blame for what happened to me. I carry no shame for the pain that was inflicted on my body. The blame is yours alone. As a child, prepubescent and naive to the ways of the world and the wiles of men, I was vulnerable to your advances and powerless to stop them. Sexual abuse, rape, intimidation, physical assault, and humiliation—these are your crimes, punishable in any state. I know now that had I known to press charges, you might have served jail time by now. Who knows the direction your life might have taken? Who knows the rehabilitation you might have received? But looking back is not my focus now—looking forward is. I have a daughter now. The experience of mothering has strengthened my conviction to speak out about the atrocities I experienced at your hands. No one should have to endure the anguish I suffered as a child. Your power trip and sadistic physical and sexual assault of my body have forever changed me as a person. That is not something I can change. What I can change is your ability to harm another child. It is for this reason alone that I write this letter. I cried at the births of each of your three daughters; I feared for their safety. The chances of your abusing again are high. As much as I struggle with direction in my life sometimes, I know now that my life has a higher purpose—to protect children from you. I will not stand idly by while you raise your three daughters. I am watching your every move. As I see it, you have a couple of options. First, I recommend that you tell your wife about your history of physical and sexual abuse of young girls. This is one of the best protections your daughters have from you. I would like her to call me after you've spoken with her so that I know you have taken this step. Second, I could call her directly and explain in great detail everything you did to me, and are still capable of doing to her daughters and other young girls with whom you have contact. Or you could share this letter with her. Third, I could speak directly with your daughters about the dangers of physical and sexual abuse. I could warn them not to let anyone touch them in ways that make them uncomfortable regardless of who the person is (family, friend, neighbor) or what they threaten (to hurt someone they love). Whichever step you take, I will certainly have this conversation with your daughters anyway. As I see it, you have very few options—but many more than I ever had as a victim of your abuse. Everyone in the family is aware of the abuse although it is not discussed. Facing it is painful and people naturally avoid pain. This is especially true for Mom, who loves you dearly and cannot reconcile her love for you with your despicable behavior and her failure to protect me from your advances. As time passes I am less concerned about the preservation of our dysfunctional family and more concerned about safeguarding our daughters' future and speaking the truth. I do not want your apology. You cannot erase the trauma of my childhood with a few short words as sincere as you might try to make them sound. Your only course of action is stepping outside of your selfish existence and putting the lives of your daughters—and other young girls who could fall prey to your evil ways—first. I will continue to interact with you as I have, until it grows too painful for me. I want you to know that your daughters are always welcome in my home and are under my watchful and loving eye at all times. I hope you will face up to what you have done and take steps now to prevent it from ever happening again."

Here's how survivors stood up to their abusers and managed to stop the abuse when it was happening to them as children:

"I remember an incident when I was 13 years old where my aunt tried to corner me again. This time something just rose up in me and I smacked her really hard across the face and got her off me. And from that point on she didn't sexually abuse me anymore. Years later I confronted her. I threw it in her face, naming what she did to me. 'You're just sick,' I told her. 'You need help. You're sexually abusing children. What kind of pervert are you?' Her mouth just dropped open. I did this in front of two of her daughters

and one of her grandchildren. I didn't stay to hear her sputter and try to explain. I just walked out the door." —Nedhera

"One day I stood up to my stepfather and told him that he wasn't my father and that he was to never touch me again. And he never touched me again." —Melissa

"After a huge fight with my stepfather where I punched him in the face to save myself, I decided to move out. I was 15." —Tammie

Choosing to confront your abuser, and those who failed to protect you from the abuse, is a big step. Only you can decide when and how you will do this. You need to assess the risk to your emotional health when you keep the abuse a secret. Whether you choose to confront in person, over the phone, or in a letter is a decision that you must make for yourself. The survivors I spoke with describe the reasons they decided to confront and how they did it. Many survivors told how, often years later, they managed to muster the courage to confront their abusers and nonprotectors.

"I kept planning in my head, If I see this guy, I'm going to confront him. *During my nephew's baptism I saw my cousin in the church. I went and tapped him on the shoulder and said, 'I need to talk to you.' He said, 'Hey, how are you! It's so nice to see you!' I said, 'No, I need to talk to you. We need to go outside.' The whole family was around and I took him by the shirt and threw him against the wall. My brother-in-law, who's a police officer, asked, 'What's going on here?' My cousin told him to go away, but I said, 'You stay right here. You need to know what this motherfucker did to me.' I said everything, and everyone was shocked because no one thought anything of this guy. I looked him in the eyes and said, 'I just feel sorry for you. Someone must have done something to you to be so messed up to be doing this to a child.' The priest went by and asked us that if we were having family problems to take it outside. I said, 'I'm not going to shut up any longer. I've been holding this for too long. I'm not going to keep quiet anymore. This is what he did to me. He sexually abused me when I was 4. And my cousin was so embarrassed that he left*

the room. During the whole mass my mother was crying. She didn't want a confrontation with the family. After the baptism I went to my mom's house feeling so good about myself. It was like such a relief. Wow! I couldn't tell you how much weight was taken off me. My brother and sister told me that he had done that to them too. I thought, God, this is a sick person we have in our family, but at least everyone in the family knows what happened now. *After that he got divorced because his wife was there at the church. He had two daughters. I don't know if he ever did anything to them."* —Diana

"I confronted my dad, and he denied it." —Jan

"When I confronted my brother and asked for validation and he couldn't give it, our relationship fell apart." —Christy

"I confronted my dad for myself and my sister. He said, 'You kids had to learn about things somehow.'" —Chris

"I wrote my father a letter before he had open-heart surgery confronting him with what he had done to me." —Mary Lou

"While I was in the survivors group I started to realize how furious I was at my uncles and aunts and any adult who stood by and let my father brutalize me. I started sending e-mails just ripping into them, telling them how angry I was and how awful they are, that they should be ashamed of themselves and that they're the awful people in the world who let child abuse happen." —Cory

"My brother was apologetic and wrought with grief for the pain he caused me." —Robin

"I was called to testify against my uncle, and he threatened me. He shot himself. I think that was a wimpy way to do it." —Debbie

"My uncle denied the abuse unless he was drunk. Then he was pretty blatant about what he did to me when we were alone." —Kristie

"My brother probably doesn't feel he did anything wrong because he would say I was consenting to sexual play. He's actually a child therapist now. I don't believe he feels he was being abusive, even though he knows I went through a bad stretch as a teenager. He wouldn't admit to any wrongdoing except to say that he was an angry child after I was born." —Dorian

"I confronted my brother through a letter and on the phone. There was a big blowout, and he denied it. He's still on drugs." —Wendy

"One of my brothers and I have a fairly good relationship. We have been able to discuss it, and he has apologized for it several times. Not a pleading apology either; it was very sincere." —Marie

Some survivors took legal action against their abusers.

"I decided that in order for me to come to completion with the priest who abused me, I needed to have a way to confront him. Though he is dead he is still being protected by my silence, as he was when I was a kid. So I decided to 'out' him. Right now I am in a process with the Professional Standards Committee of the Catholic Church that investigates all claims of sexual abuse by the clergy or in the religion. I named and exposed Father Terry." —Misha

"I went to the authorities with what my coach had done to me. The case went to trial and was plea-bargained out. He only got a year in jail and ended up serving nine months. He got his teacher's license revoked." —Delphene

"I went through the criminal 'justice' system and my abuser was found guilty, although he only served four months for four years of abuse." —Julie

Stopping the abuse was only the most urgent problem for Julie:

"When I was getting ready to go to high school I finally told my

grandfather, 'No more!' I threatened him if he ever did anything to my cousins. But I would guess that he abused them anyway."

Other survivors regretted not confronting their abusers before their deaths. They felt that now they could never have closure.

"My father died when I was 28. I never confronted him about the abuse." —Maggie

"I can't have closure. The abusers are all dead now." —Marian

For some survivors, confrontation is not something they want to do.

"My relationship with my father is actually OK. I have not told him anything about how his behavior affected me. While that is an ultimate goal for me, right now I'm just enjoying him being a somewhat active participant in my life. I think he knows he screwed up a lot as a father when we were growing up, and now he is making up for it by being more active in our lives." —Mary

"My father has never said or done anything to acknowledge that it happened. And I've never confronted him with it." —Jacque

Protecting the Children

"So long as little children are allowed to suffer there is no true love in this world."
—Isadora Duncan

As my letter to my brother indicated, my primary motivation in disclosing and confronting was to protect other children from him. When we speak out about our own abuse, we communicate our belief in the inalienable rights of children. One early childhood program director developed a Children's Rights Charter. In her program, all children have "a right to play, a right to be held, picked up, comforted, a right to feel safe, a right to play inside or outside, a right to eat when hungry, a right to privacy—to be alone, and a right not to be hurt" (Radich, 2002). How many of us were raised in environments where our rights, on all levels, were violated?

Unfortunately, choosing to confront our abusers and face the implications of what this means for the family system is not an easy decision for any of us to make. If we choose not to confront our abusers, we may try to protect our nieces and nephews and other children within our family system by offering instructions about how to protect themselves if someone is sexually inappropriate with them.

I have built my life around service to children. From my earliest experiences baby-sitting for neighbors' children and then pursuing a career in early childhood education, I have dedicated my life to them. In writing this book I have found another way to positively impact the lives of young children. When we as survivors of child sexual abuse tell the truth about our experiences, we raise awareness of the dangers of sexual predators and draw attention to individuals who have perpetrated. As Fortune warns (1983), "Sex offenders are repeat offenders and will continue to assault and abuse others until they are stopped." In addition, we learn how our own healing makes us more available to our children and may, in fact, prevent the abuse of our children.

In my conversations with survivors, we spoke of the ways in which we have each tried to make a difference in the lives of children, to protect them from friends and family members who have abused us, as well as instructed them in how to handle sexual advances by telling someone who will make these stop. Sometimes, however, we are immobilized, unable to speak out about our abuse, unable to do anything to protect others. While we may feel tremendous guilt over this, we must remind ourselves that we did the best we could at the time. We are not responsible for the abuse perpetrated on others, as we were not responsible for the abuse perpetrated on us.

Survivors described their fear that children would be abused by those who had abused them as children.

"When I warned my aunt and uncle to watch my stepfather with my young cousin, they ignored me." —Tammie

"I seem to worry about every child I ever see in an adult's lap, thinking there is something going on with that adult and that child. I'm very nervous. I have panic attacks." —Laura

"My sister has kids. I get nervous, worried when they're sitting on my dad's lap. I hope he doesn't baby-sit." —Chris

"When my sister was pregnant with her first child I literally came unglued. I pretty much lost my marbles. It was her pregnancy that really triggered everything for me. I was terrified that she was going to have a girl and that my dad would do something to her. Now she doesn't speak to my parents anymore." —Kris

Sometimes we don't know what to do, or are not conscious of our own abuse history at a time when it would have been necessary to protect or help others.

"I can only pray that none of my abusers has ever touched another child that way again." —Missy

"I actually feel guilty for not knowing what to do. I wonder if my neighbor has abused others. I'm sure he has." —Kirsten

"I sorrow over the abuse occurring to the young girl children around me, and I speak out when I feel I'm heard and cry when I'm alone." —Jan

"Nothing makes me more angry than to think of a child being abused. I was very concerned about my uncle's two daughters, but I lived several states away and had very little contact with them." —Mo

"When I was 27, my uncle who abused me was married and had a child, a daughter. I threatened to tell his wife, and I did. They divorced. My brother who also abused me has grown children. Now I'm afraid he'll abuse his grandchildren. He did abuse his own children, according to his daughter. I had no memories of the abuse until I was 29, so I couldn't have protected them." —Wendy

"I feel a responsibility to protect children, but no one would listen to me because I am 'crazy,' 'strange,' and 'incompetent.'" —Barbara

"I hope and pray that nothing would happen to my nieces. I am 99% sure that my oldest brother is not abusing his daughter. I would hope that my relationship with my niece would be close enough for her to tell me. However, I am not sure about my other brother. Nevertheless, I have not seen any signs. I do not feel a level of responsibility, but I pray they are OK." —Marie

"I just thought it was me and that my uncle wouldn't do it again, so I didn't make a big deal. When my other uncle's wife had a mental breakdown and threatened to kill the children and herself, the uncle who abused me said he'd take the kids to live with him, and he sexually abused all three." —Debbie

"I don't feel responsible, but if I can help to protect a child I would. I can't begin to answer as to whether my brother would have abused someone else. My therapist asked one time if I worried he would abuse my two nieces. But I didn't think that would happen and I didn't want to give it any energy, so I left it alone." —Whitney

Sometimes we try to protect others from the abuse, but are not able to.

"I had tried to be really bad to protect my sister, but my sister says that she was sexually abused during the day by my father and recalls what went on with me." —Tabitha

"When my sister was 14 she confided in me that Dad was doing stuff to her. I felt like I'd been kicked in the stomach and almost puked. She had more nerve than I did to ask him what he was doing. He told her he was 'teaching her how to love.' I told her if he tried it again she should scream and yell for help. I also promised to try my best not to leave her alone with him." —Jacque

"One night when my niece and nephew were living with us I found my niece putting a teddy bear between her legs like it was having inter-

course with her. I freaked and said, 'What are you doing?' She replied, 'I'm sorry, Aunt Laura, I won't do it again.' Oh, my God, I was crying and freaking out and asked her where she learned that from. Both kids responded 'Papa', my stepfather. I called my lover in hysterics and she came home immediately. We called Child Protective Services and started an investigation. It turned into a nightmare for all concerned, except my stepfather. CPS put the file on the shelf to collect dust." —Laura

"I blamed myself and beat myself up that I could have stopped my grandfather from abusing his other grandchildren." —C.J.

"I didn't tell anyone, not even my sister. And then he abused her." —Christy

"When I found out that my stepfather hurt my sister, his actual child, I was so angry. I still feel very angry about the whole thing." —Melissa

"My uncle also sexually abused my sister. For a long time I blamed myself for that because I didn't inform anyone of what happened to me until I was 16." —Kristie

Here are some of the steps that survivors have taken to try to protect children from sexual abuse:

"I do feel the need to protect children from abuse. But by the time I remembered the abuse, my father had little interaction with children. I did tell my cousins who have small children." —Katie

"My parents volunteer in a children's program. It really freaked me out when my parents told me they were doing this. I wanted to find out how much contact they really had with the kids. I called my shrink and had to see him because I was in a total panic. He was like, 'You find out what you need to find out.' I found out the program is really supervised and my parents do not have any real contact with the children. My mother and father baby-sit for friends' children, but my mother's always there. My father would never be left alone with them. I talked to the friend about it,

and she just didn't care. I said what I could. When I see her kids I'm always trying to see if they're OK or not. That's definitely a big deal to me. I feel responsible about that." —Kris

"My passion is children, and I think I am always looking for signs of abuse. I pay very close attention to comments made and also behavioral patterns when different people are around, because my situation wasn't recognized. I guess I hid it well. So I know what feelings I felt and I look for it in other children. I don't want any child's life ruined the way mine could've been." —Juli

"In my work as a psychotherapist I specialized in sexual abuse counseling and now as director of a program for youth, I have the opportunity to put in as many safeguards and as much healing as possible for our kids." —Misha

"I told a lot of my cousins that it happened to prevent it from happening to them. When I hear of it now that anger comes back full force. Now I use that anger positively and go through the proper legal measures needed to prevent it from happening to other children." —Kristie

"Ten years ago I sent a letter to my parents and siblings regarding my father's friend and what he had done to me. There are 27 children in the family and I was nervous about that." —Mary Lou

"The most I could do in terms of my own abuser and children is to let my cousins know about him and not to trust him with their daughters, which they wisely don't." —Robin

"I worked at Head Start for 13 years and have protected and provided for many inner-city children." —Naomi

"While I feel a responsibility to protect children from my father, I have had little success in this area. While my brothers, cousins, mother, and grandparents all know that my father sexually abused me for years, everyone seems fine leaving children in his care. It's almost as if it is their

belief that I was abused because of something about me and not because of his issues. Thus, in their heads, the other children are safe." —Lisa

"When I asked my abusing older brother if he intended to tell his wife or children, he said he saw no need for that. When I explained the reasons that made it seem essential to me, he said he had no problem with my telling them, but that he didn't want to. So I did. My sister-in-law seemed shocked, as did her two daughters and son. I did what I thought would help protect my great-nieces and nephews from my abuser by talking to my family about the abuse, but I'm not sure that it had the positive effect I had anticipated." —Levie

"In my personal life I never wanted my nephew to be around my grandfather. I actually cringe when I see this one picture of him holding him. I'm a social worker. What does that tell you? I am hypersensitive to the potential of sexual abuse. If I think a kid is being sexually abused, I immediately relate and want to save him or her. Eight years ago I had to leave the field for a while because I believed everyone was being sexually abused and I couldn't take it anymore. I'm more balanced now thanks to therapy." —Mary

"In my current work as a teacher I like to think of myself as being there for little girls. I didn't have a good childhood. I want to give little girls self-esteem. I see myself as the counterbalance to mothers of males." —Marian

"My family was extremely protective and wanted to share information about my grandfather with any relatives who had children in his presence." —Juli

"When I hear things about child abuse and it involves anyone I care about, it really affects me. Like when I hear parents telling their children to be quiet, which happens a lot. That's something that I want to do—to educate parents. It's not OK. It's never OK. Parents don't want to talk about it. That way she'll forget. But you never forget." —Diana

"I showed classic signs of molestation, and as a teacher I would be required to report if I had a child doing what I did. It kind of shook me

up that my mother didn't know the difference between normal and abnormal. I have hot-lined parents when I felt a legitimate concern, however unsubstantiated." —Deborah

"My mom and I don't talk about the abuse much anymore, but she did eventually come to understand. I think as a mom myself it's very complicated to feel like you repeatedly put your child in a dangerous situation." —Margie

"I am a teacher who works with at-risk children. I have called Child Protective Services on two occasions and have worked closely with the counseling services available at my school." —Elizabeth

CHAPTER 4

Lesbian Identity

"I am never afraid of what I know."
—Anna Sewell

Lesbian Survivors

In any book on lesbian survivors, the issue of *cause* is going to come up. People are always interested in discussing what causes women to be lesbian or men to be gay. Despite the fact that the origins of sexual orientation are not well understood and that it is likely a result of many factors, speculation continues. As the Boston Lesbian Psychologies Collective suggests, the question is all wrong. "Theorizing about lesbian development is still solidly in the realm of looking for 'causes' of this 'psychopathology,' " they say. Homophobic people continue to look for early trauma or developmental difficulties in the lives of gay people to explain sexual orientation. But as we know, there is no one single lesbian identity, nor a single path to lesbian identity development. Lesbians find a deeply satisfying emotional connection to women and may have political reasons too—preferring to live in more egalitarian relationships than they see in the heterosexual community. Our experiences as women loving women should be celebrated and not viewed as problems to be dealt with in psychotherapy.

Any discussion about lesbians is complicated by histories of childhood sexual abuse and the implication that the abuse somehow "caused" the lesbianism. This is part of a societal view to blame the victim. We know that sexual orientation is likely established by adolescence and is preceded by a growing awareness of same-sex attraction. Recent studies confirm that sexual behavior is changeable, but sexual identity is not. While respecting women's rights to choose a lesbian lifestyle, recent research seems to suggest that sexual orientation is determined at birth and is not changeable. Bonnie Zimmerman (1995) distinguishes sexual orientation—a condition established at birth (or at least very early childhood socialization)—and sexual preference—a choice that can be made at any time from puberty to old age."

In *The Invisible Wound*, Kritsberg and Miller—Kritsberg (1993) write, "Your sexuality is intricately interwoven into the fabric of your humanity. Your sex is a core element of who you are. When you were sexually abused, you were wounded to the very core of your being." As women we've been socialized to bury our sexual feelings. Because these feelings have been used as an excuse to perpetrate violence against us, we protect ourselves by shutting off our sexual desire. We blame the victim—ourselves.

Many survivors were angry, believing that being lesbian proved the popular myth:

"I had heard that abused girls end up as lesbians. My mom believed that and was afraid that I would be influenced by my counselor because she was gay. These allegations really made me even more confused and frustrated. I am not sure if I can explain it. I think I was afraid of coming out because it would mean that I fell into the percentages and that they all were right. It would have meant that the abuser won again." —Delphene

"I had heard people were gay because they were sexually abused. I didn't want to be a statistic. I told myself, I won't be actively gay." —Christy

"For a while I wondered if I identify as a lesbian because of the abuse." —Cristi

"I sometimes wonder if it has affected my sexual identity in a subconscious way. I try not to blame things on the abuse, but it has to have had something to do with who I am today." —Juli

"It made me question myself more. Is this why I am a lesbian? It added to my confusion and made me feel angry that the abuse affected so much of my life." —Katie

"I wanted to tell my dad, 'Look what you did to me. You made me a lesbian.'" —Chris

"When I was in the coming-out process, I went through a period of time blaming my cousin for my sexuality. I didn't want to accept it. I blamed him a lot." —Diana

It is important to say that lesbians are not more likely to have suffered childhood sexual abuse than the general population. Lesbian survivors often hear, "Oh, you're an incest survivor? That's why you're a lesbian." Some may even have said to themselves, "If I hadn't been abused, I wouldn't be a lesbian." JoAnn Loulan, in *Lesbian Passion* (1987), writes, "Childhood sexual abuse may have had a profound effect on you, but in most cases that's not why you're a lesbian." Ellen Bass and Laura Davis, noted authors of *The Courage to Heal* (1988), affirm for lesbian survivors, "What you are trying to heal from is the destructive effects of having been sexually abused, not the fact that you're a lesbian."

Researchers have found no association between child sexual abuse and the development of a lesbian sexual orientation (Bell, Weinberg, and Hammersmith, 1981). Further, the prevalence of child sexual abuse in the National Lesbian Health Care Survey (Bradford and Ryan, 1988) was comparable to that reported by Russell (1986) and Finkelhor et al (1990). Thirty-two percent of the women in the National Lesbian Health Care Survey reported experiencing child sexual abuse, compared with 38% in Russell's study and 27% in Finkelhor's study. There is no empirical confirmation that sexual abuse leads to a higher incidence of homosexuality (Zerbe, 1993). While some use research to indicate a possible link between lesbianism and childhood abuse (Cameron and Cameron, 1995; Landsdale, 1996), others, including *Queer by Choice* (2002), argue that any attempt to find a cause for homosexuality is by nature homophobic (Schuklenk et al, 1997).

Researchers (Brannock and Chapman, 1990) have found that previous traumatic experiences with men were not associated with lesbianism, indicating that such experiences may not be a significant factor in the development of sexual orientation. Others report an association between lesbianism and child sexual abuse (Lehmann, Lehmann, and Kelly, 1998; Post and Avery, 1995; Saewyc et al, 1999). Roth (1993) clarifies that sexual abuse does not determine one's sexual orientation but cuts survivors off from the normal adolescent exploration of sexual feelings and desires and leaves her unsure of her truest sexual orientation. As Katie describes, *"It did add confusion and questioning to my ability to come to terms with my sexual orientation."*

Don Clark, in *Loving Someone Gay* (1997), speculates that gay people may be "more vulnerable to the loss of awareness of our feelings than the average adult because our feelings are so invalidated from the first day we become aware of homosexual and related gay feelings." Clark writes, "It is not only the awareness of gay feelings that becomes dulled, but all feelings.... You begin to dislike your feelings. You do not trust them because they might get you into trouble." This disconnect is further complicated for lesbian survivors whose feelings of same-sex attraction are complicated by their sexual abuse experience. Being a lesbian survivor complicates the development of a healthy sexual identity and the coming-out process. According to Woititz (1989), this occurs because "Children in sexually abusive situations do not learn to feel good about their sexual selves. If you do not feel good about your sexual self and also desire your own sex, you are double damned. You now have a very large secret to keep." Lesbian survivors may feel that they need to protect their sexual identity at all costs.

Some researchers have found that one response to sexual abuse is for a woman to turn away from heterosexuality and embrace a lesbian orientation (Courtois, 1988). They found, as I did, that some women believe that their lesbianism is the direct result of their abuse experience and its aftereffects, particularly a fear and distrust of men and an aversion to heterosexual sex. In relationships with women, they seek the safety and security that they believe is impossible with men. Maltz (1991) believes that sexual abuse does not exactly cause a particular orientation, but for at least some survivors it can have a profound influence. This influence can either encourage or impede the development of a particular orientation. Survivors may move toward or against the orientation they had in the abuse (Maltz, 1991). Maltz and

Holman (1987) divided women in their study who had sexual relations with other women into two groups: (1) heterosexual women or bisexual women open to experimentation with female partners as part of either their prerecovery coping efforts or their incest recovery process; and (2) lesbians who are also incest survivors. Conversely, same-sex orientation can be blocked by anger at women (encouraged by anger at a mother who failed to protect, societal discrimination, religious nonacceptance, and a survivor's preference for celibacy as a result of the abuse (Maltz and Holman, 1987).

Survivors, lesbian or straight, go through a period where they may be conflicted about their sexual orientation. This is a natural part of the coming-out process for lesbians that is further complicated by their history of sexual abuse. When they remember having a sexual response to the abuse—a natural reaction to genital stimulation, whatever the sex of the abuser—they are often disturbed by these reactions. This negative experience of *sexual imprinting*, according to Prendergast (1996), can lead survivors to always associate sex with negative feelings. As Misha explained, "*I think that my experiences of abuse by both a woman and a man simply shut me down sexually.*" Survivors who were abused by a woman may continue to respond sexually to women and may feel uncomfortable with this and may be confused about whether or not they are lesbian. For survivors of same-sex incest, the confusion over sexual orientation can be tremendous. Sexual abuse is a form of conditioning. Munro (2002) writes, "As a result, sexual abuse survivors can be drawn to or be repulsed by things that have nothing to do with their authentic selves and have more to do with their abuse." According to Munro, "Discovering our authentic sexuality involves weeding through layers of conditioning that arose from sexual abuse, as well as other forms of conditioning, to find your deeper, more soulful self where you know who you are and what you want." As we know, sexual abuse hurts, but it can't touch our souls. Same-sex incest should not be assumed to indicate a homosexual orientation on the part of the perpetrator, but rather a traumatic reenactment of the perpetrator's own sexual molestation and therefore a traumatic stress response (Groth, 1982).

"It is not easy for me to admit that I am a lesbian because of the abuse. But I am. Before it happened I was never attracted to girls. After it happened I was never really attracted to males. I think as a result of my stepsister I became a lesbian and a sexually aggressive one." —Amy

Being abused by a man can affect a survivor's sexual orientation when she avoids relationships with men and chooses intimate relationships with women. Survivors who were abused by men may be revolted by sexual relations with men because they bring back memories of the abuse. In this way, Forward and Buck (1988) suggest that lesbianism can be a defensive flight from men. This type of reaction to incest is not the norm, but neither is it unusual.

"I think I may have had a tendency to be gay, and then [the abuse] happened. So it sort of pushed me over to that side." —Elizabeth

"My early experience made me afraid of sexual aggression in men. It took away my feelings of safety and my ability to relate sexually with men. I'm attracted to women. I find women's bodies beautiful, period. I could have been on either side of the fence, but when you take away one side... Safety with women allows me to experience sexually." —Kathy

"I'm inclined to think the abuse had no effect on my sexual identity, but maybe that's just the politically correct thing for a lesbian to think. I'm a person at the extreme end of the sexual continuum with virtually no interest in the opposite sex; in fact, it would suit me if there were no opposite sex. At the very least, though, I think the abuse was reinforcing of my inclination to prefer women. I think the fact that the persons who abused me sexually were male definitely reinforced what I consider my natural inclination to be a homosexual. I'm grateful to both of my abusers for making my choice to follow my natural inclination to be a lesbian more clear-cut." —Levie

"I think I could have gone either way, but fear has caused me to be gay." —Naomi

"The abuse was a real focus of my depression. I would ruminate on the sexual abuse and associate it with my being a lesbian. I didn't feel bad that I was a lesbian. But, in a way, I was kind of angry if indeed the abuse caused or had some connection to my sexual orientation. It made me angry that not only was the perpetrator subjecting me to abuse that caused my life to be adversely affected...not only did he abuse me, but at the time I was thinking it may have caused me to be gay—so he subjected me to not only abuse but also a lifetime of punishment and social injustice. And I didn't see it as fair for quite some time." —Lyndsey

"I turn to women because they're safer." —Kyrce

Overall, do women become lesbians because they've had bad experiences with men? If all the women who had bad experiences with men became lesbians, there would be many more lesbians than heterosexual women. The fact is, bad experiences with men do not "make" heterosexual women lesbians. Many survivors wonder if they would have been lesbian if they had not been abused. There is no way, of course, of knowing the answer to this question. But avoiding relationships with men does not make you attracted to women. As therapist Kali Munro (2002) says, "Sexual abuse cannot create your sexual desires, and cannot make you gay. Some lesbians are afraid of men because of abuse in their history or are terrified of women because of abuse in their history. Lesbian survivors' reactions to sexual abuse are not any different from those of straight women. As Elizabeth said, *"I feel a true, deeply rooted disdain for men in their late teens and early 20s, the age my abuser was."* There is, of course, nothing wrong with being lesbian, although some women still find this difficult to accept in themselves and others. The most important thing is feeling comfortable with your choice of partner and with yourself. Mental health professionals who formed a panel to discuss lesbian survivors in a videotaped program (Eide, 1993) stated that "in their practice they see no documentation or evidence of a correlation between lesbianism and a history of incest or other childhood sexual abuse."

This is how survivors describe their own struggles to reconcile their lesbian identity with their history of abuse:

"I felt dirty first of all because of the abuse and now gay too. I couldn't handle both things. It was really hard. For some people it might be easier, but for me it was harder to know that he might have been the reason for my sexuality." —Diana

"I used to think that my feelings for women were a direct result of the abuse. When I was in college, I went to therapy for the first time to 'fix my fucked-up sexuality.'" —Mo

"Am I a lesbian because my father did this? I would just not think about it." —Liz

"The weird thing about my coming-out was that it was happening about the same time I was coming out to friends and family about the abuse. So more than a few people thought the two came hand-in-hand. One friend actually said she couldn't accept my being gay because she didn't think it was 'real.' She felt it was a result of the abuse and I was just confused." —Mary

"For a long time I might have thought being queer was a result of being abused." —Pat

"In some ways the whole myth—'You are a lesbian because you've had bad experiences with men'—may be true. Why wouldn't it be true that someone could make a choice to be involved with women because they've had bad experiences with men? That makes logical sense to me. So that was something that I really had to think about, especially early on." —Margie

I was 21 when I came out to myself in the context of my first lesbian relationship. I felt tremendous shame and feared what a lesbian lifestyle meant about the dreams I had for myself and my parents' expectations for me. I was convinced that my lesbianism—as much as I reveled in my first loving relationship with a woman—was a result of my fear of and disgust with men. I believed at the time that years of sexual abuse at the hands of my older brother had turned me against men and ruined my chance for the fairy tale of marriage and "happily ever after." Before interviewing women for this book I'd never had the opportunity to ask other lesbian survivors if they wondered about their sexual identity in this way.

As we have heard, many survivors questioned their lesbianism and believed there was a causal relationship between it and their sexual abuse history. There were, however, also those who expressed no concern about any possible connection between these.

"I never questioned my sexuality. I never had a problem with it." —Julie

"I could really care less about what people think about me and who I love and how I love. Maybe the abuse has something to do with my being gay, but if it does, I really don't care because I'm happy this way." —Lyndsey

"I honestly don't think the two are related. I have never for a minute wished I wasn't gay. I'm happy about who I am, and I would never trade being gay. I like being different. I like that there is a world of diversity and not everyone lives exactly the same way. I'm never angry at 'having to be' a lesbian." —Mary

"I don't view my abuse as relevant to my sexual identity. It's more related to my personal politics and how I express my sexual identity. For the most part my inner circle has always been female." —Lisa

"I think you're born with it." —Debbie

Others believed that being a lesbian is a choice they have made.

"I think I had a choice to be lesbian or straight. I chose lesbianism." —Laura

"I feel it was my choice." —Marie

"My lesbianism was an energy thing, very positive. I wouldn't want to give the abuse that credit or power." —Wendy

"I feel that the abuse caused me to have a big mistrust of men, but I don't feel as if it has any bearing on my desire for women. I don't think it controls who you're attracted to." —Kristie

"I'm a lesbian. I don't think I would have gone through the trouble to be with women otherwise. After I had my first relationship with a woman I thought, This is the answer." —Chris

"My lesbianism has nothing to do with my having been abused." —Sue

"I don't blame anyone for me being a lesbian. I love who I am and God wanted me to be this way." —Melissa

"I made a choice not to be with men. Men make me feel connected to the abuse. I have issues with men. I have no male friends or contact with men and no desire to. I recalled the abuse when having sex with men. I'm hesitant to say I'm lesbian because I was abused. Abuse does not lead to lesbianism. The relationship is not causal. —Amanda

"The energies are more congruent in female-female relationships for me. I do not blame the sexual abusers for 'turning me gay.' I am who I am regardless of the shit they did to me. Spiritually I feel I'm gay because that is the highest path I could walk in this lifetime, and I can truly honor that in myself." —Cristi

"I think lesbianism is part of me and would have surfaced without the abuse. I think lesbianism, for me, is inherent. I am lesbian at my core, or essence, but I still had to make a choice to live that out." —Misha

What these survivors' words reveal is that questioning their lesbianism was their internalized homophobia talking. They found themselves believing society's negative attitudes toward gay men and lesbians and had turned this hatred on themselves. As Kirsten realized, *"I always say that I dislike men because of my experiences with them and that I don't date men because I'm gay. Those are two different things."*

What many lesbians described was a process in which, once they had some distance from their abuse, they were able to recognize the signs that they had been lesbian from an early age and that their lesbian identity was a positive force in their lives. The women also described their affinity for women, the way they valued their time with other women even before they identified themselves as lesbian.

"I have always known somewhere inside of me that I am a lesbian." —Pat

"I figured out that I've always had feelings for women. So I came to the conclusion that I am who I am and I was born this way." —Lyndsey

"I always had an aversion to men and a bond with girls." —Nedhera

"I was very clearly attracted to, and had very close relationships with, girls from early on. So when I became aware of that, it helped me with identity issues. The abuse was really incidental to my sexual identity." —Margie

"For me, it was a discovery. I don't believe that my aunt's abusing me sexually turned me into a lesbian. I think I would have been a lesbian whether I was abused by a man or a woman." —Nedhera

"I am glad to be a lesbian. I just wished that things had begun with consent. Not rape. I would like to be proud of the way I became a lesbian." —Amy

"Am I a lesbian survivor, or am I a survivor that happens to be a lesbian? I think the 'happening to be a lesbian' is more my orientation, rather than as a lesbian and everything coming from that. I think the fact that my abuser was a woman is almost inseparable from my desire

for nurturing. When your mother is your abuser, then your desire for nurturing is perverted. My love for closeness with women is intense, but I really don't think that the abuse from my mother made me a lesbian. I see sexual orientation as something completely different." —Jill

"I came to realize that being gay was a true part of who I am, not something that was wrong and needed to be fixed." —Mo

"I remember going through puberty, going through school, where sex was pretty much the last thing on my mind. Boys, OK, I was doing that. But I really valued my girlfriends." —Jill

"I have a deep connection to other women. It feels really good to connect spiritually with other women. I feel a lot of power when I connect with other women in that way." —Nedhera

In my own experience, I have found myself alternately disgusted with and fascinated by men. I feel a physical attraction to men at the same time that I find their physical anatomy ugly, overpowering, and offensive. I am beginning to recognize that the abuse taught me that my body had value in pleasing a man and my body continues to react in a sexual way to men's physical presence. Well into adulthood I put myself in situations where I was looking for love in sexual encounters with men. Others described an aversion to men that complemented their attraction to women.

"And that thing with men—I don't have any curiosity. I don't feel attracted to them. Even though I have many guy friends, I keep more of a distance from them." —Diana

"I couldn't figure out why all my friends were talking about boys and were starting to sleep with boys and that didn't interest me. They were talking penis size and things of that nature, and it just disgusted me. When we were in mixed parties where we were going out with guys, it was always uncomfortable for me. I never liked it. Some guy would try

and slobber on me, and I would say, 'Just get off me.' I always had an aversion to men." —Nedhera

In *Married Women Who Love Women,* Carren Strock (1998) writes, "Most of the women who knew about their feelings for other women believed that if they kept active, the feelings would go away...eventually their pent-up frustrations drove them to find a recipient for their love, or that special someone came along, making it impossible to deny their true selves any longer." C.J. explains, *"Society would like to believe that abuse makes women lesbian. But I gave it the All-American try being married for 20 years."*

It's common to have doubts and questions in the coming-out process. The key to knowing your sexual orientation is paying attention to your feelings of attraction. It can be difficult to be honest with ourselves when society is so unaccepting. More often than not, lesbians are aware of their feelings toward women long before they consider themselves lesbians. According to Clark (1977), a great deal of effort goes into explaining to ourselves why we have these feelings. We struggle with our own internalized homophobia and censor our own feelings as well as condemn others who appear or "act gay."

"It was a very, very good experience to come to the realization that I was gay." —Jill

Some women I spoke with were reassured that they could predate their lesbian feelings to a time before the abuse began.

"It made the borders a little less muddied to be able to think that this is clearly the path I was on anyway." —Margie

"I'm glad I can predate the abuse with lesbian thoughts and feelings. The abuse did not cause me to be lesbian. I didn't have the name 'lesbian' as a child, but I felt that way since I was 3 or 4. This is a women-first thing, not a fear of men." —Marty

"It makes me feel better to know that I was attracted to women early on. My body wouldn't respond to women if the attraction was only mental. I feel good and healthy around my partner. We have a normal life. If I were running, it wouldn't be that way." —Amanda

For some survivors, identifying as lesbian is uncomfortable because it's a sexual identity and they're not comfortable with sex. It can feel like being a lesbian puts an emphasis on the sexual part of you that you find unsettling. But there is more to being a lesbian than sex, of course. There's an emotional, philosophical, and spiritual connection to women. The people in your life may make being a lesbian an uncomfortable experience for you. If you're closeted and lack lesbian role models who are comfortable and relaxed in their sexual identity and you can't be open with anyone around you, the stress this creates can be particularly painful for you as a survivor. According to Bass and Davis (1988), "The secrecy, isolation, shame, and fear of exposure are very close to the feelings you had when you were abused. So if being a lesbian is the second secret you've had to keep, it can bring up unresolved feelings of terror, isolation, and pain." The concept of double invisibility—child sexual abuse and lesbianism—has been identified as unique to lesbian survivors (Hall, 1999; Hall and Lloyd, 1993; Nichols, 1987).

Reaching out to other lesbians can counter your sense of isolation. As you heal, your lesbian identity can become a strong, positive force in your life. According to the Boston Lesbian Psychologies Collective (1987), there is great variability within the lesbian experience:

> There is no single lesbian identity, nor is there a single lesbian identity development.... Some of us choose to be lesbians because we have found that in our relationships with women the spiritual qualities and psychological and emotional connections give us great satisfaction and empower us with our own potentials. Some of us choose to be lesbians for more strictly political reasons in order to counter heterosexual privilege and to develop nonaggressive and nonhierarchical structures for interpersonal relationships—that is, to live in egalitarian relationships with our lovers, friends, and community. Others of us

> feel that our connections and attractions have always been exclusively to women and that a lesbian identity has led us to discover who we are despite the lack of models available to us. Others feel we were born lesbians.... For some of us, the choice to live a lesbian lifestyle is an explicit choice not to live the lives of our parents, and more particularly the lives of our mothers.

I remember the first time I kissed a woman and realized I could be gay. It came as a surprise then, although looking back I recognize the signs of my attraction for women as early as junior high. But it wasn't until I was involved in an intimate relationship with a woman that I really allowed myself to think about what this attraction meant. I had dated boys through school and, up until the evening when I first kissed a woman, had been actively pursuing relationships with men—never mind that my relationships were always based on sex and had very little emotional connection. I believed that that was what heterosexual relationships were like. When I first kissed a woman —the woman who is now my life partner—I was amazed by her softness and the gentleness of her touch. I felt an almost spiritual connection to her that I had never experienced before in my life. It felt like coming home. It felt like knowing myself for the first time through my connection with another woman. Here are some survivors' reflections on what it means to be a lesbian.

"I am not a lesbian because I hate men; I am one because I love females." —Robin

"I have always known that I love girls." —Kirsten

Many women described the nurturing they received from women. Eileen Starzecpyzel (1987) identified "an intense longing for a nurturing, positive relationship with a woman" among lesbian survivors in her study. For the majority of lesbians Starzecpyzel counseled, there was a "conscious awareness of intense longing for mother, which is manifested through sexual desires for women and conscious wishes for the nurturing and holding of which they have never received enough." Starzecpyzel concludes, "The primary wound of incest is the loss of the mother bond." Interestingly, for lesbians, this loss of the mother causes a separation of the girl from her mother that "allows her a measure of personal power and creative flexibility in choosing more freely the appropriate personal relationship that best meets her needs." According to Starzecpyzel (1987), "It seems that a turning away from the identification with the mother and a preference for identifying with the father is sometimes an important factor in the formation of lesbian sexual identity." In describing same-sex abuse, Eide (1993) believes "abuse of a female child perpetrated by a female caregiver…complicates woman-to-woman relationships for survivors, given what is known about mother-daughter dynamics, e.g., bonding issues." The implications of same-sex abuse for women are not fully understood, although Starzecpyzel's research suggests issues around bonding in intimate relationships for lesbian survivors.

In *Growing Through the Pain* (Anonymous, 1989), an incest survivor writes:

> To reconnect, we must listen to ourselves, find our own voices for the first time." Starzecpyzel (1987) theorizes that lesbian survivors' separateness from their mothers "gives an incest survivor the empowerment to heal, and to heal with the richness and diversity that allows her the flexibility to look beyond the cultural restrictions in the life solutions she creates. For this reason, lesbian life choices may be more visible in incest survivors because the survivor's freedom leads her more easily to the choice of a woman who can provide the best and most fulfilling relationship for her. In our culture, the most empowered woman is the woman who does not need to please men.

Frequently lesbian survivors lack a clear sense of who they are and don't feel a right to define themselves. Only after they begin to acknowledge their pain and understand and accept that the abuse was not their fault can they begin to turn their lives around. We own the right to define who we want to be (Somers, 1992). Owning our lesbianism is an important piece of defining who we are.

"How could I blame my abuser for the fact that I now have a wonderful relationship with a woman?" —Mollie

"I got involved in gay organizations in college. I just wasn't sure about myself. I had never gone out with a girl. When I let a girl get close to me I said to myself, "I don't like her, but if I kiss her, I'll find out if I'm gay." But then I kissed her and it didn't mean anything. One book I read talked about how you can recognize if someone is gay by looking deep into their eyes. And I remember going into buses looking at people to see if anyone would look me in the eyes." —Diana

"I think I was lesbian from very young. In fact, one of my childhood friends asked me, 'Do you remember when your father thought we were lesbians?' That sort of tells me early on there was a perception I that I was a lesbian. I had a couple of lesbian affairs, then I got married. I had 13 years of that, and then I said, 'OK, I really am a lesbian. I've been through this fucking detour for the last 20 years. And so, let's get real!' I was in a psych hospital at the time, and I had this wonderful lesbian relationship there. It completely blew me out of the closet. It was like all of a sudden, all these things—all right, I'm a lesbian." —Jill

"I started having crushes on girls in high school. There was an incident when I was a sophomore in high school where I had my first realization that, yes, I really was a lesbian, although I didn't have that word. I remember being in the locker room, and there was a girl from one of my classes there. I've never seen a teenager of that age who had such confidence about her body. She was very muscular, not body-builder muscular, but defined. You could see muscles all over her. She was walking around the locker room talking with her friends completely stark naked. Everyone else was rushing into towels because we all had this body shyness. I was mesmerized by this girl walking around the locker room—by her confidence, by the fact that I was looking at her body. Her body was just beautiful to me and I started to get incredibly turned on. Even though I could see that people were beginning to make comments—noticing me staring—I couldn't take my eyes off her until one of her friends pointed to me. I turned away and blushed furiously. She didn't approach me, but

turned back to her friends. I was just blushing until I was purple, looking down at the floor, going into my locker, hiding my head, you know, doing whatever I could to try and save the situation and get out of there fast. Apparently, though, she said something to the teacher. The teacher understood—I suspected that she might have been a lesbian herself—and just said, 'She felt really uncomfortable when you were staring at her.' And I said, 'I'm sorry. I couldn't help it. It won't happen again.' And I started crying. And she said, 'It's OK. You didn't harm her.' She asked me if I wanted to talk with her. And I said, 'No, I can't talk.' For the rest of the semester I made sure that I got in and out of the locker room as quickly as possible. But it had just gotten branded on my brain. Then I started reading some literature and the slang that I'd heard was bull-dagger. What they were describing was a very butch woman, dressed like a man. And I thought 'I'm not a bull-dagger. That doesn't describe me.' From there, though, I found a very basic definition of lesbian—women who love women. And that sounded like me. That was in high school, I was maybe 15." —Nedhera

"I think the relationship between surviving abuse and coming out as a lesbian is an important issue. I think you have to realize that growing up in the '50s was really different. Women were pretty tightly defined. Also, sexual abuse was not discussed, so I thought I was the only person sexually abused and that it was my fault. I also thought it was really bad to be homosexual. I had a lot of confusion over these things, and I think it made it difficult to come to terms with my sexual identity and orientation." —Pat

"I was confused as to whether my attraction to women was simply a result of the abuse. But once I kissed a woman for the first time, I realized that I had been missing out. It was like, 'Wow! So this is what all the fuss is about!' I had never really been into kissing and sex and the like. I certainly was from that day forward!" —Mary

I was always the teacher's pet—to all my female teachers anyway. As early as third grade I remember having a crush on my young female teachers. I would volunteer for special privileges, give gifts for every occasion, and stay after school for additional help. I was very close to my girlfriends in school and preferred hanging out with them to dating boys. My connection with women was always at the core of my existence as it continues to be today.

The subject of lesbian survivors is controversial because people want to resolve the question of whether the abuse "caused" the lesbianism. Even discussing abuse and lesbianism at the same time is not politically correct. Marian told me, *"I am so offended by this question."* I feared that by telling people that I was a lesbian survivor they would conclude that the childhood sexual abuse had "caused" my lesbianism. "No," I wanted to tell them. "Being gay is wonderful, and while it's not a choice, I would choose it if I could." To suggest that something as ugly and painful as the abuse contributed to my ability to love another woman deeply and build a healthy and satisfying relationship with her strikes me as impossible. I recognize now that I was always gay; I suffered great pain at the hands of my brother in my preadolescent and adolescent years, but that did not make me gay. I am proud to be a lesbian. He could not have caused this. He only caused pain and anguish. It is a testament to the human spirit that I emerged from the destruction of my childhood to create a loving bond with a woman. I was abused by a man and I go to women, and other survivors were abused by women and turn to women. I think that lesbian survivors call all lesbians' sexual identity into question because we suggest that the abuse may have been a factor in our being women-loving women. Maybe it's more about public perception. As Nedhera was told by other lesbians, *"Don't tell your story because of what other people are going to think."*

"What I found surprising in recent years is how people look at this, especially in the lesbian community. They talk about childhood sexual abuse, but it's only relevant and urgent and immediate if you're not an adult survivor of it. If you're a child and you've been pulled out of the situation, then there should be concern. But if you bring it up as an adult, other lesbians, even ones who may have had the same experience, just shut you down. It's like they don't want to hear it. 'You shouldn't talk about it anymore. It's over. You should have gotten over this.' And what

you're saying to them is 'Yes, I've done the therapy, but there is going to be lasting damage.' It doesn't mean I shouldn't be able to talk about it. I should be able to tell you about all of the experiences of my life." —Nedhera

"When people say that 'lesbians are women running from bad relationships with men' I always say that if this were true, there would be a real shortage of heterosexual women!" —Pat

"If all the women who had been abused were lesbian, we'd be the majority." —Kathy

"I tell people that two of the worst relationships I've ever had were with women. So why, then, do I not run back to men? I tell them that being gay has nothing to do with who I am in a relationship with, it is about who I am. I am attracted to women. I am connected to women. I love women. That is what makes me a lesbian!" —Mary

Golden (1987) shares several definitions of lesbian that capture the variability of lesbian identity and some of the tension within the lesbian community. Adrienne Rich uses the term *lesbian continuum* to refer to the range of women-identified experiences, and Blanche Wiesen Cook defined a lesbian as a woman who loves women, who chooses women to nurture and support and to create a living environment within which to work creatively and independently, whether or not her relations with these women are sexual.

From the wreckage of their childhoods, these survivors have emerged to claim their lives again and to celebrate their sexual identity as lesbians, however they define that.

"If my cousin's abusing me was the reason for my being a lesbian, then something good came out of this. Like I told my mom, 'If you want me to be happy, then this is the way you have to accept me.'" —Diana

"I'm so happy right now. Believe me. Right now, everything's gravy." —Jill

"I'm all out, all the time." —Reg

"I came out as a full-fledged lesbian six years ago. I am currently embracing the fluidity of my sexuality, the right to exercise control over my body, and the expression of my sexuality." —Noemi

"My partner said it best. 'They raped you because you were a lesbian.' I had this energy for life because I am me, which includes being a lesbian. They wanted to steal this energy from me. I can understand why people think that lesbians are women running from men. Ignorance is bliss. People want answers for the things in life that they don't understand. I truly believe I was gay in the womb. It just took me a darn long time to come out." —Delphene

"I don't blame my abusers for my lesbianism. No way! I don't think abuse causes sexual identity." —Lynn

"I think this butchness and attraction to women would be me even if I grew up with healthy, loving parents. In fact, I see them as a saving grace for me even though it's just coincidental. All my life choices are different from those of the rest of the women in my family, which were to settle down, have a bunch of kids with an abusive man, gain a lot of weight, and be really unhappy and miserable and not know why or be able to do anything about it. I don't have that housewife mold to live up to. It's not the only reason I got myself out of the abusive cycle, but if it's related at all, it's only in a good way." —Cory

"Overall, I feel good about myself as a lesbian. I work hard on this. Sometimes I fall into the trap of feeling like I should protect people from having to deal with my lesbianism, but I have countered that by being right out there in their faces about it. I am not really openly affectionate in public, but I say what I think and let it be out there." —Pat

"It seems to me that people are just born one way or another and the only choice you have is whether you feel things deeply enough to face the truth. I am proud to be a lesbian." —Deborah

"I don't think the abuse affected my sexuality. It was just natural. I'm just me." —Julie

Levie describes the parallel experiences of being lesbian and a survivor of child sexual abuse. It is the sense of being doubly oppressed or victimized (Courtois, 1988):

"It seems to me that lesbians and survivors face a number of similar challenges. Both must deal with secrecy, isolation, grief, shame, and a sense of having been wronged, abandoned, or scorned by society. They also both have reason to feel scared, unprotected, and mistrustful. On the other hand, they are feared as possible predators or recruiters. Both are certainly misunderstood and discounted. Many in both categories feel the need to protect their families from pain and shame, and one way to do that is to distance themselves from their families. Some fear being thrown out of their families if they reveal being either a lesbian or a survivor. For women who are both lesbians and survivors the intensity of each of these challenges is automatically doubled, or even multiplied."

My whole life was dominated by having to suppress something socially unacceptable that had been done to me, and now I have this socially unacceptable sexual nature." —Tammy

I was surprised to learn from several of the women I spoke with that there is a hierarchy of lesbians out there. Despite my belief in one lesbian community, survivors told me of communities where lesbians who had had sexual relations with men—even in the context of childhood sexual abuse—were accused of not being "real" lesbians.

As Noemi told me, *"Lesbians, especially during my coming-out process, accused me of not being a real lesbian."*

Coming Out

"I had a deep, core urge or desire for a woman. I was so happy when I called myself a lesbian. Yay! This is what I really want." —Lynn

"I love women, and I don't just mean I love being in love with a woman. I really care about women and the issues we face. I respect women and like everything about them, their bodies, their hearts, souls, and minds. I like female determination and strength. I love the way I feel when I'm in a large group of women. I like power in numbers. I like being a feminine feminist." —Elizabeth

Within the lesbian community coming out is seen as a rite of passage, a celebration of our love for women and the claiming of our sexuality. For some of us, this process was a gradual realization of our love for women and a commitment to spending our lives loving women. We knew early on that we were attracted to women and coming out to ourselves was the first step in the process.

"I was fascinated with girl peers at age 4. It felt the same as it does now." —Kyrce

"I knew I liked girls when I was 4. I went to Disney World and Snow White kissed me." —Reg

"I knew I liked girls from a very young age. By high school I had experimented with two of my girlfriends. Whether I knew what to call it or not, I was a lesbian. I never had a boyfriend, never went to a prom, none of that 'boy stuff.'" —Delphene

"In fourth grade I had a female make-out partner. I always felt drawn to women." —Wendy

"I remember my friends talking about their boyfriends, and I was never interested in anyone. I would always push guy friends away for some reason. But I always had big crushes on girls." —Diana

"My feelings for other girls were already there in junior high or high school. Remember Meg Christian's song about the gym teacher? I loved my gym teacher, but it was because she was so pretty and feminine. And there was an English teacher. Oh, God, I thought she looked as beauti-

ful as Elizabeth Taylor. I brought her irises from my mother's garden." —Jacque

"I used to cruise the lingerie section of the Sears catalog as a kid. And I still remember the scent of my beautiful second grade teacher." —Pat

"I knew I was gay in sixth grade. I was vocal with my parents about it at age 12. I was a motorcycle dyke, an unabashed dyke." —Jan

"I think I knew I was gay as far back as fourth or fifth grade because I would get these terrible crushes on my female teachers." —Lisa

"When I was in junior high I watched a show on gay and lesbian people. I told my mom, 'That's what I want to be.'" —Debbie

"I like kissing women. No man has made me excited. Martina does." —Dana

"When I was 16 I met a woman. She was 24. We played softball together." —Julie

"I feel I was born a lesbian. I always felt drawn to women. I feel safer with women. When I identified as a lesbian at age 11, it was great! I felt really powerful." —Wendy

"I remember at a very young age being captivated by women. Some of the young house mothers at the orphanage would go braless and I was fascinated by the movement of their breasts under their thin blouses. I was aware of wanting the closeness of a female body. I've always known to myself that I am lesbian." —Marian

"I was out at 14. Finally, I had a name for this feeling I had. Then everyone knew. I did very little closet time." —Reg

If a lesbian manages to develop a romantic relationship with another woman during high school, she frequently does so with friends (Diamond, 2002). Often the transformation of a friendship into a sexual relationship is a woman's first experience with lesbian sexuality, as Whitney describes.

"When I was a senior in high school my relationship with my best friend turned into a sexual relationship. It was the spark of my wondering."

"Senior year of high school I met Sharon. I was 16, she was 13. She really rocked my world! We had a lot in common: softball, music. We shared a platonic and respectful relationship. I think she was priming me for what was to come. She helped me to understand that what I was feeling was normal and OK." —Whitney

For many survivors, their coming-out process was negatively affected by society's prejudice about lesbians. Although many recognized their attractions to other women, they denied these feelings because they didn't want to identify as lesbian. External pressures affecting lesbians include social stigma, prejudice and discrimination, and lack of societal and familial support and validation (Garnets, 2002b).

"I've had experiences and relationships with women since I was 15, but I never really thought I was gay. It took a long time to feel good about myself and to know this is who I am, truly." —Brooke

"I remember attachments to girlfriends and being called a 'fucking fairy.' I was closeted to myself. I came out at 27 and then it was safe not to wear layers of clothing." —Kyrce

"It took me a long time to realize that I'm actually a lesbian. I suppose that was me from a young age. I remember when I actually said, 'OK, if I'm having sex with girls, it probably means something. No one else is having sex with girls except the other girls who call themselves lesbians. I may actually be one.'" —Liz

"I was more comfortable with girls than boys when I was growing up, but I didn't want anyone to think that I was a lesbian so I never

acted on any feelings that I might have felt for a female friend." —Maggie

"I knew my whole life that I was a lesbian, but I was afraid to be me." —Sarah

"I've known for so long. I finally had to stop denying it to myself. I think the abuse helped me finally come out because I said, 'I don't want to be with a man.' I never have. I won't put up with this anymore when I can be with someone I'm actually attracted to and who will hopefully love me." —Kim

"I was not fully in touch with myself during high school. I think I was attracted to women, but I am not completely sure. I wanted to please a woman, but it was not something I thought I could pursue. In the military I struggled with the 'right' thing to do and what I was 'trained' to do with men. One lesbian tried to make an advance. I French-kissed her, but felt nothing. I became even more confused when I met my partner years later. I could stand next to her, touch her hand, hug her, or even look into her eyes and be sexually excited. I tried very hard to deny the feelings of attraction. No one has ever made me feel sexually aroused without touching! It was truly amazing once I was able to identify it. However, it was hard to accept because it was not what I was raised to know to be the 'right thing.' I was taught women were to be with men." —Marie

"I kept my coming out to myself for a while. I fought it, telling myself I was just having fun. I was so afraid to label myself because I had no explanation for what was happening. Because of the abuse, I questioned whether or not I was really coming out or just acting out sexually. Again, I didn't want to blame anything on the abuse. Not labeling myself was what helped me personally. To this day, three years later, I am no raging lesbian, but I am comfortable with who I am. I took it for what it was—an attraction to women—and I followed it." —Juli

"I knew I was attracted to girls when I was in high school, but I didn't tell anyone. I could hardly put words around it in my own head, let

alone out loud. My Catholic upbringing made it just so scary. Then I worked with a woman who was out. She was very comfortable with her sexuality, and I was able to ask her lots of questions. She was always prepared to answer them honestly and share from her experience." —Misha

"I had been attracted to women sexually—I'm particularly fond of breasts—since high school. I denied the implications, reasoning that gays cannot go to the highest heaven. I was going to the highest heaven, therefore I cannot be gay. A number of people had accused me of being a lesbian. These occurrences were derogatory and left me enraged. Finally I came to the point where I decided that if so many other people had noticed this in me, perhaps I should take an honest look at myself. So I read and I studied, and I concluded that I was indeed gay." —Cristi

"I had girlfriends when I was in junior high. In high school it was the whole lesbian thing, the uniform. I didn't think that I was what they were because I didn't want to wear the flannel shirt. I thought something was wrong with me because I wanted to wear dresses and heels." —Kris

The experience of surviving sexual abuse as a child also factors in here. In denying our sexual feelings and responses—as we were conditioned to do with the abuse—we also distanced ourselves from our growing realization that we are lesbians.

"I came out at 27 and felt a huge loss for what I had been missing all these years. I remember attachments to girlfriends, but I was very secretive about my feelings for women." —Kyrce

"I ended up in a religious Christian commune for eight years. They called it reparative therapy; it was before they had a name for Christians trying to change gays. I managed to submerge my sexuality even more. I was celibate for a whole decade and emerged from that thinking I was heterosexual." —Jill

"I had feelings for women since I was 8 or 9 and had different affairs, short ones, with women, during my marriage, but kept pushing this back.

Up until three years ago it had been 20 years since I'd been with a woman." —Margaret

"I had no idea I was gay until I was 40. I was in a circle of women in a sweat lodge in a vision quest experience when I came to knowing I'd been a lesbian my whole life." —Mary Lou

Some survivors pursued relationships with men, even marrying, before being able to understand and accept their feelings of attraction for other women.

"My coming-out process was difficult because I was engaged to be married to my high school sweetheart at the time that I was figuring it all out. I told him I was finding myself attracted to women. My feeling at the time was OK, I'm bisexual, but that doesn't mean I have to act on my attractions. *Well, that didn't work out, so he and I separated. Once I made that decision the rest just sort of happened naturally."* —Mary

"I had felt lesbian tendencies for five years before asking my husband for a divorce. I woke up one day that this is who I wanted to be. At that point I had been married to a man for 20 years. I never knew what pleasurable sex—lovemaking—was. I can count on one hand the orgasms I had in 20 years." —C.J.

"In adolescence I would find myself attracted to someone. It would go unfulfilled, and I would push the feeling down. In college I had three- to four-month relationships. I married a man for three months and moved cross-country with him." —Kathy

"I slept with my best friend of five years. It was a total surprise to both of us. When I told my husband he was hurt and tried to kill himself and then told many of our friends and family." —Tammie

"After I was married I began to realize that being a lesbian might not mean you were completely bad. And I started to realize that if I had not married, I would be with a woman." —Pat

In the context of a caring relationship with a therapist, some survivors find the courage to recognize their feelings of lesbian attraction for the first time.

"I realized I was attracted to women as a result of exploring myself openly in therapy. The attractions were there all along. I had just spent so much time focusing outwardly that I never realized my true desires." —Mary

"I had a therapist suggest I was gay. After thinking about it, I realized she was right. Admitting that lifted a tremendous weight off my shoulders. So much, quite suddenly, made a lot of sense." —Sue

I asked survivors how the abuse had affected their coming-out process. This is what they told me.

"I stupidly told my mom that maybe I was gay because of all that happened. I was scared and didn't know what else to say. My family sees my homosexuality as an aberration, not pure, and very unholy. I don't want them to think that about me." —Missy

"It took me years to accept the title society gives us. I've always hated dresses, skirts, jewelry, and makeup. So I guess those are give-aways to my lifestyle. I think many of us hate dresses and skirts because men are attracted to them more and we feel very uncomfortable when men look at us in a sexual way." —Yvonne

"I feel that if I was not abused, I would have had fewer questions about my sexuality. I think that despite the fact that I have gay friends I just thought I had to be with men because for me there was no other possibility. To me it is like a secret and I have been conditioned not to tell, so coming out is that much harder." —Rowan

"The abuse confused me, delayed it, made me think, Oh, great. Now I get to go on down to fourth class citizen, or it might get me killed, or my son taken away from me." —Tammy

"Maybe it took me longer to come out because I didn't want to add another 'freak' element to my shame pile. I wanted to be normal, and at that time and place being a lesbo was a total curse." —Tammie

"First, I decided to be asexual. Then I thought, I'll do both. *Then, finally, it was,* Fuck it, I'm just going to be a dyke." —Noemi

"I don't know if I would have experienced sexual confusion if I had not been abused, but I just accept that I am the way I am." —Maggie

"Because of the abuse by my stepsister I was seriously conflicted over being a lesbian and my attraction to straight women." —Amy

"The abuse made me less likely to come out, more fearful of other people's reactions." —Marian

Coming out has been associated with a significant reduction of anxiety and depression, higher self-esteem, greater relationship satisfaction, sense of community, and connection with family and society for lesbians (White and Martinez, 1997). Self-esteem and social support are negatively correlated with depression; it appears that lesbians with higher self-esteem and more social support are buffered from depression (Earle, 1999). A federal study conducted in 1989 found that teenagers struggling with issues of sexual orientation were three times more likely than their peers to attempt suicide (cited in Femafedi, 1994). These findings show the difficulties faced by teenagers who are coming out and suggest ways to ease that process. Further, outness is associated with better psychological health (Anderson and Mavis, 1996; Jordan and Deluty, 1998). Once we begin to accept our feelings of attraction for other women, other, long suppressed, feelings begin to reappear (Clark, 1997).

Lesbians' coming-out has been described as a multidimensional process: (1) Sexual identity formation which encompasses development of lesbian sexuality and awareness of being a lesbian; (2) Disclosure of orientation to others; (3) Sexual expression and behavior; and (4) Lesbian consciousness—how lesbians see themselves in relation to the social environment, including the lesbian and gay communities (Morris, 1997). Michelangelo Signorile (1995) explains, "Coming out of the closet doesn't necessarily mean telling everyone you run into.... What it really means is no longer worrying about being discovered. When coming out is no longer a daunting, burdensome experience but something empowering and liberating that you do every day of your life simply by living out of the closet, you'll know you have successfully completed the Outing Yourself process." Haines (1999) clarifies that a sexually empowered woman is a "woman who is embodied, whose sexual expression is part of herself, and whose sex life is self-defined."

A key to lesbians' self-acceptance is their parents' love, support, and acceptance (Mackay, 1999). Unfortunately, parents often react with shock, disappointment, and shame when they hear their child is gay or lesbian. LaSala (2000) writes, "Disclosure often precipitates a painful family crisis which can lead to cutoffs between members." Specifically, mothers' acceptance of their daughters' lesbianism has been characterized by a "nonlinear progression or sequence of reactions which included denial; feelings of devastation, loss, and self blame; struggle to tolerate; increasing acceptance; and engagement in political or social activities despite residual ambivalence" (Pearlman, 1991). While a mother may be able to accept the fact of the daughter's lesbianism, it may be more difficult for her to accept a partnered daughter, a daughter who is assertive in her lesbianism, a daughter whose appearance and behaviors do not conform to traditional female ideals, or a daughter who is openly affectionate or otherwise clearly in a sexual relationship with another woman. How much more difficult the situation is when our lesbianism is disclosed with our abuse history. Issues surrounding the abuse make lesbian survivors' sexuality particularly loaded.

Sometimes we choose not to come out because we fear the other person's reaction or because we were raised in a different time when homosexuality was more closely guarded.

"During the late 1950s we were virtually all deep in the closet, except to each other. It was similar to belonging to a secret society. I didn't come

out to my father because I feared his rejection and didn't want to disappoint him—basically the same reasons why I didn't come out to much of anyone (except other homosexuals) for about 30 years." —Levie

Coming out to family and friends can be a difficult and painful process for any lesbian. The homophobia or denial of family and friends can make our coming out combative and conflicted.

"I told my stepdad when my partner and I got together. He was initially supportive, but I realized pretty soon after that he had had a lot to drink that evening, probably while I was talking. After that he has been angry and rude to my partner, ignoring her and not allowing her to family occasions." —Misha

"My older brother is a born-again Christian. He cut me off. He won't let me have any contact with his children; he's afraid I'll give them AIDS." —Wendy

"When I came out to my parents I was excommunicated by my family and the church. My parents both died not liking me." —Jan

"My mother knows about the abuse and knows I'm a lesbian and thinks I'm bad news. My real father knows I'm gay, but doesn't know why or doesn't know about the abuse I suffered. He's too old to tell him about it now. When my stepfather found out, he wanted to see me with my girlfriends. He offered me and the lady I lived with money to have sex with his customers to keep them happy while they were in town. He wanted us to prostitute. Never happened." —Laura

"A couple of years ago I came out to my physician of 34 years. In the course of the discussion about my struggles with anxiety, she asked if I could rely more on prayer and religion. I told her that as a lesbian I feel pretty shut out from organized religion. Her reaction was comically classic. She asked if I could give up my homosexuality. When I told here that is what I am to the core, she asked if I could at least give up genital touching with my partner because that is what offends the Lord." —Levie

"My mother wasn't real happy when I came out as a lesbian. I thought she was cool with it until she said, 'Just one question. What did I do wrong?' And I said, 'Better to ask yourself what you did right.' It hurt me that she thought that this was just a phase because I hadn't found a long-term relationship yet." —Nedhera

"Telling my parents was tricky. I'm an only girl, and I didn't know how to tell them not to plan for a big wedding or that there would be no babies from me for my mom to spoil rotten. When a cousin visited and told my grandmother about me, my mother found out. She asked me, 'Are you doing something so bad that you cannot tell your father and I?' Finally, I said, 'Mom, I'm gay.' I thought as long as I told the truth it would be cool. But my mother lost it. She kept saying it was her fault and it was because I dressed and acted like a boy. She actually asked me if I wanted to be a boy. I told her 'No! Why would I want to be a boy if the girl I was with liked me because I was a girl?' It was all very confusing. For the next three years I fought with my mother about my sexuality." —Whitney

"I used to 'play nasty' with the neighborhood girls, as my mother called it. I had welts from the willow sticks where she beat me. A lot was repressed because of the beatings." —C.J.

"I'm out to my family. My brother is also gay. When I started going out with a girl in high school I was convinced that my mother was going to be OK with it. Around St. Valentine's my partner sent me flowers. When I went to the house my mom was crying. I remember she threw the flowers on the floor and said, 'You think I'm stupid? I know you're going out with a woman.' And I said, 'Yes, I am.' My mother gave me hell. It was terrible. I didn't want to be in the house. I avoided being home. It was that feeling that I had betrayed my parents, that I had disappointed them. So that just added to the depression that I was going through at the time." —Diana

"My family knew I was lesbian at 16 and didn't believe me. My mom told me to please wear makeup and go out with boys." —Sarah

"I came out when I was 19. I was seriously involved with a woman at the time. When I told my mother, she was angry and said, 'What is everyone going to think?'" —Kim

"I mailed a letter to my parents, and they both flipped out in a sad, emotional, and disappointed way. We struggled for a long time with how to deal with our differences about my sexuality. My dad is more accepting, but I think he still holds out hope that I'll 'change my mind.'" —Brooke

"When I had my first girlfriend at 19 I had to come out to my family. My mother directly asked me if I was gay, and I said yes because I don't lie. I sat at the table listening to homophobic comments for hours. Living with them was hell." —Kirsten

"My mother confronted me about living with my partner. She said, 'Is she a lesbian?' I said yes, and then all hell broke loose. We spent two days crying and yelling and arguing, and it was just awful! She is still very uncomfortable with it, and we haven't talked about it too much. I feel like I have disappointed her by being gay. My father does not know, although I think he suspects. I am afraid of rejection and of disappointing him. My dad made the abuse stop, and he's my hero. I don't want to hurt him." —Elizabeth

In coming out to our parents many of us see, yet again, their tendency to sweep uncomfortable subjects under the rug—as they did the abuse—in an attempt to keep up the charade of the happy family that has no problems.

"My mother was OK with it. She never talked about it or anything. I believe ignoring everything is her way of dealing." —Melissa

"When I told my mother that I was gay, she had almost no response and she's never mentioned it since. Where most mothers have questions, she hasn't said a thing. It bothers me because I want to know what the root of that is." —Lyndsey

"When I came out to my parents two years ago, they said they'd known for years. My mother was disgusted. Later I got a note from her that said, 'Don't worry about it. We love you.' We never talked about it. This is a theme in my family." —Amanda

"Finally, I wrote my mom a letter. I said, 'If you want me to be happy, then this is the way you have to accept me.' My mother said, 'It's not right, but no one should decide for you. Just be who you are.' After that my mother didn't say anything to me about it." —Diana

Dysfunctional family dynamics and a history of child sexual abuse—incest or otherwise—can complicate an already very complex issue. For incest survivors, coming out to family can resurrect old feelings of shame and powerlessness. Survivors' feelings of responsibility for protecting other people and their feelings—protecting them from their lesbianism as they once protected them from knowledge of the sexual abuse—can be especially painful and overwhelming. Incest survivors told me how they came out to their families.

"I knew what my parents would say, and I didn't want to hear it. When I finally told them, there was brief acceptance, then negative. I was the black sheep of the family." —Tammy

"My dad and I have never talked about my being a lesbian. I came out to my mom, but I did not come out to him. I knew my mom would tell him. And I thought that he'd take it as being because of the abuse, what he did. Now he'll make homophobic comments, stupid stuff. I know he's saying it to get at me, and I say nothing." —Kris

"I wrote my mom to tell her that I wanted to include my partner in a family gathering. She went ballistic and said it was unnatural. My sister says, 'It makes me want to vomit.' My dad couldn't handle it either, and I was officially disowned. I was afraid my father would kill me he was so homophobic. He believed we should gas gays because of AIDS." —Kyrce

"Dad was a card-carrying bigot, so that was worrisome. I feared being tossed out of the house. My folks were the last to know. I had a contingency plan for a high school teacher to take me in if my parents threw me out. Dad asked, 'Was it something I did?' I told him, 'It's not about you. I'm lesbian because I like women.'" —Reg

One of our greatest fears—whether we have accepted our lesbianism or not—is that people will think the abuse caused us to be lesbian. While we may have struggled with these thoughts early in our recovery, hearing others "blame" the abuse in this way triggers feelings of powerlessness and shame once again.

"My mom still thinks it's because of the abuse and prays that I'll find a nice man." —Brooke

"My mother knows of the abuse because of the hospital records she received (when I was hospitalized for depression and attempted suicide). Her reaction hasn't been positive. She uses the abuse to support her theory of my choosing to become gay. She attacks me with the knowledge of it." —Kirsten

"The majority of my family firmly believes my gayness is due to the sexual abuse. But I knew I liked girls from a very young age." —Delphene

Sometimes our coming-out is met with acceptance and love and we are truly blessed.

"Sometime between my first and second relationships I told my mother that I was a lesbian. She wondered if I could change and asked questions about the mechanics of intimacy between women. For a woman who had an eighth-grade education and had lived in a small rural town all of her life she was remarkably accepting and supportive. She routinely treated my partners as in-laws. Early on she advised me to just 'be who you are and hold your head high.' And this was long before anyone talked about gay pride." —Levie

"Surprisingly enough, my grandma has been the most understanding. It did not shake or alter her love for me." —Delphene

Coming out of the closet is a process involving being honest with ourselves and others about our attraction and love for women. Coming out involves telling a secret. In that way, the process of coming out as a lesbian parallels the process of coming out as a survivor. Many of the women I spoke with for this book described the anguish of telling others that they were lesbian and that they had been abused. The shame and fear that accompany these two coming-out processes make being honest with ourselves and others that much more difficult. As Joan described, *"It's a double invisibility. You're invisible because you're lesbian and you're invisible because you were abused."* Father John McNeill (1988), a gay priest, agrees, writing, "The process of coming out—telling others that one is lesbian or gay—is identical with the process of self-acceptance. The risk involved is weighed against the need for external validation." Part of this self-censure arises from the fear that people will think that the abuse made us gay despite the fact that there is no evidence to suggest that sexual abuse has an impact on whether a child has a heterosexual or homosexual orientation (Marcus, 1993).

"I am trying to deal with the shame of having been abused and the shame society imposes on same-sex partnerships." —Maggie

"The coming-out process recreated the feelings of rejection that I had experienced with the abuse. I blamed myself. I thought being lesbian was a result of being abused." —Pat

"Dealing with the abuse memories and then the process of coming out was like a one-two punch. First I was hiding because of the sexual abuse and then being gay. I see them as parallel." —Christy

"For a long time it was just shameful for me to think that I had been broken by a man. When I got to feeling really dirty, I longed for a woman. I call my girlfriend the 'perfect lesbian.' She didn't do any of this. She was

much smarter. Gosh, I wish I could've been like that. I feel like a tainted lesbian. It's just my sick way of thinking." —Tammie

Interestingly enough, survivors described more shame in coming out as a survivor than in coming out as a lesbian.

"It's easier to tell people I am a lesbian than it is to tell them I am an abuse survivor. There is just so much shame and despair in the abuse experience." —Lisa

"I didn't know who to tell about the abuse and whom I could trust. This is also the time I was beginning to find out that I was gay. When I look at everything I did in my life I feel like I might not have chosen to make some of the mistakes I made." —Melissa

"I came out as a woman who had endured incest when I was 30." — Robin

With all of the barriers to coming out and the pain and fear that often accompany it, coming out can be tremendously freeing, as these survivors attest:

"I own my lesbianism. I'm proud to know who I am and how I love others. I am a lesbian deep down within my heart and soul. I have always believed that I have been in the right place as a lesbian." —Whitney

"I told several friends about a year ago, just a sentence in passing, about my being gay. Now I have rainbows in my car and a bracelet and necklace." —Dana

"It hasn't shocked anyone yet. I'm not sure why I was so scared to come out before." —Delphene

"Things were so repressive when I was growing up in the '70s that becoming a lesbian, being a lesbian, saying I was a lesbian, was so freeing." —Jacque

"I think my nature is to be attracted to women. I feel that being a lesbian and having the balls enough to be out in the Deep South is a liberation from having to endure a life of suppressed desire and subordination to the despised male." —Tammy

"When I first came out, it was very safe and healing. Just being able to love is very healing." —Chris

"My partner and I walk hand-in-hand on the street now. It feels good to be more out." —Kyrce

Women who still feel constrained by their lesbianism talk about how they wish they could come out to others more easily.

"I am still coming out. My parents are the only relatives who know. I would like to change that, but I can't seem to find the right words to use. I don't want to hide my identity anymore." —Mollie

"Coming out has been a lifelong process for me. I am torn between thinking that my sex life is no one's business and thinking that people need to know that they have frequent—sometimes daily—contact with homosexuals without ever being aware that we are everywhere." —Levie

In the spirit of "We are Everywhere" and other campaigns to out gay men and lesbians everywhere, Bonnie Zimmerman (1995) argues that "perhaps the problem in contemporary America is not that gays and lesbians and queers are too radical, too out, too open, but that we aren't yet out there enough."

Internalized Homophobia

"I was a lesbian from birth and knew it, but the homophobia got in the way." —Dorian

Growing up and living in a homophobic society, lesbians are exposed to numerous negative attitudes, assumptions, and messages concerning homosexuality. Lesbians may experience minor, but persistent, stress from such daily hassles as having to conceal their sexual identity or hearing insulting jokes or comments about homosexuality (Beals, Impett, and Peplau, 2002). *Internalized homophobia* refers to the incorporation of these homophobic beliefs within our self-image (Frock, 1999). Internalized homophobia is associated with psychological distress and presents a significant threat to our healthy self-esteem and identity development as lesbians. General internalized homophobia has been significantly correlated with overall psychological distress as well as with depression in lesbians (Frock, 1999). Self-identification as a feminist, attitudes toward feminism, involvement in feminist activities, and coping resources were negatively related to lesbian internalized homophobia; in other words, feminist ideals were incompatible with internalized homophobia. When we experience our own power as women, we become unwilling, it seems, to be held to stereotypical notions of what a lesbian—and a woman—is.

According to Michelangelo Signorile (1995) "Every gay person has grappled with internalized homophobia"—the self-loathing, the feelings of powerlessness and hopelessness." Further, your discomfort with certain gay people is a product of your own homophobia. Signorile suggests that "in order for you to live with dignity, you must be able to politely but forthrightly stand up to people whose homophobia adversely affects you." There are those who suggest that most of the problems homosexuals experience are rooted in internalized homophobia. Johnson (2000) writes, "Transforming how we think about our homosexuality allows us to discover that the guilt and shame we feel is a shadow that belongs to mainstream society." Recognizing that that we are innocent of society's claims about us allows us to let go of the shame that generates many of our personal problems.

Internalized homophobia is positively correlated with depression; lesbians experiencing more internalized homophobia suffer higher rates of depression (Earle, 1999), and sexual identity has been identified as a cause of stress for lesbians (Bernhard and Applegate, 1999). Unfortunately, the new social visibility of gay men and lesbians in America has not conquered homophobia. According to

Byrne Fore (2000), hatred of gay men and lesbians stands as the "last acceptable prejudice."

Coming out is complicated by the fact that we live in a society where gay and lesbian people are not openly accepted. The fear and hatred of gay and lesbian people—homophobia—is part of all of us who live where intolerance, indeed violence, against us a very real problem. Tammy told me, *"I'm in middle America, and our home was vandalized. It scared us terribly. It's so awful here. We've been told a lot of BS because of where we live. But we're defiantly staying here. We do well given our circumstances."*

Even as we celebrate our love of women, we wonder how others will look at us, if our friends will still love us, and how we fit into the larger lesbian community. Facing our own internalized homophobia can be a very painful process. Recognizing the ways in which we continue to perpetuate stereotypes about gay and lesbian people, as well as trying to "pass" as straight are ways that we can be honest with ourselves about the ways in which homophobia has power in our lives.

"I hate to admit it, but I guess I still sometimes feel that to be gay is odd, freakish, dirty. Stereotypical lesbians really put me off. They seem dirty somehow. I'm not comfortable with them and I'm not comfortable feeling the way I do about them. I think I'm wrong." —Barbara

"You wouldn't know I am gay by looking at me. I don't fit the profile. In some ways that is good because it takes people like me to prove there is no profile and that being a lesbian is not about wanting to be a man. But it makes it difficult to be out and gets in the way of my being me. Also, people don't want to believe that I'm totally gay (as opposed to bi) because of the way I look." —Juli

Father John McNeill (1998) describes the challenge of internalized homophobia in our lives. "The attitudes that victimize gays are frequently taken in from the family and the church in earliest childhood. These evils are built into the very structure of heterosexual society and thus can easily become part of the gay person's identity. As a result the gay or lesbian adult may be plagued by shame and self-hatred." As

Mollie told me, *"Sometimes I also find myself wondering whether this is who I really am—because if this is who I am, maybe it makes me less of a person."*

I heard the internalized homophobia in the stories survivors told me.

"I am not 100% out in certain situations. I struggle with feeling like I should be completely out. I would love to have children, but my own homophobia worries me about bringing children into a same-sex relationship—both the how to go about it and the raising of kids." —Brooke

"Heterosexuals flaunt it all over the place. I think I try to protect people from my lesbianism." —Pat

"I fear that when I walk down the street and others see me, they will label me as being gay and reject me for that fact." —Marie

"I sometimes feel embarrassed that I am homosexual. I may be silent about my sexual orientation or even deny it." —Katie

"I was transgendered when I was a teen, celibate through my 20s, and a lesbian in my 30s. I still have masculine tendencies, but I have learned to love myself so the need to be a man is no longer there. This was homophobia, wanting to be a man loving women because then I would be straight. I got rid of the homophobia when I left the church." —Dorian

And again survivors told me how their coming out was affected by their abuse history. The two became intertwined and affected their self-esteem and willingness to be open about who they are.

"The abuse definitely delayed my coming out. If you don't like yourself then you won't face yourself or face your future." —Dana

"I think I reflect badly on the lesbian community because of being closeted and also because of my abuse, as if I am ashamed that maybe I am a lesbian because of my past." —Rowan

In addition, homophobia can have a negative effect on lesbians' relationships with their partners. While antigay prejudice can bond lesbian couples in an "us against the world" scenario and increase women's dependence on each other, the reverse is also true (Garnets, 2002b). The invisibility of lesbian relationships creates stress than can estrange lesbian couples; the social isolation and lack of legitimacy can create emotional distance in a couple and contribute to lack of commitment.

Other survivors assert their rights to be and love who they want.

"I am an in-your-face lesbian. We can't be free until we are seen on a daily basis. If my neighbors could hang me and get away with it, they would." —Jan

"I never felt shame as a lesbian. This was other people's problem." —Marty

"One of the really good things about my upbringing is that we were raised with no prejudice toward anyone. I've always had a pretty open mind and really don't feel that I'm homophobic. I think I was homophobic toward myself when I was in high school only because I wasn't ready to face it and was in fierce denial. But I never had bad thoughts toward anyone else who I thought might be gay. In fact, I was often drawn to people who were labeled 'different.'" —Mary

Finding Community

"And then I came out as a lesbian and began to meet others who came from the same planet I did."
—Marj Plumb

Given that almost 40% of lesbians are incest survivors, at some point in her life almost every lesbian will be affected by childhood sexual abuse. If they weren't abused themselves, they're very likely to find themselves in a relationship with a woman who was. That's why talking about childhood sexual abuse is so important in the lesbian community.

Lesbian and gay communities and institutions can offer support and validation for same-sex couples (Beals, Impett, and Peplau, 2002). The gay and lesbian community can offer comfort and affirmation—eliminating the stigma of being gay, changing public perceptions, and providing safe places for us to gather and build relationships (Renzetti, 1992). And the community has something very tangible to offer the lesbian woman. Michael Thomas Ford (1996) writes about the gay and lesbian community, saying, "Believe that you are not alone. There are millions of us. And believe that you are good, that being gay is a good thing you should be proud of." Anderson and Deluty (1998) found that lesbians who were more out had a larger percentage of lesbian friends and were more involved in the gay and lesbian community.

Unfortunately, a "demand for sameness" (Perlman, 1997) or conformity (Loulan, 1999) has been described within the lesbian community. Several survivors I spoke with identified these notions within their own communities, feeling outcast as survivors within the woman-identified community that they thought would embrace them. Perhaps threatened by the existence of survivors—a possible link between lesbianism and abuse—the lesbian community ostracizes survivors just when they are in greatest need of support. Reg explains, *"I haven't told a lot of lesbians that I'm a survivor. I wasn't out about it."*

"I am very proud to be gay now, but I'm not proud of having to acknowledge the abuse because of the thing of being accused of being inauthentic. I still think the abuse has a great deal to do with my sexual identity." —Noemi

"A friend was arguing recently with her partner about who would have the baby because neither had ever had sperm in her body. They were a sperm-free zone. I mean, what the fuck is that? You know, like you're the original lesbian. Like it's some badge of honor to have never had that in their bodies. There are a lot of women in the dyke community around here that act like that. If you've fucked a guy, you're just not pure anymore. It's like they think they have some corner on the

market of true lesbianism. I think that's been more detrimental to me than even some of the stuff that happened with my dad. Because when you finally come out, you think, Oh, my God, I thought this was going to be this great place, *and then,* Oh, no, it's just this place like anything else." —Kris

"I have to deal with the homophobia that exists among my peers. It's nothing new, just another challenge. What boggles me the most is the notion of working in an organization with my peers and not feeling like I can say I've been abused. We have so much pressure to prove ourselves. I find the LGBT community to be much more judgmental—you have to be outright gay because you were born that way. You have to fit within a tiny little box and not move or not stray about. While I'm not ashamed to be totally out in my work and in my regular life with heteros, I find it difficult to be out with my abuse and the fact that I'm still challenged by my sexuality with LGBT individuals." —Noemi

"I'm a very proud butch-loving femme. I'm only attracted to butch women. This has really been a problem for me. It's a very harsh climate here in the Southwest. I've been criticized by friends of mine who are lesbian, 'Why don't you just go get a boyfriend? Don't you really like men? Apparently you do because you like bull-dykes.'" —Lyndsey

Issues of isolation and invisibility are particularly keen in rural communities where lesbians often lack access to information, a public gathering space, and a local gay culture. Opportunities to connect within small informal networks of friends and acquaintances can help alleviate these problems (McCarthy, 2000). Dynamics within lesbian communities of color add another layer to this discussion. While it is beyond the scope of this book to explore the many ways that communities of color shape our lives as lesbians, there are many books that address these issues. (See the bibliography and list of resources for more titles and organizations dedicated to this topic.) Of particular note are the arguments presented in *The Greatest Taboo: Homosexuality in Black Communities*

(Constantine-Simms, 2000) that explore the politics of prejudice and the pecking order of oppression.

Isolation is still a very real problem for lesbians across the country. While there are many thriving metropolitan areas with extensive services and activities for lesbians, there are many small towns and rural communities where such support is not available. Even within larger cities, finding community can be difficult for lesbians new to the area and those who are inhibited socially.

"I have not been able to muster up enough courage to get involved in the community here. I did volunteer for Pride, but my fear, as irrational as it is, is that I won't be accepted. The third Wednesday of every month there's a lesbian issues–women's group at the bookstore. Even if I puke 14 times, I'm going to go." —Dana

"I found a gay and lesbian organization in college. I would go by every single afternoon after they had their meetings, but I never went in. I was too scared. One day I went in and sat down. Then I started volunteering with teenagers." —Diana

"There's not much of a lesbian community here. Just a few people. I don't know why that is." —Deborah

"I have no connection to the gay and lesbian community." —Tabitha

In reflecting on their healing journeys, survivors described how a supportive lesbian community might have helped.

"More lesbian women around me would have helped." —Kathy

"I recently moved in search of more truth. I came to discover myself again. In coming here I decided that I no longer want my sexuality to be a secret. In my search I agreed that I had to offer more truth to the universe in order to receive any truth back. My only hang-up before was not feeling like I was real. It was taking a lot of energy to cope with." —Whitney

"What would really help in dealing with all this is to have personal contacts here to interact with. It would be great to hook up with gals like me so we could go around our community together." —Yvonne

"I connected with some local gays and lesbians, which was therapeutic and gave me a sense of community. I tried connecting with a Mormon-oriented gay and lesbian support group, but became disillusioned with it because church doctrine did not allow for gays to be active in the church and live sexually vibrant lives." —Cristi

CHAPTER 5

HEALING

"THE WINDS AND WAVES ARE ALWAYS ON THE SIDE OF THE ABLEST NAVIGATORS."
—EDWARD GIBBON

"THERE CAME A TIME WHEN STAYING TIGHT WITHIN THE BUD BECAME MORE POWERFUL THAN THE STRAIN IT TOOK TO BLOOM."
—ANAÏS NIN

"THE GATEWAYS TO WISDOM AND KNOWLEDGE ARE ALWAYS OPEN."
—LOUISE L. HAY, *YOU CAN HEAL YOUR LIFE*

"HE THAT CONCEALS HIS GRIEF FINDS NO REMEDY FOR IT."
—TURKISH PROVERB

There are times when we become overwhelmed by the feelings we're experiencing. We fear we are going crazy. I assure you: You are not. I know it's scary, but what you are feeling is normal. You are going through recovery, and that recovery involves predictable stages and often a great deal of pain. According to Courtois (1988), healing involves acknowledging the victimization and its reality, understanding it in the context of both the family and the larger culture, and allowing and experiencing the feelings associated with the trauma. "Healing is a process," Bratton (1999) reminds us, "not an event." Matsakis (1996) assures us, "The energy you now spend suppressing the past, running from it, or hiding it from yourself and others, can be yours to invest in the present—in your goals, relationships, spiritual growth, and creativity." Now there's incentive to move forward if I ever heard one!

Therapy can offer a safe and supportive context for survivors to examine painful memories and to look at them in a new light (*reframing*). New behaviors can be learned and practiced so that survivors can experience more comfortable relationships. Cognitive techniques can be particularly effective in correcting the survivor's belief system about herself and the abuse (Courtois, 1988). Distorted or unrealistic beliefs lead to feelings and actions that are distressing and inappropriate. These include all-or-nothing thinking, overgeneralization, jumping to conclusions, magnification and minimization, and "should" statements. While survivors are often eager for recovery to happen fast, issues are considered resolved when a survivor is able to direct her mind toward or away from the trauma at will (Van der Kolk, 1987). Dayton (2000) outlines four stages of healing trauma: (1) Telling the story and bearing witness to the trauma; (2) Accepting support; (3) Linking current behavior with the original wound or trauma and separating the past from the present; and (4) Creating a new narrative and reinvesting freed energy in constructive living. In this way, healing from sexual abuse is like healing an injury to the body—both involve cleaning wounds so they can heal and bringing hurts out into the open where fresh air can cleanse them.

We want to get better right away. Dayton (2000) believes that survivors' desire for a "quick fix" arises from the following characteristics: denial, low frustration tolerance, poor impulse control, a tendency toward rash action, inability to modulate or tolerate strong emotions, and fear of emotional pain. But quick fixes, of course, are not possible. While most of us have used substances and experiences to alter our moods—and dull the pain—real healing, aimed at restoring our essential personality, takes time—and hard work. There is also a tendency among survivors to flee treatment prematurely (Courtois, 1988). Therapists who work with trauma survivors report high dropout rates (Matsakis, 1996). Sometimes survivors feel such relief at revealing their secret, venting their feelings, and being affirmed that they think they are "cured." Others enter therapy wanting the therapist to "make it all go away." Therapists can address these unrealistic expectations early in treatment by communicating an understanding of the difficulty of working through sexual abuse issues.

"I get mad. I've been in recovery for years. There was not enough abuse to justify all the time it's taking to heal." —Chris

"I've been working with my therapist for a long time on my connecting with my emotional response to what happened. I feel that we've gotten nowhere with that." —Liz

Tian Dayton (2000) offers a definition of recovery that is more inspired and far-reaching than any other that I have read. I share it here for inspiration and insight. In this definition, Dayton manages to capture the connection of mind, body, and spirit that governs sexual abuse recovery work:

> It is so often through pain that we crack through our own reserve and defense system into what is real and authentic about us. Nothing is better, no reward greater than our true connection with ourselves, and through that we can reach out and really touch another. Working through trauma pulls us from the surface of life into the wellspring from which we learn who we really are. It is this holy and good work that purifies our spirits and deepens our souls. It is in this way that we spin straw into gold and turn our wounds into wisdom.

Nicki Roth, in *Integrating the Shattered Self* (1993), believes that therapy for incest survivors is different from other psychotherapy because survivors bring a unique set of defenses, strengths, and needs. Indeed, it is the work of therapy to discover our coping strategies as a child and as an adult and help us move toward experiencing ourselves as powerful individuals. This can be achieved through therapists who function in a parenting role to the survivor, helping her to heal the damage to her sense of trust and dependency. From all that has been said thus far about the unfinished developmental tasks of childhood that survivors face and the frequently ineffective, inappropriate, or abusive parenting that survivors endured, Dayton (2000) maintains that "people with early childhood wounds have grief work to do." Unfortunately, the defenses that we use to protect ourselves interfere with our ability to feel the pain of our emotions and to heal.

There has been a lot of talk in recent years about therapy to "heal the inner child." The nature of this work is to care for the child within who was hurt—and silenced—by the abuse. Healing means accepting our vulnerability as children, which can be a very difficult for us to do. Within the context of a therapeutic relationship, however, we can receive the care we never got when we were small (Roth, 1993). We are called on to embrace that child within ourselves and become whole. Alice Miller (2001) explains, "The process of healing requires both the confrontation with childhood traumas and the uncovering of the numerous defense mechanisms that have been erected to protect the child from unbearable pain and distress." Trauma must be talked through in order for us to make sense of it. Because abuse involves the rupture of a relationship bond, the therapeutic relationship between therapist and client is the essential corrective relationship (Dayton, 2000).

We abhor our own neediness, desperately wanting to believe that we need no one and nothing. This arises from a belief that we are to blame for the abuse and that since no one answered our cries then and we were alone in the world, we must be self-reliant, always. As Missy said, "*The only therapy I can speak of is my refusal to live in fear.*" Unfortunately, this defense mechanism cuts us off from the full range of emotions that are essential to our healing. We believe that we can control ourselves, preventing our weakness from showing. In denying our weakness, however, we deny the very essence of what it means to be human, to be vulnerable, to be capable of loving another human being. Loss is part of the human experience and one that we all suffer. The blessing is in surviving our losses to love again. Putnam and Trickett found that abused girls who received individual or family therapy suffered less anxiety, felt less "stuck" in the trauma, and believed they had more options in their lives (cited in Strong, 1998).

Abuse may have caused us to get stuck in the developmental phase at which the abuse occurred. The abuse interrupts our development in very specific ways, leaving the developmental work of that stage unfinished. Erik Erikson (1963) summarized children's needs in four stages, each characterized by a unique crisis or challenge with earlier stages providing the foundation for the later stages:

- ages birth through 5: trust and autonomy
- ages 5–10: purpose and competence
- ages 10–15: identity and independence
- ages 15–20: interdependence and intimacy

Many therapists and researchers describe the importance of revisiting developmental stages where loss occurred (when the abuse happened), otherwise real progress is impossible (Bratton, 1999). In addition, "reparenting," Bratton says, "must be directed to the exact places in their lives where parenting was missing or inadequate."

Kritsberg and Miller-Kritsberg (1993) describe the recovery process in three stages. In Stage 1: Discovery—memories begin to surface, and you begin to discover how your abuse has affected your adult life. This stage is characterized by the following thoughts: *I want to remember what happened to me. I want to know how it affects my life now.* In Stage 2: Active Healing—you begin to focus less on whether you were abused and more on what you can do to heal. Your healing becomes a primary focus of your life. One of the most important goals of the active healing stage is to establish an ongoing support group. This stage is guided by the thoughts: *I am a survivor of child sexual abuse. What can I do to heal?* In Stage 3: Integration—you experience a profound sense of freedom. Rather than feeling victimized and driven by your past, you begin to view your history of sexual abuse as one of the many events and changes that have shaped your life. During Stage 3 you think: *I am a recovering survivor, continuing to heal. My life is no longer just survival—it is a steadily unfolding creation.* Wood (1993) elaborates on the three stages above in his 15 stages of recovery. He sees these as a continuous, but not linear, process common to all survivors.

- Stage 1: *Recognition of Differences* is characterized by your noticing the ways in which your life is emotionally different from those around you. You recognize that the sexual abuse and the pain you are currently experiencing may in fact be affecting your life after all.

- You enter Stage 2, *Acknowledgment of Issues*, when you realize there's a problem but you seem unable to deal with what is happening in your life. Unconsciously you know that it is safe to work on your abuse issues now.
- Stage 3: *Searching for Trust* begins with your search for a therapist or other helping professional to guide you in your healing. You establish goals together that meet your specific needs and issues.
- Stage 4: *Telling Your Story* involves recalling your abuse experiences verbally and connecting them with the feelings you experienced at the time.
- Stage 5: In *Identifying Coping Skills* you recognize the defenses you used to survive the abuse and continue to use to cope with the pain of remembering.
- Stage 6: *Dealing with Flooding* is characterized by flashbacks that carry the emotional impact of the abuse. You develop a list of things you can do to take care of yourself when you are feeling vulnerable and develop skills to help you gain control over flashbacks.
- Stage 7: In *Development of Self* you uncover your false self and begin work on developing who you are.
- Stage 8: *Feeling the Grief* forces us to face all that was lost as a result of our abuse. You grieve for the family you wish you had and the childhood that was lost and the impact these have had on your life.
- Stage 9: *Dealing with Anger* involves facing the anger we feel because of the abuse and learning to deal with it, without guilt, in positive ways.
- Stage 10: In *Confronting the Offender* you confront your offender and possibly others who failed to protect you from the abuse. This confrontation can be done in a number of ways, including writing letters or talking to the abuser who is dead.
- Stage 11: *Stabilizing Emotions* involves beginning to accept your memories without feeling like they are occurring in the present and without resorting to old coping skills.

- Stage 12: In *Exploring the Forgiveness Issues* you decide whether you want to forgive your abuser and others who did not protect you from the abuse. You forgive yourself and recognize that you were not responsible, in any way, for the abuse.
- Stage 13: *Developing Sexual Healing* involves understanding and exploring what you need and want from sexual relationships.
- Stage 14: *Finding Spiritual Healing* involves finding peace with yourself spiritually.
- Stage 15: *In Realizing Peace Within* you take control of your life and see your abuse as something that happened in the past that does not control your life now. You can now behave in self-protective ways. You have moved through the victim mentality to survivor and now thriver.

The stages identified by Bass and Davis (1988) are remarkably similar. They explain that most are necessary for every survivor, but a few (confronting your abuser and forgiveness, for example) are not applicable for every woman: The decision to heal; The emergency stage; Remembering; Believing it happened; Breaking silence; Understanding that it wasn't your fault; Making contact with the child within; Trusting yourself; Grieving and mourning; Anger—the backbone of healing; Disclosures and confrontations; Forgiveness?; Spirituality; and Resolution and moving on. Similarly, Roth's conceptualization of the therapy process (1993) includes four basic phases: validation, development of a new worldview, emotional flooding, and new hope.

Hennessy found that lesbians most often seek therapy for one or more of the following concerns: depression, childhood sexual abuse, coming out to mother, and low self-esteem (1993). Here is what survivors told me about learning patience in the healing journey.

"Over the past year I have been working with the ways that both overt and covert sexual abuse have affected my life. It is unfortunate that I waited until I was 40 years old to do this, but I could not have done it sooner." —Grace

"I was in therapy for years to learn how to cope. My friends and therapists tell me I am a miracle—that it's a miracle that I survived." —Deb

"I've learned not to push myself when it comes to my healing." —Lauren

Post–traumatic stress disorder (PTSD) is common among survivors. It is a condition that may develop after a person experiences or witnesses an extremely dangerous or life-threatening event that causes her to feel intense fear and helplessness. Not all people who experience or witness a traumatic event develop PTSD. The risk for developing PTSD is influenced by many factors including a person's:

- response to the traumatic event at the time and the intensity of the memory of the event
- coping style, personality, and past experiences in life
- age, emotional state, and the amount of emotional stress a person already feels at the time of the traumatic event
- feelings of safety and amount of support (WebMD, 2002)

People with PTSD:

- relive the traumatic event either through painful memories, vivid dreams, or believing that the event is occurring in the present time (flashback).
- try to avoid the symptoms of physical and emotional distress they felt during the traumatic event (by avoiding mental triggers, including sights, sounds, smells, or certain people). Some people with PTSD develop a condition that makes it difficult for them to feel or express emotions toward other people (emotional numbness).
- have a tendency to be on constant alert (increased arousal). They may have difficulty sleeping, frequently scan their surroundings, have short attention spans, and startle easily. They may be irritable and have angry outbursts. Others are quiet and tend to isolate themselves from other people.
- may have problems with concentration and memory. They may

not be able to remember details about the trauma.
- may experience episodes of depression.
- may have problems making decisions and planning for the future because they do not believe they have control over their lives.

Symptoms of post–traumatic stress are periods when you feel very emotionally vulnerable, where you become depressed, angry, and sad, where you're preoccupied with recurrent thoughts of the abuse, and suffer from crying spells or nightmares. Sometimes PTSD develops months or even years after the event. When it develops later it may be hard to connect the symptoms of PTSD with the traumatic event. Early treatment (crisis intervention) may prevent PTSD from developing in some people. It may also prevent other problems such as depression, anxiety, panic attacks, overuse of alcohol, or use of illegal drugs.

Treatment for PTSD includes counseling and medications. Counseling is designed to help the person deal with the traumatic event that occurred, reconnect with other people, and resume a normal life. The most widely used types of counseling are brief psychodynamic psychotherapy, cognitive-behavioral therapy, and exposure therapy. Other therapies include eye movement desensitization and reprocessing (EMDR) and group therapy. Exposure therapy is used to help a person relive a traumatic experience, confront a feared object or situation, or deal with a distressing thought while in a controlled environment. Exposure therapy is sometimes called *desensitization.* The therapist helps the person work through the physical and emotional distress that developed during the traumatic experience. This gradually reduces the person's symptoms of distress. You are also taught how to use various relaxation techniques to deal with your fear or discomfort. This helps you maintain a sense of control when you are confronted with the feared object or situation or a distressing thought or when remembering the traumatic event.

"The events of childhood do not pass,
but repeat themselves like seasons of the year."
—Eleanor Farjeon

Researchers have established an association between the experience of child sexual abuse and poor health and mental health outcomes in adult women. Depressive symptoms and manifestations of depression, such as suicidal ideation and behavior, as well as anxiety disorders, including phobias and panic disorders, are observed more frequently in survivors of child sexual abuse than in other lesbian women (Hyman, 2000).

It is possible to heal after childhood sexual abuse. It is even possible to thrive. Bass and Davis (1988) describe thriving as "more than the alleviation of symptoms, more than Band-Aids, more than functioning adequately. Thriving means enjoying a feeling a wholeness, a satisfaction in your life and work, genuine love and trust in your relationships, pleasure in your body." I asked women to tell me what therapies they had used to help in their healing. Some survivors described their mistrust of "healers" and relied only on themselves.

"I don't know that there is such a thing as 'healing.' I have learned ways to master what was done to me through reenacting it in a setting and context that is consensual." —Robin

"Self-healing only. I don't trust MDs or therapists." —Jan

"Good, bad, or indifferent, most of my healing has come from hard work within myself, by myself." —Lisa

Others described the many therapies that had been helpful to them in their healing journeys. I was impressed with the list that they gave me. From traditional talk therapy to bodywork and EMDR, survivors have found healing support in many places. The intention here is to provide information, not recommendations. As you will learn here, survivors' experiences with different therapies vary widely. It is important for you to find a type of therapy and a therapist with whom you feel comfortable.

It is often only after great suffering that we see the need to seek help. As long as we feel able to function in our daily lives, we remain self-reliant, believing *we* are all we need to get through the pain. Beverly

Engel, however, advises that "the damage caused by the abuse only increases with time.... As the damage becomes even more noticeable, your life progressively becomes more unmanageable. You begin to realize that time alone cannot heal the wounds, and that a history of sexual abuse is not something you can "learn to live with," as Katie found:

"My depression and feelings were too much for me in college, and I started to drink. This scared me so I went to a therapist who asked, 'Were you sexually abused?' Finally, someone asked the question that was haunting my mind and body. I said yes, and my recovery began."

Healing work that uses the body—the site of the abuse—as the source of the recovery process is especially helpful for many survivors. Haines (1999) describes body-oriented therapy that helps to work the trauma out of your body and to open up your emotional life. *Bodywork*, as it is called, can be particularly helpful for those of us who tend to intellectualize what happened to us to avoid getting in touch with our feelings. Haines writes,

> The abuse seemed to pour out of my body. The more I reconnected with my body, the clearer I became about what trauma was stored where. My thighs retained rage...my chest held much of the deep grief...the relief was incredible...I was coming back to me...my body actually knew things about the healing process that I didn't. In the thawing out, I got to live inside myself again.

Haines describes somatics as "an educational and transformational approach that assumes that your body, mind, and emotions are one interconnected biological system. *Soma* is the Greek word for the living body, or thought, spirit, and body as one.... Somatics recognizes an intelligence and life in the body that affects your thinking and your actions. If you change your body, or the 'holding' of trauma in your body, then your thinking, your experience of the world, and often your identity will also shift." Others have described the value of psychodrama in which the survivor works with thoughts and feelings as well as the body (Dayton, 2000). In therapy, the survivor can, for example, experience what comfort feels like. This experience becomes a "building block" for other similar experiences. Again, bodywork addresses survivors' tendency to intellectualize their feelings through extensive talking and analyzing, a common psychological defense. Kathy describes her experience with bodywork saying, "I've tried rolfing, body movement therapy, and have seen a chiropractor."

Survivors described a wide range of healing therapies that they had found helpful on their journeys.

"I have tried drug and alcohol treatment, eating disorder treatment, group therapy, experiential programming (a ROPES course), therapy, essential oils, yoga, medication, energy healing, and shamanism." —Katie

"I've tried traditional psychotherapy, guided imagery and music, psychodrama, energy work, massage, Reiki, and metaphysical tools." —Misha

"I have tried self-help, prayer, consulting with a Native-American healer, participating in sweat lodges, and telling my friends." —Tammy

"I have worked with a therapist schooled in shamanic healing and liked the result I got from that. Part of that therapy included doing what has been traditionally known as soul retrieval. When one experiences trauma it is believed that parts of one's soul can leave the body and stay unattached to one's core energy. Soul retrieval calls upon helper guides to return the misplaced energies to the person to whom they originally belonged. I felt like I should do this. I thought it was rather hokey at the outset, but have since come to see merit in this type of intervention. I feel like a lot of my core energy has returned as a result of this type of therapy. It has also helped to develop my intuitive abilities and to trust that. I feel like I've healed a lot from this childhood trauma, but I am still surprised at times when forgotten elements present themselves anew for releasing." —Cristi

"According to my therapist, 'The work we do together is a multifold investigation into all the realms of our known existence: physical, mental, emotional, spiritual, and on the level of intention. My belief about healing is that each of us is her own healer, and that healing comes primarily from within. I act as a partner in a process, a committed listener, and your mirror. I can assist you in doing various kinds of techniques which will balance your energy and enhance your sense of well-being.' I go once or twice a month. I've been going for about a year. Talk therapy helped a great deal, but I could manipulate things when it got too difficult. I find that this healing helps me to really access some painful areas that I too easily numb out with my brain. I cry a lot and feel these deep-seated wounds in a different way. It is cathartic in that way for me. Plus, it helps me realistically feel and know my pain rather than rationalize it away. It helps me connect to the universe in a larger way, accessing my spirituality and the connectiveness of everything. It seems to heal on a different level. I can literally feel the energy in my body." —Tammie

"I'm a firm believer in therapy. I have a wholistic, New Age therapist. She challenges me. She had me write a letter to my mother. I'm doing the autobiography thing now." —Sarah

Others describe the way that creating art and music helps them in their healing. In *She Who Was Lost Is Remembered*, a powerful testament to the healing power of creativity, Louise Wisechild (1991) calls healing "the task of creating ourselves." Psychotherapist Mary Bratton (1999) believes that art can be an effective way to "facilitate reconnection with the child" and aid healing. Through drawing and other creative outlets we find expression for our feelings in ways we cannot in words. Music and art therapy can help survivors to express their hidden selves (Zerbe, 1993). *Journey Notes: Writing for Recovery and Spiritual Growth* (Solly and Lloyd, 1992) and *Looking for Home: Women Writing about Exile* (Keenan and Lloyd, 1990) are good resources on writing as a healing tool. *From Surviving to Thriving* (Bratton, 1999) contains some good writing and drawing exercises and samples of survivors' poetry and artwork. In addition, many survivors I spoke with mentioned SARK's books on creativity and inspiration (see References). Through their stories, survivors shared their artwork and creative outlets with me as important aspects of their healing. Barbara self-publishes her ink drawings and poetry about the abuse. Dorian writes gay fiction. Jacque's gospel singing is a great comfort to her. Jill hand-paints book plates and bookmarks.

"Art therapy is great—write it, draw it, paint it, collage it." —Kyrce

"I'm an artist. I paint. Watercolor. I've been doing this for many years. But over the last few years I've been painting a lot more." —Jill

"I play the dulcimer." —Tammy

"On my own I do a lot of journaling, reading, songwriting, and art. Songwriting is especially powerful and empowering for me." —Mollie

"After years of therapy, I was able to rediscover my potential and to let it shine. I began to write music and sing and perform. I lost weight and started to really be myself." —Mary

Perhaps not surprisingly, traditional talk therapy was the most frequently mentioned healing therapy.

"All survivors should go to therapy. See a lesbian therapist if possible. The dynamics of therapy will pull you in different directions. Say the things you think you shouldn't say. You really bring out your demons that way. I've been in treatment with a psychiatrist for four years. We're focusing a lot on my phobia of frogs and working on my self-image, self-love, and self-care." —Wendy

"First I was in psychotherapy with a Jungian therapist. It was good, nondirective. Second was a feminist therapist. She was the best. We did deep work around the abuse, incest intensives—group and individual." —Kathy

"Therapists saved my life. Therapy was the only thing I could look for-

ward to. I was seeing a therapist weekly, now it's once a month." —Chris

"I was in therapy with a child psychologist for many, many years. We used art therapy, play therapy, role-playing, and family counseling. As an adult I find that talking, talking, and talking about it helps a lot." —Elizabeth

"I have had quite a bit of counseling—some traditional while attending university and some alternative, including soul retrieval. I did about five years of conventional therapy—one year for each year of the abuse. Part of the treatment included group therapy for survivors, eating disorders group therapy, and hypnotherapy." —Cristi

Pat describes the ongoing nature of healing when she describes her experiences in therapy:

"I have been in therapy a lot and think I have worked through a lot of my abuse issues. Early on I didn't deal very much with the abuse. The last time was the most beneficial because my therapist was better able to address the abuse issues and I was ready to deal with them. I went back to therapy recently to address my abuse history again."

Meditation is also popular.

"I chant and meditate four hours a day, from 4–8 A.M. My life force comes from that." —Jan

"I attend workshops and lectures at the health food store. I do Chi-Lel qigong. It's like tai chi; it brings energy into your body." —Sarah

Many survivors also described the benefits of journaling or writing about their experiences; committing their thoughts, ideas, and feelings to paper was a cathartic (cleansing) experience. It also served as a way of documenting their experience, validating and authenticating their life as they remembered it. Bass and Davis (1988) describe writing as "an important avenue for healing because it gives you the opportunity to define your own reality.... By going back and writing about what happened, you also reexperience feelings and are able to grieve. You excavate the sites in which you've buried memory and pain, dread and fury. You relive your history." In this way, writing is cathartic and the process of rereading what one has written is cleansing as well as reaffirming. This expressive technique can help survivors to communicate or understand their experiences (Courtois, 1988). Caution should be taken, however, so survivors don't overload themselves. Facing all the long-hidden details and accompanying feelings all at once can be quite overwhelming. Go easy on yourself as you progress in your healing. Remember, it's a process, not an event. It's not a race. Healing takes time. When you're ready, a detailed lifeline of important family and life events can supplement an autobiography or journal and reveal previously undetected patterns for the survivor.

"I journal three times a day." —Wendy

"I began journaling in high school and continue it now when I provide myself the luxury of time and reflection." —Serena

"I use writing as therapy. The experience of writing was amazing for me. It gave me the freedom to go where my life was lacking. I enjoy writing erotica because it allows me to explore my sexual self in a safe environment. It empowers me and helps to build my confidence. At times it has forced me to face my sexual demons. And the pain is still deep within me from being a sexual abuse survivor. It is definitely a catharsis to my sexual healing. I read a lot of spirituality and self-help books." —Dorian

Self-help books serve as a foundation for many survivors' healing.

"I have always been an avid reader, so early on and now that has been my best resource." —Serena

"I read self-help books (like SARK's series)." —Elizabeth

"I read books. The Courage to Heal *really helped me a lot."* —Wendy

There are many books available on the topic of child sexual abuse. The references listed at the end of this book are those that I have found particularly helpful or that were suggested to me by other survivors. It bears mentioning that with the focus on self-help books, there are two workbooks that are excellent resources for self-guided recovery efforts: *The Courage to Heal Workbook* (Davis, 1990) and *Healing the Trauma of Abuse* (Copeland and Harris, 2000). Some authors "get it" more than others and can help us by writing in an accessible way.

Many survivors describe healing of mind and body that have been instrumental in their recovery.

"Mind and body relaxation, yoga; running too." —Elizabeth

"I am in counseling now, learning how to ground myself in my relationship and not regress as much back to my childhood." —Laura

"I've used regular psychotherapy and cognitive therapy to try to treat a serious bout of depression, as well as New Age and visualization such as Louise Hay and Diane Mariechild." —Deborah

When we commit to therapy, we begin to learn how to resolve the pain rather than just recycle it (Dayton, 2000). In classic reenactment, as we have learned, we recreate the original trauma in a variety of new ways. With time, the insight of a skilled therapist, and practice, we can interrupt this cycle and learn to live in a healthier, more productive way.

"I'm not averse to checking into therapy every once in a while. I tell the therapist, 'I need to check in.' I don't want to make decisions on the basis of my sexual abuse history." —Christy

"My current therapist was recommended to me by one of my past therapists who is gay. She uses traditional therapy, but she gives me leeway since I'm a creative person. I have communicated with her through writings, drawings, e-mails and voice mail." —Kirsten

"It took my life falling apart for me to get help. I mean, I had done the drinking and all that shit. I went to therapy around that, doing a stupid drinking program. I had to really want to do this. I was pretty much on a destructive path where it was going to kill me or I was going to say, 'Hey, I need help.'" —Kris

"I'm starting to trust my therapist who I've been seeing for a year. I told her about the abuse six months ago. She has a style so different from any other therapist I've had. She has candles burning in her office. She brought me to the beach a couple of times. And once when I was cold in her office, she wrapped a blanket around me. I click with her because I can tell she really cares about me, and feeling that from her, I trust her and will do what she suggests because I know she's trying to help me." —Kim

Eye movement desensitization and reprocessing (EMDR) is a treatment that has been used to help people with a variety of psychological disorders, particularly post–traumatic stress disorder (PTSD). During EMDR, the therapist moves his or her hand back and forth about one foot away from your face. You are instructed to follow the therapist's hand with your eyes while concentrating and talking about the traumatic event, feared object, or situation, or other cause of emotional distress. After several sessions, the emotional and physical distress is expected to be reduced. Exactly how EMDR works is not clearly understood. It is thought to work like rapid eye movement (REM) sleep. During REM sleep, the brain sorts and organizes (processes) information and copes with the day's stress. After most day-to-day experiences are processed by the brain, they are forgotten. EMDR is thought to work in the same way. EMDR does not eliminate reasonable fears, nor does it eliminate all memory. It seems to reduce the amount of distress caused by a traumatic memory.

Dr. Francine Shapiro (2002), the creator of EMDR, and the executive director of the EMDR Institute, reports that substantial alleviation of PTSD symptoms was reported in two controlled studies of EMDR. The assumption is that early life experiences are stored in a dysfunctional fashion, contributing to people's inappropriate reactions to the present. According to Shapiro (2002), "When these earlier experiences are brought to mind they retain a significant level of disturbance, manifested by both emotions and physical sensations. Reprocessing these experiences with EMDR allows the client to gain insight, shift cognitive assessment, incorporate ecological emotions and body reactions, as well as adopt more adaptive behaviors. The major significance of EMDR is that it allows the brain to heal its psychological problems at the same rate as the rest of the body is healing its physical ailments. Because EMDR allows mind and body to heal at the same time, it is effectively making time irrelevant in therapy." Here are some survivors' experiences with EMDR.

"EMDR is valuable. The relationship with the therapist is essential." —Kathy

"EMDR was helpful, but not all the time. Claims of a cure and intense 10-week programs are freaky. Once every three weeks is right." —Dana

"I did EMDR and I was hopeful, but it didn't work." —Wendy

Group therapy has been an effective healing tool for many survivors, particularly for dealing with the issues of shame, isolation, and secrecy (Bass and Davis, 1988; Courtois, 1988). Reg describes her experience this way:

"I go to a Monday night group for survivors. Going to group was a huge leap for me. I think that group is pretty important. You get feedback, perspective, and validation. Other people have been through something similar. Hearing other people tell you, 'That was bad. Nobody should have treated you like that, helps. Choosing to participate in a support group probably depends on your support system."

"I tried Incest Survivors Anonymous." —Mary

Group therapy is usually recommended in combination with individual treatment, as the one-to-one client-therapist relationship is the essential vehicle for healing from abuse (Roth, 1993). Courtois (1988)

advises group therapy alone for women who find individual therapy too threatening initially, however.

"I don't think the combination of individual and group therapy is necessary. It didn't work for me. I felt bad about that. I attended a group for lesbian perpetrators of domestic violence. I found the group through a flyer for victims. I learned that the behavior stops you from healing. Once I wasn't acting out, I could deal with my feelings better. Every group has worked for me. I'm an extrovert, so groups were more comfortable for me and not intimidating. I learn a lot more through other people who have gone through it and the choices they have made, right and wrong." —Cory

Kritsberg and Miller-Kritsberg (1993) found that "Some people advocate same-sex support groups for healing, while others feel that coed support groups are more effective." I believe as they do that each survivor will find exactly what is needed for healing to take place. With that said, short-term, focused sexual abuse recovery groups offer two benefits to survivors: breaking through the isolation and learning new information about abuse and its victims. Longer-term therapy groups can help the survivor by providing information she never received in childhood. This can include life skills, how relationships work, problem-solving approaches, and explanations of emotions. In any psychotherapy group, Roth (1993) explains, the interactions among members recreate familiar patterns from their pasts. This is true of survivor groups as well. Survivors project their family members onto other members of the group and reenact positive and negative relationship dynamics. With the guidance of a skilled group leader, survivors have a chance to resolve old conflicts and learn new ways of relating.

"In the late '80s I went to a group for lesbian incest survivors. I only went a few times, but those times were a big help." —Jacque

"Other survivors are another category of women who have been helpful, mainly by showing me that they can survive and heal and that they do not deserve the shame that they feel." —Levie

"A survivor group was the best thing I've ever done. It taught me about myself." —Sarah

"Ten to 12 years ago I was in group therapy for a year. I also attended a group at a rape crisis center where I was the only lesbian in the group. I'll take help where I can get it." —Lynn

"Support groups have been very good. I felt like I was the only one. Hearing other women talk about their abuse bowled me over. I thought, There are other people this has happened to! *In high school I went to an abuse survivors group at the YWCA. In college I went to a gay support group where the topics of coming out and abuse were merged."* —Elizabeth

"We've also been in a codependents group (Co-Dependents Anonymous). There are not many Incest Survivors Anonymous groups nearby. First we went to a coed group, but we're not comfortable with men. We're in a women's group now." —Dana

"I was in a sexual abuse group for seven months." —Kyrce

Group therapy is not for everyone, and not all groups will work for all survivors. While it is the preferred treatment for many survivors, survivors with severe interpersonal difficulties or an inability to hear or react to the abuse experiences of others, or who feel too threatened by group process, should not participate in groups (Courtois, 1988). And as with all therapy, it's important to pay attention to your feelings and how you are reacting to the facilitator and other survivors.

"I became involved in a support group for women who had been molested as children. I have also attended codependency groups for lesbians and a 12-step group for survivors of sexual abuse. Neither group proved to be my cup of tea. After a few sessions with each I stopped attending." —Lisa

"In group the facilitator shared her own personal experience too much." —Dana

In their study of lesbian couples in group therapy, Groves and Schondel (1996) describe the benefits of lesbian survivors viewing their relationships dynamics as related to the abuse issues and their patterns of interacting as characteristic of other couples in similar circumstances. The goals of the series of five eight-week sessions were: to acknowledge each couple's commitment and survivor, to explore dysfunctional patterns, to enhance each couple's ability to be intimate with each other, and to learn healthier ways to be honest with each other and resolve conflict. Members agreed that a major problem in their relationships was their difficulty in communicating feelings and perceptions of their experiences. "Often each partner felt misunderstood, and old feelings of abandonment would kick in, resulting in each partner coping with defensive styles learned as survival techniques in childhood. These defensive techniques were often counterproductive to the desire to be understood, accepted, and loved by their partner." The group facilitators, lesbian survivors themselves, created a *vulnerability* contract which created a structured way for each couple to discuss personally painful issues. They found that the couples' success in the group was related to their level of commitment to confronting personal issues and willingness to work through relationship issues. Specifically they found that older couples tended to be more willing and committed to exploring alternative strategies to deal with relationship stress than were younger couples.

Sometimes we find support as Marie did, from other survivors outside of formal support groups:

"One of the best moves I ever made was when I went to school for social work. I met so many people who went through similar experiences; they became my support group. I met real friends who accepted me for who I am and not how I can please them sexually."

"I turned to friends of mine who had similar abuse histories. We started a support group which met weekly in a church. There were four of us who shared our stories—or as much as we were comfortable sharing." —Maggie

Support groups—as distinguished from therapy groups—are readily available in many communities, including on the Internet. The advantages of support groups include free membership, focus on health and competence, and a safe and therapeutic environment (Courtois, 1988). Of course, support groups have their limitations too, including not being appropriate for women in acute distress, women who have difficulty with aggressive or impulsive tendencies, or women who are overly dependent on others. Support groups are also contraindicated for the survivor who is actively suicidal, homicidal, substance-dependent, or suffering from a life-threatening eating disorder. I have included online support groups in Resources for your information.

"I've participated in Internet message boards, like Mosaic Minds for DID [Dissociative Identity Disorder]. Be careful how much you disclose. Everyone comes with their own baggage. They can push your buttons and then attack you." —Dana

Medication can be helpful if a survivor is not emotionally ready or available for therapy (Dayton, 2000). In these cases, medication becomes a "therapeutic window" through which the information gained in therapy can get through to the survivor and make the emotions more readily available for therapy. Medication may be an important part of treatment for some with PTSD. Sertraline (Zoloft), a medication used to treat people with depression and other anxiety disorders (such as panic attacks), is now being used to treat people who have PTSD. Medications that reduce the symptoms of anxiety and panic (antianxiety medications) may be useful in short-term treatment. Other medications may include medications to promote sleep and relieve depression.

MAO inhibitors and the tricyclic antidepressants that were the preferred means of treating depression have been replaced with newer drugs that have fewer side effects. Serotonin reuptake inhibitors, such as Prozac and Paxil, have been proven effective in the treatment of depression. They work by increasing the concentration of serotonin in the brain. Decreased amounts of this important neurotransmitter are present in persons who are depressed. Other popular medications are Effexor, Celexa, and Serzone. These are generally well-tolerated but can affect sexuality, appetite, and bowel function. St. John's Wort, an herb you can buy without a prescription, is also effective against mild depression. Rosenthal (2000), in *Women and Depression*, reminds us that medication can help stop the suffering in the short term, "but it can't give you insights for the long term or provide you with the emotional support you need to see what you need to see, learn what you need to learn, or go through what you need to grow through." Here are some of the experiences of survivors who are currently taking medications.

"I'm heavily drugged and will take meds for the rest of my life." —Debbie

"I suffered from major depression. I've been depressed most of my life. Now I'm on an antidepressant and love my job and my life." —Chris

"Since the '90s I've been on meds. First Zoloft for a couple years, although it really didn't help. Then nortriptyline. Synthroid because of my low thyroid, which can cause depression. Effexor, which really made a big difference for a while. And recently he's added a small dose of Risperdal because I've been kind of stuck lately." —Jacque

Others describe their desire or decision to discontinue their medication.

"I am not currently on any medication. I used to be but disliked the side effects of drowsiness, the sexual side effects, and irritability, so I stopped taking them. I got tired of trying to find the right medication and the right dosage." —Kirsten

"It's a sad commentary to live on antidepressants. It's not a compromise I'm willing to make." —Tabitha

"I've been on medication for depression. I don't really like it. I've put on a lot of weight. I'm not eating at all." —Kim

Some women swear by the antidepressant medication they are taking, believing that it keeps them alive and prevents them from taking their own lives. Others, like Reg, fear the effect that such medications would have on them, specifically that it will cut them off from the feelings they need to heal (Bratton, 1999).

"I don't want medication. My whole life has been spent not feeling. There's nothing bad about feeling bad. It's a cultural thing to take a pill to feel better. I believe it's not necessary for me."

Finding a Therapist

"When the student is ready, the master will appear."
—Zen proverb

The relationship between survivor and therapist—*the therapeutic alliance*—serves as a model of a healthy, nonexploitative, and growth-producing relationship (Courtois, 1988). As such, this relationship serves as the foundation for our work in recovery and the healing of the parent-child bond.

"Psychotherapy," explains therapist Michael Bettinger in *It's Your Hour* (2001), "is a conversation, or series of conversations, between two or more people. One or more of those individuals is a psychotherapist and the other(s) are the client(s) or patients." Bettinger warns that psychotherapy does not perform miracles. "It does not change someone into a different person.... It does, however, have an impact on how a person lives his or her life." If you involve yourself in psychotherapy, you will probably be able to say that you were the same person before and after psychotherapy but that you were able to lead a happier life after psychotherapy. Bettinger describes the unique challenges gays and lesbians face when seeking a therapist. Not only must they question the qualifications and abilities of various therapists, but they must also overcome the mistrust of others who are homophobic. In addition, they must be able to seek out a therapist who is capable of dealing with the unique needs of a LGBT client. Here, some survivors explore the issues of therapists' gender and sexual orientation.

"See a lesbian therapist if possible." —Wendy

"The therapists I have worked with in recent years have all been women. I'm not sure I could have survived without the understanding and support provided by one therapist in particular, a woman who has worked with a number of survivors and lesbians and who has been able to help me make sense of many of the aftereffects of abuse." —Levie

"I was seeing a therapist for five years, and I was getting absolutely nowhere. And I couldn't figure out why. Then I realized I was trying so hard not to say things. I didn't want to say bad things in front of a woman. That therapy was just a joke. I see a psychiatrist now, and I have no problem with him. Straight white man, wife and kids. I never thought I would have a male therapist because I don't trust men as far as I can throw them. For some reason this has worked out for me." —Kris

It may be that lesbian survivors who were abused by men will find greater comfort and safety with a female therapist, as Levie described above, although trust will still be difficult (Roth, 1993). What a survivor needs is a safe, appropriate, caring, and skilled therapist; a male therapist can fulfill these expectations as Kris described. The majority of survivors, however, will select a female therapist (Courtois, 1988; Roth, 1993). There are special considerations for male therapists, including the need for clear and rigid boundaries. "If the boundaries are permeable," Roth writes, "the client will be anticipating inappropriate behavior." Touching will be very loaded. Survivors should give the therapist permission to offer any form of physical comfort and have these boundaries respected. A male therapist who is too distant will be perceived as a threat. As Reg put it, *"I could never see a therapist who sits on the other side of the room and nods. That wouldn't feel safe to me."*

One of the best ways to find a therapist is through a referral from a friend. In most cases you will want to interview several potential therapists over the phone, describing your situation a little. Often you can tell from this initial contact if the person sounds like someone you would like to talk to.

"I actually interviewed three or four therapists. I would say something like, 'I want a therapist who will go by my timetable.'" —Jill

"My psychiatrist is funny and really down-to-earth. With my therapist we kind of clicked." —Debbie

You probably want someone you feel comfortable with, can trust, feel calm with, and feel safe with; someone who respects you, is flexible, reliable, and supportive. As Cory explained, *"You've got to find the right person. You're going to another person's core."* Survivors choose therapists for a variety of conscious and unconscious reasons, but Eide (1993) asserts that the issue of safety is first and primary for all survivors." Survivors need reassurance, encouragement, and validation at the beginning of the treatment process (Josephson and Fong-Beyette, 1987). Helpful therapists were described as patient, calm, caring, warm, nonjudgmental, empathic, honest in their responses, and interested in clients as people. Cristi describes how being open to trying something new led her to therapy using an eclectic, New Age approach that works for her:

"I preferred the more gentle approach in therapy. What worked well for me was weekly sessions where I study and journal and then share my discoveries with my therapist. I like the concept of reality therapy, where I choose who I am and believe that a healthy sense of self is not found but created. The last therapist I had was by far the most unconventional but with whom I found the most success. Along with traditional therapy, she does shamanic soul retrievals. We worked a lot with personal spirit guides and power animals bringing back the pieces of soul which had fragmented as a part of the abuse. I have also worked with people who refer to themselves as energy healers, where we look at past lives and try to release the effects of the lives which are manifesting in this life."

Mo and Cristi describe negative experiences with therapists with whom they didn't feel safe:

"When I was married I sought counseling. It was not a good experience.

The male counselor felt that I had either brought this stuff on myself or made it up. How the hell does a child bring this on herself? Why would a small child make something like this up?" —Mo

"One therapist engaged me in a therapy which I did not like. It was combative, pushing buttons until he had me in tears every session—mostly out of frustration and anger. That did not work for me." —Cristi

You will want to consider the issues that are important to you and the ways that your culture and ethnicity, sexual orientation, and other factors impact your choice of a therapist. Researchers have found that African-American women, lesbian and heterosexual, are less likely to use mental health services than are other women despite evidence of substantial emotional distress (Matthews and Hughes, 2001). Culturally-informed clinical services to address the unique needs of African-American lesbian survivors are essential (Parks et al, 2002). No relationship has been found between level of satisfaction with therapist and therapist sexual orientation (Hennessy, 1993). But Platzer (1998) believes in most cases it is difficult to establish a rapport without disclosure of sexual orientation, even if this does not directly relate to the presenting problems. Some questions that may be helpful to ask a prospective therapist of counselor include experience working with survivors of childhood sexual abuse, boundaries with clients, experience working with lesbians, and benefits of working with him or her (Haines, 1999). Of course, insight alone does not necessarily produce change (Dayton, 2000). We need to do more than "understand" how the abuse affected our lives; we need to learn new relationship dynamics that over time can recondition our responses.

Many survivors described how therapy had helped them in their healing.

"I am a survivor after years of therapy." —Tammy

"Things started changing for me for the better when I got into treatment." —Wendy

"Talking helps tremendously. I recommend getting a therapist. They kept me from wanting to hurt myself. I went to a day treatment center where there were classes to talk about anxiety, abuse, coping skills. It gets you out of the house and functioning. I see a psychiatrist and a therapist now. I found them on hospital stays." —Debbie

"I ended up working with a therapist, on and off, for 11 years. Even now I still have contact with her when I need to be grounded. She is my touchstone." —Lisa

"Last year I decided that I needed to return to counseling as a client and clear any patterns still remaining from my childhood abuse. I wanted to be as sure as possible that none of my 'stuff' would get in the way of my providing a safe and healing environment for the residents of the adolescent residential program where I work. I have tended to minimize the impact of the abuse on my life, and it's also very easy for me to slip into appeasing people." —Misha

"I sought out couples therapy for a relationship that was failing and ended up going alone to work on my own agenda, the abuse being one part of it. Without any knowledge from me, my therapist questioned me in one of the sessions about my being abused. That opened the door to the abuse agenda. Therapy was the best thing that happened to me. In therapy we uncovered and resolved many things through my dreams." —Whitney

"My therapist is open to using artwork in therapy. I do poetry and art. I don't feel pigeonholed by her." —Kyrce

"My therapist said that pain is a sign that I want to move forward. I said, 'I feel sucky, and that's a good thing?' We go once a week and have been for four years. She gives us the structure. She's taught us how to take care of ourselves. We want to be able to work on this. It takes a while in therapy. You need to find a therapist you can trust with your gut. My therapist has told me, 'Normal's only a setting on a dryer.'" —Dana

"I was slicing my arms and drinking a lot. I couldn't talk to my parents; I was the black sheep of the family. I had trust issues. I was suicidal. A friend hospitalized me. My first therapist was very cool. She worked in a community mental health center. I worked with her for nine months. I feel very fortunate to have found her." —Kyrce

"I have a male therapist. He's a former teacher of mine. It's a strong spiritual practice. This is very important to me. He uses a Rogers kind of therapy and eye desensitization. We work on inner child stuff—reliving the trauma, visual work. The questions he asks are good in helping me to see the patterns in my behavior. You can't do it alone. I didn't look for a male therapist, but wanted to deal with my relationships with men, so it was a subconscious choice. —Lynn

"I was fucked up as all get out. So over a period of time I developed a need for a therapist that was very, very supportive, nonconfrontational, and eclectic. I simply didn't feel that there was any one solution for anything. —Jill

"No one person or perspective can solve our problems. We have to be willing to let go of our certainty and be confused for a time. Most of us weren't trained to admit what we don't know. We haven't been rewarded for asking questions rather than giving quick answers. We were taught to sound certain and confident. But the only way to understand the world in its complexity is to spend more time in the state of not knowing. It is very difficult to give up our certainties—the positions, beliefs, and explanations that lie at the heart of our personal identities. And I am not saying that we have to give up what we believe. We only need to be curious about what others believe and to acknowledge that their way of interpreting the world might be essential to us."
—Margaret Wheatley

"We need to be met where we are
so that we can journey where we need to go."
—Michele Novotni

Individuals must be allowed to reveal themselves at their own speed. If professionals push too quickly, a person may feel revictimized (Zerbe, 1993).

"There was one therapist who wanted to bring my mother in. She wanted to have this big fancy meeting, and I wasn't ready for that." —Jill

"I had a bad experience with a therapist back when I was 16. She was giving advice and criticism. I was being questioned much too fast." —Cory

Committing to therapy can be a difficult process for survivors because we have trust issues and we are reluctant to remember the abuse in detail. I frequently heard how fearful survivors were to open up the proverbial Pandora's box by talking about the abuse. They feared a flood of emotions and flashbacks that they believed would overwhelm them.

"I haven't felt comfortable entering a mental health facility. They are very hurtful places. I get hurt when I try to show my feelings. I'm penalized for expressing my feelings." —Tabitha

"I have some reservations about therapy—bringing up all the rage and pain again." —Marian

These feelings are normal given the trauma we experienced at a young age (Dayton, 2000). One of the aspects of therapy, however, is learning that feelings can be experienced and described in words, instead of holding them in where we cannot identify or know them. This work is called *emotional literacy* and it builds *emotional intelligence.* It can be learned.

"Mainly, I'm bottling it up. I don't want to look at it. It would disrupt me emotionally, and it feels like a selfish indulgence. Besides, it's hard to find a therapist that doesn't focus on my being gay." —Tammy

"There are so many different approaches. I think it's really important to see a therapist. Somebody is out there with the right approach for you. Keep trying different ones until it feels right. Shop around. Trust your gut instinct. My therapist knew I was abused before I was able to tell her. I've been seeing this therapist every week for seven years. It's a personality thing. We hit it off. She gets it. She's a lesbian survivor too. I don't have to explain it to her. I feel lucky that I stumbled onto the therapist that I did." —Reg

Some survivors shared their bad experiences with therapy and their opinions that it didn't work for them.

"Psychotherapy didn't work. Too impersonal!" —Yvonne

"I saw a therapist from the ages of 3–13. I told him about the abuse. He said, 'That's an excuse. It's not real.' When my father found out I'd told, he physically punished me. Therapists are no help. I'd tell people I wanted to kill myself, and they told my parents. I have a problem seeing a male therapist, being in a room alone with a guy." —Rowan

When done right, therapy can be the key to healing from the trauma of abuse.

"In therapy I explored what had happened to me as a child. This helped me to look at my whole being more clearly, which in turn allowed me to accept things about myself that I was never open to seeing before." —Mary

"My partner encouraged me to see a therapist and went with me to the first meeting. My therapist knows what to ask to make me cry and open up. I know that it's helping. Talking about it helps. My therapist picks through what happened, examining every aspect of my abuse. Friends can't do that. My therapist has the tools to help me with my panic and depression." —Amanda

"My psychologist listens to me. I just go there and talk. As a child I didn't ever talk. It's hard, but it feels really good." —Amanda

"Before my first appointment with a therapist, I drove around the parking lot for half an hour before going in. She helped relax me to a state where if the abuse did come up, I could go to a safe place in my mind. I made a collage of sexual abuse, sex-negative stuff, then later I did it again and it was different." —Julie

Therapy can be prohibitively expensive, as these survivors told me.

"I am glad that we have help out there, but I also know that it's not always affordable." —Melissa

"I struggled with money and couldn't go for a while, then gradually saw that I was going back down to that bad place." —Amanda

"I can't afford therapy right now." —Marian

Some survivors found low-cost therapy through gay and lesbian and mental health centers. Others used their health insurance benefits to access therapy.

Issues around boundaries are critically important to an effective, professional therapeutic relationship. Blurred boundaries mirror our experiences of childhood sexual abuse and are disastrous to our recovery. Therapists who are survivors themselves should have completed extensive psychotherapy and feel sufficiently healed from the past before taking on survivors as clients. The therapist should have learned a great deal about setting and maintaining clear boundaries in relationships. Handling emotionally difficult material can trigger the therapist and cause her to distance herself from the client. This is to be expected, but good supervision can help (Roth, 1993). The therapist should not reveal her identification with the survivor until the very end of treatment, if at all. All too often therapists share too much of their own personal lives and struggles in an effort to get help with their own problems and are unavailable to their clients. This behavior is unethical, and survivors who encounter it should find a different therapist. A survivor who hears that her therapist was also abused may tone down her own story, try to draw out her therapist's story, worry about upsetting the therapist, or perceive her therapist as the ultimate role model for recovery. These all hamper the survivor's treatment. She will attempt to nurture her therapist, Roth warns, and not get the help she needs. This is codependency, and survivors are primed to fall into this trap.

"The school counselor told me detailed descriptions of how she was sexually abused. I am a visual person, and her efforts did not help my mind feel any sense of comfort. In fact, I felt even more upset. Almost violated." —Marie

"My former therapist, a lesbian survivor herself, crossed boundaries. I knew more about her life than she knew about mine." —Sarah

"Our past therapist, well, we have her cat. She made her patients her friends. It took us two years to realize how unhealthy that was. She did not have good boundaries. With my therapist now it's a 50-minute hour. She maintains that structure." —Dana

"She crossed boundaries. She took my mom on a trip to Europe. She was very controlling and freaky." —Cory

"There are some really messed up therapists out there, some who want to be my mom or take me home." —Kyrce

Sarah, who had boundary issues with a previous therapist, describes her current therapist this way: *"My current therapist doesn't answer personal questions."*

Child sexual abuse is the ultimate boundary violation. Therefore, good boundaries in therapy are critically important to survivors' healing. According to Garrett (2002), "Sexual attraction toward patients occurs widely among therapists and is viewed as a natural process in therapy." Sexual contact with patients, however, is widely regarded as misconduct and is prohibited by most professional ethics codes. It is deemed harmful, even after termination of therapy, for reasons including its similarity to incest and the power imbalance in the relationship. Roth (1993) warns that work with survivors can easily overwhelm a therapist, and good boundaries are critically important. Bass and Davis (1988) reiterate that it is "extremely damaging to engage in a sexual relationship with a client. This is a transgression of appropriate boundaries, which is far too similar to the original sexual abuse to be justified under *any* circumstances." According to Starzecpyzel (1987), "The therapist must never become part of the seduction projection, because this would confirm for the client her distorted belief that all intimacy must be obtained by sex and barter rather than the real qualities she possesses." Any sexual contact between a therapist and client is "symbolically incestuous" because it reenacts the exploitation of the abuse with another authority figure who is supposed to be trustworthy and nurturing (Barnhouse, 1978). Chris describes it this way: *"If you've been abused, therapy is a way to have an authentic healing relationship with someone who has boundaries. It's not sexual. That's so important."* Unfortunately, many therapy clients, including survivors, describe unethical practices by therapists.

"My therapist, a gay black man, said he was attracted to me and wanted a client he could be real to. I realized I needed to be needed. Then he said he was just a symbol of my problems. It devastated me. I reported him and his supervisor yelled at me, saying I had made him say those things." —Tabitha

When we describe our sexual abuse experiences, it is important for our therapists to be careful about their questioning so as not to be viewed as voyeuristic. There is a possibility that we will act in seductive ways with our therapists. This is a learned behavior and one that must be discouraged by our therapist. With a female therapist, we might perceive her as a mother or protector that we never had. A therapist's overly nurturing behavior could make the relationship more like parent and child, which could jeopardize the relationship with inappropriate boundaries. Further, the therapist's rage at the abuser must be addressed outside of the therapeutic relationship lest it contaminate and adversely affect the survivor's own healing.

Overcoming Shame

"Even the opinions you have about yourself are not necessarily true.... You have a choice whether or not to believe the voices you hear within your own mind."
—Don Miguel Ruiz, *The Four Agreements*

The more I learn about child sexual abuse and the experiences of survivors, the more inspired I am by the courage and ingenuity of survivors in surviving their assaults. We survived with no one to help us. Instead of the shame we often feel at what has happened to us, we must identify with the strength and resolve it took to survive it. Stop feeling ashamed. Stop acting ashamed. Feel proud of yourself. You survived. You found the strength to get through an unbearable situation. You were there for yourself when no one else was. That's something to be glad for. Be there for yourself once again, in your healing. Shame holds us back, as Whitney found, and keeps us from becoming who we were meant to be.

"I grew into my identity as I got older and could get past the shame and uncertainties."

As a survivor myself, I understand how difficult it is to let go of the shame. But when we understand what shame is and why we feel it, we can begin to let go of its hold over us.

Shame is a painful situation excited by guilt and disgrace. It's a master emotion in that it regulates and inhibits the expression of all other feelings. Shameful feelings are aroused most intensely when we see ourselves violating in some way the most basic values with which we identify. It becomes psychologically dangerous when it starts to color our most basic ideas about who we are and how worthy we are. Pathological shame takes the form of self-loathing and self-hatred (McNeill, 1988).

A deep sense of shame makes us feel that we are flawed in some essential way. Pathological guilt leads us to act out in self-destructive ways. We punish ourselves in order to escape the judgment and punishment we unconsciously fear. The earliest form of guilt and shame is tied to a child's need for—and absolute dependence on—the affection, acceptance, and love of her parents (McNeill, 1988). Here's what survivors told me about their feelings of shame:

"I have lived with the deeply rooted shame- and pain-based programming about who I was as a person and who I could even hope to be." —Kelly

"I think for a long time the abuse stifled me from being myself. I cut myself off from my full potential because I believed that if I let myself shine, I would attract people who would use me and thrown me away. Immediately following the abuse I cut my hair, gained weight, and withdrew from the world. I lived that way throughout my childhood and adolescence. In the last few years I can feel myself retreating again. I was getting way too close to putting pieces together about the abuse in my life, and my body wasn't ready to deal with it. As long as I carry the shame from the abuse, I stifle myself. It's a constant struggle to keep the toxins from the trauma out of my body. Sometimes I beat them. Sometimes I don't." —Mary

"I feel dirty and so unclean." —Marian

"I feel ashamed, like it was all my fault. I call these the 'hate-mes'—like little bugs that fly around my head saying, 'You're hateful. You're hateful. You're hateful,' which is just from being told that. People tell me that to keep me down." —Liz

"All the abuse stained me. I can't burn it off me no matter how deep I make the holes. I can't cut it off. I'm stained the whole way through. Sometimes when I really think about myself I feel like I don't want people to know me. Because I'm all wrong somehow. I'm ashamed of who I am. Deeply ashamed." —Barbara

"I feel there's something intrinsically wrong with me. It's my fault in a million ways. I have a deep sense of shame and worthlessness." —Lynn

"Healing in silence left me believing I was bad, tainted." —Mary Lou

In a typical pattern of offering help to others but not accepting any for ourselves, survivors described the ways in which they helped others to let go of the shame and self-blame, while unable to do this for themselves.

"I knew a lot about psychology, but I always had this thing that I would never ask for help. Why, if I can help other people—my friends would come to me and I would listen and help them become better problem solvers—did I never want to ask for help? I kept people away, anything to keep them from asking me who I really was." —Diana

"I have a friend who was abused by a neighbor. She says, 'I feel guilty because it happened more than once and I didn't stop it.' I remind her, 'You were a child.'" —Margaret

Shame keeps us from telling our stories for fear that others will think differently about us, as if being abused were something to be ashamed of.

"I am very protective of my niece. She is the daughter of my partner's sister, a Ph.D. specialist in childhood sexual abuse. I've never told her about the abuse because she might think I would abuse the baby—the whole 'abused children become abusers' thing. I wish I could tell her, but I am too afraid." —Elizabeth

It was not uncommon for survivors to tell me, as Dana did, *"I may not be what you need. I hope that if I am not that I haven't wasted your time."* Even in sharing their stories, survivors felt that they might not be good enough, that their stories might not be good enough.

For some of us, it's fairly easy to let go of the shame.

"It's not a part of my life anymore, except to console someone else. It's wasted emotion. There's no time for that in my life. I want to love and be happy. It's not the defining point of my life. I'm not letting this affect my

life. I've never had any guilt or shame about it. I was a child. I had no control. There is no shame involved." —Margaret

"One of the things a therapist did that really helped me was to really work with me on putting me in touch with myself as an adult and a powerful woman. First I visualized someone who I thought was really powerful. Then I kind of merged that with who I was. Once I was able to see myself as a grown-up and as someone who had power, and not feel vulnerable anymore, a lot of the issues around the abuse just sort of went away. Also, I was always so in touch with children that I was very clear that this had nothing to do with me in terms of me causing it or needing to feel badly about it. This was really not my fault." —Margie

Some women I spoke with had never suffered the feelings of guilt, of feeling responsible for the abuse, that many of us did.

"I don't think I ever felt any guilt about it. I just knew it was wrong, but my father was the one that was wrong. I think there's kind of a family pattern here. That's why I don't feel responsibility or guilt. I think I was just at the wrong place at the wrong time." —Jacque

"I didn't have a lot of room for shame. 'Fuck you if you'll have that impact on my life,' I thought." —Marty

Out of the pain of their suffering, the wisdom of survivors rises strong and true.

"If you don't like yourself, then you won't face yourself or your future." —Dana

Silence is one of our greatest enemies; speaking out, one of our greatest healers.

"I had a lot of shame until I found out about the abuse to the other granddaughters." —C.J.

The shame of being a lesbian who was abused by a man—resurrecting the "inauthentic lesbian" argument—is particularly painful.

"For me it was more of a battle because I'd been broken by a man. For a long time it was just shameful for me to think that I had slept with men. I feel like a tainted lesbian. I can kick myself better than anybody." —Delphene

Revictimization

"Revictimization seems to be a theme in my life." —Jen

"The abuse set me up to expect to be rejected, used, and mistreated." —Tammy

Research suggests that child sexual abuse places a woman at greater risk for further abuse in adulthood, a phenomenon called *revictimization* (Browne and Finkelhor, 1998; Messman-Moore, 2000; Runtz, 1987; Sanders, 1999; Stermac et al, 2002). Runtz (1987) suggests that traumatic sexualization, combined with overvaluation and overidealization of men, impaired ability to identify others who are trustworthy, and learned helplessness render abuse victims vulnerable to repeat episodes of sexual exploitation. With learned helplessness, victims lose their belief in their ability to influence their lives. According to Dayton (2000), "When we feel that we are powerless to change a painful situation, that nothing we can do will stop the abuse or rectify the problem, we give up." As children we froze and went numb as a defense. When we are victimized again we don't *fail* to fight back, we are *unable* to fight back (Bratton, 1999).

"I gave up and allowed myself to feel powerless. I relived the feelings of my abuse all over again! I never said "stop" or "no" because I felt powerless and almost in a state of helplessness." —Marie

"My journey to healing continues to be challenging as I struggle with frequently feeling victimized." —Jen

"I hate to say I wasn't the least bit surprised every time it happened. I kind of expected it in a strange sense. I saw that same look in many a man's face in the course of my childhood. It began to seem like they all thought these horrible thoughts." —Missy

Survivors told me, often reluctantly, how their abuse as children had been repeated later in their lives.

"After I was raped and molested from 7 until I was 15 by friends of my father and men my mother brought home, I was date-raped at 16 and my grandfather molested me until I was about 22." —Lee

"Right now I am struggling with a sexual harassment situation at work by a male coworker, and everyone has blinders on about it. I was encouraged to file a report only to have nothing done about it. The blinders phenomenon is not unusual, as my family has chosen that route in denying my abuse, which started when I was a toddler." —Jen

"There was my uncle and my cousin. When another uncle tried to pull me close, I squirmed away and ran into my cousin's room in hopes he'd leave me alone. He did. I was never alone with him again. I already had an idea of what he was capable of. Then there was a time with my stepdad's dad when I was 14. He was drunk, and I could feel instinctually what was about to happen. I broke loose." —Missy

"As a young woman I was raped twice. The first time a man asked me to use my phone, so I let him in. He made a call, then raped me. I knew there was no point in reporting it. I knew as an unwed mother on welfare with a biracial baby I would have no credibility. Two years later I was raped again, this time by a man from a neighboring apartment building. I was struggling to get my bicycle down the stairs into the basement while holding my daughter. The man offered to help me. After he put the bike away he followed me upstairs to my apartment and raped me. Again, I knew reporting it would be foolish." —Jacque

"As a child, in addition to the abuse by my mother and father, some-

one who stayed in my house, a housekeeper, made me touch her in a sexual way. Then, just last summer, I attended a group for incest survivors. The treasurer for the group, a man, took me home and raped me for nine hours. I was in a coma. I was found without clothes and no one knew my name." —Tabitha

"A woman physically abused and robbed me. It was the first time in my life that a person wasn't what she appeared to be." —Jan

"I dated a cousin for two years after high school. He tortured and abused me and was trying to kill me. I had to get his parents involved to get away. Then I dated a male teacher. He got me into drugs. He was not being very nice to me. Then I met up with a woman who stole money from me. You pick the wrong people, and people prey on you." —Debbie

"I was abused by three different men later in life." —Kim

"About 18 months ago my friend invited two men to our house. They slipped something into our drinks. One of the men asked me to walk downstairs to talk to him. When we got downstairs he pulled out his penis and tried to force himself on me. I made enough noise to get him to stop." —Kristie

"Four years ago I was seeing a male bodywork therapist, a chiropractor, who I had met in a sweat lodge. I was totally trusting of a male who said he was going to help me, which is out of character for me. He guided me to self-stimulation, and I had an orgasm. He continued to contact me. I wrote him a letter six months later telling him that what had happened didn't feel right to me. I reported him. I'm still getting over the shame and embarrassment." —Mary Lou

"My now ex-husband loved to use me as a punching bag. I was also sexually abused by a neighbor when I was 23." —Sue

"I was date-raped too. When I got a job in high school the owner sexually harassed me and felt my breasts." —C.J.

Groves and Schondel (1996) explain, "The female victim of abuse, through her experience of being silent, typically learns that women are victims. She may continue this silence when victimized as an adult or remain silenced when her child reports victimization." The association between femaleness, victimization, and weakness is consistent with a common issue related to abuse: the need to deny the abuse and remain in confusion (Saakvitne and Pearlman, 1990). "The edict to remain unaware of one's experience of abuse...is a critical part of woman's powerlessness and oppression." As Misha explains, *"I easily fall into the role of victim in my thinking if I am not alert."*

Survivors often blame themselves for this repeated victimization, believing they are branded in some way that is visible to others.

"Do I have a sign on my forehead?" —Julie

"I felt like after the first violation I had a neon sign that opened the door for others to cross my boundaries." —Brooke

Some survivors were revictimized by women as adults.

"I think numerous times I've set myself up to be abused. I've had two short (one- to two-year) relationships with women. Both women were emotionally abusive and controlling. Both times I've relocated to live with them, and then had to move to get away. I was hit or shoved in both relationships too, and their failure was always my fault. Both of my lovers used my abuse history over me." —Deborah

"Years later I was raped by a butch woman. This happened when I went to a club, got drunk, and had a woman drive me home. She raped me." —Laura

"My now ex-wife of seven years left a few bruises." —Sue

"My first real lesbian relationship became abusive. She was manic-depressive and from a similar abusive background. When she was ill she hit me once. I also hit her a couple of times, in defense." —Tammie

"In my first long-term relationship, I was physically, emotionally, and sexually abused by my partner." —Lisa

"Damn if I wasn't abused by my former spouse." —Tammy

"My coming-out relationship was abused as a child and had been emotionally abusive in past relationships. She was the one who usually initiated sex. She sometimes implied that she was healthier than I was because she was orgasmic and I was not. When I moved out, because the emotional ups and downs were exhausting, she told me that no one else could give me what she could. That she was the only one who knew what I needed. I knew it was a mistake to accept my second lover's invitation to come live with her. She had a thousand rules for all occasions. She cleaned out my bank account and hit me full in the face the day I moved out." —Deborah

Part of what happens with revictimization is that survivors tend to lose their ability to use their emotions as signals (Dayton, 2000). They misread subtle signals from other people, either over- or underreacting to what the other person is saying to them. Noemi recognized this in herself:

"I've been put through a lot of harm and even as an adult have placed myself in harm's way physically, emotionally, and sexually. Because of the way I grew up I would encounter individuals who would abuse me. The first incident was in kindergarten. It was not the last time I was raped, but because of my age and because of the person who did it—it was a boyfriend of my mother—it became a pattern. I wondered what I do that makes people or allows people to abuse me. It has affected my idea of myself."

In one study, revictimized women reported overall greater interpersonal problems than nonrevictimized women and were more socially avoidant, nonassertive, and overly nurturant (Classen et al, 2001). In healing, Haines (1999) says the survivor becomes "self-referential, meaning she trusts her own experience and intelligence over external messages." This is the emotional literacy described earlier.

Dayton (2000) describes what she calls the "pull of the traumatic bond," which is called the *reenactment dynamic.* In cycles of reenactment we tend to be drawn toward what we know, what is familiar. The information in our brains on what relationships feel like is the template from which we operate. "We choose what we knew; we do what we did." Part of this is our unconscious attempt to finally "get it right," to master situations that have crippled us emotionally and left us feeling helpless. In this way, reenactments in relationships serve as red flags marking the spot where the unfinished work is. In addition, in a cruel irony, survivors, who often feel dead inside, seek out high-risk behaviors in "a sort of unconscious attempt to jump-start their emotions" (Dayton, 2000). These behaviors may include high-risk careers, drug use, and abusive relationships. This pattern results from "sensation-seeking," the excessive physical energy and activity in the absence of the ability to modulate emotions or engage in problem solving.

"In the lesbian incest group we talked about doing deliberately risky behaviors. For me that was riding my bike along the river where maybe some guy could rape me. There was no one around. We talked about wanting to be raped. For me, it made me wonder if on some level I thought that. Because the hardest thing for me sometimes was pretending to be some holier-than-thou Christian because that was our family image, when I felt dirty and spoiled, like damaged goods." —Jacque

Recognizing the ways in which we have allowed our abusive pasts to continue to affect us is very painful. I am not suggesting that we ask for the abuse or deserve it, in any way. What I am saying is that when we do the necessary healing work —bringing our childhood wounds to our awareness and developing our abilities to keep ourselves safe and assert our rights—we may find ourselves being victimized less frequently.

"When I was young, many people took what they wanted from me because I was terrified and confused and didn't know how to protect myself." —Barbara

"I have been victimized because I let myself be victimized. I have tended to give away my power to others, and haven't stood up for myself when I should have. As my self-esteem and self-love have increased, I have gotten much better at speaking up for my needs and at not letting people treat me in abusive ways." —Cristi

Spirituality

**"We are not human beings trying to be spiritual.
We are spiritual beings trying to be human."
—Jacquelyn Small**

"My spirituality has changed over time. When I was 16 I was an atheist. I was mad at the world and I couldn't possibly believe in a God that would allow such horrible things into the world. I also remember an experience directly related to church. My cousin took me into the bus parked in the church driveway and had sex with me on the floor. So my hatred of Christianity probably started there. Through conversations with a friend I started opening my mind and accepting more possibilities. Now I have a deep spirituality. There are good things in this universe, and equally bad. So maybe for some reason I was put through all of this to teach others. To teach them it's horrible, and while they can never erase the memories, they can still live happy, satisfying lives. I don't subscribe to Christianity. I don't believe God is a being; it just is. It is everything and it is us. I guess I would say my spirituality closely resembles Hinduism. I believe in karma and repercussions. Energy, I guess, is my spirituality. Good energy goes out and so does bad, and it all comes back to its source." —Missy

When I asked women to describe their spirituality and the meaning it had in their lives, I was surprised to learn how diverse our perspectives on this topic are. While appreciating the various faiths in which we were raised, I was unprepared for the range of spiritual and religious beliefs I encountered and to learn how life-defining and transformative the power of our spirituality is. Psychotherapist and author Dina Bachelor Evan (2001) defines spirituality in the way that many survivors expressed it:

"Spirituality encompasses every aspect of life.... [It] is an internal sense of connection and harmony. It's a congruency between my values and my actions. It's an awareness that I am inextricably connected at the core to every living thing and that all of it is God, whatever you perceive God to be."

Survivors I spoke with described it this way.

"The abuse becomes incorporated into our journey through life, and we need to address it at different levels in terms of our spiritual journey. It's the issue of connection with other people and knowing that God loves us, the image of His love is created in our connections with other human beings. When your needs are not considered, it's hard to feel that connection." —Sue

"Spirituality to me is a collective sense that we all have worth." —Marian

Novotni and Petersen (2001) explain, "People who have gone through difficult experiences often rail against God. They hold grudges. They get angry. If you're going to be like that, God, then I just won't believe in you anymore! Toby Johnson, in *Gay Spirituality* (2000), contends that there is a certain kind of enlightenment that goes with being gay, a familiarity with being an outsider, a discovery that if the conventions of society are wrong about something as basic as sex, they're probably wrong about a lot of others things as well. Johnson explains, "The conflict between church teachings and the reality of gay feelings can create a spiritual crisis that causes homosexuals to reevaluate religion and the meaning of their lives." Interestingly, lesbians who attended "welcoming churches" did not become less religious as they moved through the coming-out stages as did lesbians who attended nonwelcoming churches (Chew, 1999). Psychologist Michele Novotni (Novotni and Petersen, 2001) noticed that many of her clients who were working through their anger with people had a "parallel need to work through their anger with God. Beneath the psychological issues, many of us also silently struggle with our faith."

Finney (1992) goes as far as saying, "I do not believe victims of abuse can be totally healed unless their erroneous beliefs about God are corrected." For incest survivors, the feeling of betrayal by God mirrors their feelings of abandonment and betrayal by a family member. In both instances the survivor both directs her anger at and seeks protection, direction, and love from the same place (Matsakis, 1996). These feelings can complicate the survivor's spiritual connection and cause her to question her faith.

"Become willing to see the hand of God and accept it as a friend's offer to help you with what you are doing."
—Julia Cameron

It can probably be said that one's belief in God or spiritual foundation is a product of one's environment and life experiences. For this reason, it came as no surprise to me that survivors I spoke with had varied and quite emotional reactions to my questions about their spirituality. While this is not a book about religious faith or the role of spirituality in the lives of lesbians, I felt it important to include survivors' thoughts about the role that spirituality has played in their lives. I know that for me the topic of religion has been a loaded one. Raised Catholic in an Irish-Italian family, I had a great deal of baggage about coming out as a lesbian survivor. As a child I felt like I was only going through the motions by attending church services, making my First Communion, and then being confirmed in the Catholic Church. Later, when the abuse started, I felt betrayed by God, abandoned by Him. My prayers of help went unanswered for years, or so I thought when the abuse continued. In this way I experienced what Courtois (1988) calls *religious defection*—a lack of faith in God and an unwillingness to accept a male god or religion.

As a result of our childhood trauma, we have unique issues with our spirituality that can only be understood within the context of child development. Robert Coles, author of *The Spiritual Life of Children* (1990), writes, "Children try to understand not only what is happening to them, but why; and in doing that, they call upon the religious life they have experienced, the spiritual values they have received, as well as other sources of potential explanation." Coles describes how children engage in soul-searching and attempts to make sense of their place in the universe. Buchanan et al (2001) similarly describe the struggle that lesbians face as they attempt to incorporate their sexual orientation and identity within the context of an existing religious or spiritual identity. These efforts are further complicated by the guilt and shame that many survivors feel about the abuse.

Marie Marshall Fortune (1983) sheds some light on the profound theological question that mystifies many of us—Why is there suffering? Using a theological argument, Fortune says that there is first the question of cause—the source of the suffering. God allows sinfulness because God has given human beings free will and does not intervene when they choose unrighteous acts. For victims of sexual abuse, Fortune explains that "although the inclination is to hold God or oneself responsible, there is clearly a perpetrator whose actions resulted in suffering for the victim. [The abuser's] sinful acts can be understood as a consequence of [the abuser's] own brokenness and alienation."

"I don't believe in God. I used to pray to God to make my stepfather stop, to get me out of the home while this was happening. God never answered me." —Laura

The second question is that of meaning. What meaning does the suffering hold for the victim? Here, according to Fortune, people have difficulty accepting that painful experiences happen for no good reason. So they try to create a "good reason" or seek a "greater good." Like Mary, who said:

"Working through the abuse helped me to renew my belief in God. My spirituality was stronger than ever. I don't think I ever thought, Where was God in all of this? *Because in some weird way I believe even the abuse happened for a reason. I've never questioned God working in my life; I just haven't always understood how."*

Sometimes experiences of suffering present a victim with an *occasion for a new self*—an occasion for learning and maturing psychologically and spiritually. As Juli said:

"The abuse confused me spiritually. I didn't know why God would let that happen to me. Now I believe that God has a purpose and a place for us all. I think I am supposed to use my abuse as a tool for helping others by telling my story. We can't always know what God is up to or what his motives are. He's a funny guy."

Fortune reminds us that awareness such as this is a "retrospective insight." Initially, victims do not view their experience in this way. And Fortune clarifies that "God does not send suffering in order to produce this result. God does not will that people should suffer. It is a fact of life that people do suffer."

Some survivors described feeling left alone in the midst of suffering, of feeling abandoned by God.

"For years I could not believe in a benevolent power greater than myself. I thought, If there is a loving God, why does he allow abuse to happen to innocent children? *And* If men are so troublesome in my life, how can I believe in the Judeo-Christian concept of a male deity? *I attended church for many years before I came to believe in a power greater than myself. And that was due to my experience in the 12-step program."* —Maggie

"I questioned the existence of God. This contributed to my depression—feeling so alone when other people had God. I was angry and hurt." —Amanda

"Maybe I blamed God for the abuse. I wasn't safe." —Deborah

"I felt abandoned and betrayed by God. I had this deep, ingrained guilt that God was judging me rather than my abusers. I can still believe it's my fault." —Mary Lou

Fortune (1983) explains that there are two possible sources for feelings of abandonment. One is the lack of support and involvement by family and friends. When people avoid the victim, she may literally experience being abandoned by those closest to her. She may then assume that God has also turned away. A second source of the feeling of abandonment comes from the victim's experience and understanding of suffering.

If a person believes God to be omnipotent, loving, and rewarding of the righteousness of good Christians, the suffering is either a sign of God's disfavor or a realization that God does not play by the rules. Either interpretation can lead to the feeling of being abandoned by God. This feeling of abandonment occurs for the victim who expected God to protect her from all pain and suffering. When she encounters suffering, she feels betrayed.

The sense of abandonment by God can be profound and often creates a crisis of faith for the victim. Fortune clarifies that "God does not promise to protect us from all suffering as long as we behave properly and follow the rules. God knows that we will all suffer. What God does promise us is to be present with us even in that suffering—to strengthen and carry us through." Fortune (1983) describes the need to "name the unmentionable sin, to speak the truth. And in the naming we deny its power over our lives. In naming it, the conspiracy of silence is broken. In naming it, we reclaim the truth which we know, that the way things are is not the way they have to be." Whitney explains:

"I was born and raised a Mormon. I do not believe in everything they preach or the way they function as a religion. I do believe in God and that an entity does exist. My spirituality was awakened in me in my late 20s, early 30s. My mother had been planting things inside of me all my life, but I hadn't been paying attention. I was too busy finding myself to see, hear, or feel the answers or teachings. Then one year I decided to take a closer look to what my soul was asking me. It led me to a closer relationship with my mother. I don't have exact answers and may not get them, but I have better understanding and my soul is glad that I did some personal research for some of the answers. I believe it may have awakened my soul to speak the truth."

When the abuse started, I stopped going to church and refused to participate in any conversations about religion. While I continued to identify as Catholic, I felt an emptiness inside. For years I battled with my feelings about wanting a religious affiliation and my resentment that God had left me all alone. In interviewing women for this book, I have been fortified in my belief that there is a God and that He gave me the strength that I needed to survive the abuse. Contrary to my belief that my prayers had gone unanswered and I had been left to suffer the abuse all alone, I came to realize that God was there with me when my brother was abusing me. He was helping me get through a difficult situation. Maybe in not preventing or stopping the abuse He was telling me that there was a different message for me to take out of the experience. Maybe pain is necessary. Maybe surviving abuse was the way for me to use my life to help others. I know now that God did not want me to suffer, but wanted me to survive, to be a strong, capable, and compassionate person who can help others. The lesson makes much more sense now and I am grateful for the path that I am on. It has not been an easy one, that's for sure, but one that continues to teach me every day that there are indeed mysteries of life that we will never understand.

"'Why are you doing this to me? How could you let all these bad things happen to me?' My aunt said, 'You have a purpose in life.'" —Debbie

"I was raised to believe that God is punishing, and I was terrified of God. Mom said, 'God can see you.' When I was being beaten by Dad I prayed to God, and He did not rescue me. I felt betrayed. Now I realize that I was given the tools to deal with the abuse." —Kyrce

There were many survivors who struggled as I did to make sense of their experience and to reawaken their spirituality or, for some, to find it for the first time.

"One of the initial reactions to my disclosure about the abuse was for my parents to get us all into the church. While I will admit that there was some comfort in finding God, I had great difficulty understanding why the church seemed so focused on my getting 'saved' when I was not the

offender. There seemed to be a lot of compassion and respect for my father, but I was looked at as 'something' that needed to be purified. For years I was fairly active in our fundamentalist church. In my late teens, I moved away from the church and from God as none of it was making much sense to me. I was still suffering inside while everybody seemed so happy. More recently I have started to make peace with God and am finding a place that is just for me. This has not been without a lot of hard work and a lot of bitter feelings toward God for letting the abuse happen." —Lisa

"It made me question my belief in God. And for a while I even turned away from God, the church, and my spirituality. I questioned why God would let such horrible things happen to a small child. I have come to appreciate the fact that I have very strong spiritual guides and that is why I am sane and alive today. My spirituality has been a big part of my recovery and my success." —Katie

"I still consider myself a Christian because I grew up in the Church. I don't believe that God is some white guy, but I guess I'm comfortable with my conception of God. In some old Carole King song she says, 'I know you're probably not a man or a woman, a time or a season, but I'm here and life is dear, and I guess that's a good enough reason to say just let me do what you put me here to do.'" —Deborah

"I hated God growing up. I refused to be a Catholic in elementary school and quietly wanted to know about witchcraft. As an adult I've embraced my own spirituality—the God within." —Noemi

"I never equated God with my male abuser, but being raised Catholic I believed I had to hurt for God to love me. Now I don't believe that. I've since left Catholicism." —Sarah

"I've made my peace with God." —Jacque

"I blamed God. I didn't think there was a God. I felt all alone in this. I'm not churchgoing, but I believe in an ultimate plan and believe in a God. He is all-knowing." —Dana

Being out as a lesbian is difficult in many organized religions whose doctrine contains antigay rhetoric. Reconciling one's lesbianism with one's religious beliefs is an ongoing challenge for many survivors.

"I thought for a long time that I was not worthy of God's love. As a young person I felt excluded from God's love because of the abuse and being lesbian and the terrible thoughts that I was having." —Pat

"I was very mad at Christians for a while because they said gays went to hell. Now I'm in a gay-friendly church." —Naomi

McNeill (1988) recognizes that "there are large numbers who cannot separate off their membership in the human church from their faith in God and their personal spiritual relationship with God." For these survivors, disgust with organized religion, particularly the male perspective prevalent in many religious faiths, and a sense of betrayal, alienated them from God.

"I was going to become a nun to stay within the framework of the Catholic Church and stay away from men. My family was very Catholic—a judgmental Father-God thing. I realized God was as abusive as my father. It took me a long time to get away from that oppression." —Mary Lou

According to McNeill (1988), people who cannot separate their faith and the church see only two choices: "either to remain in their church at the price of hating themselves and repressing their homosexuality as evil, or to accept themselves as homosexual and then denying or repressing their religious beliefs." Taylor (2000) found a significant negative relationship between Orthodox religiosity and negative attitudes toward lesbians and gay men. In particular, the belief that the Bible should be taken as literally as possible proved to be the strongest predictor of negative attitudes toward lesbians and gay men. In a fascinating study of gay men and lesbians' religious beliefs, Harris (2001) found that higher levels of postconventional religious reasoning—the ability to derive personal religious beliefs and to make personal religious decisions independently of other authorities, such as family, clergy, and religious reference groups—predict lower levels of internalized homophobia and higher levels of sexual identity development. It appears, perhaps not surprisingly, that our confidence in choosing a religion that fits us personally actually contributes to better feelings about ourselves as lesbians. This finding seems to suggest that lesbian survivors who are so inclined might benefit from pastoral counseling to help them heal from the abuse.

"My being fundamentalist Christian, gay, and abused are all intertwined. I was dogmatic in my Christian beliefs before. Now I'm more spiritual." —Christy

"The major obstacle for me was letting go of the rules ingrained in my brain from the religion. Once I had freed myself of that, the way was clear for me to look at my sexuality. After I had acknowledged the abuse and decided to leave the church, I was much more open to sexual experiences." —Cristi

"During my struggles in dealing with the situation I would question Why me? What did I do to deserve this? *just like a good Catholic. Now I struggle with my sexuality and if God would accept me in my relationship. Catholicism does frown on being gay. However, I know God loves me and things happen to me for a reason."* —Marie

"As a child I remember feeling that I was blessed by Jesus—despite being impoverished and not wanted by my mother! I thought that I was blessed to be healthy, smart, and athletic. When I learned that I am homosexual, all of a sudden I realized that I was not welcome in most churches. My guess is that my lack of ties to organized religion has everything to do with the homophobia not only mouthed by many churches but also actually written into their doctrine. As a child I felt firmly supported by my vague notions of a deity. Even now I feel blessed in many ways and tend to give credit for those blessings to some sort of cosmic spirituality." —Levie

There is an element of spiritual strength or religious faith in many survivors' stories. Instead of the resentment and abandonment issues that many of us experienced as a result of the abuse, many women described how their faith had always been a comfort, a source of strength that saw them through the difficult times and helped to heal the wounds. They seem to tell us what Father John McNeill writes in *Taking a Chance on God* (1988): "God's spirit is active in unlikely places, in the poor, broken, and humble places. The power of God is strongest in us when we admit our vulnerability, when we take risks and let go. To acknowledge that we are vulnerable is to acknowledge that we need God's help, and thus we make ourselves available to the power of God's love."

"I think my faith was what kept me going during the abuse." —Diana

"For me, it's never affected my belief in God. I believe that everyone has a path to live and sometimes bad things come in the way of that." —Melissa

"All my struggles are for God. God wants me to grow and gives me what I need. I've had a deep connection with God all along. My deep connection with God puts meaning in my life. I have a recognition of miracles." —Kathy

"It never affected my belief in God. It affected my belief in parents." —Serena

"Surviving abuse doesn't affect my spirituality. My faith in a higher power hasn't changed." —Kristie

"I'm a Christian and read the Bible daily. I read this morning where Jesus said, 'If you abide in me and my words abide in you, you will bear much fruit.' So I realize as I come more out of myself I can help much in His kingdom. I was fortunate to be raised in the church and came to know Jesus in 1976. So often those who need Him most seek Him more. I have the gift of intercession and have had many visions of Christ and Mary." —Naomi

"Spirituality, to me, is connectedness to spirit and nature. I believe in the Goddess and am studying Buddhism. The abuse and spirituality are connected for me. I remember praying to God for help as a child and got help, got relief. I had a spiritual experience. It kept me alive. I knew there was some protection outside of the human realm." —Lynn

"It has not affected my spirituality. I am currently pursuing being a minister with my church." —Sue

"It never affected my belief in God negatively. I've never been one of those 'God is punishing me' types or 'Why would God allow this?' My relationship with God has been consistent. My relationship with the Divine is evolving as I get older and heal some of my wounds." —Tammie

"Sometimes when my father was abusing me I would remember the gospel song 'In the Garden.' It talks about meeting and talking with Christ. My faith has been really important, prayer being one of the big things for healing. Those are two different things sometimes. I think hanging on to my faith has helped with feeling I'm a worthy person. One of the things that has really struck me, especially as I got into more accepting churches, is the idea of unconditional love. Because when you grow up with the abuse stuff you feel like My dad will only love me if I let him do this stuff to me. *If you can comprehend the idea somehow, accept the idea of God's love, I think it helps to overcome those feelings. I guess it's like saying, 'Yeah, even I'm good enough for Him. He loves me too. Even though I made mistakes. Even though I was promiscuous for a time in college. He loves me anyway.' And that gets into the idea of being saved by grace. It's not something you have to earn. He's offering it and all you have to do is accept it. Everyone's a valuable person to Him. And it doesn't matter what you've been through or what you've done. That really helps me a lot."* —Jacque

For some, their religious beliefs or spirituality became a way to connect with other lesbians and their life partners. Like C.J., who said, *"God gave me the strength. He or She put people in my life. My partner and I believe we were put into each other's lives. We were attracted to each other's spirituality."*

Other survivors were not raised with a religious or spiritual foundation and do not believe in God.

"I wasn't raised with a belief in God. I never had a relationship to the notion of a higher power, so I didn't feel either abandoned or saved by one." —Robin

"I never believed in God. It's fine for people who do. Faith is an internal thing, a feeling. It's not inside me. If it helps, that's fine, but don't use it to inflict pain on my life. Being an atheist affects the groups I'd go to. For example, I wouldn't go to 12-step programs with their belief in a 'Higher Power.'" —Reg

"Honestly, the way people think about religion, like there's some being out there that's controlling and has some say over how our lives are run and stuff, I don't believe for two seconds in anything like that. Things wouldn't happen to people the way they did if that's what it was. I can't believe some God said, 'This little girl deserves to be fucked by her dad.' There are way too many bad things that happen. For me to believe in God or something would just be denying reality. I didn't have a religious upbringing. Personally, a belief in God, like a Christian God? No. That's a crock of shit as far as I'm concerned. I was adopted. My fantasy, when my dad was abusing me, was, If it gets really bad, my birth mother will come for me. *That was like my religious substitute.* She'll be there if I really need her. *I feel a kind of spirituality and kind of a connection to the earth or something like that."* —Kris

In her book *Sexual Violence: The Unmentionable Sin*, Marie Marshall Fortune (1983) describes the need for a "clear and unflinching understanding of the ethical and theological dimensions of sexual violence to provide us with the foundation for both a pastoral and political/social response to the problem." In the Christian tradition, she writes, we find "an overall context which is both patriarchal and often misogynist, which contributes heavily to the practice of blaming the victim." Fighting this, as Dana did, brings some peace.

"The lesbian survivors I know think being a lesbian is bad, against the Bible, and that God is punishing us. But I don't believe we're going to hell because we're gay or were abused."

McNeill (1988), in *Taking a Chance on God*, refutes three traditional stances taken by the Christian community regarding gay and lesbian relationships: (1) the view that God intends all human beings to be heterosexual and that homosexuality therefore represents a deviation from God's plan; (2) that homosexuals, rather than being a menace to the values of society and the family, have as part of God's creative plan, special gifts and qualities, and a very positive contribution to make to the development of society; and (3) love between two lesbians or gay men, assuming that it is a constructive human love, is not sinful, nor does it alienate the lovers from God's plan. On the contrary, it can be a holy love, mediating God's presence in the human community as effectively as heterosexual love. McNeill argues:

> We must all mature in our faith to the point where we can separate our faith in God from the human and infallible church. We must develop our personal life of prayer so that we have our own direct and immediate contact with God. We can no longer allow our faith and belief to depend exclusively on the mediation of the church, with the result that if we become disillusioned with and scandalized by the human church, we are tempted to give up all belief.

Pat put it this way: "*The image of His love is created in our connections with other human beings.*"

Here's how survivors wrestled with the issue of separating their religious faith from organized religion and the human church.

"I have difficulty believing in organized religion. I'd like to think there is a God and that I do believe deep inside. But sometimes I wonder." —Elizabeth

"I hate organized religion in any form. The Mormon Church is very sexist and demeaning to women, and there's incest in the family. I was so disappointed in God." —Jan

"As a child your parents are like God to you. They could do no wrong. That destroys a lot when they hurt you. I'm neutral on God now. I pray a little." —Wendy

"Both of my parents were ultrasensitive to how the community judged them and the family. They made sure we went to church on Sundays, where we would often announce over the pulpit—which is the customary thing to do in the church—that we loved each other very much. I often went home feeling the lie in my heart, thinking to myself that if this is love, and I have to put up with this for eternity, I want nothing to do with it. On one hand, people—the culture in the religion and my family—taught me that God sanctioned this behavior, that He was jealous yet loving, vengeful but forgiving. Even though the philosophical heap piled itself high with contradictions, I felt in my heart over and over again that the Creator loved me unconditionally. This was one of the main focal points I held on to when I decided to leave the church and also when I decided to identify as a lesbian. Part of the reason I became so obsessed with church growing up was a way of running from the reality of the abuse. I felt so scattered and adrift that I clung to the rules with tremendous tenacity out of fear that if I didn't have some stability in my life, I would go nuts. I think on a subconscious level too I felt that if I paid extra attention to following all the rules, God would love me in spite of what I had been taught was the sin which I participated in as a sexual abuse victim. I have developed my own spirituality, finding useless much of what I was taught as a Mormon, particularly the cultural norm of sacrificing the need of the individual in the church in order to keep the organization strong and maintaining a wholesome image. Abuse in the church was largely ignored." —Cristi

"I think being raised Catholic was definitely a problem. The whole culture of Catholicism and its secrecy was actually harmful in that it

perpetuated the kind of culture that would allow abuse. I think I knew somehow that I had to distance myself from religion in order to do my healing." —Margie

"God is very problematic for me; I was always troubled by the concept. It sounds like an imaginary playmate of children—you know, the angels and the cherubs and all. Religion is man-made to serve men's needs. I hated Catholicism. Faith and religion are very negative in my worldview. I believe that men are so insecure in their lives that they create an imaginary hierarchy with God so they don't have to face their insecurity." —Marian

"I've always been able to distinguish between what Christ's teachings were and what the organized church is." —Jacque

Many survivors spoke with me about their fear that they would be blamed for the abuse by their church as they had been blamed by their family. The shame-based theology that governs many religions replicates the shame-based family systems that many of us were raised in. Part of the healing process for survivors is to heal the systems that continue to betray children with their silence and shaming. In talking to the religious community, Fortune (1983) describes what should be the "just response to the sin of sexual violence": righteous anger; compassion for the victims; advocacy for the victim; holding the offender legally and spiritually accountable for his or her sin against the victim and the community; understanding and forgiveness for the offender who has repented through rehabilitation and restitution; and prevention. All too often that is not the pastoral response that we are given. Here is an excerpt from "A Plea to My Pastor" from *I Choose to Remember* by the Violet Collective (1981):

> I need strength. I need comfort. But where can I turn? My faith provided strength and comfort in the past. It was my sanctuary. But now I find my church exposed as a traitor. It facilitated, justified, and then ignored my abuse.... I must be angry.... My anger gives me strength to stop being a victim. Please listen to

> what I am angry about.... Don't feed me the same old easy answers. They never did really work, and now I know they're lies. But I don't want to give up my spirit. I need it.... Help me to be strong. Help me to have courage.... I am in a dark tunnel traveling very fast and I can see no end. Help me believe I will survive. Don't minimize my pain by speaking quick platitudes. Don't try to make me stop hurting so you don't have to see it. Acknowledge my pain. Hurt with me. I need to know I'm not alone. Be with me (cited in Fortune, 1983).

The added insult of being abused by a religious figure—a priest or minister—was particularly devastating to survivors who had found comfort and a sense of belonging in the Church previously. The code of silence—so damaging to children—is at work here as it was in our childhoods. Rubin (2002) says, "For years people who spoke out about abuse by priests were accused of everything from outright lying to trying to destroy the church." The recent media and church attention to the abuse of children by clergy speaks to a sea change that makes us as survivors hopeful. Women spoke of how abusers would use religious rhetoric to justify the abuse in ways that were confusing to them as young children and served to alienate them from their religious beliefs.

"Spirituality is a huge area for me and I am just in the process of addressing it. Father Terry raped me spiritually, and this has affected my entire life. I was a deeply spiritual child and did my best once I became a Catholic at age 8 to live by the rules. I lost my spiritual innocence and from there I lost my way spiritually until I left the religious order in 1989. I am stronger now as I heal and am regaining my inner confidence." —Misha

"The abuse didn't help my relationship with God. My father, my abuser, was a deacon in the church. I can't think of God as a father type. I say 'Goddess.'" —Chris

"For many years I've felt extremely hostile toward religion. My abusers would talk to me about their God, especially after they sexually or physically abused me." —Barbara

"My father is a psychopathic Christian fundamentalist." —Cory

It is difficult to hear the stories of survivors who blame themselves for the abuse and who believe, as Dana does, that the abuse is proof that they are being punished on religious grounds:

"I have always believed there was something or someone that has the ultimate plan. Maybe this life I am living now is punishment for something I did in the past. Or at least punishment for betraying my mom in this life by letting my father abuse me. I hope to forgive me someday. To find the peace I do not have now. To not feel so guilty or evil."

"I must have been an abusive man in another life, and it's come back to me." —Tammy

While some survivors avoid any religious affiliation or spiritual exploration, others have found new ways to connect with their spiritual sides in ways that feel right to them as lesbians and survivors.

"I was a professed atheist from about 17 to 22, but rediscovered God through spiritually journeying into my Native-American distant past. I found a loving God as they practiced religion and found some peace and acceptance. I believe in an amorphous spiritual being. I've also explored Zen meditation and Buddhism. This has allowed the memories to come up more easily than with patriarchal religion. Gay people in Native-American tradition are in esteemed positions." —Tammy

"Now I am exploring Eastern religions—Native-American and Buddhism. In Alcoholics Anonymous I learned to be more connected and respectful of nature. Also the Michigan Womyn's Music Festival and female-identified spirituality." —Kyrce

"My partner, who studies paganism, gave me permission to explore other religions, like Buddhism." —Kyrce

"I used to be into the Indian, almost pagan, ways of belief. I also

joined a Presbyterian church in town. I found the pastor to be OK, and it was nice to know that God loved me no matter what I did. I still have a hard time with a lot of the Christian beliefs, but I still have a strong faith in a higher power, which I guess helped get me through." —Delphene

"I like Buddhism and read about it and always get something good if I go to a lecture. I see 'God' or a higher power in the beauty of a tree, in appreciating the moment, in finding gratitude for the basic things I have in life: my warm bed, clean water to drink, my car, my possessions. I see a higher power in real love and connection." —Cory

Embracing goddess spirituality is one way that survivors have made sense of their experiences. Their feelings of being disenfranchised and abused in a patriarchal society that discounts women's experiences and strength led them to a new spiritual faith.

"I always had a belief in some sort of force out there in the universe. I don't think that all of this came together by accident. I think that there was a design to it, a design to life as we know it. I have a belief in Goddess. I have a spirituality that I loosely practice. I'm a witch, a solitary eclectic. I find that that works for me. Magical things have happened, literally, since I've discovered women's spirituality and practiced it. What I see is that I have a deep spiritual connection to other women. It feels really good, and I feel a lot of power when I connect with other women in that way." —Nedhera

"I divorced the patriarchy 15 years ago. Now I have a Divine Mother spirituality and a deep belief in a spiritual source." —Mary Lou

"I believe that the energy of the goddess is the energy of the earth. It encompasses nurturing, growth-producing elements as well as those of the protector. The goddess energy is the energy of the feminine, fully actuated and honored in all its creative forms. I believe that we all carry the energy of the god and goddess within us, and it is when we tap into this inner spark that we begin to understand who we really are. I believe the god or goddess is within and that we don't need religions or gurus to show

us our path to the divine self. Each path is sacred. Each path is different, yet the same." —Cristi

"I am pagan and I study green witchcraft. It has helped me so much to learn about the divine essence and the feminine and feeling empowered. I learned about the place women had in the ancient past, their roles now, how it affects the balance, and how to restore it within myself." —Rowan

"I do not believe in God, only the goddess." —Amy

Dorian went so far as to describe the blessing of being a lesbian survivor:

"I am still a Christian, but I'm also exploring Taoism and Buddhism. I don't have a problem with it anymore because I know the truth that pertains to my life. I don't believe that being gay and a Christian contradict one another, but are just different facets of my life that make me who I am. We each have a place in this universe, and each has gifts to give. Why would a creator make everyone the same when we learn so much more about life, spirituality, and people from the different beliefs, cultures, and life experiences? Being both gay and Christian has taught me many life lessons."

Forgiveness

Society places a high value on forgiveness, and many survivors feel the pressure to forgive their abusers. The survivor is urged to let go of the anger she feels toward her abuser, release him or her from suffering any consequences of his actions, and move on with her life. But when someone has been the victim of a random and senseless act, such as robbery or assault, there is no emphasis on forgiving the perpetrator. The criminal, in these cases, is expected to be tried for the crime, to be publicly identified as having committed the act, to receive a just punishment, including possible financial restitution to the victim or prison time, and to be rehabilitated before reentering the community (Roth, 1993). Roth explains, "It would seem that asking the survivor to forgive the perpetrator is asking her to continue to take responsibility for something that does not belong to her." Were the abuser to take responsibility for his actions, Roth says, forgiveness might be a possibility. If you have adequately expressed and resolved your anger about the abuse, and forgiveness is compatible with your belief system, then it might be right for you (Roth, 1993). Courtois (1988) agrees, saying, "Forgiveness is her choice and is not something that every survivor will decide to do." Importantly, if you forgive prematurely, it becomes a way to avoid experiencing your most intense feelings about the abuse.

"The condition of the human spirit is so profound that it encourages us to build bridges."
—Maya Angelou

Perhaps no topic raised as much controversy as the issue of forgiveness. While I began the interviews with an idea of how forgiveness fit into the healing process for survivors, I had underestimated the conviction we feel about our survivor status as well as how shame can keep us from forgiving our abusers. I found Kritsberg and Miller-Kritsberg's words on the subject (1993) to be particularly helpful in clarifying the issues. They write, "To forgive those involved in your abuse requires a spiritual courage and commitment that comes from a deep love of self and of God." Of course, you don't have to forgive in order to heal. Fortune (1983) warns against rushing forgiveness when she writes, "An act of forgiveness by a victim cannot be hurried; nor can it be orchestrated by those on the outside. To expect people to move quickly from their pain to forgive those who are responsible for it is insensitive and unrealistic. Forgiveness is not merely an act of will." For Christians, Fortune clarifies, "forgiving is one means of letting go and disarming the power that the offense has over a victim's life. Forgiving means letting go of the anger and putting the experience in perspective.... Forgiveness means acknowledging the humanness of the offender. But forgiving never means condoning or excusing" what your abuser did. Forgiveness occurs within a context and takes place when a set of conditions is met (Fortune, 1983). In order to be authentic, forgiveness must be based on the following:

- a conscious choice on the part of the victim to let go of that experience of pain and anger
- empowerment of the victim through God's grace
- an experience of justice by the victim

Emotional forgiveness—when you feel forgiveness in your heart—is usually preceded by a great deal of time and energy dedicated to intellectual forgiveness (Fitzgibbons, 1986). If your abuser has acknowledged the abuse, expressed remorse, and entered treatment, there may be a way for you to truly heal the relationship—if that is what you want. Marie's experience describes how these conditions can be met:

"I think forgiveness is possible. I forgave my oldest brother because he asked for it and apologized more than once."

If forgiveness occurs in the last phases of treatment, you are more likely to feel "liberated or cleansed" by the act of forgiving (Roth, 1993). Certain motivations to forgive the abuser, however, can be unhealthy for the survivor: feeling forced to empathize with your abuser, fearing that by not forgiving you jeopardize your relationships with family and friends, or feeling that failing to forgive leaves you destined for a life of bitterness and anger. Forgiving your abuser under these conditions leaves you vulnerable to being revictimized in the future.

Forgiveness arises out of healing. According to Novotni and Petersen (2001), "Forgiveness suspends resentment or hostility." In letting go you allow positive feelings to replace the negative ones. But as Roth (1993) cautions, "the release from the pain of betrayal comes through introspection, expression, perspective, and integration" and not from forgiveness. Forgiveness is one potential outcome of the healing process, "not the process itself." Roth agrees, however, that in not forgiving our abusers we protect ourselves, sometimes too much. In not forgiving our abuser, we guard ourselves from further harm. We may try to protect ourselves by not opening up to others. Roth calls this a "victim's stance" and compares it to a "survivor's stance. The victim, Roth writes, believes that no matter how much pain someone causes her, she will eventually offer her compassion and forgiveness. A survivor, according to Roth says, "Never again will I allow anyone to have the power to annihilate me."

Renowned child abuse expert Andrew Vachss (2002) believes there is a fundamental question to ask: Are people who prey on children sick, or evil? "Sickness is a condition," he writes. "Evil is a behavior. Evil is always a matter of choice. Evil is not a thought; it is conduct. And that conduct is always volitional. And just as evil is always a choice, sickness is always the absence of choice. Sickness happens. Evil is inflicted.... Sickness should be treated. Evil must be fought."

According to Vachss, the goal for treating predatory pedophiles becomes not curing them or changing their thoughts and feelings but teaching them self-control. "To say a person suffers from the 'disease' of pedophilia," Vachss says, "is to absolve the predator of responsibility for his behavior." We want to call those who sexually abuse children "sick," says Vachss, "because sickness not only offers the possibility of finding a cure but also assures us that the predator didn't really mean it." After all, it is human nature to try to understand inhuman conduct. We believe that if we understand our abuser's motivations, we will be more inclined to forgive them. One study revealed that incest offenders' primary motives were: need for sexual gratification, outlet from present dissatisfaction, expression of anger, and inappropriate display of affection or love (Hartley, 2001). Early life experiences of offenders were characterized by physical and emotional abuse and a perception of rejection by one or both parents. Sometimes it helps us when we understand that our abusers abused because they too were abused; others among us are not so easily swayed.

"Maybe someday I will forgive him. Or maybe I will accept that there were things in his life that made him do what he did." —Mollie

"As I became more aware of the extent of the damage, I also became

more aware of the many factors that may have contributed to them becoming abusers. That understanding dilutes my anger. I feel a great deal of compassion for them and continue to be quite forgiving of them most of the time." —Levie

"I believe it's a sickness, something that can't be controlled." —Melissa

"I've forgiven my grandfather now. I guess just an awareness of how painful it must be that they feel they have to find someone that's vulnerable that they can do that to. They're such small, small people themselves and feel so badly about themselves that they have to find the smallest people to control in order to feel big. How awful and horrible it must be to be in that situation, the kind of situation that would drive you to that. There must be some point to remorse as well, and to live with that and the shame.... I understood this intellectually way before I could accept it emotionally." —Margie

"I used to think that forgiveness was not possible for me. But I've tried really hard to look at my father's life. I think a lot of how we behave is from our experiences and what happens to us. Abuse begets abuse. My father had a real strange upbringing, parents who didn't really care. I think he's had a lot of frustrations and he took them out on me." —Kris

Kristie found the prospect of explaining away the abuse abhorrent:

"I don't try to figure out why he did it. I really don't want to know. Whether he was abused when he was younger doesn't give an excuse for him to do it to others. He should've learned that if it was that horrible for him, not do it to others."

According to Vachss, the concept of evil terrifies us. "The idea that some humans choose to prey upon children is frightening." Roth explores the concept of evil as a new one to the mental health field and one that causes many therapists great discomfort. Seeing forgiveness of the abuser in the context of evil may help clarify the dilemma for survivors. "When is it ever appropriate," Roth asks, "to forgive someone who has consciously tried to kill another human being?"

According to Fortune (1983), justice for the survivor is some concrete expression of the fact that she has been wronged, that what occurred should never have happened, and that the abuser is responsible. Ideally, the abuser's repentance will provide that justice and will free the victim to forgive. Justice also can come through the legal system, as some of the survivors I spoke with found. The abuser's repentance goes beyond confession, apology, or good intentions. Repentance, according to Fortune (1983), means turning around, changing one's behavior, and not repeating the offense.

Dave Peltzer, in *A Child Called It*, warns, "When you don't forgive, you risk becoming a carbon copy of what you hate in the other person. Instead you say, 'I can't be like you.' Forgiveness cleanses you so you can move on with your life. You say to yourself, *I am letting go. I will not become like you.*" Research conducted on people who have forgiven their abusers shows that when we forgive we sleep better. In forgiving, you are giving up the hope that the past could have been any different than it was.

Some survivors described the pressure they felt to forgive when they weren't ready or did not feel the necessity of forgiving. For some, the benefits of forgiving were not readily apparent.

"I don't believe in having to forgive." —Wendy

"I don't know how I can forgive someone who hurt me when I was tiny. Especially since I don't know who it was." —Deborah

"One thing that still turns me off with religion is the forgive issue. That's a toughie for me. I think it's a lot of hype. I don't think I need to forgive. I tried it, especially during my God phase. I beat myself up for so long trying to forgive. Why can't I forgive? I even got to a point where it made me sick to my stomach. When I was going to church I would attempt to forgive. It's like in a way I felt I had to go up to the teacher or to my brother and say, 'You're just a human being, and you made a mistake' because that's what I was taught. I was like, 'I can't do that.' A lot of times I tried to get over being mad at myself for not forgiving. I remember every night and every morning I would look in

the mirror and say, 'I forgive you, Coach.' And then even that got depressing." —Delphene

"In Catholicism everyone is instantly forgiven, like it's a fast-food restaurant—drive-through forgiveness. And if you can't forgive, then it's somehow your fault. You're blamed for not being forgiving to someone who completely screwed up your life. I had to move away from that 'forgive the abuser' mentality to heal and come around to a place that I could forgive not just automatically but with a real understanding of my experiences and my abuser's experiences." —Margie

"It seems overrated in relation to me and my abusers. Several people have advised me that the key to my healing is forgiving. But so far, at least, I don't think that the considerable extent to which I have forgiven has contributed appreciably to my healing." —Levie

"I don't know that forgiveness works linearly. I don't think you forgive somehow and pow! *you're fine. I think it's a process. You have to work at it. It doesn't just happen as a result of an event like an apology or a conversation or a realization. And I'm not certain that forgiveness is the way to go for everyone. I know that those who have reached a level of forgiveness seem to be the ones most at peace, but I don't know that you have to forgive to be there."* —Mary

Others described how they want to forgive, believing as Serena does that *"it is an important step along the way to recovery."* But they aren't ready to forgive quite yet.

"I have not been able to forgive or forget my abusers." —Noemi

"I like forgiveness. It's a nice concept, but I'm not there yet. I don't know that I will ever be able to forgive my abuser for what he has done to me." —Elizabeth

"I don't know if I will ever completely forgive my parents. I guess I want to, though. My life seems to be more peaceful when I'm able to forgive." —Mary

"Forgiveness is important to me. I have lived with so much bitterness and resentment for so long—and I don't want to live that way anymore. I grew up in a very unhealthy home with an alcoholic father and a hard, withdrawn mother. They were sick and did sick things. I'd like to move on with my life." —Maggie

"If forgiveness means understanding why something happened, then I guess I am in favor of forgiveness. If it is understood to mean forgetting past hurts and allowing an offender to live and act as if there are no repercussions to his offending behavior, then I believe it is unhealthy and unfair. Ultimately, I believe each victim has to define her standards for herself and then to act in ways that honor her personal code. I neither understand my father's motives nor care to understand at this point. I have no place for him in my life, so for the most part, this is a nonissue for me. It becomes an issue for me when I start to examine my spiritual life and become conflicted about my unwillingness to forgive while asking God for the ultimate forgiveness. In this sense, it is an ongoing and sometimes painful struggle for me. I constantly seek grace to do what is right." —Lisa

"Forgiveness means moving on and is ultimately something I do for me. I need to do my work first, no carte blanche forgiveness. It's letting go of the cord or energetic connection to that person, but not forgetting. That could be reallowing it." —Mary Lou

Others have been able to forgive their abusers.

"I think it's key. Forgiveness is not about the other person, really. When I saw my stepfather last year I was reading a Bible verse that had the word forgiveness in it. I remember my entire heart feeling like it opened up and a warm feeling encompassed my body. I knew I had to let go of him and what he had done." —Tammie

"I once had a pastor who was determined to help me heal. He took me back to that time and asked me, if given the chance, what I would say to my grandpa? I told him I would ask him 'Why?' He then asked me, 'What would that do? Would that change what happened?' Then I realized that no

answer would truly help, and nothing would ever change what happened to me. So I had a choice: keep dwelling on it and wondering why, or move past it and know there is nothing I can do to make it disappear. My pastor stressed the importance of forgiveness because it is what God called us to do. I didn't understand why I had to forgive, but I was becoming active in the church and I wanted to do what I believed God would have done. Forgiveness does not mean you have to forget, nor will you. To me, forgiveness means recognizing that my grandfather had an illness and forgiving him of his faults and wrongdoings in order for me to let go of my ill feelings toward him. I forgave him in my own way, in prayer, by asking God to forgive him and admitting to myself and God that I forgave him. And I can honestly say a burden was lifted from my shoulders. I now know why forgiveness is so important. I didn't understand it even up to the moment I did it, but I was willing to give it a try. I set a specific time as a goal to be ready to forgive, or else I was afraid I never would. And I did it. I don't like what happened, but I can't change it. For me, forgiveness is the key to moving past it." —Juli

"I have forgiven my grandfather. Why not? If you forgive it's so much easier to go through your life. Nobody's perfect." —Julie

"Forgiveness was the first thing I worked on in therapy. I believe that without forgiveness I would be very angry and my spirit would be unhealthy inside. In therapy I worked on forgiving my brother because I knew that it would be a very long time before I confronted him with the abuse. I wanted to heal and move on. I wanted more positive things in my life." —Whitney

"I want freedom from the abuse memories. I see forgiveness as getting me off the hook, letting go. I have forgiven my mother for the emotional abuse and for not protecting me from my father." —Lynn

"I have come to a place of forgiveness with all who abused me. I used to think I'd never forgive my sister. I was adamant that I never would. But I decided not to carry that negative weight around with me. It was just allowing the damage to continue, and I wanted to move forward." —Brooke

Still others describe how choosing to forgive is an ongoing process.

"Forgiveness is the only answer. I dip in and out of this place on a daily basis." —Jan

"I would like to forgive. I'm working on it because I know how healing forgiveness can be for me. My therapist always says anger and resentment use up so much energy." —Kim

"Forgiveness is a key aspect for me in my healing. I feel I have developed sufficient ego strength not to decompensate as I revisit the abuse and continue the process to clear all patterns from my behavior and thinking and to clear my body of any residuals of abuse." —Misha

"When my father's helpful I can forgive. When he's mean, I can't." —Yvonne

"I think it's the only thing to do, but it's very hard." —Naomi

"Forgiveness is more of a spiritual thing. The understanding and acceptance to some extent is like the Serenity Prayer—accept the things you cannot change…and just be at peace with it." —Wendy

While Sarah and Rowan do not use the word *forgiveness*, they describe their process of letting go in the same way that Bratton (1999) describes the need to release the anger around the abuse.

"I can't forget because then I can't help anyone else. It's in the past. I made a conscious decision to let it go. My father is going through his own hell now. He chose that path. I worked on everything consciously, analyzing everything in order to change it." —Sarah

"As far as forgiveness of my abusers, I don't think I want to or should. I concentrate on letting go of the hate so I can live my life." —Rowan

Others continue to be fiercely angry at their abusers, even considering seeking revenge for the abuse they suffered.

"I can never forgive him for what he has done. I am messed up right now and trying to get my life in order, and I blame him for my relationship problems. I hope someday I can make him pay for what he has done to me and others." —Laura

"I don't forgive him. We hate him—every bone in his body. He will go to hell. I'm even angrier at Dad for how he treated our mom." —Dana

"I don't forgive the perpetrators at all. I would shoot the man who raped me." —Kathy

"I won't forgive my former boss. I would have taken legal action." —C.J.

"Despite my spiritual awakening, I still am unwilling to forgive this bastard because of what I have suffered for his misdeed." —Tammy

"I absolutely despise forgiveness in my life. It serves the perpetrator. Forgiveness is vastly overrated. I'm not willing to forgive my abusers. What they did was awful. If they were in my life I would be doing everything I could to make their lives miserable. I don't see what I would gain by forgiving them. I'm sorry they're dead now. I wouldn't mind a little revenge." —Marian

"What's appropriate for each person may be different. I don't believe in forgiveness. There are evil, horrible people in the world." —Reg

"I don't think I am capable of forgiving my uncle for what he did to me and my sister." —Kristie

"There are too many apologists for the crimes of men in this world already." —Robin

"Forgiveness is not something I'm interested in considering. I don't think it'd help me at all." —Barbara

"For me, my parents are beyond forgiveness. Every day I find some way in which I'm emotionally wounded and handicapped because of their abuse. It's not the time in my life to forgive. Maybe that will change.

Who knows? Right now I'm pretty angry at them and think they're beyond forgiveness. They are not capable of coming to me and saying 'I'm sorry.' My father has said he'd do it again. So what is there to forgive? My parents are real losers as people, and the world would be a better place without them or if they had never lived." —Cory

Dorian describes how her revenge fantasies almost ruined her life:

"Forgiveness works for both parties. I got over my hate a long time ago because it almost ruined me. I was almost a murderer."

Shortly after I confronted my brother about the abuse, my whole family went away on vacation together. It was a very difficult week for me. It was the first time that I had slept in the same house as my brother since the abuse in high school. Needless to say I didn't sleep much. Toward the end of the week, my brothers and sisters decided to go sailing. Not fond of water, I decided to stay behind. As it turned out, this decision was prophetic. No sooner had they gotten the sailboat out of the harbor than a fierce storm kicked up and capsized the boat. My brother and one of his daughters were thrown from the boat. They struggled for quite some time to get back. I was, of course, grateful to hear that my niece was safe, but I was unprepared for my ambivalence about my brother. How convenient it would have been if he had gone down with the boat. In the hours following the boating accident, I wished silently that he had. While my family comforted my brother and niece and expressed their gratitude that they were both safe, I was alone with my thoughts. Until that incident, I hadn't realized my anger at my brother had not subsided at all. While I had never put any pressure on myself to forgive him, I had secretly hoped that one day I would find forgiveness in my heart. I realize now that forgiveness, for me, is not in the near future. It may come in time as I continue to heal the wounds of my childhood, but it is not a priority. I feel that for the time being forgiveness would shift my focus away from my own healing and toward getting him off the hook for what he did. Unfortunately, that's the story of my life—letting him get away with shit. I decided once and for all that it was not my job to make his life easier. In making a new life for myself and my family of choice—far away from him—I could begin to let go of the power of the abuse over my life while letting *myself* off the hook for the abuse.

Similar to my experience, Mary describes forgiveness in language that echoes the powerlessness that she felt during the abuse. By forgiving she feels like a victim again:

"There's a part of me that feels it would be like giving up power to them again if I forgave them. Like if I don't forgive them, I somehow have power over them. That doesn't feel healthy, but it's honest." —Mary

Many survivors who are able to forgive their abusers find themselves unable to forgive those who failed to protect them from the abuse—usually a parent.

"Sometimes I'm more angry with my mother for not believing me. That actually is harder for me to forgive than what Dad did." —Jacque

"Sometimes I'm forgiving and other times I'm enraged. Enraged that my family has memories of it all happening and can do nothing to take it all back." —Missy

"I always felt that I had some reason to be angry with my mother, but I never understood the intensity of my anger until I recovered the memories of sexual abuse by my dad and brother. Then it seemed logical, albeit somewhat unfair, that I blamed her for not protecting me from the sexual abuse. In reality she had no viable means of protecting me. I'm still working on that with my mom. It's harder for me with her because I have a relationship with her and she's not overtly evil like he is. It's much more gray for me." —Tammie

Others, like Missy and Amanda, are able to forgive their nonprotectors by understanding the circumstances that surrounded the abuse.

"I have forgiveness for my mother. She made some really bad choices, but I know how hard she was trying to raise me by herself. She was 21 at the time all of this started." —Missy

"I forgive my brother for not stopping the abuse." —Amanda

Liz describes her ambivalence about forgiving her abuser, which is tied up with the fantasy of the loving and nurturing family she was denied as a child.

"I don't think it's possible to forgive somebody unless they are sincerely working on it. I don't forgive my father. To forgive him, he has to work at it too. Letting go? It's different than forgiving, I think. It would not take much for me to forgive my parents. I dream about this all the time. I dream that I'm killing them, on the one hand. Or I daydream and I think what it would be like if my father came and said, 'I have done some awful things, and I know that I hurt you in a lot of ways. This is something that I put on you that you will deal with for the rest of your life. And I'm really sorry.' If he did that, I would forgive him. But I think that's separate—I can feel myself wanting to cry just thinking about that because it's never going to happen—from saying I'm not going to cut myself anymore because that's a replay on him. I'm not going to be so scared of letting people be close to me. I'm not going to let him control me. I think that those are two different things. I need to let the anger go. But forgiveness is something that the other person has to grant to you. It isn't something that I do for my father. It's something that my father does for me. It's been easier for me to think about it that way. To tell myself that that's not going to happen. The wish for it, I can put to other things. I can wish for that feeling and get that kind of caring and acknowledgment from people other than him."

Sometimes we forgive our abusers in an unconscious attempt to heal our relationship with them and to let go of the pain of the relationship wound.

"Right now my Mother has Alzheimer's and is completely disarmed. She's just happy to have you around. And I'm getting off on that! I'm like, 'I'm going to get it for all it's worth and benefit from it. She'll be as nice as hell to me for the rest of her life. It's very ironic because now she's defenseless. It's more healing for me to give her what she couldn't give to

me than to fuck her, to screw her while she's defenseless. It makes me feel so much better to treat her the way I would have wanted to be treated when I was a child." —Jill

Some survivors, like Levie, use the defense mechanism of *idealization* in an attempt to preserve a link to the abusing parent so that the child feels less at risk (Dayton, 2000). Unfortunately, this is also the way that we continue to feel shame about the abuse, by failing to place blame where it belongs, on our abusers. Alternately, survivors may idealize people then hate them when they disappoint them in some way, seeing them as all good or all bad. This defense is known as *splitting.*

"My father died 30 years ago. I still love him with all my heart and forgive him and defend him to my family and anyone else who judges him harshly. My view of my dad is that he was my more loving parent, and the one who not only loved but also really liked me. Our relationship at the time of his death was extremely close and loving." —Levie

"It's really hard for me to call what my brother did to me a rape. I mean, it was, but it goes against everything I think about my brother. You know, I don't think he'd ever try and hurt me. But he did. I don't think he realized the impact it had." —Delphene

C.J. connects forgiveness with her faith and the strength that it has given her to move forward with her life:

"I haven't forgiven my abusers. I don't know if I ever can. Forgiveness means that I could embrace them again. But I'm not going to let what they did control me. I was raised Catholic and got pretty involved in the church when I was married. I drew a lot of strength knowing that God was all-loving and all-forgiving, opening myself up to God's forgiveness. This is about me and my happiness—knowing, understanding, and believing."

Survivors' beliefs in karma and God's ultimate plan for us all fits with their understanding of forgiveness.

"Forgiving my abusers? The friend of my parents was killed in a boating accident several years ago. And my brother is serving 55 years for murder, no parole. It is true that we all get what we truly deserve." —Sue

"Emotional, mental, and physical scars are real. I don't particularly like the word forgiveness *as that implies lessening or denying the energy of what happened. Hatred and anger, on the other hand, can rip people's lives apart on all levels. I believe it's important to come to some point of reconciliation where walking one's own path leads to health regardless of what has been done to us in the past. I still find anger cropping up at times. When I do, I try to acknowledge the emotion and look at the lesson I learn from it. I have also found it helpful to affirm that the abusive individual is walking his own karmic path: the energy which one emits into the universe returns to the sender."* —Cristi

While most of the discussion about forgiveness focused on abusers, there were some survivors, like Delphene, who believed the most important part of forgiveness is forgiving ourselves. In forgiving ourselves we let go of the shame and self-blame that belongs to our abuser and that we have carried for far too long:

"I think the forgiveness that should come should be to ourselves. We're the most important people to forgive."

CHAPTER 6

Relationships With Women

"A longing fulfilled is sweet to the soul."
—Proverbs 13:19

"You were born with the right to be happy. You were born with the right to love, to enjoy and to share your love." —Don Miguel Ruiz, *The Four Agreements*

Looking for Love

Because survivors have been deeply hurt by significant relationships in childhood, it can feel scary to become intimate with others later in life. Simultaneously, we can have a deep longing for love and connection and a deep fear of staying connected (Dayton, 2000). When we risk being in an intimate relationship, we may find that it provides an opportunity for healing and growth. Even so, we may continue to suffer contradictory fears—of being abandoned and engulfed. These fears can create anxiety around the subject of commitment. The result may be running rashly into commitments without allowing sufficient time to get to know the other person or trying to stay clear of any relationship that feels permanent. McNeill (1988) goes on to say that "in one's first experience of affectionate intimacy, one tends to become a 'hungry infant' who wants to be mothered and demands total attention and gratification. Since no adult can make that kind of commitment, the result will be intense jealousy, possessiveness, and lack of trust."

When we talk about lesbian survivors and relationships we must recognize that there is the increased likelihood that lesbians will establish partnerships with survivors since 38% of women may be survivors, and 38% of lesbian women may be survivors (Eide, 1993).

Here are some of the ways survivors describe their (failed) attempts at love.

"When I was 21 I fell in love with a woman. We became friends, and she seduced me. I became very involved emotionally as well as physically. Then I found out that she still slept with a local man just to keep her 'cover.' This hurt me a lot. It was years before I could pursue another relationship with a woman." —Deborah

"I played this game of going into a bar and looking around for someone I like. I'm the pursuer. But I always end up with people who don't know what to do sexually. They're boring." —Julie

"I like to date, although that seems problematic for many lesbians. However, no matter how honest I am about my intentions, it seems to end up with bad vibes; they want more and then get angry when I don't want the same thing." —Tammie

"I had a really screwed-up idea of what love was. I thought it was a really gross version of all the songs I'd heard. This person will take care of me, I thought, and not themselves." —Cory

Trying to find someone to love can be a very lonely and overwhelming process emotionally, as some survivors told me.

"We struggle with intimacy. We work and teach so we don't have to be social. But we are extremely lonely and afraid of being alone the rest of our life. I have lost half my life and am afraid that I won't get a chance to be in love. We don't have any social life. We don't think any woman could want us. We don't feel very attractive or appealing to anyone. I'm afraid I'm too old to come out and find someone. Can I get past this fear and find a person to share my life with?" —Dana

"I am part of a lesbian singles group at the local gay and lesbian center so I can meet women in a nonthreatening environment." —Dorian

"Sometimes I think I should just find out how to meet women online, like it seems everyone else knows how to do, and go out and find a girlfriend." —Deborah

"Dating is really hard. It's absolute hell." —Cory

"I really hate myself at times and can't look in the mirror and try to stay out of intimate relationships. I've recently started dating women again, which is difficult at times, but I'm glad I can actually be intimate with someone now." —Kim

"I've had great sexual relationships and a good platonic one. Now if I could only combine them...I haven't gotten it together yet." —Jill

"Butch-femme is the one place it's perfectly OK to be vulnerable. The problem is getting to that. And sometimes you can't get to that. But when you do, it can be really glorious. Being absolutely trusting of your partner in that way. To hold that sort of thing for your partner is very, very trusting and loving. I'm still looking." —Nedhera

Sometimes we don't have the energy to look anymore, or feel beaten down by the process.

"I don't have time. With my commute I'm gone 12 hours a day. I don't have energy when I get home. It would be nice, sure. I think I could be good in a relationship." —Reg

Codependency

"The abuse set me up to be codependent, to meet others' needs and not my own." —Kathy

According to Melody Beattie, who coined the term, *codependency* is "an emotional, psychological, and behavioral condition that develops as a result of an individual's prolonged exposure to and practice of a set of oppressive rules" (1989). These rules are enforced in dysfunctional families and are the kinds of environments in which child sexual abuse thrives. These rules say:

- Don't feel or talk about feelings.
- Don't think.
- Don't identify, talk about, or solve problems.
- Don't be who you are—be good, right, strong, and perfect.
- Don't' be selfish—take care of others and neglect yourself.
- Don't trust other people or yourself.
- Don't be vulnerable.
- Don't be direct.
- Don't get close to people.

Melissa Etheridge, in *The Truth Is: My Life in Love and Music* (2001), describes the type of codependent behavior many of us engage in when we deny our own needs and try to control others in an unconscious attempt to take care of ourselves:

> Attraction, for me, is very cerebral. It's a mental game. If I like you and you like me, then I would never go out with you. It's too easy, too predictable, too accessible. Ah, but if I like you and you reject me, like my mother or sister did, then it is a familiar place for me. I'm trying to get from other people what they are simply incapable of giving to me. Wanting it. Needing it. Craving it. Obsessing over it. But never attaching the concept of ever receiving it.

Many survivors spoke of their codependent tendencies.

"I think my ex sees us as a meal ticket. I've gotten involved in her chaos in a codependent manner." —Dana

"I feel like I'm a major caretaker and put my own needs aside. This has led to me feeling not taken care of in relationships and an unhealthy dependency from my partners." —Brooke

"My first relationship with a woman was my first real love in life. She was like an addiction. God, I was so taken with her." —Mary

"I am never afraid to give more than 100% in a relationship, which may be why the women I'm with expect a lot out of me. My mistake is not moving on when my needs and wants are not being met. I've always had the vision that women will see the good in me and replenish what they take, but it doesn't always work out that way." —Whitney

"My last relationship was nine years long and emotionally battering. The other was six years long and adulterous. I thought my worth was in helping others. 'You don't love me unless I'm doing for you.' Severe codependency messed with my relationships. Both women were survivors. 'Whatever you need to heal.'" —Kathy

"Even if the person was clearly wrong for me, I wanted to stay with her. Then I realized what a healthy relationship should be like." —Elizabeth

"Relationships have always been the reason I've been suicidal." —Chris

"I have a memory of a recent violation, a boundary violation triggered by my partner's mother. My partner and her mother have a very energetic connection. And her mom was calling every day. After eight or nine days I felt like she was taking my partner away from me." —Mary Lou

Many researchers have found, as I did, that survivors often pursue careers in the helping professions (nursing, social work, psychology) as a way to avoid their own pain. Many pursue these careers out of frustration in finding help for themselves. "Helpers" were certainly overrepresented in my sample. While these are, of course, worthwhile professions, we need to examine our motivations for getting into this line of work. Are we trying to help people out of a personal need to fix others or to feel needed? Do we want to rescue people?

"The abuse makes me want to help others. I tend to choose jobs and date people where I feel I am needed or where I think I can help or change someone. I recently tried dating someone new. She's almost perfect, an angel. I slowed things down last week because I guess there's nothing about her I can fix." —Juli

"Taking care of someone is a way of keeping distance while getting my needs met." —Liz

"People always saw me as someone who had all the answers to all the problems. But little did they know that I was doing all this because I couldn't handle what I was going through." —Diana

"I have a master's in counseling. I think I went into this to fix myself. I work with women with domestic violence and sexual abuse issues." —Kyrce

"One consequence of the abuse is that I tend to rescue people. Vulnerability is a button for me. If you're vulnerable, then you can just about bet I'm going to love you. I wish it wasn't such a turn-on for me." —Nedhera

"I used to take care of everyone else, like a good social worker. Now I'm learning to take care of myself." —Lynn

Serena described her own experience with reenactment cycles, *"I keep seeking people to repeat the same primal mistakes."* Reenactments are those relationship dynamics that get created over and over again and reveal to us where our deepest wounds lie (Dayton, 2000). Survivors whose childhood was filled with drama often recreate these dynamics in their adult lives and in intimate relationships.

"I kept stirring things up and moving around." —Deborah

"I tend to gravitate toward crisis." —Wendy

"There was way too much drama in my relationships with women or I became a 'crumb eater,' taking too much crap from my partner; dysfunction, chaos, confusion, and lack of self-esteem on my part. One woman came from a similar background, which meant we understood each other, but because she hadn't worked through any of the issues, a real intimate relationship didn't seem possible. I couldn't trust her entirely." —Tammie

"I was destroyed when my first relationship with a woman ended. I feel I have never fully recovered. It was the first time I completely let myself go with someone, and it was fantastic. But then her eyes started wandering and I couldn't hold on to her. One flirtation after another and finally she cheated on me, and my trust was forever damaged." —Mary

We also have the tendency to project our unresolved history from past relationships onto people in the present (*transference*). In relationships, our old wounds are triggered through feelings of dependency and vulnerability that are part of any intimate relationship. Survivors tend to see the world in black-and-white terms. People are either good or bad, including ourselves. This dynamic grows out of and mirrors our inner world, which alternates between high intensity and shutdown. Because we were hurt as children we may become hypervigilant in our relationships, constantly scanning for signs of a problem. As a result we can become rigid and perfectionistic in our expectations for what a relationship should be. This often includes unrealistically high standards for our partners. "Underneath," Dayton explains, "is the wish to be rescued and taken care of that grows out of unmet childhood needs." Another common couple dynamic is the distancer and the pursuer—one pursues and the other is pursued, as Juli described earlier.

Lesbian couples have been described as displaying higher levels of emotional bonding than heterosexual couples. In the extreme, this bond can create enmeshment and a lack of individuation between partners (Groves and Schondel, 1996). Group therapy with lesbian incest survivors and their partners has been successful in helping each partner respect independent thought and feeling and recognize the boundaries of the other. Couples participating in a group for survivors learned not to cut off communication and distance from each other during conflict or perceived difference. They also learned how to effectively handle conflicts which arose when both partners were simultaneously needy.

Recognizing our codependent tendencies and making efforts to break their hold on us is a first step on our road to recovery. Eide (1993) describes how "survivors of trauma have certain characteristics that may attract persons similar to themselves," but this need not be our lot in life. We can make better choices for ourselves, as the survivors below attest.

"A couple of things we may miss when forging relationships are boundaries and codependence. Even today I find myself checking and rechecking my boundaries with my friends and containing my desire to mother or become codependent with them." —Sarah

"I will never be in another codependent relationship! If people would take the time out for self-development, then they wouldn't look to their lovers to fix or fulfill them." —Dorian

"My last girlfriend told me she had met someone else. I did not want to engage in the game of waiting around to see if she would come back to me. I've learned the hard way that if a person is not happy where they are in life, trying to change them does not work and has codependent written all over it." —Cristi

"With my partner of 19 months we're not codependent. She has said she will not participate in that. She's a survivor with a lot of healing and awareness. We have good boundaries. She'll tell me when I'm trying to control." —Kathy

Violence in Lesbian Relationships

Until recently, domestic violence within gay and lesbian relationships was not researched or talked about. While many of us have heard of lesbian battering, or even suffered it ourselves, it was not a topic that was discussed. The body of research on lesbian battering is growing and contributing needed information about the dynamics of abuse within lesbian relationships. Specifically, Dayton's research (2000) reveals that survivors may be predisposed to both batter and to be battered, as Noemi attests:

"With women, the issues circled around trust and intimacy. Emotionally I found myself being an abusee or abuser."

In the first instance—when we are abused—survivors' feelings often become fused together during periods of emotional pain (Dayton, 2000). Love and violence and sex and aggression become entwined. Lesbian survivors also have a tendency to re-create intense trauma-related behaviors like shouting, hitting, sexual abuse, or acting out the behaviors they learned in childhood in subsequent relationships.

"I am drawn to controlling women who can be abusive. I start off being intimate, but then I get scared and uncomfortable. I end up breaking up with the woman because I still can't handle it too well. The relationship I'm in now is with a woman who's married, and I know she'll never leave her husband. I shouldn't have gotten involved with her when I knew. I just hoped she would leave him. I'm attracted to certain women because there's something dangerous and wild about them. I know it gets me into trouble, but that's what I like. They usually don't care about hurting someone." —Kim

"I am drawn to abusive women—verbally, physically, and mentally abusive. I was very vulnerable and drawn to situations where boundaries were crossed." —Wendy

"I've been accustomed to turmoil and mayhem since childhood. I had to get a restraining order on one woman to keep her from me. That was after a year of dealing with constant mayhem, stalking, harassment, and surveillance." —Robin

"My first lover got to be really critical and psychologically abusive. It turned out her father had raped her when she was 16. We were both so sick from the abuse, and neither of us had ever gotten any help for it, so I think it affected our dynamics. I got to the point where I got out of the relationship. I just packed up my stuff. I found the strength in that situation to do what I needed to take care of myself. Then the same thing happened with my next lover. She became increasingly verbally abusive and sometimes physically—punch and poke and stuff like that. I think I still love her, but I had to take care of myself." —Jacque

"When I found out my first girlfriend cheated on me, I was really hurt and didn't trust her at all. Staying with her was like abuse. I didn't think I was worth protecting from someone who would hurt me like that." —Melissa

"I've had two short relationships with women. Both times were failures. One woman said she had fallen in love with my 'potential.' Unfortunately, both women were emotionally abusive and controlling. Both times I've relocated to live with them and then had to move to get away. I was hit or shoved in both relationships too, and their failure was always my fault." —Deborah

"I really need to deal with the issue of me being in abusive relationships. A lot of the relationships I've been in, including the recent one, have been abusive. There's a pattern of wanting to keep the bad ones and get rid of the good ones. The good ones are people who don't express abusive behavior, that treat me with adequate respect, who respect my sexual boundaries. It's like when somebody's too nice to me. I feel uncomfortable, trapped, and I don't know what to do. Whereas with somebody who is abusive, I'll gravitate toward them in whatever subconscious way." —Lyndsey

In the second instance—when we become abusive—in an unconscious attempt to recondition our fear response, we choose people who possess qualities that mirror not only our conscious desires but also our unconscious fears.

Potential risk factors for lesbian battering include: internalized homophobia that contributes to low self-esteem, feelings of powerlessness, and difficulty establishing committed, trusting relationships (West, 2002). This list of characteristics mirrors those typically associated with survivors. The negative feelings described above are then acted out in the form of lesbian battering.

"I was willing to put up with a certain level of abuse because it was what I expected. To not be frightened I would try to be controlling of other people so that they wouldn't get me mad. It became this vicious cycle where being so controlling was actually just as abusive as what I was afraid of." —Margie

Other researchers have investigated the association between the intergenerational transmission of abuse—for example, witnessing or experiencing violence in the family of origin—and substance abuse, relationship dependency, and power imbalances. Specifically, in the case of power imbalances, Renzetti (1998) found that the greater the batterer's dependency and the greater the victim's desire for independence, the more likely the batterer is to enact more types of aggression with greater frequency. Lockhart et al (1994, cited in West, 2002) found that lesbians who reported severe levels of physical abuse perceived that their partners had a high need for social fusion, as measured by such beliefs as couples' needing to do everything together. This dynamic of domination and control is typical of relationships ruled by domestic violence.

"I had a series of nasty relationships. One wanted her own personal slave and punching bag. Somehow it was always my fault for getting her mad. At the time I had no energy to do anything about it. When we first got together I was so young and she said she cared about me. I had never had that before." —Liz

Similarly, Lockhart et al (1995) examined conflict and violence in lesbian relationships and found that conflicts over emotional dependency and sex were common. Physical abuse was triggered around issues of power imbalance or a struggle for varying levels of dependency and autonomy in the relationship. Women who perceived that their partners felt less of a need for social fusion in the relationship reported lower levels of verbal aggression/abuse. These findings are consistent with others (Miller et al, 2001) that physical aggression was best predicted by fusion in the relationship. For physical violence, control was the important predictor. Telesco (2001) found a strong positive relationship between jealousy and abusive behavior. Aggression in lesbian relationships has been described by some as mutually aggressive in nature (Lie et al, 1991). In this way, battering has been described as a response to and a reenactment of cultural oppression, internalized homophobia, and religious or psychological shame (Tigert, 2001). It appears that the shame and anger associated with oppression and prejudice contribute to aggression in relationships. This correlation has been well documented in the literature on ethnic minorities and the poor. Hansen (2001) identified five major themes related to lesbian victims of relationship violence that we can examine through the lens of the lesbian survivor. The common themes of helplessness, control, and unrealistic expectations of relationships are here.

1. Victims displayed both a vulnerability and an aversion toward helplessness.
2. Victims indicated an intense need for control, and a belief that control is obtained externally through controlling others.
3. Victims were impacted in a number of ways by their previous victimization, both childhood victimization and the victimization they experienced in their previous relationships.
4. Victims harbored a set of relationship expectations and relationship fears that were unrealistic and contradictory.
5. Victims perceived a correlation between substance abuse and violence in their relationships.

Generally speaking, the healthier the survivor becomes, the less tolerant she will be of any form of abuse. As some survivors told me, once they became aware of their pattern of revictimization and tired of the way they felt in these relationships, they made a change in their lives.

"I reached the point of saying, 'Enough already. I'm not going to have any more of this.' I realized I have a right to say no." —Jacque

"I got beaten a lot in relationships because I wouldn't stand up for myself. I'd let them beat me, and I would never fight back, until I got sick of it." —Laura

Trust

"Fear is the gatekeeper of your comfort zone."
—Rhonda Britten, *Fearless Living*

"I'm pinned down under so many old bruises, trapped beneath thick layers of scars where it's impossible to reach anyone or to be reached." —Barbara

Trust is one of the greatest difficulties for survivors. Dayton (2000) describes it this way: "If someone experienced a rupture in a 'survival bond,' subsequent bonds may be harder to form and subsequent ruptures may be more devastating because they return us to the pain of the original one."

"The people who were responsible for my care were also the people who were abusing me. And I loved deeply the people who were responsible for my abuse." —Margie

"I was abused by the people I trusted the most. These are rules of mine: Nothing good lasts forever; Don't put your eggs in one basket; Heart of steel and a bulletproof soul." —Noemi

Intimate relationships trigger unresolved pain from our past. The result is that we often project our early pain into the current relationship. That is, we see the trigger event or our current intimacy as the problem in and of itself. All too often we think the solution—or the way out of the pain—is to dump or exit the relationship.

"It affected every aspect of my life and my relationships with people—friends and lovers alike. I've sabotaged just about every close friendship and relationship I've had. It's a trust issue. When people get too close I start pushing them away or I do something totally unacceptable or unforgivable to get them out of my life." —Sue

"I was ready to run at the first sign of trouble. I always had one foot in the relationship and one foot out." —Kyrce

"I don't know what the outcome will be if I say, 'Please stay.' My immediate reaction to problems is to escape. While it's happening I don't think future-wise. I leave and feel terrible later. I feel rejected, like a core piece of my being was rejected." —Tabitha

"My adoptive mother said she hurt me because she loved me. If the price of love is being hurt, I decided I didn't want any part of it. I'm not in a relationship now. Even the word is loaded for me. It makes me think of falling in love, opening joint bank accounts, and buying a house together. It means giving up myself. I think of it as suffocation rather than commitment. It's hard to believe someone who says she cares for me." —Marian

Our understanding of the abuse is shaped by several factors: (1) our developmental stage at the time of the trauma; (2) whether it was a one-time event or a cumulative trauma that occurred over time; and (3) our sources of support at the time (Dayton, 2000). Reflecting on how old you were when the abuse occurred, its duration, and any support you had available to you can help you piece together how you have survived the abuse and how you think about it now. In addition, looking at the basic psychological response to trauma can help us to better understand our abuse experiences. According to Dayton (2000), the two-phase reaction includes protest and numbing. The protest phase is marked by anger, verbal hostility, or acting out. In time, this initial reaction is followed by numbing: a state of emotional and interpersonal withdrawal from active participation in life. The major signs of numbing include difficulty solving problems, withdrawal from social activities, and isolation.

"I struggle with not being able to communicate well during emotional situations because of overwhelming fear, and lack of skill getting my needs met and being emotionally present with other people." —Cory

During numbing, survivors lose the ability to accept support from others. To complicate matters, survivors of child sexual abuse were let down by those on whom they had come to depend for support. So they learn to go it alone, to rely on no one.

"In school I would never let friends get close to me. How much do I have to tell you for you to hurt me? I was very active, involved in lots of activities, anything possible to keep people away, to keep them from asking me who I really was. I'm very independent. I feel that I have to take care of myself and not rely on anyone. I think it's sad sometimes because you lose out. That's part of life, you know. Just like people can rely on you, you should be able to rely on people. That's part of being friends." —Diana

"I am primarily a private person and do not readily allow others into my inner world." —Lisa

Adult children of alcoholics and others who were parentified as young children may have been forced to take responsibility for themselves and siblings prematurely, affecting their ability to forge relationships well into adulthood.

A history of child sexual abuse has been shown to predict psychological adjustment and adult attachment (Roche, 1999). Maltz (1988) explains that survivors experience the long-term effects of abuse in the formation and maintenance of adult intimate relationships. In a fascinating study of abused children, psychologists, who once thought that all people had an innate ability to read facial expressions, learned that these children can be "face-blind" (Blum, 2002). They will consistently read anger into a smile and see real threat in even the mild irritation of a raised eyebrow. These children's brains show a "sudden leap in response" not characteristic of children raised in more supportive homes. Research (Harlow, 1973) suggests what many of us have experienced personally—that other, better relationships can help correct such reactions. Our childhood experiences taught us to distrust ourselves and others and to use withdrawal as a survival skill. In positive relationships with others we can let these defenses go and learn to trust again.

Recent brain research by Putnam and Trickett reveals neurological responses to the stress of childhood sexual abuse (cited in Strong, 1998). They found that girls who had suffered sexual abuse as children chronically excreted higher levels of catecholamines—the chemicals epinephrine, norepinephrine, and dopamine released by the brain and adrenal gland in response to stress—than did the nonabused girls. An excess of these chemicals in the body causes hyperarousal and has been found in Vietnam War veterans suffering from post–traumatic stress disorder. Over time, the abused girls showed signs that their stress response systems were attempting to adapt to a chronic state of anxiety and hyperarousal by becoming underresponsive to stress; their stress systems had burned out to some extent. Chronically high levels of cortisol can take a toll on the body. Too much cortisol can damage nerve cells in the brain important to learning and memory storage. Cortisol and norepinephrine also suppress the immune system, which may account for the stress-related changes in the immune systems observed in abused girls. Comparing blood samples of abused and nonabused girls, Putnam and Trickett found that abused girls had levels of autoantibodies that were twice as high as those found in the nonabused girls. Autoantibodies are thought to be possible indicators of a number of potentially life-threatening illnesses, such as lupus, in which the body attacks its own tissues.

"We can only learn to love by loving."
—Iris Murdock

"It is a very courageous act to love another, for loving requires vulnerability, an openness to the joys as well as the hurts," writes Richard Pimental-Habib in *Power of a Partner* (2002). Our experience as lesbian survivors has taught us to be guarded, and yet we have the capacity to be open to love. Pimental-Habib distinguishes between our *wanting* a relationship and being *ready* for a relationship. Readiness, he explains, requires awareness and the courage to open ourselves to another human being. Evan (2001) explains that staying present, being honest, and acting out of love, not fear, are the keys to creating real, satisfying relationships. Fear of being hurt, fear of being found unworthy, and fear of being abandoned interfere with our ability to forge healthy relationships. We coped with the abuse as children by surviving the best we could. We created layers of defenses to protect ourselves. We learned through our experience of abuse to trust only ourselves; it will take us time to learn to trust again. Trust building is an ongoing issue in sexual abuse recovery.

"I have secluded myself
from society
and yet I never meant
any such thing.
I have made a captive of myself
and put me into a dungeon
and now I cannot find the key
to let myself out."
—Nathaniel Hawthorne

When I asked survivors to describe the issues they struggle with, virtually all of them listed trust. According to Starzecpyzel (1987), "The primary issue for any incest survivor is lack of trust.... This inability to feel safe with others, either intimately or in the world, creates a profound sense of emotional isolation." Many of the defenses that survivors described earlier—detachment, dissociation, suicidal ideation, self-mutilation, tendency to sexualize relationships—cover up "underlying feeling of impotent rage." It takes trust to express rage.

"I don't think I trust anyone very much as a result of this experience." —Pat

"I hid all my emotions away. The shame, confusion, and the hatred I felt were hidden away—locked in a box hoping never to be opened. I built my own fortress around me. I hid in my room to be away from everyone. I kept to myself so no one could ever know the real me." —Mo

"At this point I'm not interested in getting involved with anyone. I just don't have the energy or the desire to take the risk." —Jacque

"I would be involved with someone but never feel as if I could truly trust them. I always expected to get hurt." —Sue

"It's hard for me to hear praise. I feel like it's a setup, that the person's only saying that so they can get something from me." —Liz

"With abuse survivors, trust is the biggest deal. I don't want to explain to other people, 'Well, my father fucked the living dog shit out of me growing up.' It's really hard for me to keep it out of the front of my mind and spend time with someone. I guess I don't want to affect other people by the weird shit that's happened to me. I'm all about control. I guess I don't have an expectation that my limits will ultimately be respected." —Kris

"I feel safer alone." —Jan

"I had many brief sexually charged encounters that fizzled out fast. I would not trust anybody with any of my real inner feelings. I was always playing games and never portrayed myself as I was. I have a female persona with an 'I don't take no shit' attitude. I thought I had a great facade, but I began to feel inauthentic and eventually suicidal." —Tammy

"I needed validation, and I was looking for it outside myself." —Christy

"I'm afraid people will hurt me, so I put up a wall when they start getting too close." —Kim

"When I was a child, my father would leave us at night on the road and drive off. Early on in my relationship with my partner I would ask my partner for the keys, so I knew she couldn't drive off and leave me." —Sarah

"I can be downright paranoid when in public and surrounded by strangers—especially strange men." —Mollie

At the root of our inability to trust is fear—fear that we will be hurt. Henri Nouwen (1986) writes, "I began to see the simple fact that those I fear have a great power over me. Those who could make me afraid could also make me do what they wanted me to do" (cited in McNeill, 1988). To break free of fear we must first recognize the connection between it and the power others have over us. When we don't feel safe with others, we feel emotionally isolated (Starzecpyzel, 1987). This loneliness, while the most painful aspect of survivors' lives, can also be the most powerful motivation to change.

Sometimes we can gain control over our fear when we manipulate situations to our own liking. When we feel in control, our fears of being vulnerable or powerless are abated.

"In all of my past relationships I was in complete control. The people were all very hardworking, loyal, kind, outspoken people, but all were willing to let me have my way." —Serena

"I have this sense that I can protect myself by knowing the rules (spoken or not), knowing directions, knowing how to do things, not being taken by surprise. It manifests as the sort of quaking antennae that lots of survivors talk about, and also as an unwillingness to acknowledge ignorance." —Marty

"I feel like I'm not protected outside. When I opened up intimately, I feared outside more. I trust the person as long as it's not too close." —Rowan

Seeking relationships with people who are unavailable or using others sexually is another way that we keep our fears at bay. If a relationship is unlikely to develop, we will not have to confront our issues with sex and love. When we keep them separate—or so we think—we can handle it fine.

"I've had nothing long-term, only one-night stands or short-term sexual relationships with straight women." —Amy

"I keep falling in love with unattainable women: straight women, celibate women. I'm attracted to people who want to be promiscuous and don't want to be with me." —Chris

"I look for women who are already taken, and sometimes straight, for love." —Naomi

"My last relationship ended because she was married." —Sue

"It used to be 'If I can have them, I don't want them.' I don't need to prove that anymore." —Julie

Survivors often live their life in extremes. We either have no sex or indiscriminate sex. We trust no one, or we trust everyone. This kind of black-and-white thinking is characteristic of survivors' rigid thought patterns and their attempts at control.

"I didn't used to trust anybody. If someone was late for a date with me, they were not to be trusted. I was really careful. Once I trust, I trust too much. I'm a lot better at trust now." —Reg

"My abuse history has had a profound effect on my ability to trust my partner and to feel secure in the relationship." —Levie

"I thought my partner would leave me because I'm sick and can't express my love. She'd give me the keys to the car to show that she wouldn't leave me. We'd leave stores if I got overwhelmed, even leaving a full basket." —Debbie

"I have a hard time understanding women. I want to be closer to them faster than what I think is the norm. I have been able to learn more about these boundaries through friends and partners who continue to teach me proper social skills and that boundaries need to be respected." —Marie

"I have trouble with boundaries: willingness to express my needs and a willingness to confront others." —Lynn

Groves and Schondel (1996) found that lesbian survivor couples struggled to cope with intimacy issues because their childhood experiences had taught them to distrust themselves and others and to use withdrawal as a survival skill. Through the group experience, the couples learned that they were not as alone or different as they believed. With time and experience they came to see that it is possible for them to learn to trust again.

"My partner is also a survivor, so it's been a big struggle. We couldn't imagine that we could be loved. Everyone should know that they deserve to give and receive love." —Amanda

"I never expected that I could rise in love until now. I really had expected to be alone forever." —Delphene

"With my partner we took it really slow and she fell in love with me. We talk it out. We don't have secrets. It's a good marriage." —Debbie

"My partner makes me feel safe and protected and cared for, and she has never been rough. Plus, she knows about the abuse and my other girlfriends did not, so that has deepened our trust level." —Elizabeth

"My partner is incredibly loving and patient. She has really helped me to see myself as a worthwhile human being. I am a strong woman, and she has helped me to grow and to heal. I know there is nothing that could come between us. She has helped me to deal with my anger, my hurt, and my pain." —Pat

"Why does our relationship work after 18 years? We're a refuge for each other. We honor each other's needs. She's one of those people who shows up and doesn't reject me. She's very much there, continuously encouraging me." —Lynn

"I've been in a relationship for nine years. She is my first steady partner. We've weathered a lot together. I can't figure out why she stays. She was so calm. She didn't act on impulse. Time is healing. I can talk to her. I've learned to trust her over time. There's mutual respect." —Kyrce

CHAPTER 7

Sex and Love: Two Separate Things

"I think that sex is how I love you." —Wendy

"I see making love as a way to feel loved, wanted, and safe." —Kirsten

Sexual abuse survivors have profound confusion around issues of intimacy and sexuality (Roth, 1993). Because we were cruelly and prematurely forced into the world of adult relationships, our understandings about love, sex, affection, and closeness are tainted and twisted. Sexuality is understood in terms of power; we believe we must submit to another person's desires. Love and sex are intertwined for us; if we are loved, then that person will want to be sexual with us. If that person does not want sex, then we are not loved. Hall (1999) found that the majority of lesbian survivors she studied experienced difficulty distinguishing sex and affection.

Survivors with unresolved issues related to the abuse tend to be either sexually withdrawn or indiscriminately sexually active (Courtois, 1988). A common experience among survivors whose feelings becoming fused together is sex and shutdown. When we are sexually abused as children, we signal our unconscious to shut down our sexual responses. Sex and fear, or sex and physical numbness, or sex and disapproval are fused. We numb our bodies, dissociate, or both (Dayton, 2000). This leaves us feeling crazy, confused, and mistrustful of our own bodies. Because the abuse represented a boundary invasion, we are susceptible to exploitation, unreasonable caretaking, and excessive submissiveness. We reject our partners because we believe that affection will ultimately lead to unwanted sex. Many of us suffer from intimacy *dysfunction.* According to Hall, survivors often have difficulty enjoying sexual contact within an established emotional relationship because this repeats the abusive one in which the survivor was emotionally close to her abuser. According to Hall, "This confusion between sex, intimacy, and love has led some of the women to oversexualize their relationships leading some into a succession of unsatisfactory relationships, searching for the 'love' which appeared to elude them." This avoidance or compulsion is common among survivors (Zerbe, 1993). We may find it difficult to touch in our relationships without feeling sexually aroused or without believing that touch will automatically lead to sex (Maltz, 1991). Sex becomes a way for us to fill a void (Zerbe, 1993).

It is often in the context of problems in an intimate relationship that survivors will enter therapy. We may become aware that the relationship is an abusive one and we need to gather the strength to leave it, or the relationship is a supportive one and we want to be healthy enough to maintain it.

Triggers

"Never fear shadows. They simply mean there's a light shining somewhere nearby."
—Ruth E. Renkel

Triggers, a category of intrusive symptoms that include flashbacks, nightmares, and body sensations, are experienced by many survivors and can be very distressing (Courtois, 1988). Physiological arousal—like during sex—can trigger memories related to trauma; these trauma-related memories in turn trigger a state of generalized physiological arousal (Dayton, 2000). Reliving traumatic events in flashbacks or nightmares causes a rerelease of stress hormones that further intensifies the strength of the trauma memories. Dr. Jane Stewart of Concordia University in Montreal believes that a hormone called corticotropin releasing factor (CRF)—levels of which increase in the brain during stress—actually increases anxiety. This may take place because CRF acts on the amygdala in ways that strengthen emotional memories once they are triggered. Psychotherapist Tian Dayton (2000) believes this is where some people get stuck. As associations intensify, stress increases along with heightened physiological arousal, and as stress increases, associations also intensify. In the most intense kind of flashback, *abreaction*, "survivors reenter the traumatic space...and relive the experience physically, psychically, and emotionally" (Bratton, 1999).

Triggers, or *associational cues*, fall into five categories: (1) Developmental crises; (2) Exposure to events which symbolize or resemble the original trauma, (3) Crises associated with recollection, disclosure, confrontation, or reporting the abuse; (4) Issues within the therapy; and (5) Life stages or cumulative life events (Courtois, 1998). When you feel as if you are reexperiencing the trauma and abuse in present time, you are having a *flashback*. Flashbacks are caused by triggers and include visual, bodily, and auditory memories. Wood (1993) says, "A good test to tell if you are having a flashback is to ask yourself if the emotions you are feeling are too intense for the situation you are in." Many lesbian survivors experience flashbacks during sex—during times of physiological arousal described above (Hall, 1999). This disrupts their sexual activity with their partners and often causes them to avoid further sexual contact.

"Intimacy was great at first, but then the flashbacks came and it was difficult for both of us. She didn't want to 'cause' the flashbacks and I didn't want to risk them, so sex slowed down." —Mary

Feeling vulnerable during sex is particularly troublesome for survivors who feel that "the past comes flooding back with all its myriad of confusing emotions" (Hall, 1999).

"My partners would do 'normal' things to show sexual attraction that would remind me of the abuse. I still have a hard time with someone getting their hands near my neck. I was terrified to get naked with a woman. A lot of the memories...in lovemaking, you're naked. I never trusted myself as to what would trigger memories and where I would go in front of this woman mentally. That thought just terrified me. I sure didn't want

to screw it up by getting naked and then having some kind of screaming fit." —Delphene

"When I was dating I would tell women about the abuse from the very beginning because I would be triggered. I would have to say, 'There's going to get to be a point because I can see that you like certain behaviors. While I'm willing to try, those things may trigger me. If I tell you stop, I really mean it. Because if you don't, you're out.' I would have to protect myself in that way. The triggering happens less frequently now unless someone gets very sexually aggressive with me. If somebody's holding me down, and I'm not expecting it, that's a big trigger." —Nedhera

"I still flinch sometimes when my girlfriend goes to touch me, especially if she has been angry. Sometimes when I trigger I get very dizzy. In extreme situations, I hyperventilate. It can be so oppressive." —Rowan

"There are sexual triggers. Sometimes it hurts to be touched. My partner's always wondered why that was. It's hard to talk to her about it because it's hard for her to hear." —Liz

"I have to be treated with kid gloves. The softer and gentler the better. I can't stand aggressiveness. It's a trigger." —C.J.

"Once, my partner and I decided to use a strap-on during sex, and I got totally freaked out. It scared the living daylights out of me. It took me about a week to recover from that experience. During that week I was distant and unfocused." —Elizabeth

"My abuser made me do oral sex on him. The first time I tried to perform oral sex on my girlfriend I felt the same as when I was violated, and I felt sick. Then I felt horrible for not being able to give pleasure to the woman I loved. I didn't want her to feel rejected. I cried and apologized repeatedly." —Kirsten

"Triggers are automatic responses connected to your past sexual abuse that can suddenly rush into the present. Certain acts, smells, words—perhaps even a tone of voice—can act as triggers that bring up images and feelings from the past.... The idea of embracing your triggers may seem counterintuitive at first.... [But] when you move yourself toward and into a trigger, you have the opportunity to then process the material and then move through it.... Triggers act as signposts to what is in need of healing" (Haines, 1999). Survivors described the many ways that they are triggered in their daily lives.

"I'm big on smell—perfume and stuff. I have to have enough stuff on me that smells pleasant so I will not be triggered by other smells in the environment that might remind me of my father or the pimp. That's my little coping thing. When it happens I'm a little kid again. I just totally flip." —Kris

"To this day I hate cottage cheese! My father was not circumcised, nor was he very clean." —Mo

"The bathroom was right next to my bedroom, so I could hear my father brushing his teeth at night. To this day I can't stand the smell of Listerine mouthwash because he always used it." —Jacque

"You wouldn't believe how often there are reminders: songs, smells, or even objects or childhood TV shows." —Yvonne

"When I watch TV or a movie I'm triggered. Triggers can be sounds like kids yelling or smells like a certain lotion. When my partner touches me I can be triggered." —Katie

"Every T-shirt I have has a stretched collar, otherwise it's the feeling of being choked. Sometimes it feels like my food's right back there. A lot of times certain foods feel too weird in my mouth." —Delphene

"No one can touch my throat or neck. I panic even when doctors put their hands on my neck. Because of the abuse I can't wear anything with a collar (something touching my neck), or a V-neck shirt (I feel vulnerable), only crewnecks. I can't stand soap or lotion because they're slimy and greasy. I have to apply lotion with only one finger." —Reg

Even all these years later I experience new triggers that bring me back, in a cold sweat, to the abuse that occurred during my teen years. The smells of Baby Magic lotion, minty toothpaste, the feel of a condom, male sweat, the crack of light that peeks from under a partially closed door, a person's hand over my mouth or the feeling of being held down, lights on during sex, the feel of lacy bras or the pull of someone removing my clothes—all will set me off. I am haunted by the sounds and smells and sensations from more than 20 years ago—the acts that introduced me to sex when I was still a child. When my brother abused me he took the pleasure out of sex, forever uniting fear and sex in a way that would interfere with my ability to form lasting relationships. Sometimes my body reacts to a trigger before I consciously register it as associated with the abuse. At times the memories are still so powerful, when all I want to do is forget. I have recently become aware of how triggering expressed anger is for me. When people—my partner, coworkers, supervisors, family members—raise their voices, I have an immediate and visceral reaction. I feel myself cowering, and I shut down. I am also very sensitive to loud noises of all kinds and I startle easily.

Survivors I spoke with described the many ways that they continue to be triggered by events in their everyday lives.

"A recent memory of my father jacking off in front of me was triggered by fear around 9/11. This was really difficult for me. He was my hero. Being aroused is a trigger for me. I was triggered a lot during sex with my partner. I still have to talk to myself about being present and not being triggered." —Lynn

"I went to the Millennium March on Washington and participated in the mass wedding. I had buried the abuse memories quite well, but had been having off-the-scale nightmares. I suffered from profound depression and was in bed for days." —Tammy

"I still believe in romance and falling in love. I don't just want to have sex. I've had sex. Unfortunately, it was with our father. Now I want to make love." —Dana

"Sometimes I have a hard time at work. I'll trigger if a man does something that reminds me of my past. Sometimes it is a smell or words or just an attitude. It makes it hard to function." —Rowan

"Up until a couple of years ago, older men in any situation alone made me nervous. I still keep my distance. I 'know' when a man is about to start something I don't want." —Missy

According to Maltz (1991), "Identifying triggers gives you power. Triggers lose their secrecy and mysteriousness once you understand them." She proposes a four-step approach to dealing with triggers: (1) **stop** and become aware; (2) **calm** yourself; (3) **affirm** your present reality; and (4) **choose** a new response. The goal is not to eliminate all flashbacks but to reduce your anxiety and improve your coping when they occur (Courtois, 1988). This includes learning new coping skills to replace those that were used in childhood that no longer serve a healthy purpose. As Pat describes, it's easy to fall into the same habits of dissociating (and using other defense mechanisms employed during the abuse), but we need to break out of this and develop healthier ways of coping:

"Early in my relationships I would not say much. I would go along with what my partner wanted, even at my expense. I would just dissociate when it got to a point of being uncomfortable."

Haines (1999) offers many helpful hints for dealing with triggers and a "Map for Recovery that includes tracking triggers, creating a trigger plan, and healing triggers in the context of sexual relationships." These may be helpful for survivors who continue to be unsettled by triggers in their daily lives.

Healing the Sexual Wounds

A history of sexual abuse can disrupt many aspects of our sexuality: how we feel about being a woman; how we feel about our bodies, sex organs, and bodily functions; how we think about sex; how we express ourselves sexually; and how we experience physical pleasure and intimacy with others (Maltz, 1991).

"The abuse has affected me: dysfunctional sex life, fear of orgasm, and lack of interest in sex, for starters. It has basically affected every attempt at a significant sexual relationship." —Mary

"I saw sex as dirty. Any kind of intimacy was very scary. Then I realized I was gay and not scared, actually extremely confident in my sexuality and in my sex with women." —Missy

Many of us struggle to understand the ways in which the abuse continues to affect our sexual behavior. Maltz (1991) lists a number of behaviors that you might recognize as resulting from your abuse history:

- I avoid or withdraw from sex.
- I fake sexual interest.
- I fake sexual enjoyment.
- I have allowed sex to be forced on me.
- I have unwanted sex.
- I usually have sex under the influence.
- I use pornography.
- I engage in compulsive masturbation.
- I engage in promiscuous sex.
- I engage in prostitution.
- I have sex in relationships that lack intimacy.
- I have sex outside a primary relationship.
- I engage in secretive sex, which generates feelings of shame.
- I have sex with a person primarily involved with someone else.
- I have sex with near-strangers.
- I demand sex from a partner.

Fearing sexual contact or separating our emotions from sexual activity—as we did when we were children—are two ways that survivors' sexuality is affected (Fortune, 1983). We may avoid sexual relationships altogether or may engage in frequent and indiscriminate sexual activity. Most sexual problems arise from survivors' fear of intimacy—emotional and sexual—which comes from their childhood experience of betrayal in an intimate family relationship. Intimacy requires taking risks and being vulnerable, both of which may be very difficult for survivors. Having been sexually exploited, it's not easy to trust again. Our sexual rights were violated, and this has a lasting impact on our sexual attitudes and behavior. Healing involves reclaiming these rights and protecting these in the future. A study of sexually abused children ages 9–13 revealed higher levels of sexual anxiety and sex-associated fears among sexually abused than nonabused children (Cohen, 1999). In this way, sexual abuse seriously harms a child's sexual development and later adult sexual behavior (Maltz, 1991). Children (and adults) have the following rights with regard to their sexuality:

- the right to develop healthy attitudes about sex
- the right to sexual privacy
- the right to protection from bodily invasion and harm
- the right to say no to sexual behavior
- the right to control touch and sexual contact
- the right to stop sexual arousal that feels inappropriate or uncomfortable
- the right to develop our sexuality according to our sexual preferences and orientation
- the right to enjoy healthy sexual pleasure and satisfaction. (Maltz, 1991)

Our reactions to sex as adults vary. We might avoid or fear sex or lack interest in having sex. We might approach sex as an obligation. We might react with anger, distrust, or guilt when we are touched or have difficulty becoming aroused or feeling sensations. We might dissociate during sex—by feeling emotionally distant or not present—or experience intrusive or disturbing sexual thoughts and images. We might engage in compulsive or inappropriate sexual behaviors, have difficulty establishing or maintaining intimate relationships, or experience vaginal pain or orgasmic difficulties (Maltz, 1991). Vaginal penetration, in particular, can be a problem for survivors for two reasons. First, vaginismus is a reflexive tightening of the muscles in the outer third of the vagina when penetration is attempted. Second, dyspareunia (painful intercourse) is the pain, burning, cramping, or sharpness that a woman experiences during intercourse. Both conditions can result from associating fear and pain of past sexual abuse with current sexual behavior. In some cases, they may be directly related to actual physical damage done to vaginal tissues, nerves, and internal organs during sexual abuse.

"I don't do penetration with women because of the abuse." —Yvonne

"I am not able to allow any vaginal penetration. My vagina needs to be healed." —Mary Lou

"Sex is the stage on which many relationship dramas are played out."
—Betty Berzon

In a cycle called *repetition compulsion*, we may unconsciously replay the sexual abuse. We try to understand what happened and resolve the stress by acting out the abuse again and again. Staging these replays can be an effort to gain some mastery and control over our experiences (Maltz, 1991).

"I notice that a lot of times I end up feeling uncomfortable with people who are patient when it comes to sex. They want to wait and be gentle about the whole situation. I tend to gravitate toward people who are not considerate in that way. I think that might have something to do with the sexual abuse." —Lyndsey

Conversely, you might avoid sex, believing that you can protect yourself from unpleasant sexual experiences or further abuse. Avoiding sex entirely, however, allows the abuse to interfere with your ability to enjoy healthy, positive sex on your own and with a partner. Touch is something that everyone needs. Virginia Satir referred to it as "skin hunger." And yet, many survivors have difficulty tolerating touch (Hall, 1999). This aversion has obvious repercussions for survivors' ability to be intimate with their partners.

"Sexual intimacy is very, very difficult for me. I am learning to relax and to enjoy touch, but I'm still light years behind most people my age. It frustrates my girlfriend sometimes because she is much more touch-oriented than I am. But she is very patient with me and says that she wants to be as supportive as she can be. I feel bad because she has to ask every time she wants to touch me. But at the same time I know it's better that she should ask than that she should do something that would frighten me." —Mollie

"I love the nurturing touch of women. However, this need for a 'mother' has been problematic for me too. I'm learning to ask for affection outside of romantic relationships. My mother never hugs or kisses me. I don't remember her being very affectionate as I was growing up either. So, I find that many of my female friends and lovers help with this emptiness and need for basic human touch. I am a sexual being, and that is important to me. I strive to express that part of myself. Amazingly, that part of me hasn't felt 'fucked up' by the abuse situation." —Tammie

Research on lesbian and heterosexual couples (not survivors) suggests that lesbian couples tend to have less frequent sex than other couples, but are more satisfied with their sex life (Rose, 1994; Schreurs, 1993). Kotulski (1996) found that lesbians engage in sex for significantly longer amounts of time than heterosexuals, engage in more nongenital physical expressions of sexuality (including kissing), and express affection in more nonphysical ways than heterosexuals (love notes and favors). In Joy Hall's study (1999), lesbian survivors acknowledged that they experienced "greater sexual freedom and willingness to experiment sexually" in their lesbian relationships. Among lesbians, however, abuse history was associated with less sexual desire. Post and Avery (1995) recommend that treatment of inhibited sexual desire in lesbians requires awareness of lesbian psychologies and the high incidence of incest and substance abuse in the lesbian community. Issues of negotiated sex and lack of spontaneity were found in lesbian relationships where both women were survivors (Hall, 1999).

Compounding the issues of shame that the survivor faces, lesbians are also particularly vulnerable to feeling that their sexual desires are secret, bad, and shameful and therefore must be hidden (Vaughan, 1999). The inability to acknowledge and express sexual needs is a universal problem for lesbian survivors (Hall, 1999). This is, of course, linked to survivors' denial of themselves as sexual in nature because of the feelings of shame and dirtiness arising from their same-sex attraction as well as their abuse experiences. As a result, many survivors reported lack of arousal and inability to experience orgasm. It is also believed that lesbians' inability to initiate sex results in large part from their socialization as women (Nichols, 1987). Lesbian survivors, specifically, who fear being seen as the abuser are often inhibited in initiating sexual contact (Hall, 1999).

"Sometimes I feel like I'm groping my partner, or if I initiate and it's not perfect timing, I really beat myself up. Instead of taking a gentle touch, I blow it way out of proportion in my mind as if it were a huge grope. I feel inhibited. I guess when it doesn't feel right I feel like the abuser. I remember being touched and pulled when I didn't even want to be touched. How could I do that? Here she is, this sweet woman." —Delphene

"One of my biggest issues has been sex—my wanting it too much or at the wrong times, her not being emotionally available." —Juli

"My biggest issue has been in not being able to perform oral sex. I feel guilty and angry that I can't. Most of my girlfriends have had no complaints about this. They were understanding and quite satisfied with how we made love. It did become an issue with one person I dated. She saw it as a reflection of her, that I didn't like her enough to do it. She even accused me of not being a 'real lesbian.' It was very hurtful and I stopped dating her." —Kirsten

Complicated by the experiences of childhood sexual abuse, it is no wonder that lesbian survivors are fearful to express their sexual desires and needs for emotional closeness. Unfortunately, the link between depression and sexual dissatisfaction and dysfunction is well documented (Hall, 1999). According to Maltz (1991), new models of sexuality should be based on a sense of choice, renewed self-respect, and a commitment to emotional intimacy. "During sex, survivors and partners need to always be prepared to stop, slow down, shift activities, and process old feelings from the abuse.... It can also be important to end a sexual encounter well.... If after sex a partner gets up quickly or rolls over without saying a word, a survivor may be left feeling bad for having had sex." Partners should immediately stop any behaviors that mimic sexual abuse or that might trigger a survivor, such as touching without consent, ignoring how the survivor really feels, and behaving in ways that are impulsive, out of control, or hurtful (Maltz, 1991). Max's breakthrough captures this perfectly:

"Once I was able to love myself and understand how very important it is to express my feelings, I am so much more alive."

In a fascinating study of the butch-femme dynamic among lesbians, Rosenzweig and Lebow (1992) found that lesbians perceive themselves as significantly more feminine when they are interacting sexually than their overall or global sex-role perception. Further, lesbians who view themselves as either androgynous or feminine in a sexual context had the highest level of sexual satisfaction. This is an interesting examination of what it means to be a sexual woman. Are the acceptable limits of female sexuality confined to being in a passive or receptive role? While we may assert ourselves and speak out in our daily lives, it appears that our female socialization greatly impacts and inhibits our behavior in the bedroom.

"Once I fully accepted my lesbianism, I refused to be a femme. I know I'm not butch, but I could never be femme, could not submit, could not be passive. I had no idea that there were all kinds of femmes out there. I had to be an androgynous lesbian. I had to be a granola girl. I identify now as femme and have now for the last 10 years." —Nedhera

I am beginning to recognize the ways in which my sexual relationship with my partner triggers me and resurrects the hurt and pain I felt during the abuse. My partner usually gets up after sex to wash her hands. I didn't realize the impact this simple action was having on me until I read the passage by Wendy Maltz. I always felt like my partner, as loving and sensitive as she is during our lovemaking, was washing me off of her. This left me feeling dirty. I rarely leave the bed after sex. Lying in bed together after is an important way for me to feel connected with her, like the sex is inseparable from the loving relationship we have with each other. In this way, I distinguish my relationship with my partner from other relationships of a purely sexual nature that I have had.

"I feel there is something unexplored about woman that only a woman can explore."
—Georgia O'Keefe

Haines, in *The Survivors' Guide to Sex*, describes her inability to "endure emotional intimacy and sex at the same time" (1999). According to Bass and Davis (1988), this is because "sexual arousal became linked to feelings of shame, disgust, pain, and humiliation." Some survivors cope by numbing these feelings with drugs and alcohol, acknowledging that they could not be sexual without getting high. This was true for me. All sex followed drinking. I never had sex sober. Not one time. I am realizing that the alcohol made it possible for me to be available sexually in a way I would not have felt comfortable if I were sober.

"Intimacy was good while I was drinking and drugging. Now I don't do street drugs or drink, and I can't make love to my lover." —Laura

Your feelings of sexual desire may scare you because they mimic the abuse (Haines, 1999). Haines clarifies,

"You may find the dynamics of power and surrender to be a turn-on. Nothing is wrong with this. The difference between childhood sexual abuse and adult consensual sex is that in adult sex, both partners are matured sexually and have the ability to make choices for themselves. In consensual sex, you are not being coerced, manipulated, or misused. Both partners' needs, boundaries, and desires are considered."

Robin describes how she was able to reclaim her sexuality by diffusing the power of her abuser's words:

"I don't avoid the things that disturb me psychically. I need to understand them, examine them, and challenge myself. I felt that if I altered my sex life to comfortably not deal with the sexual effects of trauma on my body and mind, I was letting my perpetrator win. I couldn't bear it, for instance, that because my mother's husband told me to lick his penis like it was a lollipop, the word 'lollipop' made me feel terrified and ill, and also sexually aroused and shamed. I told my lover I wanted her to lick me like it was a lollipop. After a while the word lost its power and became my *word, not my perpetrator's. After a year or less the word didn't even have the power to thrill or upset me. It was just a dumb word."*

If you were taught that the abuse was all your fault, avoiding your sexuality could seem to help you avoid the deep shame and guilt that comes with that (Haines, 1999). Avoidance includes lack of interest in sex and refusing to be an active participant in sexual encounters by passively receiving sexual attention from our partners or by dissociating during sex. In reaction to fears of sexuality, lesbian incest survivors often experience a variety of symptoms ranging from physical numbness, lack of clitoral sensations, a sense of unreality, spaciness, dissociation from their bodies, and unwanted thoughts that distract them from the sexual experience.

"I want physical intimacy, but I don't get to the point of intimacy very often." —Marian

"I woke up to my sexuality way too early, so sexually I shut my body off until my early 20s." —Kathy

"I pretty much avoided sexual awareness for a long time—into my adult life." —Jill

"It was six months into our relationship before I could let her have sex with me. And I still have this reflex when she touches certain areas." —Rowan

"I went and hid in a Christian ministry, celibate, as a nun. I came out at 28 and left the ministry for the gay lifestyle." —Dorian

"I have sexual problems. I can't talk or do sex. In therapy we've barely begun chopping at the iceberg." —Kyrce

"I have shut myself off from possibilities. My weight helps me to do this—more weight means less attractive means less sexual." —Deborah

"My partner has to deal with someone who doesn't want to have sex at all ever again." —Liz

"The abuse pops its ugly head up during each sexual relationship and prevents me from getting involved sexually with anyone." —Dorian

"I had no sexual feelings. I still feel numb in my body. I don't feel much pleasure from intercourse. When I first started dating it was hard for me to feel anything because everything was very conscious, and I was working more like a machine than with passion and emotion. My partner would try everything to let me feel pleasure, but I didn't feel much. Now I'm able to feel from my waist up. Below the waist, like going inside me, is like, 'Don't waste your time.' I don't think about it much, but telling you now, yeah, that's messed up." —Diana

"From the time the abuse stopped at age 11 until I came out at age 20, I had very little interest in sex." —Levie

"It took a long time for me to separate out that there were things that I liked about getting pleased sexually by a woman that were not

the same thing that was happening with my aunt." —Nedhera

"In fifth or sixth grade I consciously decided that I'm never going to have sex and I'm never going to get married. My goal was not to have relationships with anybody—intimate relationships or sexual relationships." —Noemi

"I had my first lover when I was 30, but I was unable to achieve an orgasm. I told her I had turned that part of me off, and now I was having trouble turning it back on." —Dorian

"I chose a celibate lifestyle until I was 42 years old. I was a nun. I wanted to live a life of service, and that was the way in the Catholic Church when I was growing up. Also, I think it was safe for me, but at a more unconscious level. The celibate lifestyle suited me. I suspect I closed down big time as a child, and I redirected that natural energy into service. I did not feel feelings of romantic sexual love until I met my partner when I was 45. I am still not particularly sexual (i.e., do not have a high sex drive). My partner accepts that, and we are very loving and gentle with each other, but not particularly sexual." —Misha

"I have finally met a wonderful woman, but I fear our relationship is in jeopardy because I am not sexual with her. She fears it's all because of her, because she's overweight. We either fight or just don't talk. She is also a survivor of sexual abuse by her brother." —Laura

"I am working through my difficulty with letting a partner pleasure me while staying focused on the physical pleasure happening in the now. I often fight the tendency to let my mind wander off during lovemaking, which often perturbs my lovers." —Cristi

Many survivors described the flood of emotions they experienced during sex.

"I cry almost every time I have sex, although it is not usually bad

crying. I get totally overwhelmed by emotion, and my method of handling it is to cry." —Elizabeth

"My abuse played a part early on in my relationships. I would have intense emotional times around sex." —Brooke

"Lots of post-trauma during sex—tears—and I'd have to stop." —Kathy

"I have these crying attacks after orgasms, which are scary and annoying. They come and go, and it makes sex a challenge." —Mary

Abuse memories can interfere with our ability to experience orgasm. Many survivors of incest find it difficult to relax and enjoy sexual encounters, making orgasm difficult if not impossible.

"I have difficulty climaxing during sex." —Elizabeth

"I still have only been able to have an orgasm the same way I did during the abuse. By that I mean the position. That mental block has only been broken down by the one person whom I loved so deeply. Orgasms are such a mental and emotional thing. Now I think so much about my ability to have one that it prevents me from having one any other way. I don't know when that will happen again. I've faked orgasms since then." —Juli

"Another result of the sexual abuse is my inability to achieve orgasm. I enjoy sex, yes, but cannot bring myself to—how shall I say this—surrender that part of me completely. That's a tough one, especially when you have to explain it to the one you're with who is doing everything right. It's humiliating, and I have no doubt that's related to the abuse." —Sue

With the help of a patient, caring partner it is possible for us to enjoy sex.

"My partner and I have worked very hard on our sexual relationship because sex is often not a comfortable experience for me. At this point I

would say our sexual relationship is way above average, which speaks to her patience and willingness to hang in there with me." —Pat

Starzecpyzel (1987) describes survivors' tendency to sexualize relationships this way:

> The incested client has a handicapping fear of closeness. In her life and in the transference [with her therapist], she protects herself from feelings of rage, abandonment, and humiliation by acting out her perceptions about intimacy and loving as they relate to her childhood predicament. Particularly disturbing for most incest survivors is the fear that closeness with someone will result in sexual interaction, either intrusion from the other or by the self. Closeness and sexuality were never differentiated in the incest survivor's home, and this association in adult life causes the survivor to defend against closeness constantly or to sexualize closeness constantly in an effort to deal with this threatening feeling of extreme danger.

Many survivors, rather than avoiding sex, become compulsive in their desire for sex, seeking it wherever they can find it in an unconscious effort to gain control over the experience, to master the sexual abuse experience by playing the role of aggressor. This compulsion arises from the survivor's inability to separate sex and love—in the same way that the two were confused during the abuse in childhood. We learn that people are not to be trusted, that they will only hurt us in the end. We come to believe that if we sabotage the relationship first then we won't be the ones who are hurt.

"While in a new relationship I would sleep with my ex-girlfriends. Not the right thing to do. I learned by the third relationship to stop cheating. My appetite for sex has always been more than any partner I have been with." —Whitney

"I think I am very odd to the degree that I am more sexual and sexually aggressive than most lesbians." —Amy

"I think I am somewhat oversexed. I crave having sex a lot no matter who I am with." —Kristie

"I remember feeling the need to be sexually satisfied at a young age. I would seek out anyone or anything to help me control the sexual urges. I really wanted to feel accepted, and one way I could help temporarily satisfy this need was to engage in sexual activity with someone, anyone. Having relations this way made it difficult for me to have friends. I was never able to learn proper social skills and nonsexual relations." —Marie

"I'm fine if I can take the lead. It's much easier for me to be the aggressor in lovemaking, as opposed to letting myself comfortably and trustingly be made love to. The abuse has affected my sexual boundaries too. I feel comfortable taking relationships to a sexual level sometimes too soon, often before I've gotten to know the person." —Cristi

"I am admired among a number of lesbian friends for my sexual prowess with straight and bi women, but I want a stable relationship. My stepsister was very sexually aggressive with me, and I was totally passive with her. I did everything she required and then some. When the abuse stopped, I became the aggressor. I am always the initiator. While I look totally feminine (clothes, cosmetics, mannerisms), I am totally butch between my legs—or in my head, or between the sheets." —Amy

"I tended to equate frequency of sexual intimacy with overall caring and love." —Levie

For an incest survivor, sex is never just sex, and it is rare—especially early in our healing process—to experience pleasure, good feelings, and the vulnerability of orgasm. Sex can become the focus of our trust issues; we struggle to believe that letting someone close will not result in betrayal or rejection, as well as a resurgence of our feelings of being powerless and bad. In an effort not to repeat the trauma the survivor uses sex to control against feelings of badness and powerlessness that are intensified in sex for her. When we withdraw from sex, and at other times give in to sex, we attempt to cope with the double messages we were given about sex. In a projection of the abuse experience, we believe we are sexually powerful and attempt to use this power to build ourselves up.

"I don't just want to have sex. I've had sex. Unfortunately, it was with our father. Now I want to make love." —Dana

"I was extremely promiscuous. I felt like sex didn't mean anything. So many male sexual partners. It wasn't important, and I wasn't important." —Amanda

"Because of my sexual appetite working so early, I was very sexual. I would get turned on very easily." —Diana

"I acted out through my teens by being a prostitute. I used my body as a commodity because I learned that giving sex was my most valuable ability." —Kris

"I fucked my way through my 20s and 30s. I was very promiscuous. I basically got any woman I wanted. I was like a kid in a candy shop." —Jan

"I was stupid and met up with a guy who happened to be a pimp, and I turned into a prostitute, just like magic, overnight. It was hard to get away from that life. I felt like that was just what I had to do, not what I wanted to do." —Kris

In a classic case of reaction formation, survivors describe how they assumed the role of aggressor in their intimate relationships in an unconscious attempt to heal the wounds caused by the sexual abuse by reclaiming the position of power.

"In some ways it was cathartic to be the one who took the power, to be the one who got to be the aggressor. Essentially, I got to be the butch in those situations. It was really liberating to not feel victimized." —Margie

"Part of being the aggressor was an experiment of sorts to see if I could find women who would be sexually attracted to me. Being the sexual aggressor and initiator took away the fear of being vulnerable. I still struggle with the belief system that I am unlovable and that someone could love me without trying to use me for their gain." —Cristi

Because sexual abuse is a boundary violation of the worst kind, survivors often have difficulty with boundaries—being able to say no.

"I continue to struggle with boundary issues, particularly dealing with things sexual in nature. For example, I have a hard time stopping people who make inappropriate advances or comments to me even though I'm extremely uncomfortable. I have trouble saying no in general, but also when it comes to sex." —Brooke

"I think I should be available when someone really wants me sexually. I have a hard time saying no to sexual advances." —Robin

"I have issues with being rejected sexually." —Kirsten 

"With sex it used to come down to 'What's the point of saying no?' It was just so hard for me to say no. Because I couldn't do it at home." —Jacque

"When I was with men I seemed more susceptible to engaging in sexual behavior that I really did not want. Now I feel that being with a woman for eight years has given me the level of comfort needed to say no and to decide when we both want sexual relations." —Marie

For some survivors, the tension around being lesbian complicated sexual boundary issues arising from the sexual abuse.

"I was promiscuous with men in college, like 20–30 men. I was only with men when I was drunk and was with each man only once. I was not attracted to men. I hated the men right afterwards. I didn't want to believe I was a lesbian. I wanted to be close to someone." —Chris

"The abuse forced the issue of sexual boundaries. I didn't understand if I was supposed to be with men or women." —Noemi

Many abused women choose to reclaim their sexuality slowly, if at all. Because they experience orgasm less often they report being less sexually responsive, and they find less satisfaction overall in their sexual relationships. According to Zerbe (1993), periods of celibacy may be necessary so that a woman who has been sexually abused can learn to establish other types of intimate bonds and feelings of empowerment. The self-help literature wisely recommends proceeding slowly in reclaiming one's sexuality, but it can be done over time, often resulting in a full sexual life.

The connection between sex and love—originally distorted by the abuse—continues to cause problems for survivors who confuse the two or act as if they are one and the same.

"I try to put sex into relationships to see if people really love me. I was very sexually promiscuous. I had trouble believing I was loved unless sex was involved." —Wendy

"One lover wasn't very understanding either and broke up with me because she viewed my inability to achieve orgasm and my masturbating—to learn how to please myself—as infidelity. I still fear a lover's rejection." —Dorian

According to Haines (1999), the decision to heal sexually is a choice to reclaim an aspect of yourself that has been wounded and used. It is a choice to make whole again a very powerful and vital aspect of your being. A lesbian partner is often better able to understand the difficulties presented in the sexual area (Groves and Schondel, 1996). Touching between women can convey emotional closeness without explicit sexual expression.

"I think that since I was abused by males there has been much less impact on physical intimacy for me as a lesbian." —Levie

"When I hit my 30s I knew that I had become a very good lover. I had confidence in myself as a strong woman and someone who could fall in love and love another woman fully and not associate that with the violence that was done to me." —Nedhera

"I feel safer with her. The pattern of abuse in my life had influenced me to find one woman whom I can feel comfortable with sexually." —Marie

"We have a beautiful love life. I still cry during and after sex. I feel so vulnerable and loved, and I guess it is still a strange feeling for me. She makes me feel safe and protected and cared for. She has never been rough. I guess the best words I can think of to describe my sex issue today is overwhelmed with love." —Elizabeth

Some survivors find the dynamics of S/M helpful to them in their sexual healing.

"Have you had anyone else talk about S/M? Are they usually bottoms? Bottom because you feel safe enough with the person. It's like you're trying to recreate the thing with your abuser. Here's some advice for survivors: Deal with your feelings about S/M. I think a lot of survivors have a desire to be in a relationship and do scenes and stuff but are really in denial because of their abuse history. It's something that with the right person can really get you past stuff." —Kris

"The most significant way that my abuse has played out in my lesbian desire is by enacting in an S/M context. I am a 'girl' to my butch, who is a 'Daddy.' In this way I have diffused the power of my perpetrator to alter my desire in negative ways. I do not avoid anything in my sexually intimate life with another female. If a sex act bugs me because it is evocative of sexual abuse, then I go headfirst into that sex act and enact it until it is not my perpetrator's act on me, but my *act with another female."* —Robin

"Freedom to me is being able to express my sexuality, whether it's leather, fetish, S/M, being fluid—all of that. I see myself more as a fluid lesbian. Allow people to self-identify. It's all about being sexually free and being able to just have that liberty and the right to be safe doing so. To know that I can be asexual if I want to." —Noemi

Others describe the reawakening of sexual desire that they have experienced in relationships with women and the sexual healing that has been possible.

"I am feeling and recognizing physical desire for the first time in my life. My girlfriend is not a therapeutic tool, but my relationship with her is helping me discover that intimacy can be a good thing, that it is not the big, huge thing with teeth that frightened me so much in my relationships with men. Her help and patience are really a magical thing—and it is equally magical that now I look forward to touching her at the end of a long day." —Mollie

"It took a long time to develop trust. My partner and I have worked very hard on our sexual relationship because sex is often not a comfortable experience for me. Now we meet each other's needs pretty well and have great fun with sex. I have a strap-on that my partner loves. I have great orgasms from her touching my clit with her hand or a vibrator." —Pat

"I do not like real human penises, but dildos are fine. Vaginal penetration with fingers is pleasurable for me with a woman." —Cristi

"One of the best things I did for my personal growth and development was to put my sexual self on the shelf, so to speak, and utilize my time and energy developing myself. I think most people run from one relationship to the next without taking time out to understand what went wrong in their former relationships and taking personal responsibility for their part in them." —Dorian

"What really helped me was that my partner was someone who really talked a lot. She would talk about everything, and I felt comfortable let-

ting her know, 'No. I don't feel anything when you do this.' So that was very important to me. That's one thing that I do. I talk. I'll say, 'I didn't feel anything you did. Let's try something else.'" —Diana

"I feel that my relationship with my partner has helped me heal the most. I've told her about my past and she is very understanding and patient with me and my difficulty in giving myself over 100% to her emotionally. I've been able to explore my sexuality in this kind, caring, soft, and welcoming way." —Elizabeth

Intimacy: Building Lesbian Relationships That Last

"Love from one being to another can only be that two solitudes come nearer, recognize, protect, and comfort each other."
—Han Suyin (Elizabeth Combin)

In *The Broken Heart: The Psychobiology of Human Contact* (1992), James Lynch writes, "Communication is vitally linked to our bodies and is probably the single most important factor that influences our health or lack of health." Recent studies have found that relationship is the single strongest predictor of long life. Unfortunately, for survivors real emotional intimacy can be difficult. We learned in childhood that trusted friends and family members would only hurt us and that those whom we relied on for protection abused us or failed to protect us from the abuse. It is no wonder that we struggle to find and maintain intimate relationships in our adult lives. According to Bass and Davis (1988), "The building blocks of intimacy—giving and receiving, trusting and being trustworthy—are learned in childhood." If children receive loving attention, they develop skills for establishing and maintaining nurturing relationships. Unfortunately, if you were abused, your trust was broken by adults who misused you. You grew up with confusing messages about the relationship between sex and love, trust and betrayal.

Our problem, according to Evan (2001), lies in not knowing how to connect deeply enough with our partner. What most of us have failed to recognize is that the chief work to be done in relationships is work we do on ourselves. No partner can give us the security, safety, or love we're looking for until we're willing to give that to ourselves first. When we focus more on what prevents us from feeling love toward our partner and less on getting our partner to be more loving, we are on the right track. In this way, we take the first step in removing the barriers to our receiving love.

Betty Berzon, in *The Intimacy Dance: A Guide to Long-Term Success in Gay and Lesbian Relationships*, writes, "The more aware you are of your own emotional underground, the more likely you are to navigate the danger zones of your relationship safely." We have to be willing to open ourselves up to our partners, to let them see what's going on inside us. We let go of our need for self-protection and learn to trust again. Intimacy grows in direct proportion to the level of openness and honesty in any relationship. Unfortunately, classic emotional triggers for survivors are the feelings of vulnerability and dependence that are part of all intimate relationships. In this way, conflict in a relationship is "an internal battle with painful baggage of an unresolved past that gets projected onto the screen of their relationship" (Dayton, 2000). While this dynamic can be found in all relationships, it is particularly evident in relationships with survivors. Here's what Jan said:

"A lot of times I felt trapped with women. It's like claustrophobia. We would break up because I needed air, like being inside a closed building. We were comfortable. I think this comes from the abuse. I was not faithful to them. I was Miss Shit America, a lesbian's worst nightmare. I didn't see that I could do it any other way. I destroyed many people along the way. I've always had wealth, and I buy my women: houses, clothes, travel. Then I was diagnosed with MS and my whole life changed. My partner wanted to care for me, but I left. That's the power of abuse. I miss the company of women."

When we are not taught as children how to build healthy relationships, this lack of experience can interfere with our ability to build intimacy as adults, as Marie discovered:

"I do not know how to be intimate emotionally, but I keep trying to learn. I just don't know when there is emotional closeness. This is still a struggle for me."

Researchers have found that close emotional connections and intimacy are highly valued and sought after by lesbians; these may be the hallmark of lesbian relationships (Biaggio, Coan and Adams, 2002). Kirkpatrick (1991) goes so far as to say that emotional intimacy may be as important as sexual satisfaction in bonding lesbian couples. While a great deal of negative information has been written about the tendency toward fusion or merger in lesbian relationships, there are two sides to this story. According to Kirkpatrick (1991), fusion or merger happen when the desire for togetherness dominates the couple's life and precludes individuality. This is seen as a consequence of a shared feminine socialization. The tendency to merge may lead to a fear of expressing differences. Causby et al (1995, cited in Biaggio, Coan and Adams, 2002) found that difficulty handling or resolving conflict, a common problem among survivors, is also seen among lesbians in merged couples. In these relationships, harmony is valued to the extent that the women deny differences and avoid conflict.

Lesbian couples have been described as more enmeshed than other couple types, presumably because female socialization and developmental dynamics gear them to be more connected than men. Only very recently have theorists proposed that two women can have relationship closeness while still maintaining individual boundaries and function effectively. Theorists distinguish between cohesion and enmeshment. *Cohesion* is a healthy emotional closeness where partners are consistently caregiving to one another and have clear boundaries. *Enmeshment*, as it is called, is "a pathological style of relating signified by intrusive closeness and lack of personal boundaries" (Roper, 1997). Differentiation is an important piece of this puzzle and involves the ability of partners to distinguish oneself from the other. In one study, lesbians reporting high levels of fusion reported less relationship satisfaction than those reporting low levels of fusion; higher levels of fusion were associated with anxious or ambivalent patterns of attachment (McBain, 1999). It seems that when we become enmeshed as couples this affects our attachment in unhealthy ways. According to Carol Rusbult, 1993, an individual's commitment to a relationship is affected by three general factors: satisfaction, the quality of alternatives to the current relationship, and investments made in the relationship (cited in Diamond, 2002). In other words, how good is the relationship, what are my options, and how much have I invested in it? The answers to these questions affect our ongoing commitment to our partners.

The flip side of the "merger as pathological" argument is found in the work of other researchers. Ossana (2000) suggested that merger may not only be desirable for lesbians in relationships but may be an adaptive response to adverse conditions (Biaggio, Coan and Adams, 2002). We find comfort and solace from a sometimes hostile world in the arms of our partners. Kelly connects this idea of refuge to survivors' sexual abuse recovery:

"My partner of nine years believes partners are a vital voice in this struggle for survivors to regain a right to our own bodies, our relationships, to making healthy choices, to learning trust, etc."

On hearing that her partner was sexually abused as a child, a woman may respond in a variety of ways. Common reactions include minimization or avoidance (Courtois, 1988). Although she might initially offer some support, she quickly drops the subject and forgets about it. Other typical responses include: rescue and protection, which may leave the survivor feeling powerless; anger and retribution, which may cause anxiety and fear; rejection, which blames the survivor for the abuse; and support and empathy, including sadness, which helps the survivor in her recovery process (Walsh, 1986).

In addition to the dynamics of lesbian couples and the unique issues of lesbian survivors, post–traumatic stress disorder also affects relationships, and in specific ways. It can be frustrating for your partner when her attempts to help you do not work. She may feel socially isolated because you don't want to participate in activities that you once did. Your partner may need information about post–traumatic stress disorder and help in dealing with her feelings. Couples counseling may be helpful also. In this way and others, partners of survivors have their own needs. While they may intellectually understand what is going on with the survivor, they may be uncomfortable with the increased demand for emotional support and restrictions on sexual behavior. As you begin to heal the effects of the abuse, your partner is forced to deal with you as a different person and in a different way than the woman she fell in love with. The rules change and partners are often left feeling out of control about the relationship. According to Maltz (1991), "In response to these feelings of powerlessness, some partners may attempt to push, control, or dominate the healing efforts." This is important because satisfaction with intimate relationships has been associated with lower levels of depression among lesbians (Oetien and Rothblum, 2000) and, of course, the reverse is also true. Further, lesbians were more likely to seek professional help for depression when depression and relationship issues were identified as occurring simultaneously (Trippet, 1994). In this way, relationship issues can serve as the catalyst for survivors seeking therapy. Maltz (1991) and Roth (1993) found that recovery work can trigger personal issues for the partner, including a new awareness of incestuous or abusive dynamics in her own family. This was Lisa's experience:

"My partner knows about the abuse, but because of her own personal struggles she will rarely engage in deep discussion about my experiences or my feelings about what happened."

Hall (1999) found that in couples where both women were survivors, there was a feeling that the abuse never went away—it remained a constant theme in their relationship. Second, there was the fear of reabusing the partner, of doing something that could be construed as abusive. While it might initially seem like a good idea to begin couples therapy instead of individual therapy when it becomes clear that there are problems in the couples' relationship, Roth (1993) counsels against this. She explains that it is not possible for a survivor to explore the depths of her personal issues in the presence of her partner. As the survivor enters the latter phases of individual treatment, however, some couples treatment may be useful in helping the couple to adjust to the changes in the relationship. Maltz (1988) disagrees, saying, "The intimate partner of the survivor is the secondary victim of the sexual abuse" and treating the couple rather than the individual is the best way to shift the focus away from the survivor to the dyad. It appears that this may be one of those issues that a survivor and her partner have to resolve for themselves.

Researchers have identified several factors that predict satisfaction in lesbian relationships. I include a discussion of these factors along with implications for lesbian survivors. Berger (1990) found that lesbians who were out to their families were more likely to report satisfaction with their intimate relationships. We can interpret this as meaning that a positive self-concept and self-esteem as a lesbian and familial support contribute to relationship satisfaction. For incest survivors, the negative implications of dysfunctional family dynamics are apparent. Dorn (1990) found that lesbian couples that were matched in level of social involvement were happier than mismatched couples. Moderately socially involved couples were the most satisfied. These findings have implications for survivors who suffer from depression and post–traumatic stress disorder and struggle with isolation and social phobia. Dorn (1990) also found that the following factors contributed to relationship satisfaction: similar class backgrounds, complementary personality styles, a sense of equality in the relationship, good conflict resolution skills, a belief in monogamy, and a similar degree of openness of sexual orientation to their families and society. Similarly, Garnets (2002b) found that acceptance of gay identity, stage of coming out, and degree of outness were common issues faced by lesbian couples. In the same vein, Groves and Schondel (1996) found that couples' success in an incest survivors group depended on their level of commitment to confronting personal issues and their willingness to work through relationship issues. Both studies highlight the importance of effective conflict resolution skills in successful lesbian partnership. Unfortunately, survivors often avoid conflict in relationships by withdrawing or shutting down. Given the importance of conflict resolution skills to successful relationships, couples would be advised to prioritize work in this area to strengthen their bond.

"My ex asked me to marry her. She was being transferred out of state and wanted me to go with her. She gave me a week to decide. I didn't like being put on a time clock. Then the bribes started. She promised to buy me a car, a house. Finally, after a few days I said, 'I cannot make the trip.' That was three years ago, and I'm still in love with her. She's a wonderful woman, but she couldn't understand what I meant when I said I just couldn't take any more." —Nedhera

"This is hard on my partner. I've almost lost her twice. Sometimes I fear she'll tell me she's tired of it and wants out. But I hope I'm thinking wrong. Intimacy is a big issue with us. We have no intimacy now, and I'm trying very hard to be intimate with her because I'm afraid of losing her. It's fear I'll be hurt, I guess. I am thankful to my lover for not controlling me." —Laura

"We have struggled with our relationship, but we continue to seek each other and resources to work through our differences. One thing I am proud of is that we continue to talk no matter what is going on between us, now matter how angry we get." —Marie

Evan (2001) explored the dynamics in lesbian couples when the women are dealing with the issues surrounding childhood abuse together. The goals of the group therapy were to acknowledge each couple's commitment as well as the survivor as an individual, explore dysfunctional patterns, enhance the couple's ability to be intimate with each other, and learn healthier ways to communicate and resolve conflict. Again we see the importance of communication and conflict resolution skills. Liz described her understanding of couples' work in this way:

"In relationships there are those things that you just ignore now. Guess what? When you've been around for 18 years, they still annoy you. You put things into piles. Here's the pile of 'I have to change because it's truly my problem that something she's doing is bothering me.' Then there's 'She really does have to change because that is really not going to work.' And 'I'm going to let it go.'"

Difficulty in communicating feelings and perceptions of experiences were a major problem in most of the couples' relationships. Often each partner felt misunderstood, and old feelings of abandonment would rise up. This resulted in each partner coping with defensive styles learned as survival skills in childhood. These techniques were often counterproductive to the women's desire to be understood, accepted, and loved by their partners.

Lesbians need relationship role models (Evan, 2002; Pimental-Habib, 2002). We need to understand that we are not the first to struggle with these relationship issues and that there are guidelines we can apply to improve our relationships. A three-pronged approach to successful relationships, proposed by Pimental-Habib, includes personal growth, rigorous honesty, and self-awareness (2002). Survivors' recovery work mirrors the work of building successful and satisfying lesbian relationships. Working at our relationships pays rich dividends, as Katie affirms:

"My abuse has greatly affected my relationship with my partner. It has affected our sexual intimacy, ability to trust, created stress, and made us struggle even more than normal. It has also brought us closer and made us stronger in the 11 years we've been together."

"I've been going back and forth with an ex-girlfriend of mine for a year. Now we find ourselves still loving each other, still connected, still interested, still attracted, and each with enough self-knowledge and healing to try and make it work. I really love this woman. I care for her deeply in my heart. We're going to go to therapy together. It's working now without any commitment to 'lasting' love." —Cory

Groves and Schondel (1996) describe the long-term effects of abuse on adult intimate relationships. As we have seen, trust, intimacy, and level of commitment are common concerns which directly impact lesbian relationships. On the other hand, the emotional bond and the understanding of the female experience can create a higher level of acceptance of the partner who is a survivor of child sexual abuse than is possible in heterosexual relationships. Many survivors I spoke with described their affinity with other women whose friendship and love made healing possible. Here's how they described their connections with other women and the impact on their healing.

"Women have been my most effective therapists and confidantes. I connect with them on a soul level better than I do most guys. Between women many of the male-female barriers are already broken down,

which allows us to trust and enjoy each other wholly. It is more of a congruence of energy than anything. I love the nurturing, loving ways of women and of the goddess." —Cristi

"Relationships with women have helped me heal so much. Women are by nature more compassionate and understanding, and that helps a lot." —Kim

"There's more intimacy and depth to a relationship with women. It's a replacement of a parental relationship with women that you don't find with men. When I'm with a woman I feel like it's simultaneously equal and parental in a certain way. With a man I'm silent and like a child. It's like I lose my sense of my third eye, my objective sense of looking out for my internal family." —Tabitha

"My relationships with women have allowed me to take control of my life and assert my inner being." —Noemi

"I feel safer doing my healing work with women." —Misha

"Women have been so incredibly compassionate and supportive of me in my healing. I received tremendous support from a woman when I decided to tell my parents about the abuse. I don't think I could have made it through it without her." —Brooke

"Women have helped me to grow. They all encouraged me in their own way to seek further insight into my thoughts, actions, beliefs, and feelings." —Marie

"Being with women lovers or friends has brought me comfort, compassion, trust, understanding, better intuition, and true love. Relationships have helped me to fine-tune my communication skills." —Whitney

"My relationships with women have been incredible. They have been lifesaving. I have been empowered by the women in my life. They have

really been there for me. I have made significant connections with women, especially other lesbians." —Katie

"In general, I think that women are gentle and soft. They are generally nonthreatening and I've been able to explore my sexuality in this kind, caring, soft, welcoming way. I really care about females and the issues we face. I respect women and like everything about them." —Elizabeth

"The comfort, love, and understanding from women have allowed me to continue living. It has helped bandage some wounds. I have learned to trust more. I have learned what loving and being loved is. I have experienced true happiness and acceptance." —Kirsten

"There are little things that I've gotten along the way—both giving and receiving nurturing from people." —Jill

"My relationships with women have been the biggest help imaginable! They have been my ears to hear me out. Women have always been my biggest source of strength and comfort through it all." —Kristie

"Being able to be safely held by a woman's energy is the greatest healing experience. Women understand female woundedness, living in a patriarchal space. There's something innate in all of us, something about woman-love. It's so nurturing, healing, compassionate." —Mary Lou

As decades of child abuse research and the personal accounts of therapists and survivors attest, healing from sexual abuse is possible. With the help of caring healers—therapists and other helping professionals—the emotional and physical wounds of childhood sexual abuse can be healed. And survivors can find love and develop real intimacy in their relationships with women too. Here survivors describe the love they found—or the love that found them.

"I am now in a wonderful relationship, and we live together in a home that we bought. We're soul mates. I never thought it could happen, but it has! Our relationship has helped me heal the most. I've told her about my

past and she is very understanding and patient with me and my difficulty in giving myself over 100% to her emotionally." —Elizabeth

"I feel like Cindy's love for me is saving me from myself. I feel worthy and loved. I now know what love feels like. It is warm and wonderful and absolutely essential to my peace of mind." —Tammy

"I think what really helped me was that my partner was someone who talked a lot, and she would talk about everything. So that was important to me. Before, the abuse was something that I kept a secret, something that I was ashamed of. Now I'm not proud of it, but it's a part of me." —Diana

"My partner is incredibly loving and patient. She has really helped me to see myself as a worthwhile human being. I am a strong woman and she has helped me to grow and to heal." —Pat

"My partner is special and understanding and supportive. She has helped me a lot. She is kind and a truly good person. She understands how deeply one is affected by abuse even though it never happened to her. She cares about me even when I'm angry, depressed, or stuck in trauma. I'd never experienced these things before her. I'd never trusted anyone before her. I guess I didn't have enough reason to." —Barbara

"I've only had one relationship with a woman. After a few months I decided a relationship with her wasn't what I wanted because I had always pictured myself with a husband, three kids, a dog, and a minivan. Several months ago I realized that this actually is what I want. I feel complete with her, and she's the only person I really want to have a relationship with. Now that we're back together I can picture myself with her, two kids, my cat, and my trusty station wagon—all of which we talk about often." —Mollie

"I feel safe with my partner in a way that I've not felt with a man. I did not feel safe as a child to reveal my pain. Now I have safe places to learn to heal. She is one of those safe places." —Maggie

"I wonder how can a relationship be this perfect. We've been together four years. We haven't had to work really hard. It's a pure, fulfilled relationship. I'm not just somebody's sex toy. It's about me. It's about us." —C.J.

"I've been in a relationship for a year. When the abuse first started coming up in our relationship my partner tried to get books on it. She was really curious about how she could help and understand me better. She's been really supportive, and I can't believe how wonderful my life is with her. I have never been in love like this before. She's nonjudgmental of my past. She lets me talk when I need to talk, cry when I need to cry, and be silent when I need to be. Now it's like, 'Holy cow! Someone really loves me and can accept everything that I couldn't even accept.'" —Delphene

"My partner of 29 years has believed my memories implicitly, telling me that they explain dozens of things about me. She has worked extremely hard to understand which of my exaggerated reactions are more directly related to the abuse than to things she says or does. She has been amazingly supportive and understanding in too many ways to enumerate." —Levie

"I have been with my partner 18 years. Why does it work? We're very different, opposites really. She is more grounded. She can see through the bullshit. I'm more emotional. I tend to spin. We're a refuge for each other. We're still in love with each other. We honor each other's different needs. She's my number 1 ally. She's been with me through all my flashbacks and craziness. She's one of those people who shows up and doesn't reject me. She's very much there, continuously encouraging me." —Lynn

"My partner has been a stronghold when I have had no strength. She has always been there for me. I owe her a lot!" —Kristie

"Being in a relationship with women, your emotional well-being is taken seriously. When there are two women in a relationship, they both can be nurturing, and there is the potential to value emotional health. There's also the potential for more egalitarian relationships. You don't have to deal with all the crap of gender roles. It really frees you from lots of the dynamics of power. And there are no written rules—literally and

figuratively. You're free to invent a relationship based on intimacy. My partner and I have been together almost 13 years." —Margie

"I'm in a six-year relationship now. It's the best one I've ever been in. It's particularly wonderful knowing where I stand. We fight and get over it. I feel completely loved and accepted. This makes a good relationship easier. It's healthy, not sick in the way my other relationships were." —Marty

"I have found that my partner brings out the emotion in me at times, much to my dismay. I have found my tears again. I am starting to find hope and love and trust, slowly, a day at a time. I have learned to share my nightmares and flashbacks with my partner." —Robin

"We've been in a relationship for two years. We met on the Internet and talked for four months before we met. We had a commitment ceremony last fall with family and friends. I've been happier in the past two years than I can ever remember." —Margaret

"I see us as two women choosing to live our lives together." —Misha

"Being with my partner has taught me that I have a right to say no, a right not to be hit, and a right not to have forced sexual relations. She helped me break the abusive hold over me. She has helped me in more ways than I could ever explain." —Rowan

As for me, I am in a loving committed relationship with my first love, a woman I met when we were working together at camp when I was just 17. We didn't get together until four years later—when I returned home to finish college and she had broken up with her girlfriend (who thought something was happening between us!). I never believed that a love like this was possible for me. I certainly never had role models for healthy relationships to aspire to. I only knew I loved her deeply and was dedicated to keeping our relationship going over the long haul. Well, it's been 18 years now and we're still going strong. It hasn't been easy, that's for sure. When I'm actively engaged in healing, my attention shifts and old defenses rear their ugly heads. I am prone to moodiness and often withdraw emotionally or shut down entirely when I become overwhelmed and sometimes lash out in anger. Lucky for us, we understand all of this by now. I know when I need space to sort things out, and she recognizes the cues that signal my need for space. I don't apologize anymore, and she doesn't blame me for the healing that I still need to do. Her patience and enduring love are two of the greatest gifts I know. Our 5-year-old daughter is another gift. In parenting her together I feel we are recreating my childhood, healing some of the old hurts and letting the joy back in. Opening my heart to love was very difficult. I was scared and anxious, fearing that I would be hurt again, wanting to shield myself from pain and remain invulnerable to further violation. What I couldn't have known at the time is that the only way to heal the pain was to trust again—on faith at first, until my heart found the way back. Now I love because I am alive. It is the very air I breathe.

CHAPTER 8

RELATING TO FAMILY

To effectively take care of ourselves, we ultimately have to examine longstanding individual and family dynamics that have presented lifelong issues for us. Decades of child abuse research demonstrate that abuse happens within a family context, and healing must take into account the ways that the family constellation made the abuse possible, perpetuated it over time, and prevented our stopping it. A primary treatment goal with survivors is fostering separation and individuation from the family and its patterns (Courtois, 1988).

For most of us, the abuse happened within the context of our family. As a result, giving up the myth of the happy family and learning to relate in new ways to our family members, if at all, are essential steps in the healing process. Psychotherapist Nicki Roth (1993) found in her psychotherapy practice with survivors that most are still in contact with their families. While many had passing fantasies of disengaging, they found themselves too tied to their families to break off these relationships. "The basic dilemma for the survivor," Roth explains, "is whether she can maintain a position of strength and health in the face of continued family dysfunction." In a classic enactment of family dynamics, changes in the survivor will be seen as a threat to the family. Any confrontation with the abuser or other family members must be carefully considered because retaliation and further abuse is likely. Finney (1992) explains, "It is a terribly lonely feeling to know that your family has abandoned you. But the truth is that they abandoned you long ago when you needed them far more than you do now."

Lesbians' relationships with their mothers are particularly complex, even within the context of mother-daughter relationships as a whole. Our experience of being mothered shapes our lives and, in many ways, guides our life choices (Donnelly, 1998). Understanding the complexity of the mother-daughter bond is essential to our healing and forging intimate relationships with women. Anger at the nonabusing parent—often a mother—who couldn't or wouldn't protect you is healthy (Bratton, 1999). Tammy describes the disruption of the mother-daughter bond in this way:

"I now know what it feels like to be held in the soft, comforting arms of a woman, something that I needed from my mother that she took away from me over the 'semen in the panties' episode. She never held me again. She never soothed me. She never acted like she noticed a damn thing was wrong. What a shitty mother! I am so in tune with my kids. How in the hell could she not have sensed that something was wrong with me?"

"I had no contact with my mother for many years because of the abuse. I was really punishing her. She was psychotic and alcoholic and I hold her accountable. The mother's role involves protectress. Had I told her it wouldn't have done any good. That's been my rage. I wrote her a letter, but I'm not getting what my child-self would like." —Mary Lou

Courtois (1988) provides rich data about mothers of incest victims who, not infrequently, were also abused. She describes three types of mothers—dependent, caretaking, and submissive. "Incest mothers," as they are called, "often suffer from sexual dysfunction and chronic depression, which may be aftereffects of their own incest."

"When I tried to talk to Mom about the abuse, she told me that she had been molested by her big brother. I tried to talk to her, and she turned it around to be about her." —Deborah

"My mom was an undiagnosed, untreated manic-depressive throughout my childhood, which explains the suicidal thoughts that she felt necessary to share with all of us. She often stated that the only reason she didn't kill herself was because she was afraid to leave us alone with our father. My mom was a victim of sexual abuse at the hands of an uncle when she was a child. I say 'victim' and not 'survivor' because I feel as though she has spent the majority of her life stuck in that victim role. She has pretty much remained tortured and victimized in all aspects of life. I

remember always feeling like I had to take care of her and that my needs as a child were never going to get met by her, so I pretty much took care of myself." —Mary

Daughters run a high risk of victimization if their mothers are absent from the family or suffer from some sort of disability, including psychiatric illnesses, personality disorders, serious incapacitating physical illnesses or disabilities, or alcoholism. Herman (1981) went so far as to say that "it appears that only a strong alliance with a healthy mother offers a girl a modicum of protection from sexual abuse." These powerless mothers are unable to prevent incest or support their daughters when they disclose its occurrence for fear that this would mean giving up their own base of security.

Our partner's relationship with our family, including our abusers, present another challenge for us. While we work through the issues related to our abuse, choosing to confront our abusers or avoid family gatherings, we must be prepared for our partner's reactions to these decisions (Roth, 1993). If we choose to maintain contact with our family, our partner may have difficulty understanding this decision and urge us to cut off all contact. This can be especially hard for us to deal with, and we may feel the need to defend our family to our partner, as Jacque describes:

"My lover had a hard time with the idea that I had anything to do with my parents after what had happened. In some ways it was really good for me to have someone being really indignant and angry on my behalf. Like, 'Wow! It really is that bad.' But it's complicated. I've still tried to have a relationship with my parents because they're the only parents I've got. The facilitator of the lesbian incest group also encouraged me to cut off all contact with my family. I remember telling her, 'No. I just can't do that.'"

Assessing Your Relationships

Most sexual abuse happens within the family. Estimates are that one in three women will be sexually abused by the time they are 18. The majority are abused by someone that they know. Kritsberg and

Miller-Kritsberg (1993) explain that child abuse it is a secret that no one talks about but everyone knows. Because of the secrecy and shame that surrounds sexual abuse, the victim is made to feel responsible for the family's problems: "If only she had kept her mouth shut, this wouldn't be happening." Kritsberg and Miller-Kritsberg assure survivors, "It is healthy to feel rage at the members of your family who were silent accomplices to your abuse." An honest assessment of our relationships with family members—and decisions about how we wish to proceed with these relationships—is one way that we take care of ourselves.

Honest assessments of our relationships with family members involve examining their words and actions and making a judgment about how our relationships with them affect our well-being. We can begin to distinguish what Dayton (2000) calls the "looking good family" and the "shadow family" and gain new perspective on the ways in which the facade of the "looking good family" contributes to our feelings of shame and craziness. In some instances, when we examine our interactions with family we will recognize for the first time the ways in which they have harmed us. For others, we will see again the negative effect that their behavior has had on our self-esteem over a lifetime.

Coming to grips with the ways in which my relationship with my brother and his abuse when we were children is only one part of the process of assessing my relationships with family. As time goes by, I come to realize the ways in which family dynamics in our household allowed and continued the abuse for many years. A demanding and often absent father, a weak and passive mother, and five children in a span of 11 years all contributed to a culture of silence. My oldest brother was the first-born son and my parents' favorite. Knowing that there is nothing I could have said or done to stop the abuse or make my parents believe me has helped me to let go of the shame and self-blame that has plagued me for years. My youngest sister recently told me how my younger brother and she would hide together, crying with me during and after the incidents of abuse, believing I was having nightmares in my sleep. My other sister, on the other hand, chooses to believe that the abuse happened because I didn't say no as she did. She does not recall the incidents where my brother abused her sexually, forcing her to perform sexually with him and me. Now that he is a husband and father she is convinced that he has outgrown whatever caused his perverted sexual desires and that his children and others are safe from him. I warn her that such thinking is naive and likely to be horribly wrong. I choose not to engage in conversations with her about the abuse anymore. She is incapable of understanding my experience and unable to offer me any support or compassion. I have decided that continuing to listen to her misguided attempts to rectify her image of the ideal family is just too painful for me now. Our family was never the way she believes it was, and I have tired of the charade.

In telling my story I have let a skeleton out of the closet. It is only one of many. I tell my story to break the silence about the abuse and to help other survivors who are as yet unable to take that step. I have no doubt that my family will view my telling as a breach of confidence, a violation of the family trust, and a major affront to the integrity of the family. While it may be all of these, so was the abuse. I maintain that it is my right to stand up and tell my story and not be shamed or scapegoated for the abuse I suffered as a child. Of course, I always believed that my disclosure would be met with denial and abandonment and support for my brother. Suffering my family's anger and withdrawal is a small price to pay after all the years of torment during and following the abuse. I did not cause the abuse, and I will not feel shame for it. My family should be ashamed of themselves for allowing the abuse to continue for so long, for not believing me when I told, and for withdrawing their love when I chose to speak out about it. Love isn't supposed to hurt. Of course, I never knew that.

Here survivors describe their interactions with family and the decisions they have made about continuing these relationships.

"No one in my family is like anyone I would have chosen to know, not like anyone I would have chosen even to know of. No way! I would stay far away from the unpleasantly distorted ones. And to the others I'd simply have nothing to say." —Barbara

"My abuser was a friend of the family. He abused my cousin and me over a period of about one year when we were 7. My parents found out about it and did nothing. I have a really hard time with that piece, especially as a parent myself. I would do something. I always knew they knew about it, but they would not talk about it until about 10 years ago when I confronted them. Their response was, 'Well, what could we do?' It is pretty scary to think you grew up with completely incompetent people as your parents. They did nothing to protect me." —Pat

"Since my family offers me nothing in terms of support or understanding, it just seems pointless to involve them in such personal discussions about the abuse." —Lisa

"My father lives in Florida and comes up here twice a year. It's still hard. I still have weird feelings of attraction and repulsion toward him." —Chris

"My parents knew about the abuse and did nothing. They participated in the abuse because of their silence. We never talked about it. There is no communication in my family; no direct communication." —Pat

"I don't have a good relationship with my mother at all. I moved out of the house at 17 before I graduated high school, and I've been standing on my own since. It's been a struggle. My mom has not offered any financial or emotional support. I don't have a lot of respect for her for that or for her denial of two very important things: the abuse and my coming out." —Lyndsey

"I was hospitalized repeatedly between the ages of 4 and 7 with bladder and kidney infections caused by the abuse. My parents didn't stay with me and gave me no explanation for what was happening. I almost died in the ICU." —Lynn

"We still don't talk in my family. When I told my mom that my symptoms were classic signs of abuse, she didn't say anything, just changed the

subject. I think the prevailing wisdom in my family is to get over it and move on, which I have tried to do." —Deborah

"I have an important relationship with my brother. We're close. We've shared the trauma of our childhood." —Amanda

"My relationship with my father? It's more than it was, but I'm still uncomfortable with it. I get so nervous before seeing him that I just don't do it." —Kris

"My relationship with my father is terse, limited, and superficial. He considers himself right in all things and refuses to honor who I am and what I believe. We have very little contact. When I do visit home the atmosphere is often tense, and Dad and I avoid each other. We rarely converse on the phone. Mom at least tries to keep some contact, but she has also said she does not want to know who I am or about the life path I now walk." —Cristi

Setting Limits

"If you were sexually abused as a child, you were not adequately taken care of. You were not taught that you could ask for or receive protection from the adults around you. Because you did not experience safety, you didn't learn that you could set boundaries and limits. You didn't know that you could say no. You didn't know that you had a right to protect yourself."
—JoAnn Loulan

Sometimes we are forced to set limits on our interactions with our family members to protect ourselves, our partners, and our children. In cases of incest, establishing firm limits about contact between our families of choice and our abusers is essential to our mental health. Many survivors are selective about which family members they see, or set stringent limitations or conditions on family interactions (Courtois, 1988). Wolin and Wolin (1993, cited in Dayton, 2000) found that children of alcoholic parents tended to locate 200 or more miles away from them, which the Wolins called the "200-mile rule." This provided the children with enough physical distance to remove themselves from the damaging effects of their parents' addiction while still keeping in touch. This strategy worked for Jacque:

"I see my parents occasionally. When I was living only 45 miles away they were quite insistent that I should come over to help them with things. My therapist actually felt it was a good idea for me to move 850 miles away because it's the only kind of boundary they recognize."

"A person needs to separate himself from family and companions at intervals and go to new places. He must go without his familiars in order to be open to influences, to change."
—Katherine Butler Hathaway

I'm not very good at setting limits in my relationships. I am nonconfrontational to a fault. I agree to do things and then resent being asked. Then I stew over how I can gracefully back out of my obligations. I often feel like people are taking advantage of my good nature and feel pressured to live up to their expectations. I am beginning to recognize my pattern of passive-aggressive behavior and understand how standing up for myself takes courage that I am continuing to build every day. Twice I have moved away from my family—each time thousands of miles—to put some distance between us as I focused on my healing. I am currently living far from family, which affords me the physical and emotional distance I need to focus on completing this book. Many of the survivors I spoke with shared their own struggles to set limits with their family members in a way that demonstrated their self-respect and unwillingness to participate in the dysfunctional family dynamics that characterized their childhood and that allowed the abuse to occur.

"One of my brothers and I do not get along very well. I actually hate him for not being able to apologize for what he has done to me. Since he

lives in another state I have no contact with him except during the holidays." —Marie

"I have a remote relationship with my father. We had no contact for eight years. He still makes passes at me. He bought my silence with his money. I won't allow the exchange of money for sexual favors anymore." —Mary Lou

"Sunday dinners continued at my grandmother's house even after I had told my family about my father's abuse. I would simply absent myself." —Lisa

"My stepfather was rude to my partner and wouldn't allow her to family occasions, so I stopped going. I confronted Dad a couple of times, and he just went berserk and accused me of trying to give him a heart attack. I backed off and now only visit him for short periods of time. He has never visited us in our home in the whole 10 years of our relationship. I wrote him a letter a couple of years ago. In response he agreed to be at least civil to my partner." —Misha

"My mother and I have maintained a rather rocky relationship through the years. Sometimes we can talk openly, but mostly I just avoid her phone calls and feel like crawling under a rock and hiding when she calls. We see each other once a year. I'd probably make more of an effort to call her or to see her if I didn't feel so amazingly drained after a conversation with her. It's still all about her, and it's exhausting. We tiptoe around topics, mostly because I think she lives in a constant state of guilt for failing to protect me as a child and for who knows what else. I resent the fact that she is unable to just listen to me without having to defend herself in some way. It's just not worth it to even attempt a conversation." —Mary

My partner and I recently moved cross-country with our daughter to start a new life for our family in California. I had found it increasingly difficult in recent years to cope with the stresses of frequent family get-togethers and obligatory gift-giving. I felt the charade of the big happy family was more than I could handle anymore.

Having confronted my brother with the abuse, I found the tension around him to be overwhelming. I lived in fear that he would abuse my daughter or his daughters, and this fear was taking its toll on me. As difficult as it was to leave family and friends behind, moving away was one of the best things I could have done, particularly as I focused my attention on writing this book. The distance from my family allowed me the space to examine my family dynamics in a way that I was unable to do when I was involved with them on a regular basis. I recognize now that the work of the developmental stage I was in when the abuse began at age 12—Identity and Independence—remained unfinished. The abuse interrupted the natural progression that occurs in young children between the ages of 10 and 15. I had not developed a healthy self-identity and had been unable, until very recently, to be independent from my family of origin. I understand now how the effects of the abuse formed an intricate web of destructive habits and experiences that I continue trying to untangle today.

Breaking Ties

"It is useless to deny that evil exists; we must frankly face its existence and refuse participation."
—Jane E. Harrison

Sometimes we are forced to break ties with our families. Their behavior may be too destructive or disrespectful for us to continue our relationships with them. When we begin to face the memories for the first time or begin therapy, breaking ties may be necessary for a specified period of time. With the help of a skilled therapist, we can decide what decision is right for us. As our understanding of family dysfunction grows we may need to take a break from our family. It may be difficult to "maintain independence against the family's efforts to reentangle [us] in the web of dysfunction and denial" (Bratton, 1999).

Some survivors have found it necessary to sever ties with their families. This was always a painful decision for them to make and one that left them with mixed emotions. Here's what they told me:

"My family is very small, and most of us don't speak to each other. We don't stay in touch much, and I can't be honest with them about my life." —Missy

"I have recently split from my mom due to her inability to accept responsibility for her part in my sexual abuse. Starting my own family and walking away from my old one has been the most healing thing for me so far." —Sharon

"I have no family contact anymore. My father is a drug addict and alcoholic. I don't know what the story is with my mother. She has said she doesn't like me. I struggle with that. My mother gave me up for adoption at one time." —Tabitha

"I left home when I was 16 and pretty much have not been in contact with them since then." —Liz

"My mother has consistently rejected and belittled me since the abuse by my neighbor. To this day we do not speak. I've been trying to understand something: So my parents rejected me when I was small. How can I extricate that from how I feel about myself now? How can I survive that?" —Tammy

"I've separated myself from the three of them—my cousins and my aunt." —Nedhera

"I had two full years when I didn't have any contact with Mother. It was sort of a symbolic effort on my part to say that I wasn't going to talk with her. Inevitably, whenever I did talk to her, even on the phone, I would regress to fully unmanageable hysteria. So it was simply self-survival that I said, 'You can't write me and you can't call me.'" —Jill

"I cut them off. I sent them a letter and then had no contact for a year." —Wendy

"We have no regular contact with the family. Our father sends us Christmas cards through our brother, and we don't even open them." —Dana

"I have no relationship with my father. I have not seen him in close to 15 years and have no plans to change. We do not communicate by phone or letter. In the event that he answers the phone when I call my mother, I simply ask for her. This arrangement is sad, but there is no real reason for me to be connected to him." —Lisa

"I attempted to have a relationship with my mother, but it did not work out. I have not spoken to or written her in four years." —Katie

"I have had no contact with my dad since 1992, nor with my sister." —Kyrce

"The issues come up over and over again. I know now that I can never have contact with my mom again." —Rowan

"I cut off relations with my family. It's not a bad thing. I'm the only one of my survivor friends who has done that. I second-guess that a lot. But I know it made me stronger, healthier, and less toxic. They are people that bring me down, that I don't respect, and that trigger me in a million different ways. I have so much anger and hatred toward them that I can't fathom having them in my life. I have decided to take the risk of loneliness and spending the holidays on my own over feeling so awful around them. I don't want to have anything to do with my family; they are just awful people. I'm embarrassed that I came from them." —Cory

"Sometimes we're stuck in trying to be the happy family. I don't need those people. It's all dead weight. I'm really happy not having any contact. I changed my name. My father doesn't have my address. He's never been to any of my houses. I don't want to put any energy into him." —Reg

"I have had no contact with my dad or my sister for 10 years." —Kyrce

"Ten years ago I told my father, 'You can have a relationship with me. I'm willing to work through it after all that happened, but you have to be sober.' I've not heard from him since." —Liz

"What has happened with me is more strategic, trying to shut out those particular individuals—by not talking to them, by not acknowledging their existence. I've also attempted to rid myself of that history." —Noemi

CHAPTER 9

The Journey Continues

Taking Care of Ourselves

"We must welcome the future, remembering that too soon it will be past; and we must respect the past, remembering that once it was all that was humanly possible."
—George Santayana

"Learning to listen to ourselves is a way of learning to love ourselves."
—Joan Borysenko

"When we truly care for ourselves, it becomes possible to care more profoundly for other people. The more alert and sensitive we are to our own needs, the more loving and generous we can be toward others."
—Eda LeShan

"Mothering myself has become a way of listening to my deepest needs, and of responding to them while I respond to my inner child."
—Melinda Burns

Courtois (1988) describes self-nurturing exercises as developmental in that survivors are encouraged to do things for themselves that are relaxing, pleasurable, and positive. This can be a new experience for us because many of us learned to be responsible for the family at a very young age with little regard for our own needs. As adults we need to learn to distinguish between *caring about* and *taking care* of others (Courtois, 1988), particularly as the caretaking role is often used to control and limit intimacy with others, preventing them from getting too close to us.

"There is no true love of self if you are abusing your health."
—Oprah Winfrey

As a defensive coping strategy, many of us reacted to our lack of nurturing by developing an awareness of others' needs for love and affection. In nurturing others we secretly hoped—and may continue to hope—that someone will do the same for us. Oprah is quoted as saying, "Weight was the symptom of a much bigger problem: my unwillingness to fully love, support and give to myself on a daily basis what I so freely give to others." Many of us choose careers in teaching, nursing, and mental health as avenues for our urge to offer nurturance. Even if we secretly wish to be taken care of, we are often extremely resistant to allow others to do so (Roth, 1993).

"I think by being a nurse I'm trying to give the help I couldn't get. We know what it's like to not be noticed. It sent me into the helping professions. I was seeking something for myself. I burned out of nursing and am now interested in ministry. I would like to minister to gays and lesbians or to women in prisons." —Tammy

"As a therapist, every time I work with a client, I am in a certain sense healing myself. I am passionate that young people have the opportunity to go to the cause of their problems rather than just be left dealing with the outcome. At another level, all the study helped me make sense of what was a very confusing inner and outer world as a result of my own abuse." —Misha

When we feel out of control a lot it's often a signal that something happened in our childhood that disrupted our ability to take care of ourselves (Strong, 1998). Being fiercely self-reliant becomes a defense against the mistrust we feel toward others. We don't ask for help, but try to figure things out on our own. While independence can help us to be successful in some areas or our life, we are often frustrated and unsuccessful in team or group situations where our success relies on our cooperation with others (Roth, 1993).

Much of the literature on healing from sexual abuse focuses on the concept of *reparenting.* Reparenting involves giving yourself the kind of emotional support and care you needed after the abuse but that you may not have received. Kathy describes it this way:

"I do a lot of reparenting of myself, speaking to the child within me. I have a good mom that I check in with my kids. I still need to be aware, despite the therapy, that the kids are roles within my personality. I need to listen to the message, when it comes, that I am not in a safe place."

Reparenting has also been called *self-care.* Learning to take care of ourselves—giving ourselves the nurturing that we didn't receive—is an important part of healing (Matsakis, 1996). Because the primary wound to survivors is self-esteem, I include here a list of suggested ways to have a better self-esteem:

1. Make a commitment to improve your self-esteem and better appreciate your worth.
2. Give yourself credit for your accomplishments.
3. Focus on your strengths rather than your shortcomings.
4. Take some time every day to see something good that you did. Write it down.
5. Tune in to your inner voice that says negative things to you. Figure out where it comes from, whose voice it is, and if it's something that you really want as part of your self image.
6. Trust your judgment of yourself.
7. Identify positive traits and talents about yourself.
8. Develop your ability to identify and verbalize your feelings.
9. Develop your ability to identify and verbalize your needs.
10. Positively acknowledge and verbally accept praise and compliments from others.
11. Develop positive self-talk messages ("I can do this." "I am good." "I am able.") (Rainbow Hope, n.d.).

Survivors I spoke with described the ways that they are learning to take care of themselves and the unexpected benefits of paying attention to their psychological and emotional needs.

"Changing my view and not seeing myself as that scared little kid helped me. When I was looking at things through the eyes of that little scared child, my perception of the world was from that teeny, very vulnerable place. Seeing the world that way, seeing everyone as a potential abuser, somehow everyone was bigger than me, was more powerful than me in some way, bigger than me in the eyes of a young child. Once I was able to recognize that and retrain myself to think No, I'm not a little girl, I'm a grown-up woman, *it changed the way I looked at things. I don't feel so frightened now."* —Margie

"I've been exercising with a personal trainer. It helps me feel better. It helps my mental health and anxiety. I want to be able to stay on my journey of introspection and self-work. I think that's going to be a lifetime journey for me, but I think that's part of my purpose on this earth. And I hope to get a greater sense of my spirituality. I just hope for the future that I can continue to keep living. I've survived many suicide attempts. So instead of resorting to that I hope I can find the strength and the spirituality and the courage and knowledge to keep on living." —Lyndsey

"I've had to learn finesse, ways of telling the truth that don't skirt the truth. It's part of speaking up for myself." —Nedhera

"I've started to date again. I'm going slow. I'm not going to jump into bed right away. We might wait six months. We're getting to know each other. She knows I'm a survivor. She doesn't judge me." —Chris

"I have 12 cats. They're pretty much my life. They're my children. It's the one thing that really makes me feel good. I come home and they're here and they're thrilled. And it helps me at night when I have nightmares and stuff. I wake up and there are five of them on top of me and they don't freak out. They're right there. I feel safe having them here." —Kris

"I have quiet time for reflection." —Tammy

Learning how to handle, reduce, or eliminate the symptoms of emotional and physical distress that occur when we remember the abuse is an important skill. Relaxation exercises, anger management strategies, and elements of a healthy lifestyle (regular exercise, enough sleep, and a healthy diet) may all help.

Another important way to heal from the abuse is to speak up and assert your needs and feelings to others. By speaking up for yourself and asserting your rights, you tell yourself and others that you deserve respect. The first step to expressing yourself, says Maltz (1991), is finding your voice and overcoming the feelings of helplessness and powerlessness that you experienced during the abuse. Survivors often struggle to express their feelings in words (Zerbe, 1993). When we learn to protect ourselves by asserting ourselves in words and actions, we counter the messages we learned as children that we were powerless and unable to protect ourselves. At its most fundamental level, this translates into learning self-defense strategies which help us feel more confident and less vulnerable, reducing learned helplessness (Courtois, 1988).

"I've let my friends use me, and I've had to disassociate from them. One friend was not keeping her promises to me. When I reflect on her comments and actions now I see them as abusive. I see disassociating from these friendships as a positive development in my life. Abusers need their targets, and I refuse to be a target again." —Marian

"My dad would come in sometimes and wake me from a deep sleep. I need to know that's not going to happen anymore. Part of the reason I'm sleeping better is because I have all these dogs around me. I know no one is going to sneak up on me now. That's why I first got dogs. I also got into self-defense workshops that helped me learn assertiveness and to take care of myself." —Jacque

"I started lifting weights two years ago and took self-defense classes. It's been four years since I was last raped, and I feel more confident that I can defend myself now. It's really empowering to feel the strength." —Kim

"I took up bodybuilding so I could defend myself." —Kyrce

"The things that seem to really help are talking to my new therapist, drawing, keeping a journal, and spending time with my nephew and pets. Listening to music helps too, especially Stevie Nicks." —Kim

"I'm really selective now about who I involve in my life." —Mary Lou

"I am very precise and particular about speech and how I use words. After living in a world where nothing was ever what it was supposed to be, I always strive to make sure that I say what I mean and that I mean what I say." —Lisa

Of course, we're not perfect. We do the best we can, even as we struggle in our efforts. Some days are better than others. The important thing is continuing to move in the direction of healing.

"Abuse affects all aspects of your life in many ways. I never take care of myself. That's something that I'm working a little on." —Diana

"Sometimes I catch myself doing it: letting men get away with shit that they shouldn't. I don't think, 'Wait a minute. I have a choice here.'" —Kris

"I lost touch with myself when I was drinking. When eating a lot and not around good people, it's hard for me to be positive." —Chris

"I suffer from a streak of self-destructiveness. I overspend my budget and don't control my weight. I tend to go on a seesaw for six to nine months. I take my vitamins every day and pay my bills. Then I stop taking vitamins and don't pay my bills. I go overboard or go in the opposite direction. Finally I have some self-awareness about this and am trying to even out the keel. My goal is to get my life in balance. No one took care of my as a child, so I had no model for self-care. I don't know how to take care of myself. I've made a lot of progress in learning about the patterns of my behavior." —Marian

People who are in touch with their feelings are less likely to rely on substances. When we feel good about ourselves, have reasonably healthy relationships with others, and have an adequate capacity for self-care, we don't need these things. We can set goals for ourselves and our lives and move toward them in incremental steps. We learn new coping strategies that allow us to let go of the old defenses that served us during the abuse but that now interfere with our moving on with our lives.

"I'll be able to pay off my credit cards by the end of the summer. I'm getting myself out of a financial bind. I want to be debt-free. I want to stay on me and keep moving forward." —Dana

"I intuitively know what I'm supposed to do and be to make myself healthier and happier." —Wendy

"I'm learning to value myself. I am sorry for the little girl inside of me that was abused. I am sorry that I did not and do not have a loving, protective mother. I have found happiness in relationships with my children, my friend, my colleagues, and fellow 12-steppers. I am accepting that I am evolving, and that evolution takes time. In the meantime I hope to extend grace and acceptance to others who are lesbian survivors of abuse." —Maggie

"I was plagued nonstop by panic and self-hate. Virtually nothing except strenuous physical activity gave me even partial relief. Until I retired, the necessity of getting up and getting ready to go to work preoccupied me enough to keep the panic at bay. But as soon as I had to begin making decisions about what needed to get done at work, the panic would take hold. Eventually I realized that if I made a careful plan for each day I struggled a bit less. I had to incorporate very doable little things to accomplish each day that I could take some sort of pride in. I make sure I have a good book to read before bed or crosswords to distract me from troubling thoughts if I'm too preoccupied to read. I review what has transpired during the day that I can feel good about—both accomplishments and things that make me feel good about myself as a person. I have a whole bag of tricks to pull out if I awaken during the night. Currently I'm into geography—naming cities in each U.S. state, foreign capitals, major

rivers, and mountain ranges. A while ago I focused on U.S. presidents and vice presidents, math problems, names of professional athletes in each sport, or poetry I had memorized. Those things work for me because they require the right amount of concentration to distract me from troubling thoughts, but they're not so fascinating that they keep me from falling back asleep." —Levie

"I have a strong spiritual center. I live two blocks from the lake now, and I can walk to the lake every day if I wish. The water was always where I would go for comfort as a child, as a teenager. And being able to do that now is a lovely thing." —Jill

"It may sound trite or cliché, but things really opened up for me when I took care of myself. Using The Courage to Heal, *I made a list of things that I love. I realized I need to cook for myself. You need to give yourself things that make you feel good."* —Cory

"I have had so many bills and things to get control of, but I am convinced that I would benefit from some therapy, so I am planning to get that started." —Deborah

"My therapist says that taking care of myself is a full-time job: exercise, food (not emotional eating to numb or comfort). I love the earth, trees, and nature. It has helped me survive." —Lynn

"We need structure in our life. We were not eating breakfast or drinking water. Our life was full of chaos. We started with a nutritionist. Now we're eating correctly, three meals a day. I also started exercising. I feel better." —Dana

Respecting Our Bodies

"The body is only a house for our soul and spirit." —Dorian

"After the abuse my relationship with my body changed. I didn't want a relationship with my body anymore." —Lynn

"At the Michigan Womyn's Music Festival I see young girls so free with their bodies. I never had that. They don't experience the stress of hoping they won't be raped." —Kyrce

"Sexual abuse," writes Marilee Strong (1998), "is the ultimate boundary violation," and it usually involves a physical assault. As survivors we have learned to distance ourselves from our bodies, to consider our physical and emotional selves as separate pieces of our total being. During the abuse we felt betrayed by our bodies, and in an attempt to protect ourselves we cut ourselves off from any appreciation of our bodies or physical sensations. As the survivor comes to know that she is lovable and did not cause the abuse, she can "embrace her body as ally and as a source of pleasure" (Roth, 1993). Using the boundary violation metaphor, addictions, sexual promiscuity, and other behaviors may be seen as attempts to "define and reestablish the body boundary" (Zerbe, 1993).

While research has shown that in general lesbians have more positive images of their bodies than do heterosexual women, this is not true for many lesbian survivors. Lesbian survivors struggle to accept their bodies for two reasons. First, the sexual abuse served to distance us from our bodies; we coped with the pain of the physical and emotional assaults by splitting from our bodies. Second, the sexual abuse confused our understanding of our sexuality. We disconnected from our sexual impulses and learned to fear our sexual responses. Lesbian survivors may suffer more intense feelings of alienation from their bodies than heterosexual women because of our experience as lesbians. Clark (1997) writes that gay men and lesbians often have "a feeling of being bombarded by their own body-associated erotic impulses...expressing a need to disrespect or disown their bodies." Our first feelings of same-sex attraction can be personally threatening and cause us to distance ourselves from them in a vain attempt to ward them off. These feelings are all too familiar to the survivor who blames her body for the sexual assaults she suffered and therefore puts up a false barrier, cutting herself off from her body.

Rosenthal (2000) found that a sexual abuse survivor whose body was invaded "often manipulates her body size to make it less appealing to future attackers." In this way, we displace our emotional struggles onto our bodies. Our eating disorders can also be ways to receive nurturance, getting others to take care of us (Zerbe, 1993). Research indicates that more than 50% of eating disorder patients struggle with *alexithymia*, a difficulty putting feelings into words—a condition that is characteristic of survivors. This difficulty may cause survivors to engage in body-oriented activity to communicate inner distress (Zerbe, 1993). We project our emotional distress onto our bodies. Renowned child abuse expert Alice Miller (2001) describes how anorexia is characteristic of this struggle. "What triggers anorexia in the first place is the tragedy of a young person unable to confide in anyone about her own feelings, to talk with anyone about how she needed to be nurtured as a child."

In families where appearances are all important, survivors may be pressured to place enormous emphasis on their physical selves to the detriment of their emotions. Looking good at the expense of feeling good and expressing true, if unpleasant, feelings can exact a high price (Zerbe, 1993). When we use food to comfort we literally swallow our feelings. Expressing our anger at our abusers and others who failed to protect us is not an option, so we swallow it. In the treatment of obesity, Van der Kolk (1987) found that integrating thoughts and feelings and healing the mind-body split was essential. The ability to put unspeakable words into feelings is an important step in healing. As children we did not have the words to describe what was happening to us. As adults many of us struggle for years, displacing our feelings onto our bodies through addictions, eating disorders, physical complaints, and sexual behaviors. Many of us distrust our body impulses and think some parts of our body are bad or unclean. Similarly, Clark (1997) describes the many ways that gay men and lesbians disown their bodies. His list is applicable to survivors who suffer the same alienation from their physical body and impulses, and, of course, particularly applicable to lesbian survivors.

You may simply tune out and ignore your body as a vague nuisance used to house and transport mind and spirit. You can take revenge on it for causing you trouble by causing it to have repeated accidents and illnesses, or simply by overfeeding or underfeeding it. Or you can reconstruct or redecorate it so as to obscure and hide it behind an artificial facade.... Whichever path you choose, your body is rejected and disowned. It becomes "it" and not "me." It is an attempt to get rid of the responsibility for those unacceptable body feelings (Clark, 1997).

As Deborah said, *"Kids don't grow up with the issues I did without having been abused. I was at a friend's house recently and watched her young children playing and running around naked. I was awed by the freedom that young children have to be naked and carefree in their bodies."*

Dissociation, a common strategy for coping with abuse, as we have learned, involves detaching from our physical selves, a state that does not allow us to experience feelings of hunger, fullness, exhaustion, sexual desire, or pain (Roth, 1993). We leave painful situations mentally, floating away somewhere up above it all. "Rather than experience the loss of control that loving brings, many of us choose to feel out of control about something that is within our control: the food we eat, or don't eat.... The issue of control—over our emotions, our feelings, other people's behavior—is central to any compulsion. The lack of control is what compulsion seems to be about" (Roth, 1991).

Pitman (1999) describes the body image concerns of lesbians, saying, "Through the inevitable process of internalized homophobia and fat hatred, both of which are institutionalized ways of keeping heterosexuality and female oppression in place, lesbians may begin to believe that there is something inherently wrong with them and their bodies." Salkin (1997) similarly describes body image development as strongly influenced by cultural forces and by personal relationships. She found that mothers have an especially strong impact on their daughters' body image. Body image was seen to improve after women self-identified as lesbians, due in part to an improved overall self-acceptance. In this way a woman's body image satisfaction is highly correlated with self-esteem (Zerbe, 1993). Pitman found that internalized homophobia and degree of outness emerged as significant predictors of body dissatisfaction and weight preoccupation. In this way research has shown that the stage of sexual identity significantly predicted body image concerns for lesbians (Braswell, 1995; Pitman, 1995a; Salkin, 1997; Wagenbach, 1998). Women who were more integrated with their lesbian identity reported feeling significantly better about their bodies than did women who were less integrated (Braswell, 1995). "Out" lesbians were more positive than less out lesbians in how they evaluate their appearance, physical health, and overall body satisfaction.

"The size that you are is immaterial. It doesn't make any difference." —Liz

Braswell (1995) stresses the importance of establishing lesbian identity as a treatment goal in psychotherapy with lesbians with body image disorders. This confirms what Zerbe (1993) writes about the relationship between a woman's body image satisfaction and her self-esteem. A renowned expert in the treatment for eating disorders, Zerbe describes the necessity of focusing both on normalizing eating and weight and the psychological problems that created the difficulty to begin with. She goes so far as to say that the long-term disastrous physical effects of obesity can be construed as a slow form of suicide that goes undetected. Obese people must address any possible unconscious investment they have in maintaining an obese body image.

At the same time, Salkin (1997) found that lesbian culture presents women with new body image questions because of the practice of typecasting and the pressures sometimes associated with butch, femme, and androgynous labels. Research, however, has shown that lesbians typically have less negative feelings about their bodies than do heterosexual women (Krakauer and Rose, 2002). And lesbians who have been out for longer report less weight concern than did those who had been out for less time. This suggests that while lesbian ideals may be less thin or less extreme than heterosexual ideals, it takes time for a woman's body weight concerns to decrease. It appears that age and coming out are factors in body weight concern.

Women's tendency to view their body as an object is an indicator of body shame (Lyders, 1999). Deborah says, *"I live out of my body. I live in my head."* Women as a group experience more body shame than men, and heterosexual women tend to experience more body shame than lesbians. But the experience of child sexual abuse, in which the body is objectified in a relentless and painful manner, would almost certainly contribute to the body shame that many lesbian survivors experience. In addition, Ludwig and Brownell (1999) found that feminine women, whether lesbian or heterosexual, reported lower body satisfaction than did androgynous or masculine-identified women. It appears that a feminine body image, which may be connected with feelings of passivity and helplessness, negatively affect women's self-image. The implication for lesbian survivors is clear here; the experience of being abused as children often leaves women feeling passive and helpless. Lesbian feminism, on the other hand, was found to contribute to positive body image (Pitman, 2000).

Eating disorders were associated with young women's perceptions that family communication, parental caring, and parental expectations were low and with those who reported sexual or physical abuse experience (Neumark-Sztainer et al, 2000). Sexual and physical abuse alone are strong independent risk factors for disordered eating. Lesbians with abuse histories also report a higher incidence of eating disorders (Griffith, 1995). In particular, a high rate of binge eating among lesbians was found that was related to the use of food for affect management (Hefferman, 1996). It appears that lesbian survivors use food to manage their emotions, especially anger and frustration, to comfort, for distraction, and to reduce anxiety. Using food regularly to comfort oneself is associated with the act of mothering and being mothered. Eating disorders are also one way that survivors try to self-regulate and assert their autonomy (Zerbe, 1993). Eating becomes a way to control. According to Rosenthal (2000), "The act of getting fat expresses an unconscious desire to gain control over one's life.… Fat is protective; it even serves to protect women from the horror of looking at her own demons and fears and, in so doing, keeps her from identifying just what it is she really wants."

"I started gaining weight in my 30s and have been morbidly obese since my 40s. When I've tried to lose weight I've gotten to the point of 20 pounds or so, and people start to compliment me. My reaction is sheer panic, gaining the weight back with a few more pounds to keep them company. I gave up dieting about 10 years ago and my weight has been quite steady since then. I know this fat suit is a coat of armor which protects me from men noticing me, but knowing that is not the same thing as being able to lose the weight and keep it off." —Jacque

"Lately I've gotten back to eating to major excess. In the last four years or so I've gained probably 30 pounds. I just don't know when to quit eating. I think a lot of it is because there were no boundaries growing up. My family was enmeshed. No one was allowed to have an identity separate from the family identity. So now I just do things compulsively and sometimes obsessively. I also think the weight is protection. I feel myself retreating again because I was getting way too close to putting pieces together about the abuse in my life and my body just wasn't ready t deal with it. Now I've got all this weight back." —Mary

Learning to take care of ourselves—some of us for the first time—involves learning how to nourish our bodies. Hirschmann and Munter, in *When Women Stop Hating Their Bodies: Freeing Yourself from Food and Weight Obsession* (1995), describe the relationship between self-trust and eating in their book. "The hunger-food connection," they write, "as it is established in infancy, is basic to developing an internal sense of security and trust. As an adult, learning to feed yourself when you are hungry serves precisely the same function because each time you feed yourself when you are hungry, you are demonstrating to yourself that you can meet your own needs. This nurturing response, repeated many times each day, ultimately makes you feel more grounded and secure."

Noemi describes the breakthrough she had in therapy when she realized the interconnectedness of the abuse, her body image, her eating habits, and her sexuality.

"I think the food and abuse are connected. When I told my therapist offhand, 'I'm going to lose weight,' she said, 'OK, let's work on your onion. There's something else that you're trying to get rid of.' Sure enough when we started talking about the weight, I had to deal with my inner demons and the abuse. I have to deal with the inside and the outside of me. They're connected. If I want to change the outside, I need to deal with the inside. It's like my whole life I've been dealing with my body, both internally and externally, in being overweight and not looking the way I wanted it to, and internally with the shame and feeling dirty. It was a way of dealing with it externally, coming out to myself, and acknowledging that I loved women

and was capable of falling in love with a woman. It continues in a wide range of ways in terms of feeling a sense of shame about my body and feeling I'm not in control over my body." —Noemi

"Fat can also be combative. Fat doesn't protect, it offends, deliberately. Fat can be a challenge to anyone who dares to penetrate the layers" (Rosenthal, 2000). This coincides with Putnam and Trickett's longitudinal research of sexually abused girls who were more likely to be obese than their nonabused peers (cited in Strong, 1998).

"It's painfully clear that I use my weight as a shield to keep people away. More weight means less attractive, means less sexual." —Deborah

Letting go of destructive habits is difficult. We learn that using substances like alcohol, drugs, and food is a signal that we want greater control over our feelings (Zerbe, 1993). Reaching for carbohydrate snacks may be an attempt to alter your mood. We also crave carbohydrates because they create sensations of being soothed and comforted, the effect we're looking for during times of emotional stress. High-fat foods are particularly desirable because of their high sensory quality. As we know, diet and our emotions work hand-in-hand. "Adequate care of our biology improves our psychology, and vice versa" (Zerbe, 1993).

Many therapists believe that if a woman admits that she has an emotional interest in being large, she is closer to stopping her compulsion to eat.

The abuse happened to our bodies. Therefore it is no surprise that our attempts to separate our mind and body continue well after the abuse has ended. It is as if we are punishing our bodies for getting us into the predicament and for any pleasure we might have experienced during the abuse. Learning to take care of ourselves necessarily includes learning to respect and take care of our bodies. We did nothing to deserve the abuse nor to cause it, and neither did our bodies. In healing our physical selves we help to heal the psychic scars of the abuse. As Haines (1999) writes, "The split between mind and body is a fictitious one. We are one body-mind-spirit."

Childhood sexual abuse literally touches your body. To leave your body out of the healing process can leave out what is potentially your surest path to well-being.

As for me, I never thought I would live very long, so I didn't pay a lot of attention to my body. High-fat foods, lack of exercise, damaging personal habits of irregular health and dental checkups were all part of the recipe for disaster. I see now that if I had been able to kill myself slowly with poor health habits, I would have. It was a passive way to end my life without having to take action. Pregnancy and the birth of my daughter six years ago began to turn this around. Although I am hardly the pillar of good health these days, I try to watch what I eat and exercise more. I know my daughter is watching my every move, and I want her to develop healthy habits and a deep respect for her body.

The disconnect I feel from my body has been difficult to live with. I feel like things happen to my body and not to me—as if my body were merely a shell. I understand now that this was a protective stance I adopted when I was sexually abused; if I disconnected from my body then I would not feel the pain of what was done to my physical self. Unfortunately, I came to realize that the pain was more than skin deep, and disconnecting my physical and emotional selves has created more, rather than less, pain. In speaking with other survivors, I learned how they too blamed their bodies for the abuse that was perpetrated against them. In particular, you can hear how femininity and the female gender were associated with weakness and powerlessness for survivors; they blame their femaleness for bringing on the abuse.

For us as lesbians there are deep implications of our hatred for the female body. First, the abuse objectifies us as weak and powerless females. We dissociate from our physical selves in a way that is psychologically and physically damaging. Second, our inability to appreciate the beauty and strength of the female body makes us incapable of accepting physical affection and sexual relations. Third, the messages we have learned about the female body cannot help but be projected onto our partners whose female bodies are reminders of our own physical failings. Many of us, in our struggles with our body image, attempt to deny secondary sex characteristics that define us as female. If we don't develop breasts and womanly hips, for example, then we will not be vulnerable to the sexual advances we fear.

"I hated females because they were so weak. I was afraid of being hurt physically, mentally, sexually, and emotionally by the males in my immediate life. I hated being female because that obviously drew much of the abuse to me." —Cristi

"For most of my years I hated being a woman because I thought that I could only be beautiful for men, and being a woman always put me in danger. I hid in my baggy clothes and wished I was a boy instead. But after my first girlfriend I realized that I could be an attractive woman for other women, that men will never have me." —Kirsten

"I have a real problem wearing dresses and skirts. It's easy access to my private parts. I always wore shorts under skirts. For years I only wore jeans." —Debbie

"I stopped wearing bathing suits and shorts after the abuse started. I felt uncomfortable going through puberty and developing breasts since my father would say it would be better when I had breasts. I started starving myself and ended up with bad anorexia, which I still suffer from. The abuse changed me by making me feel uncomfortable with my body." —Kim

Many survivors described their desire to be male, believing that that would be better for a variety of reasons related to the abuse.

"I have always wished I were a male. If I were a male I may not have been abused. My brothers would have accepted me without any need to use me to satisfy their own sexual urges. Furthermore, growing up I learned males were able to do more than girls. If I was a male I would have been able to help prevent vulnerable situations from occurring. Finally, I wish I were a male so that I could treat women the way they should be treated, not the way I was treated." —Marie

"I remember as a small child wanting to be male. I had this fantasy that I could be male if my parents would let me buzz my hair and dress in boys' clothes. I always carried a gun, even to bed." —Pat

Ironically, Marty found that after years of distancing herself from her body and blaming her female form for the abuse she suffered, she realized how much her breasts—a symbol of her womanhood—meant to her.

"I just learned that I have to have breast surgery. I was surprised by my big reaction to it. For years I hated my breasts. I thought, So they take a piece out, so what? *That's not where I am anymore. I fear for my health and I'm having a reaction about my female physicalness."* —Marty

Taking care of ourselves physically improves our emotional health and vice versa (Van der Kolk, 1987). Reclaiming our bodies involves maintaining good physical health. Efforts to make ourselves physically strong can be effective in altering our body image from weak and vulnerable (Maltz, 1991). Exercises in body awareness and appreciation that include sports, dancing, massage, self-touch, baths, and sensual experiences can help survivors reconnect with their bodies. Here are some of the ways that survivors are learning to respect their bodies.

"Teaching yoga has taught me to trust myself and increased my confidence. Doing the bridge pose in yoga in front of men and women makes me more confident in my body. Some days I feel like I'm all belly and boobs, but that's OK." —Chris

"I try to have balanced living and diet. I received dietary advice through a therapist; now my cravings for alcohol are gone." —Tammy

"I started a food diary and started exercising. I learned that my eating habits and disorder are connected with chaos." —Dana

"I'm on a macrobiotic diet now to detox my body. I've gone to Codependents Anonymous and Overeaters Anonymous. I've lost 35 pounds and gone from a size 20 to a size 14. I also became physically active; I play soccer. You can yell and kick and scream and be applauded!" —Kathy

"I think I have a lot to learn through Buddhist teachings and taking care of my body, such as dealing with being obese, which I am, and eating well for sustenance, not to numb." —Cory

"I started swimming in heated therapy pools for arthritis. I would get in the water and it was just such a strange sensation. Being in the water I felt light. I would get up on my toes and swirl around almost like a ballerina. I felt so graceful. To really focus I had to keep my eyes shut. I had to get rid of other distractions. It was probably one of the first times I felt in touch with my body and more aware of what I was doing. It's really good for me. It helps me relax." —Jacque

"I'm a purist. I only eat pure, clean food." —Jan

Grieving for the loss of our connection to our bodies is an important part of our healing. Many survivors described how observing young children's freedom with their bodies reminded them of how much they had lost and wanted to reclaim.

Activism

"The lives of children and women are the truest indicators of the strength of communities and nations. If the youngest and most vulnerable are left to find their way alone, a country violates the rights of its people and sabotages its future as an equal partner in the global economy."
—Carol Bellamy, executive director, United Nations Children's Fund

"Be the most you can be, so life will be more because you were."
—Susan Glaspell

Writing this book is an act of activism. By telling my story and helping other survivors to tell theirs I am standing up for women everywhere who have not yet found their voices. In writing this book I am saying that the sexual abuse of children will not be tolerated. We are not alone, and we will not be silenced. We are strong enough to survive the abuse and courageous enough to name our attackers and to reclaim our lives. I am spurred on by the voices of other survivors who continue their own healing and use their lives to make a difference.

Some survivors' activism is in the gay and lesbian community.

"I'm a gay activist. I go to court with victims of gay bashing." —Jill

"I work at the national level dealing with legislative advocacy on civil rights and health policy issues for the gay and lesbian community." —Noemi

"For the last two years I've been volunteering with a local gay and lesbian association." —Nedhera

Jacque is involved in animal rescue:

"I have 10 dogs and 23 cats. It's pretty crowded. I'm trying very hard not to take any more in, which is hard once people know you know how to bottle-feed kittens and things like that. They just start showing up at your door with them. I've met some really neat animal rescue people here."

Some survivors work in the area of child abuse, working with survivors or perpetrators.

"My specializing in sexual abuse came from a genuine desire to do my part to stop the cycle of abuse by being proactive." —Misha

"I'm working toward my master's to eventually do public policy and public opinion work on issues such as child abuse and family violence. I think we need to change the way people think about abuse and give them tools and ideas to act when they suspect a child is being abused. I think part of the problem is that there's this cultural norm that says you can't do anything, or shouldn't do anything, if you suspect a child is being

abused. That needs to change. There's not a survivor I know who can't look back in their history and find loving people who knew about the abuse but didn't know what to do." —Cory

"I found the lack of political activism around incest and the emphasis on therapy really disheartening. I believe activism can in itself be therapeutic. My desire to be a therapist is because I want to make political activism part of a clinical practice. I don't believe in healing but in integrating the effects of child sexual abuse into the adult life. I am an incest activist, rather than merely a survivor." —Robin

"I work with sex offenders. I also serve on the state's Battered Lesbian Task Force. My doctoral research focused on how heterosexism and homophobia impact the quality of mental health treatment provided to lesbian clients. I believe my professional path is a direct result of my abuse experiences. I work very hard to minimize the chances of my clients victimizing more people." —Lisa

Many survivors are motivated to make a difference for children and are committed to finding a way to do that.

"I'm guided to do more, to globally protect children. Abuse is a cancer. I need to have some meaning from all this, even if we help one person. I do this for my grandchildren. Now there's a critical mass, and it's blown the lid open. Look at what's happening in the Catholic Church." —Mary Lou

"I want to work with children on this issue, to be a living example of how life goes on." —Missy

Others are committed to social justice with a variety of populations.

"I have a commitment to social justice and mental health. I felt a call to work in the area of mental health. Initially I wanted to help people, then I was motivated by issues of social justice and institutional change. I was disturbed about the practice of labeling people." —Pat

"I have my own Web site with information about different causes and people to contact." —Rowan

"The majority of the ladies that I work with doing harm reduction—the working ladies who are in the sex industry—have been sexually abused. I'm in AmeriCorps now through the National AIDS Fund, which is like the Peace Corps but domestic. I hope to work for a needle exchange program and get my Masters in public health or Masters of social work. The abuse and the other things that have happened in my life, as negative as they are, have become my future, and that's a beautiful thing, actually. Doing things like volunteering and sharing your experiences with other people is empowering; it allows you to be able to do something for the greater good instead of focusing on the destructive nature of your past." —Lyndsey

"As an adult I joined the Sizes Movement, the fat empowerment movement. I joined to try and point out the inequities—perceptions of who you are as a person if you look a certain way. We know that there's a problem that American society has. But there's another layer to it when you're in the black community. It also depends on what color you are. The perception is that the lighter you are, the better you are." —Nedhera

For lesbian survivors, the personal is political. Speaking out as lesbian survivors, as I found, is an act of activism.

"I was involved with the Clothesline Project and made one of the shirts that was part of the very first display. I suppose it was purely chance that I was in the midst of acknowledging and dealing with my abuse when word went around the local women's community that the project was forming. A handful of us got together and planned an evening of shirt-making. The display was cathartic for those of us who had made shirts and for those who came to witness. For me, then, it was advocacy in the same way that simply being out as a lesbian, day in and day out, is advocacy, but not more than that. I was able to face fears for the project that I had never been able to surmount for myself." —Marty

"I have devoted more of my energy to supporting adult survivors of childhood sexual abuse—working with a coalition to promote accuracy about abuse and recovered memories, publishing comprehensive bibliographies of books concerning adult survivors, and doing some research for authors writing about adult survivors." —Levie

"I'm very interested in writing a book about my experience, to get it out there. I want to be part of something that gives back." —Wendy

"I've always wanted to help. I want to try and get the message out that this does happen and you can go on. At the time of the trial, my abuser was already working on one of my friends because the police averaged he'd had two a year. When I went to talk to the state trooper, he jumped out of my chair and gave me a big hug. He said, 'We have had too many girls come to this point and then say no.' At that point I knew for sure there was no way anybody was going to stop me from doing whatever I could." —Delphene

In using their lives, survivors demonstrate their commitment to making a difference in the lives of others. The courage to heal their own pain and then to be of service is the greatest gift they could give others—and themselves.

CHAPTER 10

HOPE

"I REALIZE THAT BEING ALIVE MEANS I WIN."
—DERI ANN GEREIGHTY

"THERE IS MORE THAN ANGER, THERE IS MORE THAN SADNESS, MORE THAN TERROR. THERE IS HOPE."
—LAURA DAVIS AND ELLEN BASS, *THE COURAGE TO HEAL*

WORDS OF ENCOURAGEMENT, WORDS OF WISDOM

We know relatively little about the factors in life that enable some people to emerge from serious trauma relatively unscathed while others bear lifelong effects. What we do know is that support from friends and family is essential to healing. In asking survivors to share what they had learned along the way, I hoped that some of our life lessons would be helpful to others. Interestingly, survivors often offered the same words of wisdom that they were initially unable to believe themselves. Those who were reluctant to reach out for help suggested that survivors reach out. Those who found it difficult to open up and talk about their experiences recommended not bottling up your emotions. It appears that in reaching out to other survivors, the women I spoke with were able to hear anew the words of wisdom and encouragement that had been shared with them. Perhaps this echo would reverberate back to help each in the end. Here's what the survivors I spoke with wanted to tell other survivors.

TELL THE STORY

"Get it out. Don't listen to other people's judgments. Don't keep it a secret. Keep voicing it. Say it out loud. Open the box. Talking about it helps. Hope will be sparked." —Kyrce

"The silence will not protect you. If you suspect it, look into it. Do something about it. If you don't deal with something, it comes out crooked. We can stop it." —Sarah

"For survivors who are in denial, talking may be a trigger, which would be a good thing." —Kris

"You never, ever forget. It's always there. You might put it away, but you're going to have to deal with it sooner or later." —Diana

Place the Blame With Your Abuser

"Send out the anger to where it belongs instead of to you or the people close to you." —Diana

"Know that it's not your fault. You've heard that a million times; believe it. You can move beyond this point—wherever you're at. You can carry the anger as long as you want, but it's only hurting you." —C.J.

"First of all, it absolutely is not your fault. Try not to feel guilty about it." —Jacque

"It's not your fault. There's nothing wrong with you." —Kim

Find Support

"You're not the only person it happens to." —Debbie

"Having one or two people who are willing to commit to you and your recovery is important. It can be overwhelming for one person. You need someone you can call in the middle of the night. It's like sponsoring in a 12-step program." —Rowan

"I know that during my healing it helped to be able to pick up what turned out to be my bible, The Courage to Heal, *and read others' accounts of healing."* —Max

"Survivors need support. Try to educate your friends; give them books. Don't put up a wall. Read books. I feel less alone now. The Courage to Heal *really helped me a lot."* —Wendy

"At times, I feel a lack of confidence in my abilities, but with positive people in my life I am able to work through most issues." —Marie

"Have a good support system. Run it by someone." —Sarah

"Find someone you can talk to about it, someone who's been in the same boat. You can just identify with someone whether it's in giving or receiving counsel." —Margaret

"If you haven't been to the Michigan Womyn's Music Festival, get your ass over there! I've got to say that it was the first place where I felt really safe. It was very freaky to me that I didn't have to worry. I didn't have nightmares there. I slept like a baby. I mean, that is totally unheard of. I have never slept for more than two hours straight since I was probably about 10. And it was just the best feeling in the world." —Kris

"I thought the answer was to kill myself or cut myself up. Then I thought of my 5-year-old nephew. He really loves me. Find support, something to live for." —Kim

"Surround yourself with loving, respectful, positive people who will believe you and trust and respect you regardless of your past or your hang-ups." —Lyndsey

Live Well

"I look back now and I wouldn't change a thing in my life. I know who I am and what I want. I have found my strength." —Julie

"Transcend survivalism and begin to live again. You get this time right now, use it. All we have is this moment, and it is precious, and so are each and every one of us. Sounds kind of cheesy, I'm sure, but that's what I've

decided for myself and here I am smiling, loving, living, and questioning and learning always." —Missy

"I feel free and happy. I'm finally not suppressing my true feelings." —Yvonne

"I feel like I'm coming around on the other side of it. That makes me feel good. Maybe I'll be one of those old crone dykes saying, 'I'm about 60 years old and am having the first good relationship of my life.' But that's OK, because I'd rather be with someone and be as whole as I feel comfortable being than dragging my baggage." —Kris

"Follow your heart, follow your spirit, and be true to your own life's path." —Dorian

"Focusing on the positives of the day—no matter how small—is important. I try to savor these things: seeing the first morning glory of the season, a tender moment with my partner, something silly that the cat did, a good TV show, a bargain at the grocery store." —Levie

"So many times I didn't have any hope. Now I love my job and my life. It's so worth it to stay alive for these times. I'd never be able to imagine things could be this good. I feel like I've landed in someone else's life. And it's good. People have said I've been attracting this to me with all the work I've been doing." —Chris

"Don't let things that happened in the past rob you of the time remaining in your life. They affected you, but they're gone. It's wasted emotion to go back and get all bent out of shape about it now. It's last week's trash. It was important when I was putting it out, but now I don't think about it. You need to put the garbage on the curb and be done with it." —Margaret

"It's so important to stay alive and try to keep going. I thought that all that life was about is pain. Just try to make it through each day. I have scars from the cutting. I'm glad I can look at the scars and know that I'm

still alive. I experience that I'm alive. And I feel lucky to be alive." —Amanda

"I would say that the best advice I could give another person who survived abuse is—as difficult as it is—focus on you and your life and what you want to make it. Take the power back into your hands and make your life something palpable, something you have control of. Don't allow that perpetrator to dictate the future of your life. I think it's important to look to yourself and the positive things that you see in yourself and focus on these things. Keep in touch with the things you truly enjoy in life." —Lyndsey

Help Others

"When you're feeling as though being you is too hard, step outside yourself. Try to see how other people are living. Because even though you've suffered an emotional and physical earthquake in your life, people have survived earthquakes. Help somebody else. To paraphrase 'Each one, teach one,' I would say, 'Each one, reach one.' Maybe somebody will read my story and recognize something and get some help." —Nedhera

"If you're able to help somebody, try to do that." —Debbie

"Doing things like volunteering and sharing your experiences with people is empowering. You can get some kind of relief from someone as they can from you. And it allows you to be able to do something for the greater good instead of focusing on the destructive nature of your past." —Lyndsey

Keep Hope Alive

"My struggles are calibrated struggles that will continue to challenge me. When a door closes, another opportunity presents itself; that I do believe." —Tabitha

"I think the abuse used to affect me negatively. Now I think it has made me a stronger person. Something I live by: If something bothers me,

I can choose to dwell on it and let it bother me, or I can move past it and move on. I choose to move past it and to stop blaming everything on it. I choose to take responsibility for my actions and get control of myself and who I want to be. I wasn't going to let my abuser control the rest of my life. If someone thinks I am not capable of doing something and I think I can, I take it upon myself to do it. For the first time ever, I don't wake up in the morning and question who I am or what I'm doing." —Juli

"I'm not going to say it's been easy. It's been very hard for me sometimes to beat back those things that really have haunted me from being damaged by the abuse. But I would say that although I'm not necessarily anyone's role model, I've certainly tried to live a pretty good life." —Nedhera

"I think that in some way I am always going to have to struggle and work through abuse emotions that come up just experiencing the problems of life that everyone faces. But I really feel confident I can handle these and not have them be bombs that go off in my life but difficult and uncomfortable feelings that every human being has to work through." —Cory

Celebrate Your Strength and Courage

"You survived. That means you're strong. You're beautiful because you had the grace and dignity to continue on in spite of it all." —Lynn

"We are utterly an amazing people, no? We are the backbone of everything that has true substance. The world would be truly a dull place were we not to be here. I guess that is why we came." —Jan

"We're the strongest people that there are. We have to go through so much to recover. We're courageous and strong and creative." —Chris

"I feel as if I am a stronger person and I feel that I can handle most things that come my way." —Marie

"On the one hand I lost my innocence and confidence. And on the other hand, I am a strong and passionate woman." —Misha

"I've done a lot of personal work and have healed from my issues of abuse to the point where I can now see the gifts received—not from the actual abuse, but from my being metaphorically thrown 'out of the box' of any illusion of safety, any belief that some prince would rescue me, or any tolerance for further victimization. It was a strange way to arrive at a feeling of comfort in my life with women and an acceptance of men, but it happened and I am grateful." —Carol

"Being a survivor makes you stronger." —Debbie

Embrace Your Spirituality

"It's important to reach out to your spirituality as you understand it." —Lyndsey

"God be with you through your journeys in life." —Laura

Take Prescription Medication if Necessary

"Take medication if you need to." —Debbie

"I'm on an antidepressant and love my job and my life." —Chris

Seek Therapy

"Go to therapy or something like a healing body thing. I definitely didn't do enough time in therapy, although I think I've done a hell of a job on my own." —Delphene

"See somebody twice a week." —Debbie

"The first thing you need to do is acknowledge that you've been damaged badly. Don't try and sugarcoat it with 'I'm fine.' If you're having strange reactions and you can't figure out where they come from, instead of getting angry at the people who point them out to you, instead of getting angry at yourself for having them, get some help as quickly as possible." —Nedhera

"Don't be afraid to go to a therapist even if it's difficult. It's difficult to detail what happened. The sooner you can face it, confront it, maybe you won't have so many problems. You have to get rid of the guilt and shame—Why did I let it happen? Why didn't I say anything?" —Julie

Explore Creative Healing Techniques

"Find the things that work for you. Art therapy is great—write it, draw it, paint it, collage it." —Kyrce

"Try writing." —Debbie

"I have found that I communicate about the abuse better through writing." —Grace

"Find something therapeutic to nurture: music, gardening. I live in my aunt's old rock farmhouse. I'm turning my gardening into a small business." —Tammy

Redefine Family

"Starting my own family—and walking away from my old one—has been the most healing thing for me so far." —Sharon

"My good friends are like a family to me now." —Amanda

"Remove yourself from the negative stuff in your family." —Sharon

Commit to Healing

"Now I realize, either I move forward and take chances or I sit home with my cats. Don't bottle it up. Don't believe that you're so damaged that people will judge you. You're wasting your time. I wish I had created a time—a leave of absence—to really focus on this issue. It's like the bad weed I keep cutting up that keeps coming back." —Dana

"It's a long-term process with no way to be short-term. Remember the 12-step adages 'Don't quit five minutes before the miracle happens' and 'Keep showing up.' You all deserve the healing. Damage was done on many levels, and work is needed on many levels. Betrayal happens in relationships; work one-on-one to heal that. To heal the physical injury, experience safe touch, nurture your body, and express the feelings that are in it." —Kathy

"When a woman turned to me after an Alcoholics Anonymous meeting one night and told me that she had just discovered that she was a survivor. I said, 'Now that knowledge can free you up and take you where you can't go without it. It's scary and disturbing, but you can embrace it and get through it.' I would encourage other survivors to take breaks. It can't all be done at once; it's a spiral. You address the same issues over and over again, and they look different." —Marty

Margie describes the distinction between acknowledging our abuse history and being stuck in the victim mode. As Bratton (1999) puts it, "The abuse will become 'something that happened to me,' a far cry from 'the abuse is me.'"

"This might come out sounding much more judgmental than I mean it, but I'm just going to say it. You need to move on. I think that there's this culture of survivors, people who've been victimized and still feel victimized and get stuck there and identify in that way. I don't identify as a survivor because it has nothing to do with what I have become. It's no longer a powerful part of my identity. I don't choose to identify by deficits. The abuse doesn't have that power for me anymore, although it's still part of my experience. It's incorporated into who I am, but it's not one of my primary identities."

Be Good to Yourself

"It will not happen again. It's not happening now. What you feel is normal and caused by the abuse. Don't listen to the 'hate-mes.'" —Liz

"Sexual abuse takes away a lot of your trusting and loving feelings, your self-love and self-acceptance. When we accept ourselves, we can give ourselves that gift back." —Christy

"Get to know yourself." —Rowan

"Keep following your gut instinct no matter what the messages are. There's something else there. Whatever happened to you can't hurt you now." —Kyrce

"We are the hero of our own story."
—Mary McCarthy

In specifically addressing the needs of lesbian survivors, the women I spoke with had this to say:

"I think being abused and being homosexual go hand-in-hand. If you're striving to work on the abuse issues, don't neglect who you are as a person and as a lesbian." —Christy

"You go, girl! Do it for you. My healing journey from the addictions has brought me me back and has brought such miracles in my life. It brought me to my lesbianism. Now I can love someone else. The journey is so worth it. Be true to yourself. I wouldn't trade me for anything. I live my journey. Blessings on your journey." —Mary Lou

"The abuse has to change people. But I also firmly believe that one can take what life gives them and can build strength from it, regardless of how painful or debilitating it may seem at times. Learning to clear the helpless energies I took on from the abuse has made me a stronger and wiser person and has helped me to understand who I am. Being able to face and conquer a bajillion fears has given me the gift of peace and self-love which is something that I sought for quite some time. As I become more comfortable with the male and female aspects of myself, I am finding that I am even more attracted to women than I have been in the past." —Cristi

Parenting (Protecting) Our Children

"If a survivor hasn't remembered her abuse or acknowledged its effects, she may not be able to recognize signs that her children are in danger or may not be able to respond effectively."
—Laura Davis and Ellen Bass, *The Courage to Heal*

"When you are a mother, you are never really alone in your thoughts. You are connected to your child and to all those who touch your lives. A mother always has to think twice, once for herself and once for her child."
—Sophia Loren

Many of us are parenting and doing a very good job at it. This despite a lack of good parenting role models and the ongoing stress of dealing with abuse issues. As survivors who are parenting, many of us recognize the need for parenting role models because we did not have good examples growing up. We want to do better by our children than our parents did for us. This is only possible when we bring to consciousness our abuse memories and resolve the issues related to it. We do this work for ourselves and, ultimately, for our children. In a study of risk factors for child sexual abuse, McCloskey and Bailey (2000) found that girls whose mothers were sexually abused were 3.6 times more likely to be sexually victimized; maternal sexual abuse history indicates a strong potential for the intergenerational transmission of child sexual abuse. It seems that mothers who were themselves abused as children are unavailable to their children in ways that puts them at risk. Sarah came to the startling realization that her mother would never be there for her in the way that she needed her to be. *"I found out that my mom had sexual abuse in her past. So if I had told her about the abuse, nothing would have happened."*

Calao and Hosansky created "A Child's Bill of Personal Safety Rights," healthy guidelines for children that may be helpful for us to reflect on as we raise our young children (cited in Bass and Davis, 1988). Because many of us were raised in families where our rights were not honored and respected, it can be difficult for us to recognize the need for such guidelines and to implement them in our homes now. Children's rights include the rights:

- to trust one's instincts and one's funny feelings
- to privacy
- to say no to unwanted touch and affection
- to question adult authority and to say no to adult demands and requests
- to lie and not answer questions
- to refuse gifts
- to be rude and unhelpful
- to run, scream, and make a scene
- to bite, hit, or kick
- to ask for help

As parents we all want the best for our children. We worry that we aren't doing all we can to insure our children's happy and successful future. Homophobia rears its ugly head when we encounter society's prejudice against gay and lesbian families and the false assumption that gay and lesbian families produce gay and lesbian children. (As if that were a bad thing!) Despite no empirical evidence that children raised in gay and lesbian families develop homosexual orientations or fare worse than children in heterosexual homes—in fact studies actually demonstrate that our children perform better socioemotionally—prejudice against our families continues.

In fascinating work on lesbian parenting issues, Judith Stacey and Timothy Biblarz from the University of Southern California (2001) reviewed the literature exploring the effects of parental gender or sexual orientation on children's sexual preferences and behavior. In reviewing the findings from 21 psychological studies conducted between 1981 and 1998, they found some interesting differences among children based on the sexual orientation of their parents. For example, children of gay and lesbian parents, especially daughters, did not follow gender norms in play or career choices. This might be expected given lesbians' commitment to gender neutrality and freedom from the constraints of gender roles. Hoeffer (1981) also found that lesbian mothers' preferences for their children's play were gender-neutral. In this way, it appears that the children of lesbian mothers experience the same freedom from the constraints of gender-typed behavior that their mothers enjoy. While this research was not conducted with children parented by lesbian survivors specifically, it would be interesting to explore how lesbian survivors' parenting experiences differ, if at all, from lesbian mothers' as a whole. While I have presented research here that describes the impact of sexual abuse on the development of lesbian women, it is unclear how the experience of early childhood trauma affects lesbian survivors' parenting ability and choices. Of particular interest would be an examination of the ways in which survivors' tendency to be more feminine and passive (nonassertive) in their personal interaction styles contrasts with lesbians who did not suffer sexual abuse as children.

Being raised in a lesbian family can create stress for children, but researchers have found that this stress does not cause undue harm. Garnets (2002b) found that: (1) lesbian mothers are likely to be good parents; (2) lesbian mothers have no ill effects on their children because of their sexual orientation (mental health of children, personal development, social relationships, sexual identity, risk of sexual molestation, and social stigma); and (3) parental disclosure of sexual orientation appears to have positive effects on parent-child relationships. Patterson (1994) found that children ages 4 to 9 with lesbian mothers expressed more stress than did those of heterosexual mothers, but at the same time they also reported a greater sense of overall well-being (Stacey and Biblarz, 2001). Patterson speculates that children may experience more social stress at the same time that they gain confidence from their ability to cope with it. Children from lesbian-mother families also appear more willing to express their feelings—positive and negative. Children raised by lesbian coparents grow up to be more open to same-sex relationships. As my 6-year-old daughter said at breakfast one morning, "Mom, why do some girls want to marry boys?" Lesbian mothers were found to be more sensitive to issues surrounding their children's sexual development and to the possible teasing their nonconforming children might experience, as well as more open to discussing sexuality with their children and more affirming of their questions about sexuality. Again, these studies were conducted with lesbian parents who were not specifically survivors. The ways in which lesbian mothers' abuse experiences impact their parenting around these issues of sexuality and sexual development have not been examined.

The myth that abused children become abusers haunts many survivors. This despite ample evidence that the majority of adults who abuse children are heterosexual men (Garnets, 2002b). Baker (2002) maintains, "There are more abused children who will live their lives without harming another person than there are abused children who become perpetrators." Several survivors I spoke with described their fear that they were capable of abusing children in the way they had been abused. Here I share what survivors told me of their personal anguish, their fear that they were capable of abusing children.

"At one point I was scared about how much my family trusted me with their kids. You know, people have this idea of gay people being very sexual and with me being abused and remembering what I tried to do to a cousin when I was 6, I thought, 'My gosh, no.' I'm thinking I wouldn't want my child to have the freedom that they let their kids go out with me. I felt so honored that they trusted me with their kids. I was always very careful. I watched myself because of what had happened to me." —Diana

"I feared I would become the abuser. Somehow very early on I got the idea that I was capable of doing what had been done to me. I was terrified of myself. I knew that I was capable of being physically and emotionally abusive. I think that parenting my son was really the road out of that for me because by parenting I realized that I really could not be abusive, that it was just so not who I was." —Margie

While these are natural fears, it is extremely unlikely that you will abuse children if you are actively engaged in healing (Bass and Davis, 1988; Bratton, 1999). Chris told me, *"I'm afraid of abusing kids. If I'm in therapy, I won't."* While statistics show that many perpetrators were abused as children, not all survivors will abuse. In fact, the vast majority of survivors grow up to be fierce protectors of children, determined that no other child will ever be hurt as they were (Sanford, 1990). The key appears to be an awareness of our triggers and seeking help right away when we recognize a problem.

Another important piece of protecting our children is addressing our personal abuse issues so that we are available and consciously aware of potential threats and injuries to our children. According to Bass and Davis (1988), "If a survivor hasn't remembered her abuse or acknowledged its effects, she may not be able to recognize signs that her children are in danger or may not be able to respond effectively." Unfortunately, this describes Mary Lou's experience in parenting.

"My daughter and son were abused by their father, whom I divorced 14 years ago. I was in total denial about my own abuse at the time."

In a fascinating study of survivors' experiences with breast-feeding, Halliday-Sumner and Kozlick (1996) found that breast-feeding triggered sexual abuse memories, and sensations during breast-feeding reminded mothers of past abuse and experiencing loss of control over how her body was used or touched. As the authors suggest, "[Childbirth and breast-feeding] are clearly sexual events in a woman's life involving the anatomical sites that have been the focus of past abuse and trauma." Given my own experience in breast-feeding my daughter for 16 months I can identify with some of what the researchers found, and yet my experience of nurturing and nourishing my daughter in this way helped me to heal in ways that I could not have anticipated. In giving birth to a daughter and nourishing her with my body, I reclaimed my sexuality and womanliness and redefined the purpose and aesthetic of my sexual anatomy.

If you were abused by one of your relatives, you may wonder if you have a right to deny your children access to your family. Bass and Davis (1988) are adamant in giving survivors permission to set limits or break ties with their families of origin if their children's welfare is at stake. "Maintaining family ties for the sake of tradition does not help your children. You do not owe your child the opportunity to bond with a child molester. Let the abuse have the repercussions it merits." Courtois (1988) concurs and describes how survivors who maintain contact with the abuser must be vigilant and explain to their children why unsupervised contact is not allowed. Below, survivors describe how they limited or banned contact between their abusers and their children.

"I keep the girls away from my father, except for Christmas and his birthday." —Sarah

"My children knew from very young that their grandmother is married to a man who sexually abused me and is a threat to children, so they can never meet him. My mother's husband is not allowed contact with me or my family, or my mother will no longer be allowed to see my children. I established this rule after my first child was born. It's sad that I have to use my children as bartering chips with my mother. But since she chose to stay married to him and not protect me, she now has to police him in order to protect the well-being of me, my children, and my partner." —Robin

As for me, I'm telling my story so my daughter will know what happened to me and be protected from this happening to her. As I wrote in the letter to my brother, "For the record, my daughter will never spend time alone with you. You are not to be trusted." I tell the story of my abuse so she'll be proud of me and the steps I've taken to reclaim my life. In telling, I prove to myself that no harm will come to me and my family if I speak the truth about my childhood. I'm telling my story for her, my sweet baby girl. Here is how Margie described her efforts to empower (protect) her daughter.

"We don't do 'Stranger Danger' stuff with our daughter because we feel very strongly that still at this point in time, in her kindergartner life, it's our job to protect her. And we are very careful about who she's with. We've created a situation with her where she's only with people we know. Having been abused makes it feel even more like children have the responsibility for preventing abuse—like they're somehow supposed to keep this from happening to them. As if you could do that in your 6-year-old wisdom and body. Empowering our children to be the deciders about their body and emotional health is important. My partner and I have been very intentional about that with our kids, about saying, 'You get to make that choice.

You don't have to go around and blanketly kiss everyone. We don't need you to do that for our purposes. You know what's comfortable for you.' There have been times when adults have been playing with her in a way that made her frightened, and she's turned around and shouted, 'I don't like the way you're playing with me.' People would ask us, 'Well, aren't you going to say something?'—like she's being fresh. And we say, 'Yeah, we're going to say 'Good job!' It's like with issues around food. It is so clearly your body. Don't ever doubt that for a second. It's the opposite of the message that was given us as kids, which was that your body belongs to everyone else and you just happen to be living in it."

Being overprotective and hypervigilant with our children was a theme in many survivors' stories. In trying to protect our children, we sometimes project our own experiences and fears onto them in an unhealthy manner.

"I was extra-protective of my kids. If someone molested my kids, I'd kill them in front of the judge and everyone." —Margaret

"I'm a determined, hawkish, and hypervigilant mother who loves unconditionally and protects fearlessly both of my children, with whom I have warm and loving relationships." —Tammy

"I'm very protective of my children. Everything threw up a red flag." —C.J.

"I was overprotective of my children. One time I flew into a rage when my husband was disciplining our oldest daughter. He closed the door behind him and was intimidating her verbally. I forced myself into the room and screamed at him to never close the door behind him when he went into her room. My husband and daughter were shocked because they knew nothing about my abuse history, and my reaction seemed out of proportion to what was happening." —Maggie

Pat shares how dealing with her abuse issues helped her to be a better parent.

"My partner and I have an adopted 12-year-old daughter. I have been in therapy a lot and I think I have worked through a lot of abuse issues. I am glad I waited until I was older to be a mom, otherwise I might have sucked at it! My parents found out about the abuse by a friend of the family and did nothing. I have a really hard time with that piece, especially as a parent myself. I would do something. I try to be sensitive to my daughter, attuned to her, and get her to talk with me. She's pretty quick to tell us what's going on with her. I feel we've been reasonable in our protectiveness. We try to be rational. You can't raise a healthy child otherwise. She doesn't know about the abuse yet, but I will tell her."

Dr. Leigh Baker (2002), child abuse expert and founder of the Trauma Treatment Center of Denver, describes the most common characteristics of sexual predators and how they lead their victims through the stages of sexual abuse—invaluable information for parents in preventing abuse. Arming yourself with information about sexual predators helps you to identify these individuals before they harm your children.

Some survivors shared their abuse histories with their children in an effort to protect them from abuse. Telling our children about our abuse history is a good idea, but experts advise that the information be geared to the child's age and maturity level (Courtois, 1988). Such disclosure is indicated especially in cases where the mother's abuser is perceived as a continued threat to children.

"I am sorry I had to tell my daughter stuff about Dad fairly early on. I told her she needed to be careful about Grandpa touching her. I always watched like a hawk and tried not to let him be alone with her. I was worried that it would give her a general distrust of men. I tried so hard to protect her from ever having to go through anything like I did. I feel good I was able to do that, to keep her safe. I don't know if she comprehends or appreciates what that means. I hope so." —Jacque

"I had the self-desire to get the damn victim thing off my head and to be a good mom. If my daughters ask me, I'll tell them everything when they're much older. I'll tell them that some people are not really good at being par-

ents, but I turned out OK. I fear the girls reaching the age at which I was abused and wanting to have sleepovers. When will it be over?" —Sarah

"I told my children about the abuse. Absolutely." —Mary Lou

Sometimes we find it necessary to forgive ourselves for our inability to protect our children. Sometimes despite our best efforts, our children are abused.

"When I found out my son's stepmother was physically abusing him, I could've and would've killed her. The only thing that stopped me was I had no vehicle then and I lived three hours away from her." —Sue

"I feel like I have to work on my own shit to be able to help my 15-year-old daughter, who just told me she was raped. She's in therapy now. She told me how she wore her new pajamas to my mom's for Christmas with a bra under them. My brother had unfastened her bra three times. My mom had seen it and said something to him, but I felt that as her mother I needed to stand up for her and protect her too. I told her, 'You have my permission to slap anyone who does something like that to you!'" —Deborah

Unfortunately, some of the survivors I spoke with had lost contact with their children or even lost custody of them. This was, of course, devastating for them, something that caused deep emotional reverberations in their lives.

"I'm the single parent of a 15-year-old daughter who was taken away legally. My sister took custody of her and is seeking to adopt her. My daughter is very angry with me. I said, 'Don't use me as an emotional punching bag.' There are ways I really hurt her. It's painful and liberating not having my daughter with me." —Tabitha

"Maybe I say too much to my daughter. She's not talking to me right now. It's kind of hard for me to see it because the only way she's going to get any place is to pick herself up and get on with it." —Jacque

The challenge of lesbian survivors raising sons is a particularly fascinating topic. Discussions of sex role socialization and our fears of generalized hatred toward men were powerful examples of survivors' efforts to grapple with the difficult issues of parenting boys.

"I'm raising a son conceived through donor insemination by a friend. I'm trying to toughen him up. He sees his dad as weak and his moms as strong. I will instill compassion in him. It will always be with him—his loving kindness. He's a big bruiser of a kid who's gentle. I'm concerned that with the hormonal changes of adolescence this might change. Raising children—loving them and nurturing them—has been healing. They've blossomed in a nontraditional home. I certainly didn't learn to parent by example. I'm OK, or they wouldn't be OK." —Tammy

Some women told how their decision not to parent, or reluctance to involve children in their life, arose from their abuse history. Kris went so far as to make the decision not to have children—the only way she knew for certain to protect them from her parents. *"I knew when I was little that I would never have children because of what was going on with my dad. I was worried if I had a child it would be around my parents."* Others, like Elizabeth, are interested in parenting, but want to explore all the issues first. *"My partner and I want to have children in a year. We want to be prepared, not overly protective. We want to explore all the issues first."*

"I've always wanted to be a mom, but I'm afraid of how I will parent. I have a terrible temper and want to spank. My dad would spank and then apologize." —Rowan

"One of the reasons I didn't have children is because I would have aborted a son or drowned it at birth. And I could only do so much to protect a daughter. I realized how awful and hard it was to be a little girl." —Marian

"I am basically alone in life as I have chosen not to have children. I fear that I would not be a good parent because of what I experienced as a

child. I also chose not to have children because I don't have an adequate support system in which to rear a child." —Lisa

Giving Thanks

The process of writing this book has been more difficult and more rewarding than I ever imagined it could be. What began as a personal exploration quickly became a search for community and support among lesbian survivors. The writing was emotionally grueling at times and the gratitude of the women I spoke with spurred me on when my emotional reserves ran low and when the devastating effects of my own abuse threatened to overwhelm me. To all of you who shared your stories—I owe you as much thanks as you extended to me. I share with you here survivors' reflections on telling their stories. I hold these comments close to me, like the bright flame of a lit candle, caressing and soothing me with its warm glow. Your generous spirit and tremendous courage are a daily inspiration to me.

"We need to know we are not alone."
—C.S. Lewis

"Thank you for being willing to write on such a hidden issue." —Erin

"I wish you the best of luck in your endeavor. I think what you're doing is a great thing!" —Mary

"Your words were so warm and sensitive. You gave me some peace and hope. Thanks, dear person. Best wishes for your book." —Barbara

"I have wished that a book for and about lesbian survivors existed. Thank you for putting this together." —Grace

"I think this is a great thing that you are putting together. I know I could have used a book to read when I first came out." —Katie

"I think this is a great endeavor, and I am so thankful that you are writing this book. Thank you for allowing me to be a small part of it." —Meg

"Thank you for giving me the opportunity to go back to that time and once again realize the importance of forgiveness. The questions themselves were insightful for me." —Juli

"I appreciate your opinion of my heart, truly perceptive and intuitive. Thanks, it made me smile. It made me look at some things I hadn't thought about directly in years, and made me learn more about myself and how I feel about the past. Anyway, wow, I have a lot to think about now. Thank you. I've been looking for a book like this for years, one that speaks to my specific culture of lesbians. I have the utmost respect." —Missy

"Writing and reading decrease our sense of isolation. They deepen and widen and expand our sense of life. They feed the soul. It's like singing on a boat during a terrible storm at sea: You can't stop the raging storm, but singing can change the hearts and spirits of the people who are together on that ship."

—Anne Lamott, *Bird by Bird: Some Instructions on Writing and Life*

"Books were one of the primary ways I healed, so it's great to be able to give back something." —Cory

"It's helpful for me to pull it all together like this." —Jacque

"I think what you're doing is really a good thing. And, hey, I'll be buying copies. I know this is going to be a tough project. I hope it goes well for you." —Kris

"I'm honored that you picked my story. I appreciate it." —Lyndsey

"Writing this down for the first time has helped. I have never really told anyone the whole story. I don't know how people can just tell people out loud." —Melissa

"Thanks for speaking to me. It was healing to just answer your questions. It made me cry as I remembered once again. I guess that means I'm not there yet, whatever that means. Thanks for entering my world." —Jan

"You're doing a great thing here." —Sharon

"Thanks for the gentle interview." —Sarah

"Thank you for letting me, finally, get my story out there in the world. I feel a lot better letting someone else know the pain, the abuse, and how it has affected me through my life, all the struggles I have." —Laura

"Thank you for taking the time to listen to my story and offer your insight and support." —Tabitha

"Thank you for doing this. I need to get this outside of myself. The discussion is helpful for me. I think it's going to be a great book." —Lynn

"Thank you for responding to my story with such sensitivity, warmth, and kindness." —Barbara

"I'm grateful for the opportunity to revisit this. It felt good talking about it. I felt a little traumatized by our conversation initially, but that has since worn off. I have to periodically look at the rage and the pain. It's beneficial. Writing helps too, to get it out of your system." —Marian

"Going through this process has been important to me." —Elizabeth

"Thanks for talking with me. It made us feel like we have started to give something back." —Dana

"I am very interested in your project and would help in any way I could. This has been interesting, writing this anyway. I'm really proud of us both." —Deborah

The experience of hearing the survivors' stories was both affirming and overwhelming. Learning (yet again) that I am not alone in my experience was very empowering. Hearing the pain and suffering of so many women was very difficult. As a result of my work on this book I decided after many years out of therapy to recommit to my own healing. There are new issues for me to face now. With the insights I have gained through my conversations with other lesbian survivors, I have a different perspective on my childhood experiences that will help me on my journey.

Afterword

Writing this book has been an incredible journey for me, personally and professionally. It demanded more from me than I believed I was capable of giving. It stretched me in ways that I was—at least initially—reluctant to be stretched. I have learned a great deal about myself in the process, and appreciate more fully the amazing healing journey I am on. I am optimistic about my future and hopeful that other survivors will find what they need for themselves and for their lives. I hope that this book has taken you on a journey of your own. I anticipate that this book will spark exciting conversations about the nature of sexual identity development and the sexual abuse recovery process, and I look forward to participating in these. I am also hopeful that my research will spark others to examine the experiences of lesbian survivors in the following ways:

- larger-scale studies like this
- exploration of sexual intimacy and relationship dynamics in lesbian couples where both partners are survivors
- exploration of the butch-femme dynamic among lesbian survivors
- exploration of the meaning of sexual dysfunction in the lesbian community
- exploration of issues unique to lesbian survivors of color
- exploration of lesbian survivors' parenting experiences
- a look at the wide range of sexual expression for lesbians and lesbian survivors, including gender-queer, lesbian, bisexual, and transgendered

While I have tried to provide answers to some of the questions about lesbian survivors' experiences and to offer resources to answer others, there remain many unanswered questions about the nature of sexual abuse recovery and lesbians' sexual identity development. I hope that in reading this book you will be encouraged to begin research and writing of your own on this subject or to encourage others to explore these important issues. I would love to hear from you about your reactions to this book and your own writing and activism on child sexual abuse in general, or the experiences of lesbian survivors in particular.

I wish you well on your journey. Take good care.

BIBLIOGRAPHY

Aaron, D.J., Markovic, N., Danielson, M.E., Honnold, J.A. Janosky, J.E. and Schmidt, N.J. (June 2001). Behavioral risk factors for disease and preventive health practices among lesbians. *American Journal of Public Health, 91*(6), 972–975.

Abbott, L.J. (November 1998). The use of alcohol by lesbians: A review and research agenda. *Substance Use and Misuse*, 33(13), 2647–2663.

Ainley, R. (1999). *What is she like? Lesbian identities from the 1950s to the 1990s.* London: Cassell Academic.

Ainscough, C., and Toon, K. (2000). *Surviving childhood sexual abuse: Practical self-help for adults who were abused as children.* Cambridge, Mass.: Fisher Books.

Allender, D.B. (1990). *The wounded heart: Hope for adult victims of childhood sexual abuse.* Colorado Springs, Colo.: NavPress.

American Association of Suicidology (2002). Understanding and helping the suicidal person. Online: www.suicidology.org/understandingsuicide.htm

Anderson, M.K., and Mavis, B.E. (1996). Sources of coming out self-efficacy for lesbians. *Journal of Homosexuality*, 32(2), 37–52.

Anonymous (1989). *Growing through the pain: The incest survivor's companion.* Park Ridge, Ill.: Parkside Publishing Corporation.

Arata, C.M. (January 1999). Cope with rape: The roles of prior sexual abuse and attributions of blame. *Journal of Interpersonal Violence*, 14(1), 62–78.

Arnup, K., ed. (1995). *Lesbian parenting: Living with pride and prejudice.* Charlottetown, Canada: Gynergy Books.

Atkins, D., ed. (1998). *Looking queer: Body image and identity in lesbian, gay, and transgender communities.* Binghamton, N.Y.: Harrington Park Press.

Back, G.G. (1985). *Are you still my mother? Are you still my family?* New York: Warner Books.

Baker, L. (2002). *Protecting your children from sexual predators.* New York: St. Martin's Press.

Baker, R.A., ed. (1998). *Child sexual abuse and false memory syndrome.* Amherst, N.Y.: Prometheus Books.

Baker, R.A. (1998). The statement of the problem. In R.A. Baker, *Child sexual abuse and false memory syndrome* (pp. 9–14). Amherst, N.Y.: Prometheus Books.

Barker-Collo, S.L., Melnyk, W.T., and McDonald-Miszczak, L. (April 2000). A cognitive-behavioral model of post–traumatic stress for sexually abused females. *Journal of Interpersonal Violence,* 15(4), 375–392.

Barnhouse, R.T. (1978). Sex between patient and therapist. *Journal of the American Academy of Psychoanalysis, 61,* 533–546.

Bass, E., and Davis, L. (1988). *The courage to heal: A guide for women survivors of child sexual abuse.* New York: Harper and Row.

Beals, K.P., Impett, E.A., and Peplau, L.A. (2002). Lesbians in love: Why some relationships endure and others end. *Journal of Lesbian Studies,* 6(1), 53–63.

Beals, K.P., and Peplau, L.A. (March 2001). Health relationship issues for lesbians' social involvement, disclosure of sexual orientation, and the quality of lesbian relationships. *Psychology of Women Quarterly,* 25(1), 10–19.

Bear, E. (1989). *Adults molested as children: A survivor's manual for women and men.* Seattle: The Safer Society Press.

Beardslee, W.R. (2002). *Out of the darkened room: When a parent is depressed: Protecting the children and strengthening the family.* Boston: Little, Brown and Co.

Beattie, M. (1992). *Codependent no more.* Center City, Minn.: Hazelden.

Beattie, M. (1990). *The language of letting go.* Center City, Minn.: Hazelden.

Beattie, M. (1989). *Beyond codependency.* Center City, Minn.: Hazelden.

Bell, A.P., Weinberg, M.S., and Hammersmith, S.K. (1981). *Sexual preference: Its development among men and women.* Bloomington, Ind.: Indiana University Press.

Bencosme, W.L. (2002). Tending the depressed soul. Online: www.soultenders.com/depression.html

Bennett, S.E. (February 2000). Heterogeneity in patterns of child sexual abuse, family functioning, and long-term adjustment. *Journal of Interpersonal Violence*, 15(2), 134–157.

Bepko, C. (1991). Feminism and addiction. New York: Haworth Press.

Berger, R.M. (July 1990). Passing: Impact on the quality of same-sex couple relationships. Social Work, 35(4), 328–332.

Berman, L.A., Berman, J.R., Bruck, D., Pawar, R.V., and Goldstein, I. (October 2001). Pharmacology or psychotherapy? Effective treatment for FSD related to unresolved childhood sexual abuse. *Journal of sex and marital therapy*, 27(5), 421–425.

Bernhardt, L.A., and Applegate, J.M. (July–August 1999). Comparison of stress and stress management strategies between lesbian and heterosexual women. *Health Care for Women International*, 20(4), 335–347.

Berzon, B. (1996). *The intimacy dance: A guide to long-term success in gay and lesbian relationships.* New York: Penguin Putnam.

Bettinger, M. (2001). *It's your hour: A guide to queer psychotherapy.* Los Angeles: Alyson Publications.

Biaggio, M., Coan, S., and Adams, W. (2002). Couples therapy for lesbians: Understanding merger and the impact of homophobia. *Journal of Lesbian Studies*, 6(1), 129–138.

Blum, D. (October 6, 2002). Young brains shaped by abuse. *Los Angeles Times*, M1–3.

Blume, E.S. (1990). *Secret survivors: Uncovering incest and its aftereffects in women.* New York: John Wiley and Sons.

Boston Lesbian Psychologies Collective, eds. (1987). *Lesbian psychologies: Explorations and challenges.* Chicago: University of Illinois Press.

Bradford, J., and Ryan, C. (1988). *The national lesbian health care survey. Final report.* Washington, D.C.: National Lesbian and Gay Health Foundation.

Bradford, J., Ryan, C., and Rothblum, E.D. (April 1994). National mental health care survey: Implications for mental health care. *Journal of Consulting and Clinical Psychology*, 62(2), 228–242.

Brady, M. (1991). *Daybreak: Meditations for women survivors of sexual abuse.* New York: Hazeldon/HarperCollins.

Brannock, J. C. and Chapman, B.E. (1990). Negative sexual experiences with men among heterosexual women and lesbians. *Journal of Homosexuality*,19(1), 105–110.

Braswell, P. (1995). The influence of self-monitoring on the body attitudes of lesbians at different stages of lesbian identity formation. *Dissertation Abstracts International, 56-06,* 3434.

Bratton, M. (1999). *From surviving to thriving: A therapist's guide to Stage II recovery for survivors of childhood abuse.* New York: The Haworth Press.

Brogan, D.J. (Winter 2001). Implementing the Institute of Medicine report on lesbian health. *Journal of the American Medical Women's Association*, 56(1), 24–26.

Brown, K.J. (August 2001). Evaluation of Project Chrysalis: A school-based intervention to reduce negative consequences of abuse. *Journal of Early Adolescence*, 21(3), 325–353.

Brown, L.S. (1987). Lesbians, weight, and eating: New analyses and perspectives. In the Boston Lesbian Psychologies Collective, eds., *Lesbian psychologies: Explorations and challenges* (pp. 261–282). Chicago: University of Illinois Press.

Browne, A., and Finkelhor, D. (1998). The impact of child sexual abuse: A review of the research. In R.A. Baker, *Child sexual abuse and false memory syndrome* (pp.355–383). Amherst, N.Y.: Prometheus Books.

Browning, C., Reynolds, A.L., and Dworkin, S.H. (April 1991). Affirmative psychotherapy for lesbian women. *The Counseling Psychologist*, 19(2), 177–196.

Buchanan, M., Dzelme, K., Harris, D., and Hecker, L. (October 2001). Challenge of being simultaneously gay or lesbian and spiritual and/or religious: A narrative perspective. *American Journal of Family Therapy*, 29(5), 435–449.

Burch, B. (1993). *On intimate terms: The psychology of difference in lesbian relationships.* Chicago: University of Illinois Press.

Burstow, B. (1992). *Radical feminist therapy: Working in the context of violence.* Thousand Oaks, Calif.: Sage Publications.

Butke, M. (1995). Lesbians and sexual child abuse. In L. Aronson, ed., *Sexual abuse in nine North American cultures: Treatment and prevention* (pp. 236–258). Thousand Oaks, Calif.: Sage Publications.

Butler, S. (1978).*Conspiracy of silence: The trauma of incest.* San Francisco: New Glide Publications.

Cabrera, J. (August 6, 2002). Forgiving the unforgivable. *Family Circle*, 160.

Cameron, R., and Cameron, K. (April 1995). Does incest cause homosexuality? *Psychological Reports*, 76(2), 611–621.

Chew, C.M. (1999). The relationship between religion and psychological adjustment in gay men and lesbians. *Dissertation Abstracts International*, 60-08, 4208.

Cicconi, P. (2000). *Lasting effects of sexual abuse on mental health of heterosexual and homosexual women.* Masters thesis, California State University, San Bernadino.

Clark, D. (1997). *Loving someone gay.* Berkeley, Calif.: Celestial Arts.

Clark, D.B., De Bellis, M.B., Lynch, K.G., Cornelius, J.R., and Martin, C.S. (October 18, 2002). *Physical and sexual abuse, depression, and alcohol use disorders in adolescents: Onsets and outcomes.* Online: www.sciencedirect.com

Classen, C., Field, N.P., Koopman, C., Nevill-Manning, K., and Spiegel, D. (June 2001). Interpersonal problems and their relationship to sexual revictimization among women sexually abused in childhood. *Journal of Interpersonal Violence*,16(6), 495–509.

Clausen, J. (1997). *Apples and oranges: My journey to sexual identity.* Boston: Houghton Mifflin.

Clunis, D.M., and Green, G.D. (1988). *Lesbian couples.* Seattle: Seal Press.

Cogan, J., and Erickson, J., eds. (1999). *Lesbians, Levi's, and lipstick: The meaning of beauty in our lives.* Binghamton, N.Y.: Harrington Park Press.

Cohen, J.B. (July 1999). Examining sex-related thoughts and feelings of sexually abused and nonabused children. *Journal of Interpersonal Violence*, 14(7), 701–712.

Coles, R. (1990). *The spiritual life of children.* Boston: Houghton Mifflin.

Constantine-Simms, D. (2000). *The greatest taboo: Homosexuality in black communities.* Los Angeles: Alyson Publications.

Cooper, C.D. (1995). *Childhood sexual abuse and depressive symptoms in a lesbian population: An exploratory study.* Doctoral dissertation, University of Southern California, Los Angeles.

Copeland, M., and Harris, M. (2000). *Healing the trauma of abuse: A women's workbook.* Oakland, Calif.: New Harbinger Publications.

Courtois, C.A. (1998). The memory retrieval process in incest survivor therapy. In R.A. Baker, *Child sexual abuse and false memory syndrome* (pp. 259–274). Amherst, N.Y.: Prometheus Books.

Courtois, C.A. (1988). *Healing the incest wound: Adult survivors in therapy.* New York: W.W. Norton and Company.

Crowe, M. (September 1996). Cutting up: Signifying the unspeakable. *Australian New Zealand Journal of Mental Health Nursing,* 5(3), 103–111.

D'Augelli, A.R., and Grossman, A.H. (October 2001). Disclosure of sexual orientation, victimization, and mental health among lesbian, gay and bisexual older adults. *Journal of Interpersonal Violence,* 16(10), 1008–1027.

Davis, L. (1992). *Allies in healing: When someone you love was sexually abused as a child.* New York: HarperCollins.

Davis, L. (1990). *The courage to heal workbook: For women and men survivors of child sexual abuse.* New York: Harper and Row.

Dayton, T. (2000). *Trauma and addiction: Ending the cycle of pain through emotional literacy.* Deerfield Beach, Fla.: Health Communications.

Descamps, M.J. (1998). *Mental health impact of child sexual abuse, rape, intimate partner violence and hate crimes in a national sample of lesbians.* Doctoral dissertation, University of Vermont.

De Vidas, M. (1999). Childhood sexual abuse and domestic violence: A support group for Latino gay men and lesbians. *Journal of Gay and Lesbian Social Services,*10, 51–68.

Diamond, L.M. (2002). "Having a girlfriend without knowing it": Intimate friendships among adolescent sexual-minority women. *Journal of Lesbian Studies,* 6(1), 5–16.

Diamond, L.M. (September 1998). Development of sexual orientation among adolescent and young adult women. *Developmental Psychology*, 34(5), 1085–1095.

DiLillo, D., Giuffre, D., Tremblay, G.C., and Peterson, L. (February 2001). A closer look at the nature of intimate partner violence reported by women with a history of child sexual abuse. *Journal of Interpersonal Violence*, 16(2), 116–132.

Dinsmore, C. (1991). *From surviving to thriving: Incest, feminism and recovery.* Albany, N.Y.: State University of New York.

Donnelly, N. (1998). *Mom: Candid memoirs by lesbians about the first woman in their life.* Los Angeles: Alyson Publications.

Dorn, B.A. (1990). An investigation into factors that contribute to successful long-term lesbian relationships. *Dissertation Abstracts International*, 51-07, 3560.

Duncan, R.D. (September 2000). Childhood maltreatment and college dropout rates: Implications for child abuse researchers. *Journal of Interpersonal Violence*, 15(9), 987–995.

Dworkin, S.M., and Gutierrez, F.J. (1992). *Counseling gay men and lesbians: Journey to the end of the rainbow.* Alexandria, Va.: American Counseling Association.

Dyer, W.W. (2001). *There's a spiritual solution to every problem.* New York: HarperCollins.

Earle, H.A. (1999). The relationship of internalized homophobia, level of outness, perceived social support and self-esteem to depression in lesbians. *Dissertation Abstracts International, 60-09*, 4885.

Eichberg, R. (1990). *Coming out: An act of love.* New York: Penguin.

Eide, M. (September 1993). Issues concerning incest and lesbian survivors: A review and sneak preview. *Above a Whisper*, 3(4), 1–3.

Elder, L. (1998). *Beginnings: Lesbians talk about the first time they met their long-term partners.* Los Angeles: Alyson Publications.

Emerson, J. (1994). *In the voice of a child: One woman's journey to healing from sexual abuse.* Nashville: Thomas Nelson Publishers.

Engle, B. (1989). *The right to innocence: Healing the trauma of childhood sexual abuse.* Los Angeles: Jeremy Tharcher, Inc.

Erikson, E. (1963). *Childhood and society.* New York: Norton.

Etheridge, M. (2001). *The truth is: My life in love and music.* New York: Random House.

Evan, D.B. (2001). *Break up or break through: A spiritual guide to richer relationships.* Los Angeles: Alyson Publications.

Evert, K., and Bijkerk, I. (1987). *When you're ready: A woman's healing from childhood physical and sexual abuse by her mother.* San Luis Obispo, Calif.: Launch Press.

Evosevich, J.M., and Avriette, M. (1999). *The gay and lesbian psychotherapy treatment planner.* New York: John Wiley and Sons.

Faderman, L. (Winter 1984). The new gay lesbians. *Journal of Homosexuality*, 10(3-4), 85–95.

Feiring, C., Coates, D.L., and Taska, L.S. (December 2001). Ethnic status, stigmatization, support, and symptom development following sexual abuse. *Journal of Interpersonal Violence*, 16(12), 1307–1329.

Femafedi, G. (1994). *Death by denial: Studies of suicide in gay and lesbian teenagers.* Los Angeles: Alyson Publications.

Finkelhor, D., Hotaling, G., Lewis, I.A., and Smith, C. (1990). Sexual abuse in a national survey of adult men and women: Prevalence, characteristics, and risk factors. *Child Abuse and Neglect, 14*(1), 19–28.

Finney, L.D. (1992).*Reach for the rainbow: Advanced healing for survivors of sexual abuse.* New York: Berkley Publishing Group.

Fitzgibbons, T.P. (1986). The cognitive and emotive uses of forgiveness in the treatment of anger. *Psychotherapy*, 23, 629–633.

Fontes, L.A. (1995). *Sexual abuse in nine North American cultures: Treatment and prevention.* Thousand Oaks, Calif.: Sage Publications.

Ford, M.T. (1996). *The world out there: Becoming part of the lesbian and gay community.* New York: The New Press.

Fore, B. (2000). *Homophobia: A history.* New York: Henry Holt.

Fortune, M.M. (1983). *Sexual violence: The unmentionable sin. An ethical and pastoral perspective.* New York: The Pilgrim Press.

Forward, S., and Buck, C. (1988). *Betrayal of innocence: Incest and its devastation.* New York: Penguin.

Fossum, M.A., and Mason, M.J. (1986). *Facing shame.* New York: W.W. Norton and Company.

Fraser, S. (1988). *My father's house: A memoir of incest and of healing.* New York: Ticknor and Fields.

Frock, S.D. (1999). The relationship between internalized homophobia and psychological distress in lesbians. *Dissertation Abstracts International, 61-01*, 0529.

Garnets, L. (Winter 2002 a). From abnormal to normatively different: Psychology's changing views of gay men, lesbians, and bisexual people. Online: www.sscnet.ucla.edu/02w/womenm147a-1/wo2handouts.htm

Garnets, L. (Winter 2002 b). Lesbian and gay parenting: Major findings. Online: www.sscnet.ucla.edu/00W/women185-2/Parenting.htm

Garnets, L.D., and Peplay, L.A. (2001). A new paradigm for women's sexual orientation: Implications for therapy. *Women and Therapy*, 24(1-2), 111–121.

Garrett, T. (2002). Inappropriate therapist-patient relationships. In R. Goodwin and D. Cramer, eds., *Inappropriate relationships: The unconventional, the disapproved, and the forbidden* (pp. 147–170). Mahwah, N.J.: Lawrence Erlbaum Associates.

Gayles, J.M. (1998). *The dating game: A guide for women dating women.* Transformation Works Publications.

Gil, E. (1992). *Outgrowing the pain together: A book for spouses and partners of adults abused as children.* New York: Bantam Doubleday Dell.

Giorgio, G.A. (2001). Contesting the utopia: Power and resistance in abusive lesbian relationships. *Dissertation Abstracts International, 62-08*, 2904.

Girshick, L.B. (October 2001). Sexual violence within lesbian battering. *Off Our Backs, 31(9)*.

Golden, C. (1987). Diversity and variability in women's sexual identities. In the Boston Lesbian Psychologies Collective, eds., *Lesbian Psychologies: Explorations and challenges* (pp. 19–34). Chicago: University of Illinois Press.

Goldman, L. (October 21, 2001). Cut to the core: Self-injurers add damage to the deep wounds within. *Chicago Tribune*, Section 13, p. 3.

Goodloe, A. (1993). Lesbian identity and the politics of butch-femme roles. Online: www.lesbian.org/amy/essays/bf-paper.html.

Graber, K. (1991). *Ghosts in the bedroom: For partners of survivors.* Deerfield Beach, Fla.: Health Communications.

Greene, B. (1997). Lesbian women of color: Triple jeopardy. *Journal of Lesbian Studies, 1*(1), 109–147.

Greene, B., and Herek, G.M., eds. (1994). *Lesbian and gay psychology: Theory, research, and clinical applications.* Thousand Oaks, Calif.: Sage Publications.

Griffith, P.L. (December 1997). MMPI-2 profiles of women differing in sexual abuse history and sexual orientation. *Journal of Clinical Psychology,* 53(8), 791–800.

Griffith, P.L. (1995). Characteristics, symptoms, MMPI-2 profiles of women comparing sexual orientation and childhood sexual abuse history. *Dissertation Abstracts International, 560-7,* 4015.

Groth, A.N. (1982). The incest offender. In S.M. Sgroi, ed., *Handbook of clinical intervention in child sexual abuse.* Lexington, Mass.: DC Health.

Groves, P., and Schondel, C. (1996). Lesbian couples who are survivors of incest: Group work utilizing a feminist approach. *Social Work in Groups,* 19(3), 93–103.

Gust, J., and Sweeting, P. (1992). *Recovering from sexual abuse and incest.* Bedford, Mass.: Mills and Sanderson.

Guyer, C.L. (2000). Evaluating relationships between personal perceptions, self-esteem, and childhood sexual abuse experienced by gay men and lesbians. *Dissertation Abstracts International,* 61-04, 2200.

Guyer, C.L. (2000). *Childhood sexual abuse in gay men and lesbians.* Doctoral dissertation, Walden University.

Haines, S. (1999). *The survivor's guide to sex: How to have an empowered sex life after child sexual abuse.* San Francisco: Cleis Press.

Hales, D., and Hales, R.E. (May 5, 2002). When a teenager is sad…Pay attention! *Parade Magazine,* 4–5.

Hall, J. (February 1999). An exploration of the sexual and relationship experiences of lesbian survivors of childhood sexual abuse. *Sexual and Marital Therapy,* 14(1), 6–70.

Hall, J.M. (May 1999). Lesbians in alcohol recovery surviving childhood sexual abuse and parental substance misuse. *The International Journal of Psychiatric Nursing Research,* 5(1), 507–515.

Hall, J.M. (1998). Lesbians surviving childhood sexual abuse: Pivotal experiences related to sexual orientation, gender, and race. *Journal of Lesbian Studies*, 2(1), 7–28.

Hall, J.M. (January 1996). Pervasive effects of childhood sexual abuse in lesbians' recovery from alcohol problems. *Substance Use and Misuse*, 31(2), 225–239.

Hall, L., and Lloyd, S. (1993). *Surviving abuse*. London: Falmer Press.

Hall, J.M., and Powell, J. (February 2000). Dissociative experiences described by women survivors of childhood abuse. *Journal of Interpersonal Violence*, 15(2), 184–204.

Hall, L., ed. (2000). *Lesbian self-writing: The embodiment of experience*. Binghamton, N.Y.: Harrington Park Press.

Halliday-Sumner, L., and Kozlick, D. (September 1996). Impact of past sexual abuse on breast-feeding. www.breakingthesilence.com/breast.html

Hamming, J.E. (August 2001). Dildonics, dykes and the detachable masculine. *European Journal of Women's Studies*, 8(3), 329–341.

Hancock, M., and Mains, K.B. (1987). *Child sexual abuse: Hope for healing*. Wheaton, Ill.: Harold Shaw Publishers.

Hansen, I.M. (2001). Lesbian relationship violence: A qualitative study of victims who became offenders. *Dissertation Abstracts International*, 62-10, 4787.

Hansen, P. (1991). *Helping the relationships of sexual abuse survivors*. San Francisco: Heron Hill.

Harlow, H.F. (1973). *Learning to love*. New York: Ballantine Books.

Harne, L., and Miller, E. (1997). *All the rage: Reasserting lesbian feminism*. New York: Teachers College Press.

Harris, J.I. (December 2001). Religious variables relevant to internalized homophobia and sexual identity development. *Dissertation Abstracts International, 62*(5-B), 2516.

Hartley, C.C. (May 2001). Incest offenders' perceptions of their motives to sexually offend within their past and current life context. *Journal of Interpersonal Violence*, 16(5), 459–475.

Hausen, P. (1991). *Helping the relationships of sexual abuse survivors*. San Francisco: Heron Hill.

Hefferman, K. (July–August 1998). The nature and predictors of substance use among lesbians. *Addictive Behaviors*, 23(4), 517–528.

Hefferman, K. (1997). Binge eating, substance use, and coping styles in a lesbian sample. *Dissertation Abstracts Internationa*l, 58-07, 3924.

Hefferman, K. (March 1996). Eating disorders and weight concern among lesbians. *The International Journal of Eating Disorders*, 19(2), 127–138.

Hennessy, K. (1993). Psychotherapeutic issues of lesbians. *Dissertation Abstracts International, 54-05*, 2754.

Herbert, S.E. (1996). Lesbian sexuality. In Cabaj, R.P., and Stein, T.S., eds., *Textbook of homosexuality and mental health* (pp. 723–742). Washington, D.C.: American Psychiatric Press.

Herman, J. (1981). *Father-daughter incest.* Cambridge, Mass.: Harvard University Press.

Hirschmann, J.R., and Munter, C.H, (1995). *When women stop hating their bodies: Freeing yourself from food and weight obsession.* New York: Fawcett Columbine.

Hoffman, J.M. (1997). *The prevalence of sexual abuse, depression, and relational difficulties in adult homosexual women: Implications for mental health care needs* Doctoral dissertation, Fuller Theological Seminary.

Holmes, D.S. (1998). The evidence for repression. In R.A. Baker, *Child sexual abuse and false memory syndrome* (pp.149–168). Amherst, N.Y.: Prometheus Books.

Holt, K. (2002). *Can you see me?* Chiaro Publishing.

Hughes, T.L., Johnson, T., and Wilsnack, S.C. (2001). Sexual assault and alcohol abuse: A comparison of lesbians and heterosexual women: *Journal of Substance Abuse*, 13(4), 515–532.

Hyman, B. (February 2000). The economic consequences of child sexual abuse for adult lesbian women. *Journal of Marriage and the Family, 62*(1), 199–211.

Jaffe, C. (1998). Alcoholism and internalized homophobia in lesbians. *Dissertation Abstracts International*, 59-09, 5088.

James, J.W., Friedman, R., and Matthews, L.L. (2001). *When children grieve.* New York: HarperCollins.

Janseen, M. (1991). *Secret shame: I am a victim of incest.* Minneapolis: Augsburg Fortress.

Jeffreys, S. (November 2000). 'Body Art' and social status: Cutting, tattooing and piercing from a feminist perspective. *Feminism and Psychology,* 10(4), 409–429.

Johnson, J.D. (1993). *The long term impact of childhood sexual abuse on sexual functioning of lesbian women: A project based on independent investigation.* Master's thesis, Smith College of Social Work.

Johnson, S.E. (1990). *Staying power: Long term lesbian couples.* Tallahassee, Fla.: Naiad.

Johnson, T. (2000). *Gay spirituality: The role of gay identity in the transformation of human consciousness.* Los Angeles: Alyson Publications.

Jordan, K.M., and Deluty, R.H. (1998). Coming out for lesbian women: Its relation to anxiety, positive affectivity, self-esteem, and social support. *Journal of Homosexuality, 35*(2), 41–63.

Josephson, G.S., and Fong-Beyette, M.L. (1987). Factors assisting female clients' disclosure of incest during counseling. *Journal of Counseling and Development, 65,* 475–478.

Kamsner, S. (December 2000). The relationship between adult psychological adjustment and childhood sexual abuse, childhood physical abuse, and family-of-origin characteristics. *Journal of Interpersonal Violence, 15*(12), 1243–1261.

Kang, S., Magura, S., Laudet, A., and Whitney, S. (June 1999). Adverse effect of child abuse victimization among substance-using women in treatment. *Journal of Interpersonal Violence, 14*(6), 657–670.

Kaufman, G., and Raphael, L. (1997). *Coming out of shame: Transforming gay and lesbian lives.* Main Street Books.

Keenan, D., and Lloyd, R., eds. (1990). *Looking for home: Women writing about exile.* Minneapolis: Milkweed Editions.

Ketring, S.A., and Feinauer, L.L. (April–June 1999). Perpetrator-victim relationship: Long-term effects of sexual abuse for men and women. *American Journal of Family Therapy, 27*(2), 109–120.

Kirkpatrick, M. (August 1991). Lesbian couples in therapy. *Psychiatric Annals, 21*(8), 491–496.

Kleindienst, K., ed. (1999). *This is what lesbian looks like: Dyke activists take on the 21st century.* Ithaca, N.Y.: Firebrand Books.

Klinger, R.L., and Stein, T.S. (1996). Impact of violence, childhood sexual abuse, and domestic violence and abuse on lesbians, bisexuals, and gay men. In R.P. Cabaj and T.S. Stein, eds., *Textbook of homosexuality and health* (pp. 801–818). Washington, D.C.: American Psychiatric Press.

Kominars, S.B., and Kominars, K.D. (1996). *Accepting ourselves and others: A journey into recovery from addiction and compulsive behaviors for gays, lesbians, and bisexuals.* Center City, Minn.: Hazeldon Information Education.

Kotulski, D.S. (1996). The expression of love, sex, and intimacy in lesbian and heterosexual couples: A feminist inquiry. *Dissertation Abstracts International,* 57(6-B), 4090.

Krakauer, I.D., and Rose, S.M. (2002). The impact of group membership on lesbians' physical appearance. *Journal of Lesbian Studies, 6*(1), 31–43.

Kritsberg, W., and Miller-Kritsberg, C. (1993). *The invisible wound: The new approach to healing childhood sexual abuse.* New York: Bantam Doubleday Dell.

Krystal, H. (1968). *Massice psychic trauma.* Madison, Conn.: International Universities Press.

Kurdek, L.A. (September 2001). Differences between heterosexual-nonparent couples and gay, lesbian, and heterosexual-parent couples. *Journal of Family Issues, 22*(6), 728–755.

Kushner, L.P. (1984). *Dragonchild: One lesbian's journey of survival through a childhood of battering and sexual abuse.* Iowa City, Iowa: Iowa City Women's Press.

Landsdale, S. (1996). *The issue of choice for lesbians. Dissertation Abstracts International, 56*-12, 7079.

LaSala, M.C. (Spring 2000). Lesbians, gay men, and their parents: Family therapy for the coming-out crisis. *Family Process, 39*(1), 67–81.

Lehmann, J.B., Lehmann, C., and Kelly, P.J. (April 1998). Development and health care needs of lesbians. *Journal of Women's Health, 7*(3), 379–387.

Leventhal, B., and Lundy, S.E. (1999). *Same-sex domestic violence: Strategies for change.* Thousand Oaks, Calif.: Corwin Press.

Lever, J. (August 22, 1995). Lesbian sex survey. *The Advocate*, 23–30.

Lie, G.Y., Schilt, R., Bush, J., Montaigne, M., and Reyes, L. (Summer 1991). Lesbians in currently aggressive relationships: How frequently do they report aggressive past relationships. *Violence and victims*, 6(2), 121–135.

Lightner, K., and Viger, T., eds. (1996). *The new Our Right to Love: A lesbian resource book.* New York: Touchstone Books.

Lobel, K. (1986). *Naming the violence: Speaking out about lesbian battering.* Seattle: Seal Press.

Lockhart, L.L., White, B.W., Causby, V., and Isaac, A. (December 1994). Letting out the secret: Violence in lesbian relationships. *Journal of Interpersonal Violence, 9*(4), 469–492.

Loulan, J. (1999). Lesbians as luvbeins. *Journal of Lesbian Studies, 3*

Loulan, J. (1987). *Lesbian passion: Loving ourselves and each other.* San Francisco: Spinsters/Aunt Lute.

Ludwig, M. R., & Brownell, K. D. (1999, January). Lesbians, bisexual women, and body image: An investigation of gender roles and social group affiliation. *The International Journal of Eating Disorders, 25*(1), 89-97.

Lyders, G. C. (1999). Body image and attitudes toward eating: The influence of objectified body consciousness and variations of gender and sexual orientation. *Dissertation Abstracts International,60-04*, 1861.

Lynch, J. (1992). *The broken heart: The psychobiology of human contact.* Ornstein & Swencionis.

Mackay, J. L. (1999). The relationship between parents and their gay and lesbian children. *Dissertation Abstracts International*, 61-03, 897.

Madwin, G. (1999). The implications of "gay gene" studies for queer by choice people. [Online] Available: www.queerbychoice.com/gaygene.html.

Maltz, W. (1991). *The sexual healing journey: A guide for survivors of sexual abuse.* New York: HarperCollins.

Maltz, W. (1988). Identifying and treating the sexual repercussions of incest: A couples therapy approach. *Journal of Sex and Marital Therapy, 14*(2), 142-170.

Maltz, W., & Holman, B. (1987). Incest and Sexuality: *A guide to understanding and healing.* Lexington, MA: Lexington Books.

Mantilla, K. (1998, September). Biology, my ass. Off Our Backs, [Online] Available: www.offourbacks.org/Feature.htm.

Marano, L. (2002, September 17). *Affluent kids: Both pressured and ignored.* United Press International. [Online] Available: http://upi.com/view/cfm?StoryID= 20020917-030837-5850r

Marano, L. (1999, March/April). Depression beyond serotonin. Psychology Today.

Marcus, E. (1993). *Is it a choice: Answers to 300 of the most frequently asked questions about gays and lesbians.* New York: HarperSanFrancisco.

Matsakis, A. (1996). *I can't get over it: A handbook for trauma survivors.* Oakland, CA: New Harbinger Publications.

Matthews, A. K., & Hughes, T. L. (2001, February). Mental health service use by African American women: Exploration of subpopulation differences. *Cultural Diversity & Ethnic Minority Psychology,* 7(1), 75-87.

Matthews, A. K., Hughes, T. L., Johnson, T., Razzano, L. A. & Cassidy, R. (2002, July). Prediction of depressive distress in a community sample of women: The role of sexual orientation. *American Journal of Public Health, 92*(7), 1131-1139.

McBain, S. M. (1999). The role of fusion and patterns of attachment in the relationship satisfaction of lesbians. *Dissertation Abstracts International,60-08,* 4304.

McCarthy, L. (2000). Poppies in a wheat field: Exploring the lives of rural lesbians. *Journal of Homosexuality,39*(1), 75-94.

McCloskey, L. A., & Bailey, J. A. (2000, October). The intergenerational transmission of risk for child sexual abuse. *Journal of Interpersonal Violence, 15*(10), 1019-1035.

McClure, M. B. (1990). *Reclaiming the heart: A handbook of help and hope for survivors of incest.* New York: Warner Books.

McNeill, J. J. (1988). *Taking a chance on God: Liberating theology for gays, lesbians, and their lovers, families, and friends.* Boston: Beacon Press.

Messman-Moore, T. L. (2000, May). Child sexual abuse and revictimization in the form of adult sexual abuse, adult physical abuse, and adult psychological maltreatment. *Journal of Interpersonal Violence, 15*(5), 489-502.

Miller, A. (2001). *The truth will set you free: Overcoming emotional blindness and finding your true adult self.* New York: Basic Books.

Miller, D. H. (1998). *Freedom to differ: The shaping of the gay and lesbian struggle for civil rights.* New York: New York University Press.

Miller, D. H., Greene, K., Causby, V., White, B. W., & Lockhart, L. L. (2001). Domestic violence in lesbian relationships. *Women & Therapy*,23(3), 107-127.

Morris, J. F. (1997). Lesbian coming out as a multidimensional process. *Journal of Homosexuality*, 33(2), 1-22.

Munro, K. (2002). *Am I gay because of the abuse?* [Online] Available: www.kalimunro.com/article_gay_abuse.html

National Depression Screening Day. (2002). Screening for mental health. www.mentalhealthscreening.org/dep/dep-sample.htm

National Mental Health Association. (1999). Recognizing childhood depression is first step to saving lives. www.nmha.org/newsroom/system/ news.vw.cfm?do+vw&rid=109

Neisen, J. H., & Sandall, H. (1990). Alcohol and other drug abuse in gay/lesbian population: Related to victimization. *Journal of Psychology & Human Sexuality,3*(1), 151-168.

Nestingen, S. L., & Lewis, L. R. (1991). *Growing beyond abuse: A workbook for survivors of sexual exploitation or childhood sexual abuse.* Minneapolis: Omni Recovery.

Nestle, J., Wilchins, R., & Howell, C. (2002). *GenderQueer: Voices from beyond the sexual binary.* Los Angeles: Alyson Publications.

Neumark-Sztainer, D., Story, M., Hannan, P. J., Beuhring, T., & Resnick, M. D. (2000, November). Disordered eating among adolescents: Associations with sexual/physical abuse ad other familial/psychosocial factors. *International Journal of Eating Disorders,28*(3), 249-258.

Nichols, M. (1987). Lesbian sexuality: Issues and developing theory. In the Boston Lesbian Psychologies Collective (Ed.), *Lesbian psychologies: Exploration and challenges* (pp. 97-125). Urbana and Chicago: University of Illinois Press.

Novotni, M., & Petersen, R. (2001). *Angry with God.* Colorado Springs, CO: NavPress.

Oetien, H., & Rothblum, E. D. (2000). When lesbians aren't gay: Factors affecting depression among lesbians. *Journal of Homosexuality, 39*(1), 49-73.

Ogilvie, Beverly A. (2004). Mother-daughter incest: a guide for helping professionals. Binghamton, N.Y.: Haworth Press.

O'Neill, M. R. (1998, October). Depression vulnerability in gay, lesbian, and bisexual young adults. *Dissertation Abstracts International,59*(4-B), 1864.

Orbach, S. (1978). *Fat is a feminist issue: A self-help guide for compulsive eaters.* New York: Berkeley Books.

Osborn, S. (1992). *Surviving the wreck.* New York: Henry Holt.

Otis, M. D., & Skinner, W. F. (1996). The prevalence of victimization and its effect on mental well-being among lesbian and gay people. *Journal of Homosexuality, 30*(3), 93-121.

Owens, G. P. (2001, February). Cognitive distortions among women reporting childhood sexual abuse. *Journal of Interpersonal Violence,* 16(20), 178-191.

Pace, C. (1999). The influence of ritual use, institutional support, and conflict resolution style on lesbian couples' relationship satisfaction. *Dissertation Abstracts International, 60-06,* 3019.

Parks, C. W., Cuttts, R. N., Woodson, K. M., & Flarity-White, L. (2001). Issues inherent in the multicultural feminist couple treatment of African-American, same-gender loving female adult survivors of child sexual abuse. *Journal of Child Sexual Abuse,* 10(3), 17-34.

Pearlman, S. F. (1991). Mothers' acceptance of daughters' lesbianism: A parallel process of identity formation. *Dissertation Abstracts International,* 52-03, 1733.

Pelzer, D. (2000). *Help yourself: Celebrating the rewards of resilience an gratitude.* New York: Dutton.

Penelope, J., & Wolfe, S. (1989). *The original coming out stories.* Freedom, CA: The Crossing Press.

Perlman, S. F. (1997). The saga of continuing clash in lesbian community or Will an army of ex-lovers fail? In J. White & M. C.

Martinez (Eds.) *The lesbian health book: Caring for ourselves.* Seattle: Seal Press.

Petersen, B. (1991). *Dancing with Daddy: A childhood lost and a life regained.* New York: Bantam Books.

Pimental-Habib, R. (2002). *The power of a partner: Creating and maintaining healthy gay and lesbian relationships.* Los Angeles: Alyson Publications.

Pimental-Habib, R. (1999). Empowering the tribe: A positive guide to gay and lesbian self-esteem. New York: Kensington Publications.

Pitman, G. E. (2000). The influence of race, ethnicity, class, and sexual politics on lesbians' body image. *Journal of Homosexuality,* 40(2), 49-64.

Pitman, G. E. (1999a). Body image, compulsory heterosexuality, and internalized homophobia. *Journal of Lesbian Studies, 3*(4), 129-139.

Pitman, G. E. (1999b). The relationship between body dissatisfaction and internalized homophobia in lesbians. *Dissertation Abstracts International,* 59-9, 5105.

Platzer, H. (1998, March). The concerns of lesbians seeking counseling: A review of the literature. *Patient Education and Counseling, 33*(3), 225-232.

Plumb, M. (1997). Blueprint for the future: Lesbian health advocacy movement. In J. White & M. C. Martinez (Ed.) *The lesbian health book: Caring for ourselves* (pp.362-377). Seattle: The Seal Press.

Post, L. L., & Avery, J. E. (1995). Therapeutic approaches to inhibited sexual desire in lesbians. *Counseling Psychology Quarterly,*8(3), 213-219.

Prendergast, W. E. (1996). *Sexual abuse of children and adolescents: A preventive guide for parents, teachers, and counselors.* New York: Continuum Publishing.

Queer by Choice. (2002). The implications of "gay gene" studies for Queer by Choice people. [Online] Available: www.queerbychoice.com/gaygene.html

Queer Press Collective. (Ed.). (1991). *Loving in fear: An anthology of lesbian and gay survivors of childhood sexual abuse.* Toronto, Ontario: Queer Press NonProfit Community Publishing of Toronto.

Radicalesbians. (1970). The woman identified woman. [Online] Available: http://scriptorium.lib.duke.edu/wlm/womid/

Radich,J. (2002). *Children's Rights Charter.* [Online] Available: http://webmail.aol.com/msgview.adp?folder=Su5T1g=&uid=3316 482

Radomsky, N. A. (1995). *Women, chronic pain, and abuse.* Binghamton, NY: Haworth Press.

Rafkin, L. (Ed.). (1990). *Different mothers: Sons and daughters of lesbians talk about their lives.* Pittsburgh and San Francisco: Cleis Press.

Rainbow Hope. (n. d.). What you can do to have a better self-esteem. [Online] Available: www.rainbowhope.org/~site/selfesteem.html

Rankow, L. J. (1997). Long time cumming: Notes on chronic illness, sexuality, shame, and desire. In M. C. Martinez *The lesbian health book: Caring for ourselves* (pp. 106-113). Seattle: The Seal Press.

Rayside, D. (1998). *On the fringe: Gays and lesbians in politics.* Ithaca, NY: Cornell University.

Reinfelder, M. (Ed.). (1996). *Amazon to Zumi: Toward a global lesbian feminism.* London: Cassell Academic.

Renzetti, C. M. (1998). Violence and abuse in lesbian relationships: Theoretical and empirical issues. In R. K. Bergen (Ed.), *Issues in intimate violence.* Thousand Oaks, CA: Sage.

Renzetti, C. M. (1992) *Violent betrayal: Partner abuse in lesbian relationships.* Thousand Oaks, CA: Sage Publications.

Renzetti, C. M., & Miley, C. H. (Eds.). (1996). *Violence in gay and lesbian domestic partnerships.* Binghamton, NY: Haworth Press.

Ristock, J. L. (2002). *No more secrets: Violence in lesbian relationships.* New York: Routledge.

Roberts, S. (1996). *Roberts' rules of lesbian living.* Duluth, MN: Spinsters Ink.

Roche, D. N. (1999, February). Adult attachment: A mediator between child sexual abuse and later psychological attachment. *Journal of Interpersonal Violence, 14*(2), 14-207.

Roper, K. D. (1997). Lesbian couple dynamics and individual psychological adjustment. *Dissertation Abstracts International, 58-05,* 2698.

Rose, S. (1994). Sexual pride and shame in lesbians. In B. Greene & G. M. Herek *Lesbian and Gay Psychology: Theory, research, and clinical applications: Psychological Perspectives on Lesbian and Gay Issues* (71-83). Thousand Oaks, CA: Sage Publications.

Rosenfeld, I. (1999, September 19). When the sadness won't go away. Parade Magazine. [Online] Available: www.parade.com/current/editor _picks/ sadness.html

Rosenthal, M. S. (2000). Women and depression. Los Angeles: Lowell House.

Rosenzweig, J. M., & Lebow, W. C. (1992). Femme on the streets, butch in the sheets. Lesbian sex-roles, dyadic adjustment, and sexual satisfaction. *Journal of Homosexuality*, 23(3), 1-20.

Roth, G. (1991). *When food is love: Exploring the relationship between eating and intimacy.* New York: Penguin.

Roth, G. (1984). *Breaking free from compulsive eating.* Indianapolis and New York: The Bobbs-Merrill Co.

Roth, N. (1993). *Integrating the shattered self: Psychotherapy with adult incest survivors.* Northvale, NJ: Jason Aronson.

Rothblum, E. D., & Cole, E. (1989). *Lesbianism: Living boldly.* Binghamton, NY: Haworth Press.

Rubin, B. M. (2002, April 28). Abuse victims find way to heal: Survivor groups gain support amid priest scandal. *Chicago Tribune*, Section 4, pp. 1, 5.

Runtz, M. G. (1987). *The sexual victimization of women: The link between child abuse and revictimization.* Paper presented at the annual meeting of the Canadian Psychological Association, Vancouver, BC.

Russell, D. E. H. (1986). *The secret trauma: Incest in the lives of girls and women.* New York: Basic Books.

Saakvitne, K. W., & Pearlman, L. A. (1993). The impact of internalized misogyny and violence against women or feminine identity. In E. R. Cook (Ed.), *Woman, relationships, and power: Implications for counseling* (pp. 221-247). Alexandria, VA: American Counseling Association.

Saewyc, E. M., Bearinger L. H., Blum, R. W., & Resnick, M. D. (1999, May-June). Sexual intercourse, abuse and pregnancy among adolescent women: Does sexual orientation make a difference? *Family Planning Perspectives, 31*(3), 127-131.

Sage Publications. (1992). *Positively gay*. Thousand Oaks, CA: Author.

Salkin, N. B. (1997). A qualitative study of body image and lesbian self-identity. *Dissertation Abstracts International,58-07*, 3947.

Sanders, B. (1999, February). Childhood maltreatment and date rape. *Journal of Interpersonal Violence,14*(2), 115-124.

Sanford, L. T. (1990). *Strong at the broken places: Overcoming the trauma of childhood abuse.* New York: Random House.

SARK. (1994). *Living juicy: Daily morsels for your creative soul.* Berkeley, CA: Celestial Arts.

SARK. (1992). *Inspiration sandwich: Stories to inspire our creative freedom.* Berkeley, CA: Celestial Arts.

SARK. (1991). *Creative companion: How to free your creative spirit.* Berkeley, CA: Celestial Arts.

Schilt, R., Lie, G. Y., & Montaigne, M. (1990). Substance use as a correlate of violence in intimate lesbian relationships. *Journal of Homosexuality, 19*(3), 51-65.

Schreurs, K. M. G. (1993). Sexuality in lesbian couples: The importance of gender. *Annual Review of Sex Research, 4*,49-66.

Schuklenk, U., Stein, E., Kerin, J., & Byrne, W. (1997, July-August). The ethics of genetic research on sexual orientation. *The Hastings Center Report, 27*(4), 6-13.

Shapiro, F. (2002). EMDR in brief. [Online] Available: www.emdr.com/brief.htm

Shaw, R. (Ed.). (2000). *Not child's play: An anthology on brother-sister incest.* Takoma Park, MD: Lunchbox Press.

Shaw, J., & Erhardt, V. (1997). *Journey toward intimacy: A handbook for lesbian couples.* Couples Enrichment Institute.

Signorile, M. (1995). *Outing yourself: How to come out as lesbian or gay to your family, friends, and coworkers.* New York: Random House.

Singh, D., Vidaurri, M., Zambarano, R. J., & Dabbs, J. M. Jr. (1999, June). Lesbian erotic role identification: Behavioral, morphological, and hormonal correlates. *Journal of Personality and Social Psychology, 76*(6), 1035-1049.

Sisley, E., & Harris, B. (1977). *The joy of lesbian sex.* New York: Simon & Schuster.

Slater, S. (1995). *The lesbian family life cycle.* New York: The Free Press.

Smith, S. S. (1995). Relationship satisfaction in lesbian couples. *Dissertation Abstracts International, 57-01,* 0766.

Sojourner, S. (1997). *Psychic scars... And other mad thoughts..* In J. White & M. C. Martinez (Ed.) *The lesbian health book: Caring for ourselves* (pp.233-251). Seattle: The Seal Press.

Solly, R., & Lloyd, R. (1992). *Journey notes: Writing for recovery and spiritual growth.* New York: Ballantine Books.

Somer, E. (1995). *Food and mood: The complete guide to eating well and feeling your best.* New York: Henry Holt and Company.

Somers, S. (1992). *Wednesday's children: Adult survivors of abuse speak out.* New York: Putnam/Healing Vision Publishing.

Stacey, J., & Biblarz, T. J. (2001), April). (How) does the sexual orientation of parents matter? *American Sociological Review, 66,* 159-183.

Stark, E., & Holly, M. (1998). *Everything you need to know about sexual abuse.* New York: The Rosen Publishing Group.

Starzecpyzel, E. (1987). The Persephone complex: Incest dynamics and the lesbian preference. In The Boston Lesbian Psychologies Collective *Lesbian Psychologies: Explorations & Challenges* (pp. 261-282). Urbana and Chicago: University of Illinois Press.

Stermac, L., Reist, D., Addison, M., & Miller, G. M. (2002, June). Childhood risk factors for women's sexual victimization. *Journal of Interpersonal Violence,* 17(6), 647-670.

St. John, S. (1994). The homophobia healer: A primer for gays, lesbians, and the families and friends who love them. Denver, CO: Tickerwick Publications.

Stolinsky, S. A. (2002). *Act it out: 25 expressive ways to heal from childhood abuse.* Oakland, CA: New Harbinger Publications.

Strong, M. (1998). *A bright red scream: Self-mutilation and the language of pain.* New York: Penguin.

Strock, C. (1998). *Married women who love women.* Los Angeles: Alyson Publications.

Struve, J. (n.d.). Clinical considerations in working with gay and lesbian sexual abuse survivors. [Online] Available: www.atlantapsychotherapy.com/ articles.struve4.htm

Sullivan, G. E. (2000). An exploratory study: *The relationships of the sense of difference in the pre-coming out stage of lesbians and childhood sexual abuse: A project based upon independent investigation.* Master's thesis, Smith College School for Social Work.

Szymanski, D. M. (2001). Lesbian internalized homophobia in relation to same-sex relationships, feminist attitudes, and coping resources. *Dissertation Abstracts International*, 62-08, 2691.

Taylor, T. S. (2000). Is God good for you, good for your neighbor? The influence of religious orientation on demoralization and attitudes toward lesbians and gay men. *Dissertation Abstracts International ,60*-12, 4472.

Taylor, J., & Chandler, T. (1995). *Lesbians talk about violent relationships.* Scarlet Press.

Teicher, M. H. (2002, March). Scars that won't heal: The neurobiology of child abuse. *Scientific American*, 68-75.

Telesco, G. A. (2001, December). Sex role identity and relationship factors as correlates of abusive behavior in lesbian relationships. *Dissertation Abstracts International, 62*(5-A), 1945.

Tigert, L. M. (2001). The power of shame: Lesbian battering as a manifestation of homophobia. *Women & Therapy, 23*(3), 73-85.

Thompson, B. W. (1994). *A hunger so wide and so deep: American women speak out on eating problems.* Minneapolis and London: University of Minnesota Press.

Thompson, M. P., Kaslow, N. J., Lane, D. B., & Kingree, J. B. (2000, January). Childhood maltreatment, PTSD, and suicidal behavior among African American females. Journal of Interpersonal Violence, 15(1), 3-15.

Trippet, S. E. (1994, July-August). Lesbians' mental health concerns. *HealthCare Women International*, 15(4), 317-323.

Uhrig, L. J. (1984). *The two of us: Affirming, celebrating, and symbolizing gay and lesbian relationships.* Boston: Alyson Publications.

Vachss, A. (2002, July). What we must do to protect our children: A call to action. *Parade*, 4-5.

Van der Kolk, B. A. (1987). *Psychological trauma.* Washington, DC: American Psychiatric Press.

Van Gelder, L., & Brandt, P. R. (1996). *The girls next door: Into the heart of lesbian America.* New York: Simon & Schuster.

Van Meer, J. A. (1990). *The lesbian survivor: Long term implications of sexual abuse on lesbian identity development and sexual functioning.* Doctoral dissertation, California School of Professional Psychology.

Vaughn, S. C. (1999). The hiding and revelation of sexual desire in lesbians: The lasting legacy of developmental traumas. *Journal of Gay & Lesbian Psychotherapy, 3*(2), 81-90.

Wagenbach, P. M. (1998). The relationship between body image, sexual orientation and gay identity. *Dissertation Abstracts International, 60-01*, 0403.

Walsh, C. P. (1986). *The self-concept and sex-role orientation of adult females in therapy with and without incest history.* Unpublished doctoral dissertation, University of Florida, Gainesville.

Waters, E., Merrick, S., Trebouz, D., Crowell, J., & Albersheim, L. (2000, May). Personality and social development attachment security in infancy and early adulthood: A twenty-year longitudinal study. *Child Development, 71*(3), 684-689.

WebMD. (2002). Post-traumatic stress disorder. [Online] Available: http://aolsvc.webmd.aol.com/condition_center_content/apd/article/2950.1505?z=2951

Westerlund, E. (1992). *Women's sexuality after childhood incest.* New York: W. W. Norton & Co.

Whealin, J. M., & Jackson, J. L. (2002, August). Childhood unwanted sexual attention and young women's present self-concept. *Journal of Interpersonal Violence, 17*(8), 854-871.

Whiffen, V. E., Judd, M. E., & Aube, J. A. (1999, September). Intimate relationships moderate the association between childhood sexual abuse and depression. *Journal of Interpersonal Violence, 14*(9), 940-954.

Whiffen, V. E., Thompson, J. M., & Aube, J. A. (2000, October). Mediators of the link between childhood sexual abuse and adult depressive symptoms. *Journal of Interpersonal Violence, 15*(10), 1100-1120.

Whisman, V. (1995). *Queer by choice: Lesbians, gay men, and the politics of identity.* New York: Routledge.

Whittington, S. A. (2000). Effects of coming out, age, mental health, and abuse on alcohol-related behaviors in lesbians. *Dissertation Abstracts International, 61-02*, 1067.

Wijma, K., Soderquist, J., Bjorklund, I., & Wijma, B. (2000, September). Prevalence of post-traumatic stress disorder among gynecological patients with a history of sexual and physical abuse. *Journal of Interpersonal Violence, 15(9)*, 944-958.

Wilson, M. (1994). *Crossing the boundary: Black women survive incest.* Seattle: Seal Press.

Wilton, T. (1999). *Good for you: A handbook on lesbian health and well-being.* London: Cassell Academic.

Wisechild, L.M. (Ed.). (1991). *She who was lost is remembered: Healing from incest through creativity.* Seattle: The Seal Press.

Wisechild, L. M. (1988). *The obsidian mirror: An adult healing from incest.* Seattle: Seal Press.

Woititz, J. G. (1989). *Healing your sexual self.* Deerfield Beach, FL: Health Communications.

Wood, W. A. (1993) *Triumph over darkness: Understanding the trauma of childhood sexual abuse.* Hillsboro, OR: Beyond Words Publishing.

Worthington, E. (2001). *Five steps to forgiveness.* New York: Crown.

Wylie, M. S. (1998). The shadow of a doubt. In R. A. Baker *Child sexual abuse and false memory syndrome* (pp. 49-75). Amherst, NY: Prometheus Books.

Zerbe, K. J. (1993). *The body betrayed: Women, eating disorders and treatment.* Washington, DC: American Psychiatric Association.

Zimmerman, B. (1995, Spring). Introduction. *NWSA Journal 7*(1), 1-7.

Resources for Survivors

The resources listed here are among those either suggested to me or those I have come found along the way. The appearance of resources on this list in no way constitutes an endorsement of the organization or the information it presents. Neither does the omission of any organization from this list represent anything other than an oversight on my part.

Advocates for Abused and Battered Lesbians (AABL)
www.aabl.org

American Academy of Pediatrics
141 Northwest Point Blvd., P.O. Box 927
Elk Grove Village, IL 60007
(800) 433-9016

American Humane Association
63 Inverness Drive East
Englewood, CO 80112-5117
(800) 227-4645
www.amerhumane.org
(This organization provides professionals and concerned citizens with facts, resources, and referrals needed to help children and families in crisis and to prevent child abuse in their own neighborhoods.)

Asian and Pacific Islander Wellness Center
www.apiwellness.org

Astraea Foundation
www.astraea.org
(lesbian philanthropic organization)

Body Positive
www.bodypositive.com

(Web site dedicated to feeling good about the bodies we have. Inspiration, support, newsletter, message boards, support groups)

Child Abuse Legislative Study Project
www.childabuselegislation.org
(political action for the victims of child abuse, incest, and domestic violence. A nonprofit organization dedicated to tracking bills, laws, and legislative action on child abuse, incest, and domestic violence)

The Child Abuse Prevention Network
www.child.cornell.edu
(the Internet nerve center for professionals in the field of child abuse and neglect)

ChildHelp USA
15757 N. 78th Street
Scottsdale, AZ 85260
24-hour crisis hotline: (800) 4-A-CHILD or (480) 922-8212
(ChildHelp is dedicated to meeting the physical, emotional, educational, and spiritual needs of abused and neglected children.)

Child Protection Project
www.childpro.org
(focuses on abuse within the Mormon Church)

Classic Dykes Online
www.classicdykes.com
(resource and meeting place for lesbians in midlife and beyond. Bibliography, Ask an Expert, personals, therapist, and much more.)

Coming Out
www.hrc.org/ncop/guide/index.asp
www.emptyclosets.com
www.org.au/outreach/out1.htm

Debtors Anonymous
www.debtorsanonymous.org

Eve's Garden
119 W. 57th Street #420
New York, NY 10019-2383
(800) 848-3837
www.evesgarden.com
(woman-oriented store and catalog of toys, books, and videos)

Family Pride Coalition
P.O. Box 65327
Washington, DC 20035-5327
(202) 331-5015
www.amilypride.org
(national organization whose mission is supporting and protecting the families of gay, lesbian, bisexual, and transgender parents. Sponsors family events, coordinates local parenting groups, publishes newsletter, and more.)

Fat Acceptance Stuff
www.casagordita.com/fatacc.htm
(links, resources, and organizations)

Fat Girl
www.lustydevil.com/fatgirl
(the magazine for fat dykes and the women who want them)

The Gay and Lesbian National Hotline
PMB #296
2261 Market St.
San Francisco, CA 94114
(888) THE-GLNH
www.glnh.org

Gay/Lesbian/Bi/Trans Narcotics Anonymous
wwwglweb.com/glna

Gay Lesbian International Therapist Search Engine
www.glitse.com
(free and anonymous database of referrals and tips for finding a therapist)

Girls Fight Back
www.girlsfightback.com
(inspires, motivates, and educates women and girls of all ages to take a proactive stance opposing and combating violence against women. Conducts presentations to businesses and schools, publishes an e-newsletter, and provides links to self-defense training nationwide.)

Good Vibrations
www.goodvibes.com
(retail stores in San Francisco and Berkeley and mail-order catalog of books, toys, and videos)

Healing Journey Survivor chat room
www.healing-journey.net/chat.html

The Healing Voice
c/o Heidi Kuhl
Center for Creative Arts and Healing
601 Allen St.
Syracuse, NY 13210
e-mail: HealingVoiceNews@aol.com or Heidikuhl@aol.com
(newsletter for survivors of sexual trauma and their allies)

Human Rights Campaign
919 18th St. NW, Suite 800
Washington, DC 20006
(202) 628-4160
www.hrc.org

Incest Survivors Anonymous
P.O. Box 17245
Long Beach, CA 90807-7245
(562) 428-5599

KaliMuno.com
www.kalimunro.com
(online psychotherapist with resources for healing for survivors including self-help tips, inspirational poetry and quotes, and self-help articles on: relationships, lesbian and gay issues, articles for survivors and their friends, body image/issues with food, addictions, emotions/feelings. Also writes a newsletter for survivors, Healing Words.)

Kristen's Place
www.nhhi.net/kp
(tools for lesbian and straight survivors of sexual abuse/assault: recovery, support forum and chat, online counseling.)

Lesbian.com
www.lesbian.com
(comprehensive reference for lesbian information)

Lesbian Connection
EPI, P.O. Box 811
East Lansing, MI 48826
(517) 371-5257
elsiepub@aol.com
(free worldwide forum of news and ideas for, by, and about lesbians. Includes letters, listing of conferences and other events, marketplace)

Lesbian Mothers Support
www.lesbian.org/lesbian-moms

LGBT People of Color
www.members.aol.com/gendervariant/index.htm
(books, resources, and Web rings)

Llego: The National Latino/a Lesbian, Gay, Bisexual and Transgender Organization
1420 K St. NW, Suite 400
Washington, DC 20005
(202) 408-5380
www.llego.org
(events, publications, programs, resources)

National Association of Anorexia Nervosa and Associated Disorders
P.O. Box 7
Highland Park, IL 60035
(847) 831-3438
www.anad.org
(The oldest nonprofit dedicated to alleviating eating disorders and promoting healthy lifestyle. Offers referrals, counseling, education, newsletter, conferences, and consumer advocacy.)

National Association to Advance Fat Acceptance
www.naafa,org
(nonprofit, human rights organization dedicated to improving the quality of life for fat people)

National Center for Child Abuse and Neglect (NCCAN)
Office of Human Development Services
Department of Health and Human Services
P.O. Box 1182
Washington, DC 20013
(703) 821-2086

National Center for Lesbian Rights
www.nclrights.org

National Center for Missing and Exploited Children
1835 K Street NW, Suite 700
Washington, DC 20006
(800) 843-5678 or (202) 634-9836

National Center for Post-Traumatic Stress Disorder (PTSD)
www.dartmouth.edu/dms/ptsd

National Child Abuse Hotline
(800) 442-4453
1345 N. El Centro Ave.
Hollywood, CA 90028
(provides on-the-spot telephone counseling to any child being abused physically or sexually and offers immediate assistance, information, and referrals to anyone concerned about abused children)

National Clearinghouse on Child Abuse and Neglect
330 C St. SW
Washington, DC 20447
(800) FYI 3366
www.calib.com/nccanch
(national resource and clearinghouse that collects, stores, organizes, and disseminates information on all aspects of child maltreatment.)

National Coalition Against Domestic Violence
Information Line: (800) 799-7233
National Office: (303) 839-1852

National Coalition for Black Lesbians and Gays
P.O. Box 19248
Washington, DC 20036

National Committee to Prevent Child Abuse
332 South Michigan Ave.
Chicago, IL 60604-4357
(800) CHILDREN or (312) 663-3520

National Council on Child Abuse and Female Violence
1155 Connecticut Ave., Suite 400
Washington, DC 20036
(800) 222-2000 or (202) 429-6695

National Eating Disorders Association
(800) 931-2237

National Gay and Lesbian Task Force
1700 Kalorama Rd. NW
Washington, DC 20009
(202) 332-6483
www.ngltf.org

National Institute of Mental Health
www.nimh.nih.gov
(fact sheets, brochures, reports and other educational materials about mental illness and mental health including post-traumatic stress disorder, depression, eating disorders. Some information available in Spanish.)

National Latina Lesbian and Gay Organization
PO Box 44483
Washington, DC 20026

National Mental Health Awareness Campaign
(877) 495-0009
www.nostigma.org
(crisis intervention and referrals)

National Organization for Lesbians of Size
www.nolose.org
(support, social, and networking group for women who identify as lesbians and who are fat or fat positive. Offers bulletins, news, resources, and links.)

National Organization for Victim Assistance (NOVA)
1757 Park Rd., NW
Washington, DC 20010
(202) 232-6682
(provides crisis intervention, short-term counseling, medical and legal advice, and referrals to victim assistance programs across the country, including battered women's programs and rape crisis centers.)

National Resource Center on Child Sexual Abuse
106 Lincoln St.
Huntsville, AL 35801
(800) KIDS-006 or (205) 533-KIDS

Old Lesbians Organizing for Change
P.O. Box 98042
Houston, TX 77098
www.oloc.org
(quarterly newsletter, support groups, seminars, and workshops)

Overeaters Anonymous
World Service Office
P.O. Box 44020
Rio Rancho, NM 87174-4020
(505) 891-2664
www.overeatersanonymous.org
(national 12-step organization offering meetings/support, subscription magazine, and annual convention)

Pandora's Box
www.prevent-abuse-now.com/index.htm
(forum for child abuse information, including child protection resources, research and statistics on child sexual abuse, prevention resources, legal information, and poetry)

Parents Anonymous
6733 South Sepulveda Blvd., Suite 270
Los Angeles, CA 90045
(800) 421-0353 or (213) 410-9732

Prevent Child Abuse America
200 S. Michigan Ave., Suiite 17
Chicago, IL 60604
(312) 663-3520
www.preventchildabuse.org

(This agency provides information about child abuse prevention, programs, education, training, research, and advocacy directed toward reducing all forms of child abuse.)

Pridelinks.com
www.pridelinks.com
(gay, lesbian, bi, trans search site)

Pride Senior Network
www.pridesenior.org
(quarterly newspaper for the aging LGBT community, research initiatives, provider directory, and resource center)

Rainbow Alliance of the Deaf
P.O. Box 14182
Washington, DC 20044-4182

Rainbow Hope
www.rainbowhope.org
(offers online support group for lesbian survivors of abuse and their partners)

Rape, Abuse, and Incest National Network (RAINN)
635-B Pennsylvania Ave., SE
Washington, DC 20003
Telephone: (800) 659-HOPE
www.rainn.*org*
(free, confidential national sexual assault hotline that operates 24/7)

The Recovered Memory Project
www.brown.edu/Departments/Taubman_Center/Recovery
(Internet-based research project directed by Professor Ross E. Cheit of the Taubman Center for Public Policy and American Institutions at Brown University. This site hosts numerous academic articles debunking the claims of the False Memory Syndrome Foundation. Contains resource publications and archive of recovered memory cases.)

Recovered Memories of Sexual Abuse
www.jimhopper.com/memory/
(excellent compilation of articles and opinions about the indisputability of recovered memories.)

Safe Alternatives Program (Recording)
(800) DONT-CUT

The Safer Society Foundation, Inc.
P.O. Box 340
Brandon, VT 05733
(802) 247-3132
www.safersociety.org
(This agency is dedicated to the prevention and treatment of sexual abuse. Safer Society offers publications for professionals, families, victims, and offenders related to sexual abuse.)

Sex Offender Registration and Community Notification Internet Access
(For information on the registered sex offenders in your community contact your local sheriff's office or police department. Check with local law enforcement for a web site that lists registered sex offenders n your community. Online information regarding registered sex offenders is available.)

Sibling Abuse Survivors' Information and Advocacy Network (SASIAN)
www.sasian.org
(features articles, papers, and links of interest to survivors of sibling abuse)

Soul Survivors
www.geocities.com/awaygirl/Intro.html
(for black men, women, and children across the globe who have been affected by sexual violence)

Standing Against Global Exploitation (SAGE)
www.sageinc.org

(medical care, housing referrals, job training, and drug treatment for women who want to leave prostitution)

STOP IT NOW!
P.O. Box 495
Haydenville, MA 01039
(413) 268-3096
www.stopitnow.com
(This organization is based on the idea that adults, especially abusers and potential abusers, must stop sexual abuse. It works to help abusers seek help, to educate adults about the ways to stop sexual abuse, and to increase public awareness of the trauma of child sexual abuse.)

Suicide Hotlines
National Hopeline Network (800) SUICIDE
Prevention Hotline (800) 827-7571

Survivor Connections
Frank and Sara Fitzpatrick
52 Lyndon Rd.
Cranston, RI 02905-1121
(401) 941-2548
(an activist organization for survivors of clergy abuse and those who support them)

Survivors Healing Center
2301 Mission St., Suite C-1
Santa Cruz, CA 95060
(831) 423-7601
(Founded by Ellen Bass and Amy Pine, this center provides resources, classes, and healing support for survivors of childhood sexual abuse.)

Survivors Network of those Abused by Priests (SNAP)
www.teleport.com/~snapmail/
(self-help organization of men and women who were sexually abused by priests, brothers, nuns, deacons, teachers, etc.)

Survivors of Incest Anonymous
(301) 282-3400

Trikone: Gay and Lesbian South Asians
P.O. Box 21354
San Jose, CA 95151

VOICES in Action, Inc. (Victims of Incest Can Emerge Survivors)
P.O. Box 148309
Chicago, IL 60614
(312) 327-1500
www.voices-action.org
(an international network of male and female incest survivors, local groups, and contacts that offers free referrals to therapists, agencies, and self-help groups endorsed by survivors.)

Web by Women for Women
www.io.com/~wwwomen/sexuality/index.html
(a group of sex-positive, anti-censorship feminists created this site in order to give voice to women's stories about sex and sexual identity)